Empathy and Business Transformation

Due to its potential transformative nature, empathy has increasingly received attention in business, psychology, neuroscience, education, medicine, social sciences and design, to mention only a few. During the last two decades, discussions about the role of empathy in design and creative research and practice have developed, with empathy perceived as a key instrument in human-centred design and design thinking. This book revisits the powerful concept of empathy in the new post-pandemic era in which ubiquitous digitalisation presents challenges to retaining human-centredness when developing products and services.

The book presents a practical four-step approach to the challenges presented concerning how organisations can turn from merely feeling empathy with or for people, to actions of empathy and compassion that can be implemented with and by communities. A wide range of organisations and organisational settings can benefit from the presented case studies and research methods. Through them, the book explores how to discover, share and act with empathy and compassion in the new digitally driven post-pandemic era to innovate across a wide range of organisations, including for-profit and not-for-profit businesses and those in the public and third sectors.

This edited volume will appeal to global researchers in the fields of product and service design and digital, social innovation, as well those interested in organisational development. The practical, interdisciplinary nature of the book and innovative four-step approach will also appeal to upper-level students.

Melanie Sarantou is an adjunct professor in social design and senior researcher at the University of Lapland, investigating how arts and narrative practices impact marginalised women in communities in Namibia, Lapland, Russia and Australia. Her current research focuses on the role of arts in societies that exist on the margin of Europe in the European Commission-funded Horizon 2020 project titled 'Action on the Margin: Arts as Social Sculpture'.

Satu Miettinen is professor of Service Design at the University of Lapland, Finland, with research interests spanning the themes of design methods in engaging with the Arctic region, service design methods for inclusion, the participatory development of services and socially responsible art and design methods.

Empathy and Business Transformation

Edited by
Melanie Sarantou and Satu Miettinen

Routledge
Taylor & Francis Group
LONDON AND NEW YORK

First published 2023
by Routledge
4 Park Square, Milton Park, Abingdon, Oxon OX14 4RN

and by Routledge
605 Third Avenue, New York, NY 10158

Routledge is an imprint of the Taylor & Francis Group, an informa business

British Library Cataloguing-in-Publication Data
A catalogue record for this book is available from the British Library

Library of Congress Cataloging-in-Publication Data
A catalog record has been requested for this book

ISBN: 978-1-032-13076-7 (hbk)
ISBN: 978-1-032-13078-1 (pbk)
ISBN: 978-1-003-22755-7 (ebk)

DOI: 10.4324/9781003227557

Typeset in Bembo
by Taylor & Francis Books

Contents

Figures

Tables

Contributors

Daria Akimenko is a Russian researcher, artist and cultural manager currently based in Italy. Her research and artistic interests include narrative-based art, communities of practice and place, migratory practices and the related identity work. Daria holds an MA in Spatial Design from the Ural State Academy of Architecture and Art (Russia) and a Doctor of Arts degree from the University of Lapland (Finland).

Mira Alhonsuo (Doctor of Arts) is a postdoctoral researcher in service design. She has been working as a researcher and service designer for multiple cases in social and healthcare services, digital services and tourism. Her research interests include design methods, empathy and user experience.

Rosa Maria Ballardini (LL.M, PhD, Docent) is a professor of IP law and Vice Dean (research) at the University of Lapland/Faculty of Law. Rosa's research interests focus on the interface between law, technology and sustainability. Her research approach is multidisciplinary, combining law, technology and business using different methodologies.

Caoimhe Isha Beaulé is a doctoral researcher at the University of Lapland. Her background is in visual arts and design, sustainability and creative processes, with a focus on design in Northern environments. Her current research aims to increase knowledge on trust-building processes in collective design practices involving communities and culture.

Marina Bos-de Vos is an assistant professor of Ecosystem Innovation at the Design, Organisation and Strategy Department of Industrial Design Engineering, TU Delft. In her work, she focuses on the roles and value creation processes of creative professionals in interorganizational projects. Drawing from her experience as an architect, she synthesizes insights from research into tools that design students and young professionals can use when collaborating across organizations.

André Casanova Silveira is a PhD candidate at the School of Physical Education and Sport at the University of São Paulo in the Endurance Performance Study Group. He works on topics related to exercise and looks at how environmental factors (e.g., air pollution) could limit performance. In addition, he is a cyclist with six years of experience.

Marcelo Corrales Compagnucci (LL.M, LL.D) is an attorney specializing in privacy, data protection and information technology law. His research interests are the legal issues involved in disruptive innovation technologies and biomedicine. He is currently an associate professor at the Centre for Advanced Studies in Biomedical Innovation Law (CeBIL), Faculty of Law, University of Copenhagen, Denmark.

Timothy K. Craig is an experienced pharmaceutical research and development leader who has held multiple leadership positions in both large and small pharmaceutical companies, including Pfizer, Novartis, Roche, Harker-BIO, Proteros, TimPharma LLC and Emerald Bio. He obtained his PhD from the University of Texas Southwestern Medical Center at Dallas in Molecular Biophysics.

Luiz E. P. B. T. Dantas is a tourism cycling and urban biker enthusiast. He holds a Doctorate in Human Movement Pedagogy from School of Physical Education and Sport (USP). He has professional experience in school and university teaching and research in the field of Physical Education and Sports.

Marija Griniuk is a performance artist and doctoral candidate at the University of Lapland, Faculty of Art and Design. Her research concerns the new channels of performance documentation derived from typically invisible biometric data, such as brain activity.

Päivi Hanni-Vaara holds a master's degree in Tourism and Hospitality Management and belongs to the Culture-Based Service Design Doctoral Program at the Faculty of Art and Design at the University of Lapland. Hanni-Vaara is a Senior Lecturer at the Lapland University of Applied Sciences. She contributes her research to applied research, which values her background in the tourism business as a travel agent. Hanni-Vaara's research focuses on empathy in a digital customer journey of tourism and hospitality, interconnecting digital services and human centricity.

Maria Huhmarniemi is an artist and a teacher in the University of Lapland, Faculty of Art and Design. She engages with questions concerning the North and environmental issues such as the relationship between people and nature and environmental responsibility. Her research tackles political contemporary art and education for sustainability through art.

Juha Iso-Aho holds a Master of Arts, majoring in Theatre Research. Since 2000, he has worked at the Humak University of Applied Sciences as Lecturer in Cultural Management. In recent years, he has chiefly worked as a project manager and expert in various development projects dealing with event production, culture tourism and creative economy.

Katja Juhola is a curator, visual artist and researcher. For her, instead of art objects, the process is important. Her basic aspirations stem from the principles of equality and an ecological way of life. Juhola believes in the possibility of art making a social and environmental change.

Katri Konttinen (MA, Arts) is a designer and doctoral candidate at the University of Lapland. She is also a member of the Service Design Research Group Co-Stars. Konttinen worked as a researcher on the SEEYouth: Social Innovation through Participatory Art and Design with Youth at the Margins project. She is interested in multidisciplinary actions and their impacts taking place between art and design.

Mikko Koria is a professor and the director of the Institute for Design Innovation at Loughborough University London. His key areas of interest include design-driven entrepreneurship, innovation in policymaking and services and the management of design and projects in global organisations.

Krista Korpikoski is a PhD candidate at the University of Lapland in the Culture-based Service Design Doctoral Programme. In addition, Korpikoski acts as a university teacher in the Service Design Master's Degree Programme PAMA and as a project manager in the LEADBEHA project. She is also a member of Service Design Research Group Co-Stars.

Tatiana Kravtsov is a doctoral candidate in the Faculty of Art and Design at the University of Lapland, Finland. Her artistic education and practice vary from visual arts to ceramics and environmental art. Her interests include art-based research methods, traditional and contemporary handicrafts, natural materials and connectedness with nature.

Outi Kugapi is a doctoral candidate in tourism research at the University of Lapland, Multidimensional Tourism Institute. Currently, she works at Education and Development Services, University of Lapland. Her research interest is tourism experiences in craft tourism, and she has coauthored several articles on the topic.

Maria Cecilia Loschiavo dos Santos is a philosopher and full professor of Design at FAU-USP. Her current research is Discarded Products, Design and Homelessness in Global Cities, and she is deeply committed to design and social responsibility issues. She is the SEEYouth Project Principal Investigator in Brazil.

Nina Luostarinen holds a master's degree in Culture and Arts and has worked with cultural management projects at Humak since 2007. She is also a doctoral candidate at the University of Lapland (Faculty of Art and Design). She is interested in the narrative experience related to places, serendipity and the power of playful attitude.

Enni Mikkonen (Dr. Soc.Sci) is a postdoctoral researcher in social work at the University of Lapland, Finland. She is currently studying whiteness and racialised structures in the social work profession in Finland and Nepal. Previously she has worked in multiple interdisciplinary research projects focusing on migration and integration, and the intersections of arts and social work, such as the research project SEEYouth, Social Innovation through Participatory Art and Design with Youth at the Margins in 2020–21. She is particularly interested in decolonial, feminist and transnational social work; critical whiteness and race studies; and Global South-North collaboration.

Smaranda-Sabina Moldovan is a visual artist and PhD assistant at West University Timisoara, Faculty of Arts and Design. Moldovan focuses her research on the relationship between objects and social spaces, working in the areas of environmental art and object painting. She uses monochrome and colour fields and minimalistic objects to encourage living with less.

Bruna Montuori is a designer and PhD candidate at the School of Architecture, Royal College of Art, funded by CNPq, Brazil. She investigates narratives and spatial justice at Redes da Maré organisation, Rio de Janeiro. Bruna holds an MSc. in Architecture (FAU-USP) and is cofounder of the 'Por um design relacional' research group.

Ludovick Myumbo was born in Iringa (Tanzania). He is a lecturer in the Department of Sociology at St. Augustine University, Tanzania. He received his PhD in Social Sciences at the University of Tampere (Finland). His research interests focus on gender-based livelihoods, civil society organizations and sustainable development.

Heidi Pietarinen (PhD in Arts) is a professor in the Faculty of Art and Design at the University of Lapland, Finland. She holds a PhD degree in textile design, and her research emphasises knowledge and methods of textile art, design and history. She is also curious about the narratives and multiple cultural influences told by textiles. The cultures teach us to find contrast of materials, colours and textures within the simplest forms. Stories should not be thought of only as written history, but as what we do – doing is thinking.

Tarja Pääkkönen, MSc. (econ) completed her doctoral thesis at the University of Lapland. Intrigued by how designers think and how organizations make sense, her research combines design with organisation and management studies. She is a senior lecturer with a working history of 20 years in Finnish higher education.

Eduardo Rumenig Souza has been an enthusiast of active mobility and cycling commuters for 20 years. He holds an undergraduate degree in Physical Education and Social Sciences. Currently, he is a doctoral candidate at EEFE-USP. He has professional experience in teaching and research in physical education and urban anthropology, emphasising active mobility and health.

Mariluz Soto Hormazábal is a researcher and professor of Universidad del Desarrollo, Chile. She has experience as a researcher and consultant in design and communication in projects in Chile, Latin America and Finland. Her research interests are service design, community, emotions, cocreation, nature and creative-artistic exploration.

Albert Tibaijuka is a lecturer at St. Augustine University of Tanzania (SAUT), serving the faculty of Social Sciences and Communication. He received his PhD in African Studies at the University of Basel, Switzerland. His experience centres in researching the fields of organization–stakeholder relations, corporate social responsibility and media operations.

Eija Timonen is professor of Media Studies at the Faculty of Art and Design at the University of Lapland and a docent at the Aalto University Department of Film, Television and Scenography. She has led several research projects and served as a member of the executive team at international and national conferences and for academic journals. Alongside the research, she has an active art career in photography and fiction writing. The results of the work have been featured in many exhibitions, as well as in ice art-based research articles (see www.lightofice.net).

Rosana Vasques is a lecturer at FAU-USP, teaching industrial and service design. She is also a research fellow in the SEEYouth Project and the InovaUSP. Her current research and professional practice include design research, social innovation and sustainability, service design and service ecosystems in the creative economy.

Pekka Vartiainen holds a PhD and has been working as a teacher and researcher in Humak in the Department of Cultural Management since 2001. He is also a docent at the University of Helsinki (Comparative Literature). His publications include fictional texts and several academic articles and books on arts and culture.

Maria Luiza Viana is a PhD candidate in Design at the School of Architecture and Urbanism, University of São Paulo, FAU-USP. She teaches in the Design programme at the Federal University of Minas Gerais. She is a member of the research groups at UFMG and FAU-USP. Her research areas are art, design and communities.

Robert van den Hoven van Genderen is a professor at the Law Faculty University of Lapland (Finland) and Vrije University Amsterdam. He is also a visiting professor at Kyushu University, Japan, and a partner at Switch legal international lawyers. He worked as the director of international regulatory relations in the telecommunication industry before returning to the academic world, concentrating on the legal and ethical aspects of intrusive technologies in AI and robotics.

Michelle Olga van Wyk is currently a lecturer in the Design department at the Cape Peninsula University of Technology, Cape Town, South Africa. Her background in jewellery design informs her research interest in decolonising research practices and creative making processes, and is also the foundation of her practice-led PhD at the University of Lapland, Finland. She enjoys exploring non-traditional materials through the lens of handmade jewellery and Indigenous crafting.

Mari Viinikainen holds a Bachelor of Arts and is completing a master's degree in Sociology at the University of Lapland. Her research interests include research ethics, new materialism and Indigenous studies. She is currently working with topics like Indigenous food sovereignty and food security, local environmental observations and Indigenous design and innovations.

Yangyang Zhao is currently an associate professor at the Department of Informatics at the University of Oslo. In addition, she has been an associate professor in the Department of Science and Industry Systems in University of Southeast Norway since 2013. She has gained global industrial experience in process management and entrepreneurial experience in IT.

Acknowledgements

The editors thank the anonymous peer reviewers of the manuscript for providing meticulous and helpful comments in the initial stages of the manuscript. In addition, we thank the following reviewers for critically reading the manuscript and suggesting substantial improvements on earlier chapter drafts.

Ashley Colley
Soili Haarala-Nysten
Mirja Kälviäinen
Kalle Lempiäinen
Mari Mäkiranta
Enni Mikkonen
Heidi Pietarinen
Piia Rytilahti
Tiina Seppälä
Yang-Yang Zhao

The editors acknowledge funding support for this manuscript by the Faculty of Art and Design of the University of Lapland.

The editors also acknowledge funding support received to produce this manuscript under the *AMASS* project, which has received funding from the European Union's Horizon 2020 research and innovation programme under grant agreement No. 870621.

1 Introduction

Melanie Sarantou and Satu Miettinen

Over the past decade, the discussion on empathy has grown, producing such an abundance of available material that one wonders what else could be contributed. There has, however, been a clear call from scholars around the globe to produce more case studies on the phenomenon of empathy and its role in building the social fabric of organisations and communities (Gökçiğdem, 2019). For example, Tunstall (2013) wanted to see practical case studies from the peripheries of society to illustrate the functioning of empathy and compassion within our organisations and societies. Young (2015, p. 135) asked workplace leaders, process facilitators and designers to integrate empathy carefully and realistically into everyday working and organisational practices. Wetter-Edman (2013, p. 108) asked designers to seek out empathy and find inspiration from a 'deep understanding of latent needs, dreams and expectations' of individuals and communities to be used as the initiators of creative processes, for example, through empathic design methods. These direct calls for action are addressed in this book.

Empathy and Business Transformation targets the lack of descriptive case studies by discussing and sharing new knowledge. It asks the following: How can we discover and share empathy to create innovation within organisations, whether they are for-profit or not-for-profit businesses or in the third, public or private sectors? The book draws on theory and novel data to explore the dynamics of human empathy in creating a strategic vision and leadership in organisations (Chapman, 2015; Patnaik, 2009; Ventura, 2019). It also explores the topic of empathy from a practical perspective by considering a wide range of case studies and the role empathy plays in technological and digital approaches within organisational settings.

We define empathy as the capacity to understand the elements that underpin the realities and situations that are experienced by people (Ashworth & Lucas, 2000; Rumble et al., 2010; Saarikivi, 2018). Empathy is an essential ingredient of our social cognition and can be defined as the ability 'to understand and share another person's inner life' (Brink et al., 2011, p. 1). This capacity includes the understanding of emotions and feelings that underpin the associated meanings connected to personal circumstances. By using empathy, we can think of the needs of people and act on them (De Lille et al., 2012). In

DOI: 10.4324/9781003227557-1

short, we are empathic if we are able to, as Patnaik (2009) explained, reach outside ourselves to perceive, grasp, understand, sense and respond to the inner and emotional states of others.

In practice, empathy is a complex psychological phenomenon (Powell & Roberts, 2017); it can stimulate participation because it requires detachment from a current lifeworld while opening that of another (Ashworth & Lucas, 2000). Participation is the result of empathic and 'imaginative engagement with the world' (Ashworth & Lucas, 2000, p. 299). It is a skill that humans employ to understand other people's emotions, and it is a skill that service-providing organisations can use to engage their customers and staff in empathic interactions and dialogue to identify the challenges and opportunities in their service delivery (Wetter-Edman, 2013). Through empathy, service providers can prototype proactive solutions to add value and create new business.

Empathy is the only skill with which we can understand emotions; thus, it supports our collective intelligence (Saarikivi, 2018). The neural network most closely associated with empathy is the frontal mirror neuron system (MNS), a 'simulation mechanism' of our neuron networks that enables us to perceive others' actions, similar to when we are engaged in them ourselves (Brink et al., 2011, p. 2). Empathy can be seen as the glue of connectedness, and it comes about and is created by paying attention and being present, having the motivation to create understanding by relying on relevant previous experiences and displaying enactment and interaction (Saarikivi, 2018).

In keeping with Ekman (2007), Powell and Roberts (2017, p. 137) and Riess and Neporent (2018), we approach empathy through a 'tripartite classification'. This classification includes cognitive empathy, or the ability to recognise what others are feeling; affective empathy, which is known as emotional empathy or emotion sharing by sensing and feeling with others; and compassionate empathy, which occurs when we assist people to cope with their emotions and circumstances. Cognitive empathy is the ability to understand the intentions of another person (Baron-Cohen & Wheelwright, 2004; Bloom, 2017; Brink et al., 2011; Shamay-Tsoory et al., 2005). Affective empathy is 'the ability to imagine or "experience" a situation from another person's point of view' (Brink et al., 2011, p. 2); it promotes emotional responses and our acknowledgement of another person's affective state (Brink et al., 2011). Compassionate empathy is known as empathic concern (Bloom, 2017; Riess & Neporent, 2018). Here, Ekman and Ekman (2017, p. 41) have maintained that empathic concern is connected to a larger view of global compassion seeking to 'alleviate the suffering of anyone, regardless of their nationality, language, culture or religion' and 'widening our sphere of concern beyond our families'.

The notion of kinaesthetic empathy, a fourth classification of empathy, is an emerging discussion in the field of performing arts and design frameworks and needs mentioning. It is defined by Reynolds and Reason (2012, p. 18) as a 'key interdisciplinary concept in our understanding of social action and communication in creative and cultural practices'. As a broader definition, kinaesthetic empathy 'can be used to evaluate and generate a wide variety of movement interactions' (Cuykendall et al., 2015, p. 305). This book deliberates on the role movement plays in eliciting this kind of empathy in embodied service design practices and interactions with users.

However, there are also arguments against empathy. Baron-Cohen (2012) and Bloom (2017) warned against the darker side of empathy when a lesser or severe lack of cognitive empathy is misused by those who have the power to observe others and make educated guesses and to engage in manipulation or seduction to a greater or lesser degree. When it comes to our ability to make appropriate judgements or analyses regarding our moral obligations, cognitive empathy can fail. For affective empathy, there is the danger of its narrow 'spotlight nature' (Bloom, 2017, p. 31) influencing the interactions with people who seem to be similar to us. Such sentiments can strengthen notions of 'us' against the 'other' to support classism or racism. Bloom upheld that realities of life exist in which cognitive empathy may not help us as much as we would have hoped, for example, in social policymaking.

In feminist theory, Lather (2000, p. 18) warned not to attempt to 'reduce otherness to sameness within a personalised culture' because we do not have the capacity to do so, and we may never assume to know everything through a so-called 'empathetic approach to understanding' (see Sommer, 1994). Lather (2000) reasoned for a 'methodology of getting lost', one in which we explore the possibilities for empathy beyond the obvious (p. 19) because not all can be understood or shared between people (see Gair & Moloney, 2013; Sommer, 1994). Bloom (2017) also provided a more complex concept of 'diffuse compassion' (p. 35), requiring careful deliberation, intelligence, a 'desire to do the right thing' (p. 44) and self-control instead of responding emotionally to sentimental appeals. His call for 'rational compassion' is based on impartial reasoning (p. 51) and a more critical view towards empathy because its benefits are generally perceived as obvious, being widely acknowledged without requiring justification.

The concept of empathy that was deployed in design research in the 1990s was revisited by Mattelmäki et al. (2014). The role of experiences, emotions and meaningful everyday practices were studied by Mattelmäki et al. (2014) to understand how to stimulate innovation and human-centred solutions. Here, empathic design is an interpretative approach used for creating new solutions in users' lives (Batterbee et al., 2014). Innovation can be unlocked once organisations seek the deep emotional needs of users and try to understand them to transform organisational processes and functions (Batterbee et al., 2014). The design factors for creating empathic, inclusive and novel cultural experiences in museums have been illuminated by Gökçiğdem (2019), and these factors include, for example, intentionality, intersectionality, curiosity, communication, optimism, play and storytelling.

A growing need exists for embedding empathy into all spheres of business (New & Kimbell, 2013; Tzouramani, 2017). For example, empathy is widely discussed as an entrepreneurial skill (Galinsky et al., 2008; Humphrey, 2013) and the main ingredient in successful service delivery (Goleman, 2003), but also as a skill that can advance socially sustainable practices and the design for social and cultural contexts (Gökçiğdem, 2019; Rumble et al., 2010). This means that more empathic services and interactions should exist among organisations, but also among their employees and users. Empathic design (Leonard & Rayport, 1997) is especially meaningful when applied in depth to gain an understanding of complex cultural underpinnings and situations. With a variety of case studies, this book illustrates how to work with empathic design in practice and a wider notion of empathy when applying empathy in different cultural settings.

The role of empathy in organisational development and values-based management has been emphasised by Pavlovich and Krahnke (2013). In their book *Organising through Empathy*, they explored the role of empathy beyond the capitalist point of view that solely stresses profit and productivity; they sought to understand how empathy can sustain organisations and our broader societies in terms of intellectual, ecological, spiritual and aesthetic well-being. The need for empathy has been widely discussed in business leadership, but the notion has also been criticised for its superficial approach (New & Kimbell, 2013; Ohren, 2014). Organisations can draw on empathy for the development of user-centric services while enabling users to express their needs for customised services through empathic dialogues between them and the businesses. Therefore, the mechanisms and methods of empathy-building through creative and digital approaches in a variety of organisations is central to this book.

Digital and technological approaches to organisational management, product and service delivery and the role empathy plays in these organisational processes have been examined. Saarikivi's (2018) research has shown that any flat-screen interface can mean the death of empathy, yet Archer and Finger's (2018) research has indicated that the use of immersive digital formats, for example, 360-degree video and virtual reality (VR), generate more empathy in viewers than nonimmersive formats such as screens. The use of various interfaces – or a combination thereof – is explored as an approach for enhancing empathy between organisations and their users. One of the practical challenges addressed is online and off-grid work in the post-COVID-19 global digital environment, especially for the inclusion of users and organisations who live at the margins of society.

Approaches to mediating empathy

This book addresses empathy in different business, societal and organisational contexts through mediation. Empathy can be mediated among people through the use of objects or through a combination of processes and objects (Marchetti et al., 2020). The book illustrates case studies that are connected, for example, to tourism, education, law, digital business and service development, manufacturing industries and automation, as well as cultural and third sectors. The case studies span geographical peripheries, such as the northernmost reaches of Lapland, and marginalised local communities of Rio de Janeiro and rural South Australia, to name a few. Addressing this wide spectrum of user groups and their needs is possible when using the varied tools from cross-disciplinary fields such as arts and design, social work and law and business and management studies.

The case studies reveal how arts-based methods (ABMs), storytelling, design, digital approaches and tools can contribute to new ways of communicating and understanding empathy; these methods can have a concrete role in mediating emotions and empathy in organisations, for example, in projects, workshops or interventions, using tactile and visual means in learning (Knochel et al., 2018). Young's (2015) and Wetter-Edman's (2013) ideas about generating a deep understanding of user and community contexts show the importance of the collection of information by the actors themselves through dialogue and deeper context descriptions. Hence, the results have been delivered by ABMs, storytelling and listening (Miettinen et al., 2019). Deep understanding that leads to learning forms part of the design phases and design thinking toolkits, helping generate insights about the difficulties users or communities face, their environmental realities and their resulting behaviours (Dam & Siang, 2020). These case studies represent not only solution-driven development and methods, but also innovative, customised methodologies that use ABMs to enable empathy generation within these specific contexts. These case studies enable and encourage the application and development of new tools that the reader can apply in their own organisational or community interactions.

In this book, some of the case studies present ABMs and design tools that enable collaborative and participatory engagement in action that can help communities create connections and disclose meaningful narratives of past and present experiences in initiating empathy. The value of ABMs, such as utilising the sensory modalities of light, sound, taste, pressure and temperature, is that kinaesthetic empathy can emerge through these methods in jumps, turns or acrobatic movements. In creating empathy, ABMs sometimes enable processes that other methods are not able to. Further, the chapters that take a critical look into capitalising on empathy, whether culturally, economically or socially generated, offer more perspectives on empathy in the context of sustainable practices.

Collaborative, arts-based and storytelling approaches encourage solution-driven development, but they also stimulate empathy (Brink et al., 2011; Saarikivi, 2018). Existing methods, such as the 'empathy story' (Archer & Finger, 2018; Brink et al., 2011; Faver & Alanis, 2012); narrative empathy (Juntunen & Saarti, 2000; Moore & Hallenbeck, 2010); 'improstory', which refers to the use of a combination of performance art, music, improvisation and storytelling (Karppinen et al., 2018), present only a short list of the methods that have been used to enhance empathy among organisations, coordinators, project participants, researchers and the researched. These methods incorporate performance and embodied practice into a place-connected process in which it is possible to mediate empathy among people.

The noteworthy methods introduced by Gaver et al. (1999) employ cultural probes that create empathy by contextualising user experiences. A model for creating empathy has been proposed by Kouprie and Visser (2009) and Miettinen et al. (2016); this model is based on the cycles of discovery, immersion, connection, detachment and planning. Several design tools have been developed to create empathy and user insights as well. Riess and Neporent's (2018) *EMPATHY* tool aims to address empathic communication through seven steps that use nonverbal cues and actions and that can be used in communication, including eye contact, facial expression, posture, vocal tone, listening and response.

The role of technology is discussed in many of the case studies, exploring empathy construction through digital tools in the context of research and design with individuals and communities. Although ABMs and creativity feed the imagination and stimulate empathy through aesthetic experiences, rhythm, music and fiction, digital interfaces are believed to inhibit empathy (Saarikivi, 2018). Computer-based communication is often believed to suppress empathy, but Powell and Roberts's (2017) study has shown that contextual and situational factors need to be taken into consideration because the situational variables in personal communication can impact empathy processes, as well as the kind of – if any – empathy that is generated. In addition, their study found that empathy can be experienced at multidimensional levels, depending on the particular digital interaction. For example, some interactions may stimulate various kinds of empathy: cognitive, affective and/or compassionate (Powell & Roberts, 2017, p. 145). Often, computer-based communication is used in a complementary fashion to other forms of conversing, with cognitive empathy being experienced most often during digital interactions (Powell & Roberts, 2017, p. 145). Creative methods, tools and digitalisation will be featured in this book to exemplify the navigation of empathy actions in a variety of organisational contexts.

The organisation of the book

The book presents a practical four-step approach to the challenges presented concerning how organisations can turn from merely feeling empathy with or for people to actions of empathy and compassion that can be implemented with and by communities. These steps describe a process (Figure 1.1) that engages in empathic action through cross-disciplinary and creative approaches to find solutions to societal and organisational needs, including creating connections for generating empathy through ABMs (step 1), creating emotional insights through storytelling (step 2), wayfinding and initiating action with beneficiaries through the role of design for services, products and experiences (step 3) and scaling up empathic action through digital approaches (step 4). Each section of the text uses practical case studies to exemplify real-life actions for the four steps. The sections offer examples of field research and findings, project outcomes, concepts, frameworks and novel and creative methods and tools.

Step 1 explores the role of creativity and the arts in creating connectivity and generating empathy with beneficiaries. Empathic immersion into the contexts

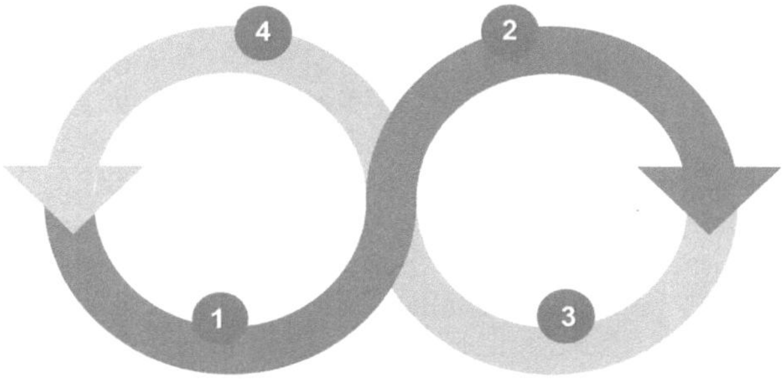

Step 1: Create connections for generating empathy

Step 2: Create emotional insights

Step 3: Wayfinding and initiating action with beneficiaries

Step 4: Scaling up empathic action

Figure 1.1 Process for empathic action through cross-disciplinary and creative approaches to find solutions to societal and organisational needs.

and lives of beneficiaries is explored, with the objective of understanding the perspectives, needs and aspirations of the beneficiaries through creative experiences and arts-based practices. Here, beneficiaries are understood as those who will benefit from the empathic action – groups, users, communities, customers, participants, consumers and vulnerable populations. Step 2 explores the role of stories and local and personal narratives in creating emotional insights with the beneficiaries. This section looks at the wider implications of stories and narratives in understanding the feelings, emotions and dreams of the beneficiaries, here with the aim of stimulating a deep understanding of generating empathic actions. The focus of step 3 is to draw on the role of design for wayfinding with beneficiaries through the empathic process with the objective of collectively determining opportunities for empathic action in service delivery and organisations. This section reviews the possibilities for bottom-up action, collective vision and leadership development through cocreation and mapping. Finally, step 4 examines the role of digitisation and technology in empathic action in terms of scaling it up to deliver value, care and compassion to the beneficiaries. In the final section of the book, a wide range of practical creative, design and digital tools that can be applied in organisational settings by business practitioners and project managers to respond to the needs of the users will be discussed.

Section A – the role of creativity and the arts in creating empathy – consists of four chapters in which arts-based approaches and their potential in fostering empathy are explored. In Chapter 2, from the perspective of NGOs, Enni Mikkonen and Katri Konttinen discuss how refugee youth's well-being and integration into societies can be strengthened through creativity and arts-based approaches, here as a way to strengthen their sense of belonging and connection to new environments. In Chapter 3, Tatiana Kravtsov, Maria Huhmarniemi and Outi Kugapi discuss the use of birch bark weaving to design a culturally sustainable creative tourism service in Finnish Lapland. The authors explore how in the context of creative tourism, empathy can come about through creative workshops in which the participants can make objects with aesthetic and cultural value that stimulate dialogue, sharing and learning. In Chapter 4, the authors Katja Juhola, Marija Griniuk and Smaranda-Sabina Moldovan discuss how empathy can be created through various approaches to digital participatory artworks through artistic workshops and performances. In Chapter 5, Daria Akimenko, Melanie Sarantou and Satu Miettinen discuss the application of a collaborative art and storytelling initiative in the form of a method titled 'Life Story Mandala', which is an empowering tool for generating empathy in social design processes.

In Section B, the role of stories in creating empathy explores the creation of emotional insights through storytelling and narrative practices. In Chapter 6, Rosana Vasques, Mikko Koria and Maria Cecilia Loschiavo dos Santos discuss how love and hate letters were used to gauge customer satisfaction and build empathy through digital business. In Chapter 7, Albert Tibaijuka and Ludovick Myumbo discuss how the regulations used in educational contexts, specifically universities in Tanzania, can be adapted to better serve student communities; they propose that emotional insights into a student's narrative recounts can assist in developing more empathic, compassionate and lenient educational assessment regulations that may be better suited to local cultural contexts. In Chapter 8, Caoimhe Isha Beaulé and Mari Viinikainen explore the notion of generating trust through storytelling because such practices can foster supportive environments and collaboration in translocal or transdisciplinary organisational contexts, where team members are from diverse – including Indigenous or minority – backgrounds. In Chapter 9, Juha Iso-Aho, Nina Luostarinen and Pekka Vartiainen explore the relationship between historic and local stories, place making and empathy; this chapter uses stories to illustrate how they can facilitate empathic processes and connections between people because narrative practices can facilitate an understanding of being in someone else's shoes. From a personal perspective, Michelle Olga van Wyk uses empathy as a form of knowledge with the aim to identify potential pathways for enhancing creative learning journeys for both students and learning facilitators that can encourage connections and healing through a storytelling method. Van Wyk transfers her personal experiences of working environments in which tensions exist to an organisational level in Chapter 10.

In Section C, the role of design in creating empathy explores how design–whether product or service design – can find opportunities to initiate action with the beneficiaries of organisations and social endeavours. In Chapter 11, Mira Alhonsuo and Mariluz Soto focus on a south–north service design collaboration to gain insights into the service prototyping experience in a Chilean context; they explore how empathy can be better defined in service prototyping processes to improve and clarify empathy adoption into organisational processes. In Chapter 12, Tarja Pääkkönen and Marina Bos-de Vos engage in a theoretical exploration of the benefits and drawbacks of 'empathy work' by professional designers in multidisciplinary collaborations. Organisational development needs are explored in Chapter 13, also from the perspective of service design in the manufacturing industry; here, Krista Korpikoski seeks to understand how organisations can become more receptive to empathic development approaches. In Chapter 14, Bruna Montuori, Maria Luiza Vianna, Rosana Vasques and Maria Cecilia Loschiavo use two Brazilian case studies to present a critical perspective on whether empathy is enough as a design method to engage with marginalised groups. They argue that empathy can fall short of understanding the complexities of systems and legacies of oppression in peripheral contexts. The section concludes with Chapter 15 by Heidi Pietarinen, Eija Timonen and Melanie Sarantou, who address how materiality can mediate empathy among people in cross-cultural contexts, for example, in tourism.

In Section D, the role of technology in creating empathy and scaling up empathic action is the focus. In Chapter 16, Päivi Hanni-Vaara explores empathy in a digital customer tourism journey; she analyses a leisure traveller's experiences of empathy by drawing on the perspectives of cognitive and affective empathy. In Chapter 17, Yangyang Zhao and Timothy Craig explore how to digitally transform venture-wide operations by using empathy in strategic planning. The authors propose five design principles and practical activities that can guide organisational (re)design for embedding empathy into business processes. In Chapter 18, through an ethnography with delivery cyclists in Brazil, Eduardo Rumenig Souza, Luiz Eduardo Dantas, André Casanova Silveira, Rosana Vasques and Maria Cecilia Loschiavo dos Santos deliberate whether digital platforms are led by values of morality, mutual aid and solidarity, or instead whether such platforms are driven by apathy and competitiveness instead of human-centred and empathic approaches. The final chapter of the book, Chapter 19, by Rob van den Hoven van Genderen, Rosa Maria Ballardini and Marcelo Corrales, delivers a fresh perspective, exploring the role of empathy in the regulation of AI innovations in terms of user-centric perspectives on intellectual property rights and privacy. Through this lens, the authors discuss the perceived lack of empathy in the application of the law, which is expected to maintain objective views, despite its instrumentality in creating communications and relations between people.

Although the book is divided into four sections to illustrate the process of empathic action proposed in Figure 1.1, readers should be aware that we do not propose four sections that are detached from one another. Empathy is often generated and continued throughout processes that often need to overlap, flow and extend. At the same time, empathy can be interrupted or even end in the same processes. That is why we do not wish to create explicit sections throughout the book, but we do indicate where our readers can find chapters related to a specific topic in the Table of Contents. Readers will also notice that some chapters span over several of the steps we propose. Chapter 4, for example, focuses on empathy generated through creativity, artistic processes (step 1), but it also addresses how empathy works in digital environments (step 4). The themes of Chapter 5 again flow into steps 1 and 2 of the proposed process of empathic action. We seek to understand how empathy comes about through practical implementation and doing, which often entails unique interpretative and intuitive shared processes. Each chapter provides two practical summaries that provide readers with knowledge of how empathy can be practically applied in different organisational contexts. Additionally, readers are presented with two summaries at the end of each chapter in which the authors give a synopsis of the practical implications offered for organisational and business contexts.

References

Archer, D., & Finger, K. (2018). Walking in another's virtual shoes: Do 360-degree video news stories generate empathy in viewers? Columbia Academic Commons Report 2018, Tow Centre for Digital Journalism. https://academiccommons.columbia.edu/doi/10.7916/D8669W5C.

Ashworth, P., & Lucas, U. (2000). Achieving empathy and engagement: A practical approach to the design, conduct and reporting of phenomenographic research. *Studies in Higher Education*, 25 (3), 295–308.

Baron-Cohen, S. (2012). *The science of evil: On empathy and the origins of cruelty*. Basic Books.

Baron-Cohen, S., & Wheelwright, S. (2004). The empathy quotient: An investigation of adults with Asperger syndrome or high functioning autism, and normal sex differences. *Journal of Autism Development and Disorders*, 34 (2), 163–175. https://doi.org/10.1023/B:JADD.0000022607.19833.00.

Batterbee, K., Suri, J. F., & Howard, S. G. (2014). Empathy on the edge: Scaling and sustaining a human-centered approach in the evolving practice of design. Innovation Design Engineering Organization (IDEO). http://www.ideo.com/images/uploads/news/pdfs/Empathy_on_the_Edge.pdf.

Bloom, P. (2017). *Against empathy: The case for rational compassion*. Random House.

Brink, T. T., Urton, K., Held, D., Kirilina, E., Hofmann, M., Klann-Delius, G., Jacobs, M. A., & Kuchinke, L. (2011). The role of orbitofrontal cortex in processing empathy stories in 4- to 8-year-old children. *Frontiers in Psychology*, 2, 80.

Chapman, J. (2015). *Emotionally durable design: Objects, experiences and empathy*. Routledge.

Cuykendall, S., Soutar-Rau, E., Cochrane, K., Freiberg, J., & Schiphorst, T. (2015). *Simply spinning: Extending current design frameworks for kinesthetic empathy*. In Proceedings of the Ninth International Conference on Tangible, Embedded, and Embodied Interaction (pp. 305–312). TEI '15, Stanford, CA, USA, 15–19 January; ACM New York.

Dam, R. F., & Siang, T. Y. (2020). Design thinking: Getting started with empathy. Interaction Design Foundation. https://www.interaction-design.org/literature/article/design-thinking-getting-started-with-empathy.

De Lille, C., Roscam Abbing, E., & Kleinsmann, M. (2012,). *A designerly approach to enable organizations to deliver product-service systems*. 2012 International Design Management Research Conference, 8–9 August;Boston, MA, United States.

Ekman, P. (2007). *Emotions revealed. Recognizing faces and feelings to improve communication and emotional life* (2nd ed.). Holt Paperback.

Ekman, P., & Ekman, E. (2017). Is global compassion achievable? In E. M. Seppälä, E. Simon-Thomas, S. L. Brown, M. C. Worline, C. D. Cameron, & J. R. Doty (Eds.), *The Oxford handbook of compassion science* (pp. 41–49). Oxford University Press.

Faver, C. A., & Alanis, E. (2012). Fostering empathy through stories: A pilot program for special needs adoptive families. *Children and Youth Services Review*, 34 (4), 660–665.

Gair, S., & Moloney, S. (2013). Unspeakable stories: When counter narratives are deemed unacceptable. *Qualitative Research Journal*, 13 (1), 49–61. https://doi.org/10.1108/14439881311314568.

Galinsky, A. D., Maddux, W. W., Gilin, D., & White, J. B. (2008). Why it pays to get inside the head of your opponent: The differential effects of perspective taking and empathy in negotiations. *Psychological Science*, 19 (4), 378–384.

Gaver, W., Dunne, T., & Pacenti, E. (1999). Design: Cultural probes. *Interactions*, 6 (1), 21–29.

Gökçiğdem, E. M. (2019). Preface: Designing for empathy and the oneness mindset. In Gökçiğdem, E. M. (Ed.), *Designing for empathy: Perspectives on the museum experience* (pp. 15–21). Rowman & Littlefield.

Goleman, D. (2003). What makes a leader? In L. W. Porter, H. L. Angle, & R. W. Allen (Eds.), *Organizational influence processes* (pp. 229–241). M. E. Sharpe.

Humphrey, R. H. (2013). The benefits of emotional intelligence and empathy to entrepreneurship. *Entrepreneurship Research Journal*, 3 (3), 287–294.

Juntunen, A., & Saarti, J. (2000). Library as the student's cornerstone or obstacle: Evaluating the method of empathy-based stories. *Libri*, 50 (4), 235–240.

Karppinen, S., Poutiainen, A., Kairavuori, S., Rusanen, S., & Komulainen, K. (2018). ImproStory: Social improvisation and storytelling in arts and skills subjects in teacher education. *International Journal of Education & the Arts*, 19 (9).

Knochel, A. D., Hsiao, W. H., & Pittenger, A. (2018). Touching to see: Tactile learning, assistive technologies, and 3-D printing. *Art Education*, 71 (3), 7–13.

Kouprie, M., & Visser, F. S. (2009). A framework for empathy in design: Stepping into and out of the user's life. *Journal of Engineering Design*, 20 (5), 437–448.

Lather, P. (2000). Against empathy voice and authenticity. *Kvinder, Køn & Forskning*, 4. https://doi.org/10.7146/kkf.v0i4.28384.

Leonard, D., & Rayport, J. F. (1997). Spark innovation through empathic design. *Harvard Business Review*, 75, 102–115. https://cem.nd.edu/assets/171111/peter_zapf_spark_innovation_through_empathic_design.pdf.

Marchetti, A., Miraglia, L., & Di Dio, C. (2020). Toward a socio-material approach to cognitive empathy in autistic spectrum disorder. *Frontiers in Psychology*, 10 (2965). https://doi.org/10.3389/fpsyg.2019.02965.

Mattelmäki, T., Vaajakallio, K., & Koskinen, I. (2014). What happened to empathic design? *Design Issues*, 30 (1), 67–77.

Miettinen, S., Sarantou, M., & Akimenko, D. (2016). Collaborative art and storytelling as an empowering tool for service design: South Australian case study. In P. Rytilahti & S. Miettinen (Eds.), *For profit, for good: Developing organizations through service design*. University of Lapland Press.

Miettinen, S., Sarantou, M., & Kuure, E. (2019). Design for care in the peripheries: Arts-based research as an empowering process with communities. *Nordes*, 8. https://archive.nordes.org/index.php/n13/article/view/467/438.

Moore, R. J., & Hallenbeck, J. (2010). Narrative empathy and how dealing with stories helps: Creating a space for empathy in culturally diverse care settings. *Journal of Pain and Symptom Management*, 40 (3), 471–476.
New, S., & Kimbell, L. (2013). *Chimps, designers, consultants and empathy: A theory of mind for service design.* In Proceedings of the Cambridge Academic Design Management Conference (pp. 1–14), 4–5 September.
Ohren, D. (2014). The limits of empathy in business ethics education. *Business Ethics Journal Review*, 1 (18), 113–119.
Patnaik, D. (2009). *Wired to care: How companies prosper when they create widespread empathy*. FT Press.
Pavlovich, K., & Krahnke, K. (Eds.). (2013). *Organizing through empathy*. Routledge.
Powell, P. A., & Roberts, J. (2017). Situational determinants of cognitive, affective, and compassionate empathy in naturalistic digital interactions. *Computers in Human Behavior*, 68, 137–148.
Reynolds, D., & Reason, M. (Eds.). (2012). *Kinesthetic empathy in creative and cultural practices*. Intellect Books.
Riess, H., & Neporent, L. (2018). *The empathy effect: Seven neuroscience-based keys for transforming the way we live, love, work, and connect across differences*. Sounds True.
Rumble, A. C., Van Lange, P. A., & Parks, C. D. (2010). The benefits of empathy: When empathy may sustain co-operation in social dilemmas. *European Journal of Social Psychology*, 40 (5), 856–866.
Saarikivi, K. (2018). Empathy, emotion, technologies and human experience. The Evolving Role of Service Design, HKISDNC18. https://www.youtube.com/watch?v=gufub7Ee480https://www.bing.com/videos/search?q=Saarikivi+Katri+2017+youtube+empathy&view=detail&mid=2CAA151A10E26A4ABBFB2CAA151A10E26A4ABBFB&FORM=VIRE.
Shamay-Tsoory, S. G., Tomer, R., Berger, B. D., Goldsher, D., & Aharon-Peretz, J. (2005). Impaired 'affective theory of mind' is associated with right ventromedial prefrontal damage. *Cognitive Behavioural Neurology Sciences*, 18, 55–67.
Sommer, D. (1994). Resistant texts and incompetent readers. *Poetics Today*, 15 (4), 523–551.
Tunstall. E. (2013). Decolonizing design innovation: Design anthropology, critical anthropology. In G. Wendy, T. Otto, & R. C. Smith (Eds.), *Design anthropology, theory and practice* (pp. 232–250). Bloomsbury Academic.
Tzouramani, E. (2017). Leadership and empathy. In J. Marques & S. Dhiman (Eds.), *Leadership today* (pp. 197–216). Springer.
Ventura, M. (2019). *Applied empathy: The new language of leadership*. Hachette UK.
Wetter-Edman, K. (2013). Relations and rationales of user's involvement in service design and service management. In S. Miettinen & A. Valtonen (Eds.), *Service design with theory: Discussions on change, value and methods* (pp. 107–116). Lapland University Press.
Young, I. (2015). *Practical empathy: For collaboration and creativity in your work*. Rosenfeld Media.

Section A

The role of creativity and the arts in creating empathy

Step 1: Create connections for generating empathy

2 'We really have quite a lot to say …'

Fostering agency of youth with asylum-seeking backgrounds by arts-based methods and dialogue as actions of empathy

Enni Mikkonen and Katri Konttinen

Introduction

People fleeing from wars, conflicts and other adversities and seeking asylum in a new country are often presented as political and demographic challenges, using terms such as refugee 'flood' or 'wave' (Seppälä et al., 2020). In addition, many studies have demonstrated that, in popular political and governmental rhetoric, young people are often perceived from the perspective of risk (Hart, 2009). Young people with asylum-seeking backgrounds carry the double burden of being viewed as inclined toward radicalisation, thus being a potential societal threat to be governed and controlled (Hart, 2009). This nativist and racialised problem-oriented view, in addition to being harmful by feeding social polarisations and racism, disregards young people and their communities' internal diversities, agencies, creativity and capabilities (Jennings et al., 2008). When seeking transformative human-centred solutions to current global challenges – such as forced migration – new approaches and methods with social and participatory aspects need to be developed, which widen the discourse about youth to view them as capable of handling and transforming their difficulties into solutions and empowerment (Canuday, 2009). In this chapter, we reflect on the potentialities of interdisciplinary and multiprofessional arts-based methods (ABM) and dialogues by addressing *empathy* in a non-governmental, not-for-profit organisational context to foster the agency of youth with asylum-seeking backgrounds and to deconstruct the social divisions.

When new services in an organisational setting are developed at short notice as the global crises emerge, the importance of strengthening professional practices based on the principles of human rights, social justice and empowerment is highlighted. We focus on the third sector, which has been a crucial 'partner' of the public sector, to varying degrees in different societies, in providing services for promoting the well-being of people at the margins. However, in recent years, the third sector has increased its collaboration with private organisations in order to grow the business sector's social responsibility (Levitt, 2016). In the time of the 'refugee crisis' in Europe in 2015 (Seppälä et al., 2020), the third

DOI: 10.4324/9781003227557-3

sector, along with public and private service providers, responded to the growing need for organising reception and integration services for newcomers. This chapter is based on our arts-based research (ABR) collaboration with a non-governmental organisation (NGO) that had established a family community home for unaccompanied young asylum seekers during the 'crisis'. Our NGO perspective focuses on the improvement of youth's well-being and integration by strengthening their sense of belonging and building connections to their new environments.

We build on an interdisciplinary approach combining socially engaged and environmental arts-based methods (ABM) (Kester, 2005; Leavy, 2009, 2018; Sederholm, 2000) with a critical social work perspective (Dominelli, 2010; Fook, 2016; Jennings et al., 2008). We address arts-based dialogues as reflective and reflexive spaces of mutual learning, unlearning and relearning (Leavy, 2018) across disciplinary, professional, cultural and ethnic boundaries. These processes and spaces are multidimensional and multisensory, including actions based on creativity and interconnectedness via bodily, interactional and visual exercises. We seek to analyse the dimensions of empathy that ground those exercises and interactions, but also discuss how they can generate empathic action in the NGO setting for designing measures adapted to the degree of agency and self-determination of youth in rapidly changing environments (Massey et al., 2008).

Empirically, the chapter is based on a qualitative, ethnographic and participatory study implemented as a part of an international research project, SEEYouth – Social Innovation through Participatory Art and Design with Youth at the Margins: Solutions for Engaging and Empowering Youth with Trans-Atlantic Mirroring – that responds to the societal challenge of marginalisation of young people in different contexts across the globe. The analysis builds on our collaboration in designing and implementing an arts-based workshop with the NGO partner and seven young people with asylum-seeking backgrounds in Southern Finland in the spring and summer of 2020. This workshop formed an important basis to build trust and continue collaboration with the youth later on via online and face-to-face workshops and an art-exhibition that are analysed in more detail elsewhere (Konttinen et al., forthcoming).

We view empathy through an interdisciplinary approach. First, we build on its links with arts regarding art education (Bertling, 2015), theatre (Blair, 2009) and dance (Katan-Schmid & Gillette, 2017). Empathy has been considered from the perspectives of *embodiment* – in physical reactions and actions; *affection* – in being able to feel what another person is feeling; *cognitive capacity* – in taking the perspective of another person (visualisation and imagination of the other's situation); and *monitoring mechanisms* – in separating one's feelings from those of the other (Blair, 2009). By building on these perspectives, we approach empathy as a dialogical process by engaging in mutual arts-based exercises to gain a better understanding of oneself and the other, which increases critical self-reflexivity and is an ethical ground for ABR. Second, we build on the notion of empathy as carrying social responsibility, a core element in social work (Cipolla & Bartholo, 2014). While the importance of empathy is incorporated in social work practice, it is not sufficiently researched as a social work skill (Lynch et al., 2019). By reflecting on practising empathy through ABM, this chapter provides new approaches to social work and not-for-profit organisations' professional skills.

We discuss empathy in terms of actions and dialogues with youth to strengthen their capabilities and creativity and to gain more control over their own lives. By building on a critical paradigm (Dominelli, 2010; Fook, 2016; Jennings et al., 2008), we emphasise the structural dimension in this action: to address power hierarchies, structural obstacles and social injustices that may hinder youth's agency in their social environments and integration processes. In this light, we seek to respond to the following research question: *How can arts-based methods (ABM) and dialogue using a critical social work paradigm create practices building on empathy and foster the agency of youth at the margins?* Based on our findings, we consider empathy as *social and environmental interconnectedness* in reflective ABM and dialogues. We discuss interconnectedness that leads to creating a 'third space' (Bhabha, 2004; Soja, 1996) in the arts-based workshops, which functions as an ethically sensitive, mutually trustful basis for building empathy and fostering agency with the youth from asylum-seeking backgrounds. This chapter provides insights to transformative potentials of interdisciplinary and multicultural professional action and dialogues in an NGO setting to seek for coherence in fragmented social systems.

Building empathy through socially engaged and environmental arts-based methods with the critical social work perspective

The theoretical premise of the chapter lies in our interdisciplinary framework combining the critical social work paradigm and ABR. As ABR focuses on discovering the potentialities of the arts by combining them with the humanities and sciences (Leavy, 2018), we build on the approaches of *socially engaged* and *environmental art* that both highlight the importance of multidisciplinary processes (Hiltunen, 2020). They also communicate well with *social work* (Dominelli, 2010) as they build on active participation, communication and interaction with communities in the arts-based processes. We intertwine these approaches in participatory methods leading towards youth-centred arts-based dialogues that form the core of our knowledge production. In this study, collaboration of a social work researcher, an artist-researcher and an advisor on multicultural youth work from an NGO was achieved in reflective conversations, based on the premise of being 'context providers' rather than 'content providers' (Kester, 2005) and thus creating space for youth's agency, expertise and perspectives.

One of the premises of *socially engaged art* is to bring transformation in the consciousness of participants through dialogues (Kester, 2005). Different methods can be utilised in socially engaged art practices, which are often context bound, dealing with issues that affect people's everyday lives (Sederholm,

2000). Those arts-based activities contain a component of dialogue as their core element (Edwards et al., 2016) in which youth's contribution as experts by experience is utilised by sharing their knowledge intertwined with creative working. Dialogue via ABM provides visual and embodied tools for reflecting emotions, thoughts and senses on the environmental and social aspects.

As it is enmeshed with the social aspect of ABM, we utilise *environmental art* that connects with places through meaning-making rather than merely creating an object placed in an environment. This art form deepens our experience of place and creates interaction between people and places (Huhmarniemi & Jokela, 2018). We build on methods that focus on opening senses and observing one's environment from the point of view of inspiration, belonging and identity. Both socially engaged and environmental art are often driven by the ideas of change and temporariness, highlighting the uniqueness of the situation (Sederholm, 2000) and place, which characterise the artworks and the processes. Our approach to arts-based dialogue reflects on different topics in innovative and sometimes provocative ways that can lead to unexpected and even emancipatory outcomes, according to Edwards et al. (2016). They also noted that arts-based dialogues combine environmental and social aspects in a contextual manner. These dialogues are not led by an artist or a researcher, whose role is to place youth's voices at the core and deconstruct obstacles to their expression and self-determination and provide tools and methods that foster dialogue.

Our approach is based on the facilitators' participation in the exercises with a critical dialogue in working towards new understandings and insights, empathy and connectedness with youth (Edwards et al., 2016; Mikkonen et al., 2020). This approach draws upon the *critical social work paradigm* that is premised on the importance of deconstructing social injustices and advocating for structural change, as opposed to seeing social problems as individual issues (Dominelli, 2010; Fook, 2016). In this light, ABM and dialogue need to reflect critically on epistemic and social power relations amongst facilitators, youth and their social contexts (Mikkonen et al., 2020). It is particularly important to pay attention to the specific vulnerability of youth with asylum-seeking backgrounds, as the question of their empowerment and agency links with the complexities of integration, including temporal, institutional, social and experiential dimensions (Mikkonen, 2019). By recognising these complexities, critically reflective ABM and dialogue aim at active community participation in advocating for socio-political transformation (Jennings et al., 2008; Canuday, 2009), which deconstructs the risk-based discourse of the youth at the margins. These processes are both physical and reflective, which we approach as characteristics to develop empathy and embodied understanding (Katan-Schmid & Gillette, 2017) beyond different boundaries.

In our interdisciplinary approach to *empathy*, we acknowledge its complexity and multidimensionality (Lynch et al., 2019; Blair, 2009). Amongst the three identified dimensions of empathy, the emotional, cognitive and behavioural (Lynch et al., 2019), we especially focus on the behavioural aspect in order to address it as actions taking place via *interconnectedness* on social, cultural and environmental levels, which enable dialogical and relational encounters (Bertling, 2015). Our methodological and theoretical framework supports this approach first, through the critical social work paradigm and socially engaged art to acknowledge cultural, ethnic and language differences and create connectedness across them via dialogues (Lynch et al., 2019). The actions that are based on multidimensional interconnectedness function as a prerequisite for empathy, and they include social relevance (Bertling, 2015). Second, we utilise environmental arts for building empathy that highlights an aspect of creating connectedness beyond an anthropocentric perspective – via enjoyment of nature, empathy for creatures and a sense of oneness and responsibility towards the environment (Bertling, 2015).

The benefits of empathy are obvious (connectivity and potential for a positive change), but there is also a need for a critical examination of it (Blair, 2009; Cipolla & Bartholo, 2014). Providing straightforward interpretations of empathy without a critical approach risks simplification of complex issues or projection of ourselves into another's situation, 'overfeeling' or 'consuming' another's situation and remaining concerned only with emotions rather than participating or promoting change (Blair, 2009). Empathy can also contrast with inclusion in the risk of disregarding the other's subjectivity via aiming to 'know' the other, which is, however, never fully possible as empathy is built on dialogues with a person(s) with their unique perspectives and agency (Cipolla & Bartholo, 2014). By building on the critical paradigm, we highlight that empathy requires reflection on multiple and intersecting power structures – such as those based on racialised, colonial, socio-economic, cultural or gendered hierarchies – and 'blind spots' that a person with privileges may carry, including a risk of being overprotective of or victimising the other, thus disregarding their agency (Dominelli, 2010). Through reflective discussions and ABM crossing disciplinary, cultural, social and language barriers, we go on to address the development of tools and spaces for building empathy to generate new social processes and dialogues that deconstruct power hierarchies and support the agency of young people at the margins.

Arts-based research involving youth with asylum-seeking backgrounds

The empirical basis of the chapter lies in ethnographic and participatory ABR involving youth with asylum-seeking backgrounds in Southern Finland. The methodological frame was built on an interdisciplinary approach, resulting in carefully planned and structured, intensive workshop activities with the youth. The process started by negotiating with the advisor on multicultural youth work from the NGO context, as he had been a manager of a family community home and an instructor of the youth when they had first arrived in Finland one to five years earlier. The collaborator's commitment to the project's aims and purpose was pivotal in defining the spaces, structures and framework of the workshops. He provided critical insights into the benefits and risks of youth participation, resulting in insightful interprofessional discussions throughout the process. His role in reaching the youth, communicating and translating the project into the 'youth's language' formed a cornerstone in gaining trust and legitimating the workshop activities from the youth's perspective. The NGO collaborator's knowledge on youth's needs, wishes, challenges and skills guided us for contextual sensitivity, thus functioning as an ethical basis of the project.

As the COVID-19 pandemic broke out prior to the workshops, digital communication and tools took a central role in the planning process. After identifying the participants, we connected with them via a WhatsApp group. However, building trust with the youth also required face-to-face meetings to increase their commitment and gain a deeper mutual understanding. The participants were 18–20 years old, six boys and one girl, originally from the Middle East and Africa, with residence permits in Finland. Their Finnish language skills were sufficient for communicating in plain language, and some discussions were translated into English. In the meeting prior to the workshops, we 'travelled' on the Google Earth site to introduce the roots of the participants and the project's international partners, to orientate to the workshop's emotional and social space.

The workshop methods were designed after the first meeting, considering the specificity of the group. In reflective negotiations with the NGO collaborator and the youth, participatory methods through socially engaged and environmental arts formed the basis for the activities addressing themes that related to challenges and future prospects of the youth. The workshop was designed to be a 'camp' – in the youth's terms – over a weekend. The chosen site was a villa in the countryside, as the environment was considered an important aspect for interaction, communication and co-reflection via embodied and dialogical exercises. Especially after the COVID-19 isolation, the space away from the youth's daily contexts and the face-to-face interaction functioned as a basis for intimate and in-depth reflections. The themes of the workshop were divided into two categories, starting from the past and present, proceeding towards the future, namely: *identity, worries, challenges, global connection* and *future, dreams, hopes and inspiration.*

The first workshop, entitled 'Me and My Environment', began with lighting a candle as a symbol of a 'global campfire' to lead into a workshop mode. The participants – including the facilitators – presented photographs and visual items to tell about themselves, with the intention to evoke the emotional and visceral responses in the group via representing their memory (Leavy, 2009) and to create a sense of connectivity and intimacy. The second workshop addressed the theme of 'Our Space', utilising various materials such as wooden discs, paints and coloured pencils to express one's place in the world. This workshop took a different turn than planned, and the youth started to use the given materials on their own terms, resulting in colourful pictures about their homes of origin, families, dreams and the emotional processes of 'needing and sharing warmth' in their lives.

Figure 2.1 The 'camp' consisted of multiple communal, embodied and symbolic exercises. Photographs by Katri Konttinen and Mikko Ylisuvanto.

The third workshop, 'Let's Move Together!', created space for physical activity and freedom for the youth to design their own activities. They acted as workshop facilitators and chose to go for a ride on fat bikes and presented relaxed and happy responses afterwards. At the end of the first workshop day, we gathered around the campfire to discuss the youth's worries and their universality. The youth expressed their worries in their mother tongue through writings that were collected in a wooden box. At the end, the collected worries were cast into the fire as a symbol of letting go of them. The reflective discussion was insightful and in-depth, and youth found it particularly meaningful regarding their fears, racism, challenges of integration and identity.

The fourth workshop, 'Forest Pond', started the second day of the camp. This activity began with a 'path of senses', a multisensory walk in the countryside ending at a small lake, during which we focused on different senses, and the youth created their own inspiration jars from small findings in the surrounding environment, which were later shared with the group (Waara & Konttinen, 2013). In the fifth workshop, 'Future', we utilised creative letter writing for 'future me' (Bolton, 2004), inspiring the youth to imagine what their wishes, dreams and goals would be regarding their lives after five years.

The workshop sessions created a continuum, and at the end of each session, there was a reflective moment that proved to be the core of the in-depth interaction; the youth expressed their ideas and reflections, which indicated their creativity, wisdom and capabilities. Having time and space for two days was important in deepening the reflection and communication, as the NGO collaborator reflected:

> this was lovely regarding time as there is a night in between so you can make kind of a continuum to this. It was really nice as you could finish one thing. To put those worries there and tomorrow is a completely other thing. Then your brain has processed over the night what was done during the day. It's not only a two-hour workshop and you go.

The research data consisted of the audio recorded and transcribed discussions with the youth and the collaborative partner, photographs, video clips, artefacts of the youth and reflective diaries on participatory observation of the researchers. The data analysis was based on multiple methods, starting from the content analysis (Neuendorf, 2011) by open coding and thematic categorisation of audio-recorded and transcribed reflective discussions. The ethnographic analysis method (Davies, 1999) was used for reflective and reflexive research notes on participatory observation, and visual analysis (Pink, 2009) was used for the material produced in the workshops: photos, videos and artefacts. An analysis framework was formed via identifying the themes by mirroring the data to the research questions and the interdisciplinary reflections.

Ethical considerations were important, as the research involved youth from multiple margins. The main ethical premise was to ensure that the participants' knowledge and agency were centralised and that they could take an active role in creating their own narratives based upon their experiences and expertise. The researchers aimed at continuous *critical reflexivity* and establishment of trust with the participants, enabling them to control the information they wanted to share. *Informed consent* was obtained from the youth after explaining their rights in participation (the right to withdraw from the project at any time, anonymity and safety) in an inclusive and interactive process.

Findings: Social and environmental interconnectedness for building empathy by arts-based methods

Our findings illustrate that empathy through ABM was based on *interconnectedness* that enabled dialogical and relational encounters with the youth and the NGO collaborator (see also Bertling, 2015). We identified two major dimensions of interconnectedness regarding youth's agency in our intercultural workshop space: *the social and environmental*. These dimensions were overlapping and related also to other dimensions, such as economics, which, however, was not widely reflected on by the youth in the workshop. We discuss our findings by illustrating the main themes regarding these dimensions of interconnectedness and how they emerged through ABM in the workshops.

Social interconnectedness

Interconnectedness on a social level took multiple forms, intersecting with societal, cultural, economic, ethnic and gendered structures (Dominelli, 2010). These dimensions were reflected in the question of *identity* that became the main theme of the workshops, which the youth discussed particularly regarding the question of *belonging*. Via creative visualisations, writing and reflective dialogues, the youth presented in-depth insights on their 'in-betweenness' of different cultures. They identified themselves as being partly Finnish and partly belonging to their country/culture of origin, as this data extract indicates:

> Finnishness. I visited there [*in his country of origin*] and people were always talking to each other. Always. – for example, you go to a shop and the cashier talks with you. She is a best friend with you. Like that. But it was a bit weird to me. I would not like to share my information with them. Who are they? I don't know them. Like all that Finnish culture has impacted. Yes, I am a multicultural person, and I am in between them.

This youngster reflected on cultural differences and his relation to individuality as a virtue in Finnish society versus communality in his country of origin, resulting in describing his multicultural identity as being fluid and dynamic. In terms of building social interconnectedness in Finnish society, the youth presented challenges related to racism (and fear that it awakens) and the cultural value of independence that causes loneliness. In spite of the youth being located at the margins by ethnicity, language, and religion, their active agency, openness and creativity in the arts-based activities and dialogues built connections to each other and the facilitators and, symbolically, to youth in other contexts. The reflections on these connections could be harnessed to also strengthen social interconnectedness in wider contexts and to develop professional working methods in the third sector.

Identity questions were also present in the reflections on the *meaning of place*. Exploring the participants' hometowns via Google Earth was an important moment of sharing intimate and original details of oneself. The discussions, followed by our cross-world travels online and other exercises, showed various interpretations of meaningful places. As the youth described their home countries, cities and villages, the value of *home* and *roots* was strongly present. Despite the experiences and circumstances that had forced the youth to leave their homes, they described the places through positive memories and wishes to return one day. However, traumatic experiences and difficult emotions were also shared, especially worries about their families back home. We reflected on these worries with the participants by utilising social work and the NGO collaborator's professional knowledge to emotionally support the youth. Visualising memories via creative methods strengthened the youth's agency and indicated social interconnectedness to their origins. These memories were intertwined with the current place and moment in their narratives and expressions. Thus, social interconnectedness contained the meaning of place and home in temporal and spatial dimensions, as past and present were intertwined via the meaningfulness of the youth's original and current home countries.

In building social interconnectedness, the questions of differences and diversities are crucial (Dominelli, 2010). Our findings show that social interconnectivity by ABM and dialogues created space for innovative communication methods, which included the potential to transcend professional, cultural, ethnic and language barriers. One of the participants reflected on his painting that illustrated social interconnectedness via a colourful image:

> There is some green and here some yellow, meaning different situations in life. Sometimes there can be situations where we feel bad or there are problems, let us say hundreds and thousands of things. But, for example, this spring or when it's cold outside, you see some people who come and help you. This is what I mean, to bring warmth to your life.

Thus, social interconnectivity as an aspect of empathy builds on mutual respect and support in a creative space and unique time and place. The holistic theme behind the camp was the ideal of a 'global campfire'. Via its symbolic meaning, we built connections to the wider context to mirror challenges and solutions with youth in different parts of the world. The campfire functioned as a space to be present and to encounter each other without diminishing the differences but with respecting and celebrating them.

Figure 2.2 Visual expressions of social and environmental interconnectedness. Photograph by Katri Konttinen.

Environmental interconnectedness

The meaning of interconnectedness beyond the anthropocentric sphere was highlighted in the environmental arts-based exercises and closeness of nature in the camp. The youth expressed their views via the exercises that guided them to 'open' their *senses* – focusing on smelling, hearing, feeling and seeing on the nature path – and to utilise natural materials for their inspiration besides visual and embodied expressions. Environmental interconnectedness was also illustrated in their free exploration of the surroundings, which expressed their enjoyment of nature and responsibility towards the environment (Bertling, 2015). The outdoor activities emphasised the importance of the senses in getting to know new places and surroundings, which was reflected on by the youth during these activities. The exercises illustrated how opening one's senses to environments could also open them to self-knowledge, helping to root oneself to a place, which can be an empowering and healing experience for the youth at the margins, as the NGO collaborator explained to one of the participants who lay on a large rock during our reflective discussion:

> Now when you are lying here [*on a rock*], we have done those exercises, where we learn to ground ourselves when we are feeling stressed or have experienced a trauma.

The importance of *space* and *embodiment* are intertwined in the environmental interconnectedness that fosters empathy (Blair, 2009). Interconnectedness expanded beyond physical to social and psychological spheres, forming a safe space where the youth could freely express themselves with confidence and feel they would be heard and respected. Their body language in the exercises indicated *safety, trust* and *affection*. They did not withdraw from the discussions or the activities; instead, they chose active and open participation. A carefully selected environment together with a well-structured programme played an important role in creating a sense of respect towards the time that the youth provided by participating in the workshops and the views and creativity they contributed to the project. The closeness to nature in early summer greenery created a unique atmosphere that was one of the cornerstones of the participatory arts-based action for creating empathy.

The nature connection included a potential to overcome sadness and feel joy and beauty, as two of the youth expressed after the exercise of collecting natural materials for the 'inspiration jar':

> There [*in a glass jar*] is water. Water is important for life, it makes me happy. When I am feeling sad or shy, I drink water. It makes me feel good. There are flowers and a tree. A park.

> This is the aquarium of life. There are all sorts of things inside, some stones and a small lawn, not real one. Then there are flowers. I just made it look nice, without any specific meaning ... I just wanted to make a beautiful scene.

The interconnectedness to nature was a shared experience; the youth spoke about the importance of protecting it and the vitality of water as a symbolic and concrete prerequisite of life. Also, their narratives of home included multiple nature elements. Environmental interconnectedness as a part of creating practices for empathy draws on the meaning of being responsible and sustainable, simultaneously building on social interconnectedness beyond different contexts to aim at transformation for a better future.

Discussion: 'Third space' as a context for empathy through mutual action and dialogue

An important element that made the workshop into a meaningful and inspiring space for co-creation was – in the words of one of the participants – its wider purpose. This purpose was symbolic, developed around the concept of a 'global campfire', aiming to create a safe and inspirational 'third space' (Bhabha, 2004; Soja, 1996) that was based on dialogic processes, which proved to be the core element of building empathy through ABM. The third space was a reflective place for addressing global interconnectedness and challenging topics from the youth's perspective. We view the third space via the sense of radical openness and hybridity, paying attention to the uniqueness of each person, actor and context (Bhabha, 2004). As the critical social work paradigm sheds light on the processes for deconstructing social injustices and advocating for structural change (Fook, 2016), we argue that this unique third space, building on social and environmental interconnectedness, has a potential for transformation through capturing the shifting and changing milieu of ideas, events, appearances and meanings (Soja, 1996).

The workshop space was identified as the creation of 'our place – a meaningful place' (Cresswell, 2004, 7) for discussion and sharing with mutual trust. The evaluation of the workshop showed that by merely stepping out of the expert's role and giving space for the youngsters to share their thoughts and creating a space in their own – yet shared – terms, remarkable results were achieved. The third space as a sense of sharing was strongly present, for instance, when sitting around the campfire and the discussion flowed freely. In such a space, also the quieter youth started to speak about their worries and wishes, which proved that arts-based dialogue could lead to unexpected and emancipatory outcomes (Edwards et al., 2016). This space of in-depth reflections was re-created exercise by exercise in a flexible and reflexive process where social and environmental interconnectedness was practised and strengthened in a tangible way.

The third space for building empathy was based on collaboration crossing professional, disciplinary, cultural and social boundaries, where the voices of the youth were placed at the core. For the facilitators, the third space was about learning, unlearning and relearning together with the participants (Baldacchino, 2013; Leavy, 2018). The youth shared insights about their everyday lives, cultural knowledge and the challenges they face. For example, their reflections on racism showed that it was a shared worry, yet it does not represent a similar worry for people embodying whiteness, which indicates the normativity of whiteness in a Finnish society. These insights were based on the youth's expertise derived from experience as they added their creativity, perspectives and strengths to this collaborative space; thus, they acted to generate empathy through mutual action. Dialogue drawing upon arts-based activities became a central part of the process and can be seen as an outcome in socially engaged art (Kester, 2005). ABM supported and inspired the dialogues, building and strengthening empathy within the group and providing visual forms for the topics the youth wished to address.

Building empathy through socially engaged and environmental ABM with a critical social work perspective was based on a symbolic 'third space' where the agency of the youth was considered as a potential that could be harnessed to drive for transformation not only in their personal lives but also on a wider perspective, such as political spheres. Social interactions, intertwined with an environmental aspect, can produce new social phenomena (Massey et al., 2008), such as novel actions and systems for social justice and coherence. The 'third space' with a mutually predetermined purpose can retain the creative force of empathy as a basis for the youth to participate in designing new solutions for encountering global challenges. For the third-sector organisations working with young asylum seekers, it can provide novel tools to address human needs and act with empathy that fosters youth's agency to act on their own terms.

The reflections on empathy through action provide in-depth insights for utilising ABM in developing professional tools that strengthen social and environmental interconnectedness and promote the holistic well-being of youth. Using interdisciplinary reflections such as our collaboration generated, NGOs could create new spaces for empathy through action, where the structures, environments and social relations could be developed to utilise the youth's expertise that is often disregarded in public discourses perpetuating a risk-oriented view of youth. In those spaces, the youth's statement that 'we really have quite a lot to say ...' provides possibilities for them to flourish. Ultimately, in building empathy through arts-based action and dialogues that aim at generating new social processes for deconstructing power hierarchies and supporting agency of young people at the margins, the question is about creating spaces where youth can feel warmth, happiness and joy.

Summary 1: Lessons learned that can contribute to the organisational or business context

- A strong, long-term and trustful connection between the professionals from the NGO and the youth was at the core in building empathy by arts-based methods amongst the researchers, artists and youth. This was a timely process that required continuity, constant negotiations and a critical approach.

- When building empathy action by arts-based methods with youth at the margins, the main aspects were about prioritising the youth's time, needs, wishes and creativity, and acknowledging the unique, situated and contextual dimensions with ethical considerations; via clear structures, comfortable facilities and a safe environment and space (not overly regulated), the trust with the youth was established.

Summary 2: Contribution to organisational or business knowledge or practices

- By working with an interdisciplinary and multiprofessional approach (such as combining social work, arts-based research and multicultural youth work approaches) with youth from asylum-seeking backgrounds, organisations could develop their methods to harness interactional creativity and create a safe 'third' space for youth's agency and interconnectedness that can transcend social, cultural, ethnic, and language barriers in novel ways.
- The contribution of arts-based methods can be observed through actions that endorse youth's creative skills via providing tools for visualising and expressing their ideas, generating in-depth reflections. Thus, empathy action through arts support their well-being and sense of belonging and can contribute to organisations' work for creating social justice and preventing marginalisation.

References

Baldacchino, J. (2013). Willed forgetfulness: The arts, education and the case for unlearning. *Studies in Philosophy and Education*, 32, 415–430. https://doi.org/10.1007/s11217-012-9339-y.

Bertling, J. G. (2015). The art of empathy: A mixed methods case study of a critical place-based art education program. *International Journal of Education & the Arts*, 16 (13). http://www.ijea.org/v16n13/.

Bhabha, H. K. (2004). *The location of culture*. Routledge.

Blair, R. (2009). Cognitive neuroscience and acting: Imagination, conceptual blending, and empathy. *The Drama Review*, 53 (4), 92–103.

Bolton, G. (2004). *Writing cures: An introductory handbook of writing in counselling and psychotherapy*. Brunner-Routledge.

Canuday, J. J. (2009). Beyond powerlessness: Celebrating the power of the displaced. In A. K. Giri (Ed.), *The modern prince and the modern sage: Transforming power and freedom* (pp. 249–270). SAGE India.

Cipolla, C., & Bartholo, R. (2014). Empathy or inclusion: A dialogical approach to socially responsible design. *International Journal of Design*, 8 (2), 87–100.

Cresswell, T. (2004). *Place: A short introduction*. Blackwell.

Davies, C. A. (1999). *Reflexive ethnography: A guide to researching selves and others*. Routledge.

Dominelli, L. (2010). *Social work in a globalizing world*. Polity Press.

Edwards, D. M, Collins, T. M., & Goto, R. (2016). An arts-led dialogue to elicit shared, plural and cultural values of ecosystems. *Ecosystem Services*, 21, 319–328.

Fook, J. (2016). *Social work: A critical approach to practice*. SAGE Publishing.

Hart, S. (2009). The 'problem' with youth: Young people, citizenship and the community. *Citizenship Studies*, 13 (6), 641–657.

Hiltunen, M. (2020). Taiteelle ominainen työskentely rakentaa tekijäänsä ja maailmaa ympärillämme [Working for art builds its maker and the world around us]. *Opetushallitus*. https://www.oph.fi/fi/koulutus-ja-tutkinnot/taiteelle-ominainen-tyoskentely-rakentaa-tekijaansa-ja-maailmaa-ymparillamme.

Huhmarniemi, M., & Jokela, T. (2018). Ympäristötaide taiteilijan soveltavana ja integroituna osaamisena [Environmental Art as an applied and integrated competence of an artist]. In T. Jokela, M. Huhmarniemi, C. Haataja, & T. Issakainen (Eds.), *Ympäristötaidetta Lapin matkailuun* [*Environmental Art for Lapland Tourism*] (pp. 107–121). University of Lapland.

Jennings, L. B., Parra-Medina, D., Hilfinger-Messias, D. K., & McLoughlin, K. (2008). Perspectives on participation: Toward a critical social theory of youth empowerment. *Journal of Community Practice*, 14 (1–2), 31–55.

Katan-Schmid, M., & Gillette, E. (2017, 19–22 April). *Dance for empathy: Embodied practice and the physical-mental act of understanding*. Dance Fields Conference, University of Roehampton. https://www.academia.edu/31534528/Dance_for_Empathy_Embodied_Practice_and_the_Physical_Mental_Act_of_Understanding_Book_of_abstracts_Dance_fields.

Kester, G. (2005). Conversation pieces: The role of dialogue in socially-engaged art. In Z. Kucor & S. Leung, *Theory in contemporary art since 1985* (2nd ed., pp. 153–165). Wiley-Blackwell.

Konttinen, K., Mikkonen, E., & Ylisuvanto, M. (forthcoming). Dialogues for plurality – arts-based exchange for strengthening youth's role as agents of change. In S. Miettinen, E. Mikkonen, M. Sarantou, & M. C. Loschiavo dos Santos (Eds.), *Artistic cartographies and design explorations towards the pluriverse*. Routledge.

Leavy, P. (2009). *Method meets art: Art-based research practice*. The Guilford Press.

Leavy, P. (2018). *Handbook of arts-based research*. The Guilford Press.

Levitt, T. (2016). *Partners for good business, government and the third sector*. Routledge.

Lynch, A., Newlands, F., & Forrester, D. (2019). What does empathy sound like in social work communication? A mixed-methods study of empathy in child protection social work practice. *Child & Family Social Work*, 24, 139–147.

Massey, D., Valkonen, J., Lehtonen, M., Rantanen, P., Valkonen, J., & Rovio, J. (2008). *Samanaikainen tila* [Simultaneous Space]. Vastapaino.

Mikkonen, E. (2019). Arts-based approaches to challenge cultural otherisation in social integration processes. *På Spissen/Dance Articulated*, 30–32.

Mikkonen, E., Hiltunen, M., & Laitinen, M. (2020). My stage: Participatory theatre with immigrant women as a decolonizing method in art-based research. *Art/Research International: A Transdisciplinary Journal*, Special issue on 'Encountering Artistic Research Practices: Analyzing their Critical Potentialities', 5 (1). https://doi.org/10.18432/ari29474.

Neuendorf, K. A. (2011). Content analysis: A methodological partner for gender research. *Sex Roles*, 64, 276–289.

Pink, S. (2009). *Doing sensory ethnography*. SAGE Publishing.

Sederholm, H. (2000). *Tämäkö taidetta?* [Is this art?]. WSOY.

Seppälä, T., Nykänen, T., Koikkalainen, S., Mikkonen, E., & Rainio, M. (2020). In-between space/time: Affective exceptionality during the 'refugee crisis' in Northern Finland. *Nordic Journal of Migration Research*. https://doi.org/10.2478/njmr-2019-0029.

Soja, E. (1996). *Thirdspace: Journeys to Los Angeles and other real-and-imagined places.* Blackwell.

Waara, S., & Konttinen, K. (2013). RiverSounds – JoenÄäniä. Creating new connections between contemporary art, design and traditional cultures. In G. Coutts, M. Huhmarniemi, E. Härkönen, & T. Jokela (Eds.), *Cool: Applied visual arts in the North* (pp. 167–171). Lapland University Press.

3 Encouraging empathy in creative tourism

Tatiana Kravtsov, Maria Huhmarniemi and Outi Kugapi

Introduction

This chapter approaches empathy from the perspectives of creative tourism and participatory art. We explore the transformative and educational potential of art workshops to increase both travellers' and locals' empathy towards and awareness of Arctic nature and cultures. Dialogue and transformative experiences are the key values of our study. In recent years, creativity in tourism has received significant attention from scholars and practitioners alike (Kugapi et al., 2020; Richards 2011, 2019, 2020; Sarantou et al., 2021). Creativity can be enhanced by creative people working as activity facilitators as well as through tourism experiences that engage participants (Kugapi & Höckert, 2020; Kugapi et al., 2020; Richards, 2011; Sarantou et al., 2021). Creative tourism offers opportunities for cultural encounters, dialogue and knowledge exchange (Duxbury & Richards, 2019; Miettinen, 2007; Richards & Wilson, 2006) and can encompass many fields of art and culture, including literature, cultural events and education, to name a few (Richards, 2011). In this chapter, we discuss how challenges to the development of sustainable tourism are addressed in Finnish Lapland. More specifically, we focus on the design of a creative tourism service that enhances cultural exchange and nature connectedness. Culture, along with cultural sustainability, is both an enabler and a driver of the economic, social and environmental dimensions of sustainable development (Soini & Birkeland, 2014). The art and heritage sector constituted the organisational context of our study. The creative tourism service is designed to be marketed and sold by art museums and galleries in Lapland, with the aim of employing artists and crafters in collaboration with art and tourism agencies.

Discussing empathy, Peloquin (1996) explains that "a person who hopes to be empathic must pursue an experience that awakens the sense of fellowship" (pp. 660–661). Empathy involves the capacity to adopt the perspective of the (human or non-human) other, to establish an emotional bond with that other and to understand the other's emotions (Brown et al., 2019). Our study was motivated by new models both for stimulating people's empathy to increase their awareness of sustainability issues and for exploring interactions between place, identity and empathy (Brown et al., 2019).

DOI: 10.4324/9781003227557-4

In Finnish Lapland, discussions on sustainable development have a practical orientation with the aim of solving local and regional problems in tourism, such as seasonality, un-ecological motor-based tourism services and the appropriation of the Indigenous Sámi culture. Scholars have also used the concept of Arctification to point out stereotypical images of the North that overlook the cultural diversity of the region (Chartier, 2018; Rantala et al., 2019). Northern and Arctic communities also face issues related to the effects of climate change, globalisation, unemployment and shifting demographics, all of which require culturally sensitive solutions, such as developing services in a place-specific and participatory manner (see Olsen et al., 2019; Rantala et al., 2019). New activities in the tourism sector should, therefore, be developed locally and based on local knowledge. For example, these activities should increase tourists' and locals' awareness of the cultural richness of Lapland, enhance their authentic experiences of nature and culture and stimulate empathy towards local nature, culture and people. Landscape painting courses, nature photography activities, crafting workshops and gallery tours that include dialogue and creative activities are some potential means of developing art-based activities for tourists visiting Lapland that also provide possibilities for empathic bonding with a place and its people. Cultural sensitivity, which includes avoiding cultural appropriation, must be carefully considered when designing services to be used by the growing tourism sector.

In this chapter, we present a case study of birch bark weaving from Finnish Lapland, with a focus on designing a culturally sustainable creative tourism service. Two testbeds were used: the first in an outdoor environment and the second in a gallery space (Figures 3.1 and 3.2). Due to travel restrictions caused by Covid-19, in both testbeds, the group of participants included locals and newcomers but not actual tourists. The case study was part of the Art-Based Services for Tourism project, 2019–2021, funded by the European Regional Development Fund (ERDF). The project focused on helping artists, crafters and designers in Lapland develop new tourism activities and products. It supported artists as well as art gallery and art museum enterprises in collaborating with the tourism industry and mediating creative tourism services for tourism clients and agencies. Arts-based research methods (Jokela, 2019) and action-research approaches were implemented in the Art-Based Services for Tourism project. The focus was on participatory art to encourage meaningful and transformative tourism experiences, the celebration of local cultures' and human diversity and the stimulation of empathy towards nature and people.

The ERDF programme (2014–2020) was intended to strengthen economic and social cohesion in the European Union by correcting imbalances between regions. The programme invested in innovation and research, the digital agenda, support for small- and medium-sized enterprises and the low-carbon economy. The case study presented in this chapter was part of a development project that supported small enterprises, such as art galleries, and non-commercial associations in Finnish Lapland, where tourism creates jobs and income without, until now, sufficiently benefiting artists (Kugapi et al., 2020).

Figure 3.1 Birch bark weaving workshop, in outdoor environment, August 2020, Rovaniemi. Photographs by Tatiana Kravtsov.

Crafting and dialogue for revitalisation and empathy

Scholars have conducted research on artistic practices based on narrative and dialogue for the place-bound identity-building of individuals and communities (Akimenko, 2018; Hiltunen, 2010). Akimenko (2018) describes how empathy and narrative sharing can be created using an arts-based approach to tacitly impact the identity work of individuals and communities beyond verbalisation. Similar place-based strategies have been studied as part of the new genre of public art (Lacy, 1995), relational aesthetics (Bourriaud et al., 2002) and participatory art (Matarasso, 2019). Competitiveness and creativity have also been examined in the rural–urban framework (Huggins & Clifton, 2011). Place-based strategies involve using the capacities of places and communities to foster regional development (Daniels et al., 2015; Dredge & Jenkins, 2003). In tourism scholarship, such approaches are usually described as participatory tourism development (Höckert, et al., 2021; Saarinen, 2010). In sustainability research, the value of empathy, place and identity interactions is similarly considered to be highly significant (Brown et al., 2019).

In this article, we consider how place-making offers development possibilities to remote, rural and peripheral places that function as centres for their inhabitants, giving communities control and ownership of their cultures, as discussed in tourism research (Saarinen, 2010), and capacities for empowerment and regional identity, as proposed in arts research (Hiltunen, 2010). Creative tourism applies place-making strategies to allow artists and designers to earn a sustainable living and establish new businesses in collaboration with art institutions and organisations as well as tourism enterprises (Kugapi et al., 2020). The development of arts- and crafts-based participatory activities has been motivated by sustainability studies, where sustainability is considered not merely as economic and ecological well-being but as including cultural and social principles.

Richards and Raymond (2000) emphasise participation in creative experiences as a characteristic feature of creative tourism, with creativity offering new opportunities, innovation and mobility. Tourists' participation in creative activities, Pine and Gilmore (1999) suggest, can make their experience more valuable, enjoyable and memorable, while Du Cros and McKercher (2015) highlight the participatory element as requisite for successful cultural tourism attractions. A deep connection between the visitors and the culture and place occurs when the visitors observe and participate in traditional craft-making, which involves emotions and senses.

Creative workshops allow participants to make objects with aesthetic and cultural value and offer possibilities for dialogue, sharing and learning, as well as encountering nature through tactile practices with natural materials. As Peloquin (1996) argues, the activation of bodily senses in artistic activities is necessary to increase empathy. In the workshop discussed in this study, stories and experiences related to birch trees and bark were shared between hosts and guests, locals and visitors, with the aim of fostering empathy, cultural exchanges and fellowship. Sharing narratives allows the imagination to envisage new perspectives and increases understanding of the other. Peloquin (1996) suggests that only after such involvement can a person enhance their capacity to respond, feel and make connections.

While fellowship, empathy and a sense of community among art workshop participants is a common aim of artists (Akimenko, 2018; Matarasso, 2019), the need to also extend empathy to non-human actors through art is currently being studied by many scholars (Flynn & Reed, 2019; Raatikainen et al., 2020). Northern ecoculture – the tradition of knowing and feeling with nature – offers an interesting context for such studies; in our case, the context involved material harvested from the forest. Throughout generations, people living in the North have developed strong bonds with the forest, which are reflected in folklore, traditional beliefs and everyday life. According to Pallasmaa (1987), the forest, which has provided raw material for buildings, tools and household objects, has been a source of imagination and spirituality, inhabited by mythical creatures: "The forest was a sub-conscious sector of the Finnish mind, in which feelings of both safety and peace, and fear and danger lay" (p. 16). During the last several decades, the lives of many Finns have shifted from natural to urban environments. Consequently, their closeness to and unique sense of the forest, tacit knowledge of natural materials and ability to listen and observe nature have been lost or forgotten among the routines of urbanised life.

We wanted to find out whether these values and this bond with nature could be revitalised (along with the revitalisation of crafting skills) and whether Northern ecoculture could be shared with guests, as Huhmarniemi and Jokela (2020b) propose. Moreover, in developing the new creative tourism service, we were especially interested in crafts and heritage. Our aims were to study, represent and reform local traditions, create novel meanings with them and incorporate local knowledge into fresh forms of expression and innovation.

In Asia, North America and northern Europe, birch bark craft traditions have been developed and passed down through generations since ancient times. However, in current-day Finland, only a few knowledge holders of these traditions remain. To preserve this expertise, old methods for working with birch bark, such as weaving and folding, could be transmitted as cultural heritage via our tourism service. While creative activities and pedagogical encounters should be attuned to local particularities and global concerns, tourism services do not need to be the same as in traditional cultures; traditions can be transmitted respectfully while addressing contemporary needs and practices (Huhmarniemi et al., 2021).

The role of empathy in pro-environmental actions and pro-social behaviour has been identified and considered by several researchers (Brown et al., 2019; Lord-Kambitsch, 2014), who have shown that empathy for others is not sufficient for action and that place attachment can both promote sustainability and act as a barrier to change (Brown et al., 2019). To ensure planetary survival, a sense of empathy has to be expanded from humans to other animals and elements of nature (Keto, 2018). In our study, we developed and experimented with an art-based method for stimulating empathy in the context of creative tourism in Lapland. Due to the scope of this chapter and our research data, we do not evaluate the activity's long-term impact on emphatic relations or on pro-environmental and pro-social behaviour. However, sustainability is interwoven with the development of creative tourism services because participatory arts and crafts are ecologically less harmful than tourism services based on fossil fuels and because the employment of artists and craftspeople in the tourism business supports social and economic development in Lapland.

Method: Arts-based action research

Our study followed the principles of arts-based action research (ABAR) (Jokela, 2019; Jokela & Huhmarniemi, 2018). This approach guides the progress of our research in the testbed cycles and uses art as a catalyst for development work. The ABAR method was invented mainly based on regional development projects, in which the challenges of peripheral villages and undeveloped creative industries and cultural services constituted the need for interventions, social change and empowerment though art and art education (Hiltunen, 2010; Jokela et al., 2015; Jokela et al., 2019). Long-term ABAR projects have also involved winter art in collaboration with snow and ice engineering and tourism industries; such developments have created work opportunities for snow and ice builders and carpenters and resulted in new kinds of tourism sites and services, such as snow and ice hotels (Jokela et al., 2014). Another ongoing long-term ABAR project concerns cultural sustainability in Lapland (Härkönen et al., 2018; Härkönen & Stöckell, 2019).

The ABAR strategy is useful when the goal is to create practical change, as well as valid, justified knowledge and understanding related to the change (Jokela et al., 2015; Jokela et al., 2019). The aim of knowledge in arts and art education is transformational; ABAR research is typically meant to develop increasingly functional working and teaching methods or artistic productions. The enhancement of sustainable development is closely linked to the ABAR strategy as ABAR research projects aim to develop methods, practices and models of activities that allow stakeholders, local communities and society in general to develop sustainably (Jokela et al., 2019). The roots of this research strategy can be traced back to action research, artistic research focused on artists' skills and art-based research (Leavy, 2009).

The Art-Based Services for Tourism Project includes developing performances and art workshops targeted at international tourists and sharing the cultural heritage of Lapland. For the project, the University of Lapland hired seven freelance artist-researchers with whom many university students and staff members collaborated, conducting parallel research cycles. The research process included identifying the needs, challenges and expectations of partner galleries and museums regarding tourist attractions for summer and attracting tourists to the galleries. The development work started with co-design sessions, in which artists, students and representatives of the art galleries and museums brainstormed new services. The sessions took place at the galleries and museums and involved presentations of art collections, facilities and surroundings as well as customer analyses. The sessions varied in length from a few hours to a few days. Numerous ideas and preliminary concepts were formed during the workshops, and some were chosen for further development and testing. The services mainly targeted international customers and diverse groups of locals and tourists.

In this chapter, we analyse one case from the Art-Based Services for Tourism project, which was designed and tested across two design cycles by Tatiana Kravtsov. The idea behind the birch bark weaving activity included continuing the birch bark crafting tradition by making contemporary wristbands in a participatory workshop.

During the first of the two design cycles, benchmarking was conducted to map creative tourism services offered by art museums in remote areas of the world, and theoretical knowledge was explored regarding nature connectedness, participatory art workshops and creative tourism. The collected visual and theoretical materials were analysed, and the main direction for designing the service was identified. Subsequent research revealed a fascinating world of birch bark traditions, and weaving techniques were selected for development into a creative service. The work with natural material was intended to facilitate experiences involving bodily senses that could potentially enhance nature connectedness. The first testbed for the service took place on a sunny August day at a park by a church pond in Rovaniemi and involved four participants – two locals and two newcomers from northern Russia. In the second design cycle, the data from the first testbed were analysed. The second testbed took place at a gallery, with the participants comprising a similar group of locals and newcomers.

During the two testbeds set up by artist-researcher Kravtsov, research data were collected via observations and video, audio and photographic documentation. The collected data were analysed to identify the strengths and weaknesses of the service for further development and improvement. In ABAR, participants' or users' experiences are not observed from a third-party perspective; rather, the researcher is at the core of the projects and has agency to promote development, reflection and evaluation. In our case, the data were analysed collaboratively by the authors, and one author participated in the second testbed.

Empathy increases in dialogue with participants and natural materials

Birch bark weaving is a creative tourism service conceived by the artist-researcher Kravtsov, in which birch bark traditions are shared by crafting a wristband. As one of the northernmost deciduous trees in the Arctic, birch is important for local ecocultures. Traditionally, all parts of the birch tree were used to create items essential for life in the Arctic area. Birch bark is a resistant, renewable and sustainable material that can be carefully harvested by skilled craftspersons without harming the tree (Gårdvik et al., 2014) and thus is suitable to use when developing sustainable tourism services. Common in the nineteenth and early twentieth centuries, the weaving, bending and folding of birch bark were key techniques for crafting a wide variety of artefacts, such as containers, baskets, shoes and fishing net weights (Ranta, 2016). While such knowledge has been carefully passed down generations until recent times, very few people now maintain this tradition. Therefore, the new tourism service has the potential to revitalise the cultural heritage, crafting skills and traditional nature connectedness that are typical to Northern ecoculture. The service was designed for galleries and museums (Figure 3.2) but could also be performed in outdoor settings, such as parks or forests, to enhance the bodily senses and support connectedness with nature (Figure 3.1).

The testbed consisted of four parts: introduction, discussion, crafting and feedback. During the introduction, the artist-researcher, Kravtsov, presented and discussed with the participants various types of birch, its physical and spiritual uses of the tree in Finland and other Northern cultures. Harvesting techniques and times, preservation methods and various uses of birch bark were introduced based on knowledge gathered during the literature investigation. After the discussion, the participants were given a small piece of birch bark to feel the unprocessed material and its layered structure of various textures and colours (Figure 3.1). The design of the birch bark bracelets was based on a basic

Figure 3.2 Birch bark weaving workshop, December 2020, Gallery Napa, Rovaniemi. Photographs by Tatiana Kravtsov.

weaving technique common in Finland, Russia and other Northern places. The knowledge of shared traditions increased the sense of fellowship among the workshop participants, who did not know each other before the event. One participant described her previous experiences related to birch bark traditions as follows:

> I come from the North European part of Russia, and it is a tradition there as well, but I have never done this before; of course, I knew about the shoes made of birch, baskets and so on.

During the crafting part of the activity, Kravtsov demonstrated a basic technique known in many Northern cultures. In Finland, for instance, this technique was used to weave decorative bands for birch bark hats, while in Russia, it was used to make headbands (Rutanen & Öljymäki, 2015). For the service, the woven band was reshaped into a bracelet. Following the instructions, the participants could weave a band themselves, adjusting its length to their wrist sizes (Figure 3.1). The results were jewellery pieces that transformed traditions to suit contemporary needs and cultures. The workshop demonstrated how revitalisations of past traditions could be intergenerational and intercultural (Huhmarniemi & Jokela, 2020a) and transmit traditional knowledge, arts and ecocultures to new generations and visitors in Lapland. Dialogue about the material's physical and spiritual features and the hand-making process together formed an experience that the participants appreciated and believed they would remember. Following the activity, one participant stated:

> The story deepens our [*in tourists'*] hearts while we are doing [*the activity*]. It leaves something when tourists go back to their home. The story stays with them. Whatever they make and take with [*them*], it continues to affect [*them*]. I see it as something that combines, unites the world.

The dialogue was intended to foster discussion and cultural exchange between the participants, who shared stories and knowledge related to birch trees and bark traditions in different cultures. Crafting offered the participants tactile experiences of a tradition rooted in close contact with nature. One participant pondered how she would bond with trees if she continued crafting: "With respect, with honour and with love".

The participation of both locals and newcomers enabled a conversation about traditions related to birch and bark. At the first testbed, after the bracelets were ready, the participants were asked to reflect on the workshop's structure and to share feedback regarding their experiences as well as ideas for improvements. The participants made the following suggestions: selling sets of materials with instructions that customers could bring home as souvenirs; designing postcards with birch trees or objects made of birch bark along with stories; and designing other objects with the same technique, such as hair decorations and belts. All the participants agreed that the outdoor environment was pleasant and made it easy to connect to birch trees which were visible in the surroundings. In the second testbed, one participant mentioned that after the creative activity, she would look at birch trees in a different way, feeling more connected to her local environment:

> I sense some beautiful holiness in this: respecting the material and wanting to honour, respect the work. And this is good for concentration, and you can see the beauty through your hands. I can see the beauty that comes – it is a huge aspect. It totally works for me. I sense a new way now even to see birches and other trees, but these individual birches, I see [*on my mind*], ah, there is my beautiful bracelet and this material.

The participants stated that they would be interested in similar activities when travelling themselves if the services were based on local cultures:

> If it is something like this, I would go, for example, as here are many birch trees. For me, it is something I could relate to Finland; that's why I would go. But if it is something that has nothing to do with the destination, I probably wouldn't go. It has to be unique.

Discussion

Birch bark weaving combines participatory arts, crafts and design. In the Arctic, these forms of expression are often intertwined with activities that embrace tradition and innovation and intermix participatory art, service and product design while enhancing Arctic sustainability (Kugapi et al., 2020). Making crafts items from natural materials is an essential part of ecocultural life in the North and differs from dualistic Western thinking, in which various practices are separated into isolated disciplines (Huhmarniemi & Jokela, 2020b). The approach is parallel to *Sámi duodji* (Guttorm, 2015), community art of crafted sustainability (Härkönen et al., 2018), and socially engaged art that combines service design and co-design (Härkönen & Vuontisjärvi, 2018).

Many educational philosophers and health and well-being researchers have emphasised the deep importance of personal and cultural reconnection with nature. For example, Lumber et al. (2017) examined the relationship between connectedness with nature, well-being and pro-environmental behaviour and suggested involving "contact, meaning, emotion, compassion and beauty" in activities designed as pathways to nature connectedness. These features were also part of the birch bark weaving workshop. We agree with artist-researcher Jan van Boeckel (2006), who demonstrated art's capacity to facilitate the experience of nature via our emotions, senses and creativity. Van Boeckel (2006) stated that art activities "can sharpen and refine our perception and make us sensitive to the mystery of the things around us" (p. 72). The participants similarly believed that activities such as this workshop could impact on their environmental attitudes:

> Here, we make something that we treat with respect, and we don't have to have this much – just one is enough – and it's easier now to treat it well, so it stays for years and years, and it's an honour to show them – the decorations.

Based on our case study of developing the creative tourism service, we recommend stimulating empathy towards local cultures and non-human nature through participation in creative activities involving arts and crafts. This can be done by involving the bodily senses by engaging natural materials, such as birch bark, as was done in this case study. Empathy can also be stimulated by promoting dialogue among workshop participants and inviting them to share their narratives, experiences and cultural knowledge on, for example, the materials at hand. Our study also shows how in relation to creative tourism, arts and crafts have the potential to encourage cultural continuation, support local cultural identities, revitalise Northern ecocultures and nature connectedness and inspire empathy towards Arctic nature, cultures and peoples. Participants' positive experiences in creative activities can also prompt their interest in creative tourism services offered by art museums and galleries and thus support the sustainable development of the Arctic tourism business. Art and craft institutions should employ artists to develop such services further. We consider the enhancement of empathy, cross-cultural dialogue and transformative experiences in relation to nature connectedness to be essential to increasing cultural sustainability in Lapland and elsewhere in the Arctic region.

Summary 1: Lessons learned that can contribute to the organisational or business context

The art and heritage sector constituted the organizational context of our study. Creative activities offered by art museums and galleries will support the sustainable development of the Arctic tourism business. Employment of artists and crafters in collaboration with art and tourism agencies can be achieved by applying place-making strategies in creative tourism sectors. Arts and crafts in creative tourism have the potential to encourage cultural continuation, support local cultural identities, revitalise Northern ecocultures and enhance empathy towards Arctic nature, culture and people.

Summary 2: Contribution to organisational or business knowledge or practices

In our study we applied art-based methods for stimulating empathy in the context of creative tourism in Lapland. Our study demonstrates how such creative activities in tourism can support social and economic development in Lapland. We argue that new arts- and crafts-based creative tourism services can bring together locals and tourists via creative and empathic practices, introducing local traditions to visitors and transforming cultural heritage into creative tourism and contemporary culture.

References

Akimenko, D. (2018). *Narrative spaces: On identity work and placeness through arts-based narrative practices* [Doctoral thesis, University of Lapland]. Acta electronica Universitatis Lapponiensis. https://lauda.ulapland.fi/handle/10024/63503.

Bourriaud, N., Pleasance, S., & Woods, F. (2002). *Relational aesthetics.* Les presses du reél.

Brown, K., Adger, W. N., Devine-Wright, P., Anderies, J. M., Barr, S., Bousquet, F., Butler, C., Evans, L., Marshall, N., & Quinn, T. (2019). Empathy, place and identity interactions for sustainability. *Global Environmental Change*, 56, 11–17.

Chartier, D. (2018). *What is the "Imagined North."*Presses de l'Université du Québec.

Daniels, J., Baldacchino, G., & Vodden, R. (2015). Matters of place: The making of place and identity. In K. Vodden, R. Gibson, & G. Baldacchino (Eds.), *Place peripheral: Place-based development in rural, island, and remote regions* (pp. 23–40). ISER Books.

Dredge, D., & Jenkins, J. (2003). Destination place identity and regional tourism policy. *Tourism Geographies,* 5 (4), 383–407. https://doi.org/10.1080/1461668032000129137.

Du Cros, H., & McKercher, B. (2015). *Cultural tourism* (2nd ed.). Routledge.

Duxbury, N., & Richards, G. (2019). *A research agenda for creative tourism.* Edward Elgar Publishing.

Flynn, A., & Reed A. (2019). Building ecological ontologies: Ecojustice education becoming with(in) art-science activism. In R. Foster, J. Mäkelä, & R. Martusewicz (Eds.), *Art, ecojustice, and education: Intersecting theories and practices* (pp. 124–140). Routledge.

Gårdvik, M., Stoll. K., & Sörmo, W. (2014). Birch bark: Sustainable material in an authentic outdoor classroom. In T. Jokela & G. Coutts (Eds.), *Relate North 2014: Engagement, art and representation* (pp. 146–168). Lapland University Press.

Guttorm, G. (2015). Contemporary duodji: A personal experience in understanding traditions. In T. Jokela & G. Goutts (Eds.), *Relate North: Art, heritage and identity* (pp. 60–76). Lapland University Press.

Härkönen, E., Huhmarniemi, M., & Jokela, T. (2018). Crafting sustainability: Handcraft in contemporary art and cultural sustainability in Lapland. *Sustainability*, 10 (6), 1907. https://doi.org/10.3390/su10061907.

Härkönen, E., & Stöckell, A. (2019). Cultural sustainability in art-based interdisciplinary dialogue. *International Journal of Art & Design Education*, 38 (3), 639–648.

Härkönen, E., & Vuontisjärvi, H. (2018). Arctic art and design education and cultural sustainability in Finnish Lapland. In T. Jokela & G. Coutts (Eds.), *Relate North: Practising place, heritage, art & design for creative communities* (pp. 86–105). Lapland University Press.

Hiltunen, M. (2010). Slow activism: Art in progress in the North. In A. Linjakumpu & S. Wallenius-Korkalo (Eds.), *Progress or perish: Northern perspectives on social change* (pp. 119–138). Ashgate.

Höckert, E., Kugapi, O., & Lüthje, M. (2021). Hosts and guests in participatory development. In A. Harju-Myllyaho & S. Jutila (Eds.), *The future of inclusive tourism* (pp. 15–32). Channel View Publications.

Huhmarniemi, M., & Jokela, T. (2020a). Arctic arts with pride: Discourses on Arctic arts, culture and sustainability. *Sustainability*, 12 (2), 604. https://doi.org/10.3390/su12020604.

Huhmarniemi, M., & Jokela, T. (2020b). Arctic art and material culture: Northern knowledge and cultural resilience in Northernmost Europe. In L. Heininen, H. Exner-Pirot, & J. Barnes (Eds.), *Arctic yearbook 2020: Climate change and the Arctic: Global origins, regional responsibilities?*Arctic Portal. https://arcticyearbook.com/.

Huhmarniemi, M., Kugapi, O., Miettinen, S., & Laivamaa, L. (2021). Sustainable future for creative tourism in Lapland. In N. Duxbury, S. Albino, & C. Pato Carvalho (Eds.), *Creative tourism: Activating cultural resources and engaging creative travellers* (pp. 239–253). Cabi International.

Huggins, R., & Clifton, N. (2011). Competitiveness, creativity, and place-based development. *Environment and Planning A*, 43 (6), 1341–1362.

Jokela, T. (2019) Arts-based action research in the North. In G. Noblit (Ed.), *Oxford research encyclopedia of education*. Oxford University Press.

Jokela, T., Härkönen, E., & Yliharju, A.-J. (Eds.). (2014). *Snow design in Lapland: Initiating cooperation*. Lapland University Press.

Jokela, T., Hiltunen, M., & Härkönen, E. (2015). Art-based action research: Participatory art for the North. *International Journal of Education Through Art*, 11 (3), 433–448.

Jokela, T., & Huhmarniemi, M. (2018). Art-based action research in the development work of arts and art education. In G. Coutts, E. Härkönen, M. Huhmarniemi, & T. Jokela (Eds.), *The lure of Lapland: A handbook of Arctic art and design* (pp. 9–23). Lapland University Press. https://lauda.ulapland.fi/handle/10024/63653.

Jokela, T., Huhmarniemi, M., & Hiltunen, M. (2019). Art-based action research: Participatory art education research for the North. In A. Sinner, R. L. Irwin, & J. Adams (Eds.), *Provoking the field: International perspectives on visual arts PhDs in education* (pp. 45–56). Intellect.

Keto, S. (2018). Mihin jengiin kuulut? – Eli miten sosiaalisuutemme rajat vaikuttavat empatian piirimme laajuuteen [Which gang do you belong to? That is, how the boundaries of our sociality affect the extent of our empathy]. In S. Keto & E. Aaltola (Eds.), *Empatia: Myötäelämisen tiede* [*Empathy: The science of compassion*] (pp. 249–265). Into.

Kugapi, O., & Höckert, E. (2020). Affective entanglements with travelling mittens. *Tourism Geographies*, 1–18. https://doi.org/10.1080/14616688.2020.1801824.

Kugapi, O., Huhmarniemi, M., & Laivamaa, L. (2020). A potential treasure for tourism: Crafts as employment and a cultural experience service in the Nordic North. In A. Walmsley, K. Åberg, P. Blinnikka, & G. T. Jóhannesson (Eds.), *Tourism employment in Nordic countries: Trends, practices, and opportunities* (pp. 77–99). Palgrave Macmillan. https://doi.org/10.1007/978-3-030-47813-1.

Lacy, S. (1995) Debated territory: Towards a critical language for public art. In S. Lacy (Ed.), *Mapping the terrain: New genre public art* (pp. 171–185). Bay Press.

Leavy, P. (2009). *Method meets art: Arts-based research practice*. Guilford Press.

Lord-Kambitsch, E. (2014). Introduction to empathy: Activation, definition, construct. *Think Pieces: A Journal of the Arts, Humanities, and Social Sciences*, 1 (1), 1–8.

Lumber, R., Richardson, M., & Sheffield, D. (2017). Beyond knowing nature: Contact, emotion, compassion, meaning, and beauty are pathways to nature connection. *PloS One*, 12, e0177186. https://doi.org/10.1371/journal.pone.0177186.

Matarasso, F. (2019). *A restless art: How participation won, and why it matters*. Calouste Gulbenkian Foundation.

Miettinen, S. (2007). *Designing the creative tourism experience: A service design process with Namibian craftspeople* [Doctoral thesis, University of Art and Design Helsinki].

Olsen, K. O., Abildgaard, M. S., Brattland, C., Chimirri, D., De Bernardi, C., Edmonds, J., Grimwood, B. S. R., Hurst, C. E., Höckert, E., Jæger, K., Kugapi, O., Lemelin, R. H., Lüthje, M., Mazzullo, N., Müller, D. K., Ren, C., Saari, R., Ugwuegbula, L., & Viken, A. (2019). *Looking at Arctic tourism through the lens of cultural sensitivity: ARCTISEN – A transnational baseline report*. Lapland University Press. http://urn.fi/URN:ISBN:978-952-6620-39-8.

Pallasmaa, J. (1987). Architecture of the forest. In K. Tapper, S. Sarajas-Korte, A. Ruusuvuori, E. Rauske, J. Pallasmaa, S. Heikkilä, & T. Periäinen (Eds.), *The language of wood: Wood in Finnish sculpture, design and architecture* (pp. 16–22). Museum of Finnish Architecture.

Peloquin, S. M. (1996). Art: An occupation with promise for developing empathy. *American Journal of Occupational Therapy*, 50 (8), 655–661. https://doi.org/10.5014/ajot.50.8.655.

Pine, B. J., & Gilmore, J. H. (1999). *The experience economy: Work is theatre & every business a stage.* Harvard Business School Press.

Raatikainen, K. J., Juhola, K., Huhmarniemi, M., & Peña-Lagos, H. (2020). "Face the cow": Reconnecting to nature and increasing capacities for pro-environmental agency. *Ecosystems and People*, 16 (1), 273–289. https://doi.org/10.1080/26395916.2020.1817151.

Ranta, S. (2016). *Ylimuistoinen tuohi: Käytön kulttuurihistoriaa* [*Memorable birchbark: The cultural history of its usage*]. Maahenki.

Rantala, O., de la Barre, S., Granås, B, þór Jóhannesson, G., Müller, D. K., Saarinen, J., Tervo-Kankare, K., Maher, P. T., & Niskala, M. (2019). *Arctic tourism in times of change: Seasonality.* Nordic Council of Ministers.

Richards, G. (2011). Creativity and tourism: The state of the art. *Annals of Tourism Research*, 38 (4), 1225–1253. https://doi.org/10.1016/j.annals.2011.07.008.

Richards, G. (2019). Creative tourism: Opportunities for smaller places? *Tourism & Management Studies*, 15, 7–10. https://doi.org/10.18089/tms.2019.15SI01.

Richards, G. (2020). Designing creative places: The role of creative tourism. *Annals of Tourism Research*, 85. https://doi.org/10.1016/j.annals.2020.102922.

Richards, G., & Raymond, C. (2000). Creative tourism. *ATLAS News*, 23, 16–20.

Richards, G., & Wilson, J. (2006). Developing creativity in tourist experiences: A solution to the serial reproduction of culture? *Tourism Management*, 27 (6), 1209–1223. https://doi.org/10.1016/j.tourman.2005.06.002.

Rutanen, E., & Öljymäki, J. (2015). *Tuohitöiden käsikirja* [*Handbook for bark crafts*]. Minerva.

Saarinen, J. (2010). Local tourism awareness: Community views in Katutura and King Nehale Conservancy, Namibia. *Development Southern Africa*, 27 (5), 713–724.

Sarantou, M., Kugapi, O., & Huhmarniemi, M. (2021). Context mapping for creative tourism. *Annals of Tourism Research*, 86, 103064. https:/doi.org/10.1016/j.annals.2020.103064.

Soini, K., & Birkeland, I. (2014). Exploring the scientific discourse on cultural sustainability. *Geoforum*, 51, 213–223. https://doi.org/10.1016/j.geoforum.2013.12.001.

Van Boeckel, J. (2006). Forget your botany: Developing children's sensibility to nature through arts-based environmental education. *The International Journal of the Arts in Society*, 1, 71–82.

4 Empathy in digital participatory artworks

Katja Juhola, Marija Griniuk and Smaranda-Sabina Moldovan

Introduction

In a digital era, particularly with the new emphasis on digital communications due to COVID-19, we need to enhance our creativity, confidence and resilience to handle unexpected situations. We will focus on practices in creative participation and how to utilise digital channels to communicate and increase empathy and creativity in real time in different participatory contexts, such as art performance, art symposia and art events. One part of our study arose from the human–nature dialogue and how this exercise was conducted using online participation. We present digital empathy from the position of an artists' ability to connect and share experiences and feelings with the audience or co-participating artists through technology used during art events. The *Power of Nature* (PoN) study case shows that researchers will meet nature as an equal participant, as posthumanism or transhumanism describes it (Valera, 2014).

This study extends the long-term arts-based action research of Finnish artist researcher Katja Juhola and Lithuanian artist researcher Marija Griniuk. The third author is an art educator and artist researcher Romanian Smaranda-Sabina Moldovan, who participated as an artist of Juhola's long-term research in the International Socially Engaged Art Symposium (ISEAS) and the *PoN* workshop. People will have to change their consumption habits. We see digitalisation as an opportunity to form a new community activity that includes nature as a participant. Our study presents cross-border and arts-based action research into communicating empathy and compassion through digital connections in participatory art. We explore the patterns of challenges and possibilities in digital communication in art. Artists' responses can play a meaningful role in enhancing and communicating empathy in digital connections involving humans and non-humans. In the artwork, these responses interconnect towards the emotionally safe and welcoming common space of creativity, despite the difference in the backgrounds of the involved participants and facilitators. Thus, art can be used to develop empathy because it is based on the kinship of the common functions of both practices: response, emotion and connection (Peloquin, 1996). According to Trott's (2017) definition, radical innovation is based on introducing new technology to service production. We see using

DOI: 10.4324/9781003227557-5

digital channels in art practice or curating as filling these criteria. However, according to Sarantou (2020), challenges tend to inundate processes. Sarantou argued that overcoming challenges requires innovative strategies supported by empathetic art-based approaches (2020). This provides new opportunities for re-examining and adapting the most effective ways to expand artistic practices.

We present two case studies: socially engaged art and performance art. We used the arts-based action research (ABAR) method to develop two different kinds of research. In both studies, digitality embraces empathy. The first case study is the August 2020 *International Socially Engaged Art Symposium* (ISEAS), which featured international online participation for the first time. ISEAS shows how arts-based methods can create emphatic attitudes towards nature. The second case study presents the performance *Territory* by Griniuk, realised in 2018. Here, performance art meets digital channels to communicate empathy and interconnectedness between the artist and the audience using visual or audio outcomes in real time during the performance.

We ponder what factors could strengthen the conditions for success in digital participation and provide recommendations on how to make it more motivating and successful using empathy as a key tool. Arts-based research (ABR) (Barone & Eisner, 2012; Leavy, 2017, 2018; McNiff, 1998; Rolling, 2013) uses art as a tool to access research results. Art can be used to illuminate things that might otherwise be hidden or difficult to express verbally. ABR is inherent in the researchers' interests and methods of art. ABR can be used through conversational art (Bhabha et al., 1998; Kantonen, 2005, 2010; Kester, 2004). Juhola's research focuses on developing an intensive art symposium (ISEAS) (see Table 4.3). Griniuk steps into the context of technology-based participation in real time during a performance from the perspective of a performance artist. Embodied experience is at the core of her study as bodily sensations happen in the action space. Griniuk's research focuses on developing methods through which these moments of bodily involvement and creative enlightenment can be transferred to digital sociomateriality during an art event in real time. Both cases share performative and participatory acts of art.

We aim to jointly find new digital methods and recommendations to enhance motivation within participation based on developing empathic ways in the field of socially engaged art (SEA) and performance art. Our research question arises from the current global social and artistic context and pro-force technology-based innovations: How can digitality be applied to art workshops and artistic fieldwork? We also examine how arts-based methods could be used in the wider field of organisations, where art could be used as a method to develop empathic actions towards nature.

How empathy can be used to develop a participatory artwork

Digital empathy comprises five types of empathy (Friesem, 2016b). These five different types of empathy layered our structural stages of constructing a digital-art event. Kester (2004) argued that empathic vision is an essential part of dialogical aesthetics in participatory art. He suggested that empathy is a necessary basis for communicating and understanding race, sexuality or ethnic origin, which is essential in cross-border and cross-cultural art events. Empathy towards nature (see Table 4.1) is the ability to consider 'Others'– non-humans, and thus, 'ecocentric orientation' was developed (Lithoxoidou et al., 2017). As posthumanism sees all living beings on an equal footing, the 'ecocentric orientation' makes people's needs less important to secure other living beings.

Thompson (2012) claimed that SEA had revealed numerous tensions over the past 40 years, primarily by shaking the foundations of art discourse and sharing techniques and ideas in fields far from the forms of classically perceived art. In the 1990s, Lacy (2010) highlighted the struggle between the SEA and more traditional art. Lacy argued that participatory art is a competitive option where artists connect with a wide and diverse audience, and each group contributes to the discussion. Lacy's art pattern is based on the relative aesthetic (Bourriaud et al., 2002) and the dialogical aesthetic (Kester, 2004).

Performance art focuses on participatory practices centred on the artist's role as a facilitator. Schechner (1977) claimed that performance is artistic action, consistent with a ritual, where transformation happens in a liminal space. Participatory performance is discussed by Bishop (2004) as artwork in which the audience can become a collaborator and transgresses the threshold of spectatorship. In this study, we used 'participatory performance' and 'art' to describe artworks containing participation and interconnectedness between all involved in real-time action, including nature. Kinaesthetic empathy (Kim, 2015) as empathy-in-movement is applied in performance artwork. Miettinen et al. (2016) stated that the storytelling narrative function is a crucial tool that facilitates empathic processes, primarily in service design.

McKenzie (2001) argued that a liminoid space is a meeting between technology and performance. Liminoid space includes cultural, organisational and technological performances, which are digitally remediated and united in the performative space (McKenzie, 2001). Trott (2017) introduced technology-based innovation,

Table 4.1 Definitions of empathy used in this study, developed by the authors of this study based on the previous research (Friesem, 2016a; Kim, 2015; Lithoxoidou et al., 2017).

Term	*Explanation*
Digital empathy (Friesem, 2016a)	Empathy between humans immersed in digital and media activities.
Kinaesthetic empathy (Kim, 2015)	Empathy is based on encounters with aesthetic objects or experiences and one's feelings relating to them.
Empathy towards nature (Lithoxoidou et al., 2017)	Empathy in which humans put nature needs above their personal interests to promote environmentally friendly values.

which can be applied to techno-performance (McKenzie, 2001), focusing on the cyber-spatiality of bodies immersed in interactions by technological means. This technology allows the performer or artist facilitator or a curator-facilitator and participants to experience bodily sensation in playing the performative action, which happens in this liminoid space. Hobye and Lowgren (2011) showed that connectedness and empathy within the digital performance space have three key points: the performer strategy, the social play in the performance space and the narrative built in the interactions (Hobye & Lowgren, 2011). According to Salen and Zimmerman (2004), sounds and images impact the motivation to participate in social play, which is determined by a safe and non-judging environment that allows empathic connections between the facilitator and participants. Both of our cases show narrative playfulness that has been created using empathy to create a truthful atmosphere for creating something new.

Methodology

ABAR was developed at the University of Lapland (Hiltunen, 2008; Jokela, 2019). ABAR comprises research cycles due to its action research approach (Arslan-Ari et al., 2020). Each cycle operates independently and evolves based on the evaluation and results of previous cycles. The research question also evolves as research progresses. ABAR learns during each cycle, and its research questions can be reformulated. Each cycle of ABAR involves the design, artistic implementation, reflection, analysis, publication of research results and setting new goals (see Table 4.2).

This study is based on a loose collaboration between two separately developing ABAR processes (see Table 4.3). One of them is to develop art–science symposia as socially engaged art by artist-researcher Juhola; the other ABAR process involves Griniuk's performance art research based on various digital devices whose importance is to contact the public.

PoN research data were collected while participating in ISEAS 2020. ISEAS includes photographers and videographers, facilitated conversations every day, art in action, and reflections collected afterwards from the participants to be analysed from the perspective of digital participation and emphatic action towards nature. The data also include participants' written reflections, collected via email by Juhola, Juhola's recorded conversations and research diary. Juhola also participated in one of the third *PoN* experiences during ISEAS.

Table 4.2 ABAR. Common steps for the researchers Griniuk and Juhola, developed by the authors of this study.

Step 1	*Step 2*	*Step 3*	*Step 4*	*Step 5*
Defining the goals for the research cycle	Planning the artistic event to test and gather the data	Realising the artistic event and gathering data	Analysing the collected data and extracting the results	Defining the goals for the new cycle

Table 4.3 ABAR cycles in the research by Griniuk and Juhola, developed by the authors of this paper.

Griniuk's ABAR cycles	*Description of the cycles*	*Juhola's ABAR cycles*	*Description of the cycles*
1. Pre-study 2015–2019 Cycle 2019–2021	Defining the framework of the study, test performances and presentations using electro-encephalogram (EEG) (Griniuk, 2021d, in print). Exhibition at the gallery Kilo (Rovaniemi, Finland) was followed by an article based on reflexive research as a strategy (Griniuk, 2020).	1. Pre-study and cycle 2013–2016	Participating in eight international symposia. Organising the first art symposium in Finland 2014. Organising the first ISEAS 2017. One article was written about these experiences (Juhola & Moldovan, 2020).
2. Cycle 2020	EEG and DIY electronic instruments on the body as the tools for connecting with the audiences during live events (Griniuk, 2021b).	2. Cycle 2017 and 3. Cycle 2018	ISEAS 2017 had a case study in nine locations (Juhola et al., 2018). The 2018 ISEAS with performance art focused on collective methods of improvisation (Juhola, 2020).
3. Cycle 2020–2021	The role of the artist as a teacher. EEG as a monitoring tool. Performance pedagogy project The Nomadic Radical Academy (Griniuk, 2021a; Griniuk, 2021c,).	4. Cycle 2019	ISEAS in Nature 2019 resulted in five articles, themed around reconnecting to nature, ethics of gathering, creativity within knowledge engagement and circular economy (Juhola, 2019; Raatikainen et al., 2020; Juhola et al., 2020; Huhmarniemi & Juhola, forthcoming; Juhola, 2021).
4. Cycle 2021	Collaborative performance. EEG as the tool for communication and documentation during the performance (Griniuk & Mosich, 2021).	5. Cycle	In August 2020 and January 2021, ISEAS in Western Lapland resulted in data gathering to develop arts-based methods for environmental conflict mediation.

Moldovan's research was conducted using autoethnographic methods; while participating online in ISEAS 2020, in 2021 she attended ISEAS in person and gathered data through her experience, which was analysed and further developed in the visual arts and presented in the Korundi art museum. Griniuk's data were collected as video and photography, alongside the artist's notes from 2018 during the performance art event.

ISEAS Power of Nature

ISEAS 2020 was held in August 2020 in Äkäslompolo, Western Lapland, Finland, and focused on developing conversational art in meditating conflicts arising from using natural resources. ISEAS's goal was to design, experiment and evaluate artistic, interdisciplinary, community-based and artist-driven approaches. ISEAS is based on multi-level conversations. All research data were collected and analysed with written permission.

The team *PoN* workshop focused on strengthening people's relationships with nature. Empathy towards nature was an essential tool. The work began with online meetings in early 2020. The team included Finnish artist Maria Huhmarniemi, English shamanism researcher Francis Joy, Romanian artist Smaranda Sabina-Moldovan and Chilean dancer–choreographer Hugo Peña. The planning was curated, guided and facilitated by Juhola during the online meetings on Messenger. Due to COVID-19, Moldovan participated in the 2020 symposium online.

The goal of the *PoN* team in ISEAS 2020 was to enhance connectedness towards nature and expand dialogue and a sense of community between humans and non-human nature and nature spirits. This project focused on sharing spiritual knowledge and practices that would help participants enhance, communicate and strengthen links between people and nature by Joy's (2018) understanding of how nature has a hidden spiritual side. Arts-based methods were created by Moldovan together with her team. Workshops started by Joy explain how to communicate with trees and continue by Peña inviting participants to dance with nature. These artworks are related to affective learning in the contemporary art field (Snellman, 2018). The team decided to use the same practices in Romania and Lapland and to share their experiences via online video meetings. Moldovan explains her experience in the feedback on ISEAS:

> I began my experiment by searching for trees with interesting shapes in their crowns. The crowns initially had a decisive impact on my choice of tree for my first experience. After that, I was getting closer and closer to the triangular 'tree gate'. I felt warmth and a feeling of levitation, although I knew that my feet remained on the ground. My hands, positioned in front of my body, perceived a new, trustworthy atmosphere. As I came out from under the crown, its influence diminished, and slowly, the ordinary air of the place was reinstated.
>
> Later, I had discussions in a video meeting with the team and participants from the workshop. Meanwhile, I discovered that my experience of the white willows near the water could be linked to the feminine presence and white elements that help to treat depression. An online dialogue with the participants started from the story of this experience. I started mirroring

the shared images using visual metaphors [*as explained in Anderson & Anderson, 2009 , and presented in Figure 4.1*] The identification created a bond between the participants. I used happiness and optimism in communication. Creating a joyful environment in a virtual space was necessary for everyone to avoid fearing the pandemic spread globally.

(Moldovan, August 2020)

A participant in the Lapland workshop described their feelings as follows:

I approached the tree carefully, walking around and feeling the plough. Then, I introduced myself to the tree. The tree was an old pine tree with

Figure 4.1 (From top right, clockwise) Hugo Peña during a tree connection. Photo credit: Touko Hujanen, 2020. Smaranda-Sabina Moldovan meditating under the white willow. Photo credit: Marcello Maggioli, 2020. Screenshots during ISEAS 2020. These photos were made during the same workshop reproductions made by the PoN team in Äkaslompolo. Smaranda-Sabina Moldovan archive, 2020.

> several small pine benches underneath. I hugged a tree and asked the tree if he could advise me on next weekend's 'Vision quest' in Rautavaara. The tree replied that he would communicate to the trees that would help me there. He himself cannot help me in any other way. I felt a tree stroking my hair.
>
> In the second session, we had to feel the wood and go around the wood still feeling. We had to wrap around the tree. I felt like it was a sexual dance with a tree.
>
> (Anonymous participant, August 2020)

After the symposium, all ISEAS artists were asked for feedback on Moldovan's online participation. The feedback strongly highlighted empathy for Moldovan and admiration for her positive attitude. The artists had experienced participation in the symposium as a self-reinforcing experience, and they found it very unfair that Moldovan could not participate physically. However, all ISEAS residents stated that Moldovan was present among them; although they had not physically met her, they felt that she was already their friend and part of a very personal reinforcing experience, as explained in the two quotes:

> Many times, I wondered what it would feel like to be there myself, participating online. However, she [*Moldovan*] always looked brisk and good-natured, although I might have been sad and felt like a true outsider if I had stayed home and hung out from there.
>
> (Anonymous participant, October 2020)

> Smara's online participation was also a reminder of the real world in the symposium's universe; there is a world in the background that is now controlled by a coronavirus. Yet it also reminded us how important it is for humans to be social, near others and participate online, at least, so that we can all be together somehow. I see us, and that is what ISEAS represents to me – being together as people.
>
> (Anonymous participant, October 2020)

This experience enhanced our creativity, confidence and resilience in approaching unexpected situations. Our biggest challenges were technical issues (i.e., stable internet connection, telephone signal). The ISEAS 2020 allowed us to experiment with digital tools and observe how empathy between artists was present in digital communication in art. The empathic response of all artists to the ABR methods (storytelling, dialogical art, sharing images and videos) played a meaningful role in finding a way to enhance and communicate empathy in digital connections.

Digital performance

The performance *Territory* at the festival Terytoria in Torun in Poland in 2018 explored communal territory and sensual, mental space. By remediating interhuman connections through technology, the performance integrated innovative performance practices from the perspective of the foreign artist participant, who interacted with the audience of the international performance art event. This enabled the artist to connect with the audience despite language barriers or feelings of unfamiliarity with the artist's culture of participation.

Performance is built on the concept of interhuman embodied interactions (Dourish, 2001). It is inviting, motivating and playfully focused on connecting with the audience and inviting it into active cocreation of the artwork, even in events and environments unfamiliar to the artist. Developing an encouraging, motivating and empathic space of interaction and participation is at the core of participatory performance. Including digital and electronic channels to make the moments of interconnection visible or sonified in real time can reduce doubt within participants' decision-making on whether to join the performance (Hobye & Lowgren, 2011). Actively and non-verbally engaging the participants in performative action can make artworks completely accessible to international audiences, thereby bypassing the obstacles to equal participation commonly posed by linguistic or cultural barriers.

The performance created an empathic connection with the participants and highlighted how every decision they made could affect performance. Griniuk utilised digital channels and wearable devices connected to physical actions and movements to remediate empathic connections with her audience (see Figure 4.2). These costumes are based on work by Steve Mann (1997) and include sound, multi-coloured lights and other electronic devices mounted on the performer's body.

Territory explores the remediation of interhuman connectedness by incorporating DIY technology into the aesthetic outcome based on image and sound. The performance was realised as a solo performance facilitated by one performer. It comprised vocal and movement-based sequences, accompanied by sound based on the distances between the performer, surfaces, objects and audience members. Griniuk presented the performance in which electronic devices with motion and distance sensors were attached to her body, which responded to the distances between the performance body and the viewers using sequences of light and sound. Additionally, the viewers could play a tune on the performer's body using an electronic device that sent a weak electric charge throughout the body of the performer and the body of the interacting audience member. The performance created a dialogical space where communication took place by electronic means and where the public influenced the course of the performance. Griniuk also appeared to be vulnerable, where trust and empathy for dialogue matter (Figure 4.2). The performance was designed to highlight the prevailing networks in society that are also controlled by electronic means.

Recommendations for digital participation in international contemporary art

Technology has entered and occupied a huge part of our creative and communicative processes. We proved that empathy relates to the artistic area, as the intentionality, stratification and concretisation of the creator's intentions relate

Figure 4.2 *Territory* by Marija Griniuk (2018). Video still. Credit: Centre of Contemporary Art, Toruń, Poland. Editing: Marija Griniuk.

to the viewer's or participant's reaction at an intimate, subjective level (Peloquin, 1996). Our findings showed that empathetic human connections can be formed using current technology.

Digital empathy is a new concept designed to emphasise social, emotional and cognitive practices as part of digital and media literacy. It is classified into five different stages: empathic concern, cognitive empathy, projective empathy, affective empathy, psychological empathy and aesthetic empathy (Friesem, 2016b). Our two case studies revealed similar structures between empathy phenomena in works of art that arise from empathic pre-planning, encounters with another artist during artwork and reflection on works. Our analysis shows that there are benefits to using digital tools in art activities. We suggested that third-sector organisations could leverage the kinship between art and empathy to create functional new ways of working digitally based on the following findings.

First, an online art experience can never replace a face-to-face one. However, we found that there are certain prerequisites for the successful involvement of participants through virtual channels:

1 Understanding the reasons and contexts of all the participants involved is core. This impacts the desire for successful outcomes of online meetings. Participants' attitudes and motivation for active participation are among the most important prerequisites.
2 When we cannot use senses other than seeing and hearing, an empathic way of working is required. Sharing one's background and situation helps to create an empathic approach: the willingness to communicate and share experiences is crucial to this. Cognitive empathy and affective empathy are part of the process and should be fully developed.
3 Visual images and conversations can increase the imaginative, empathic spectrum of connections among group members. Activating both video and sound connections in virtual events is important.
4 Optimism is part of the empathic concern and is a great tool for creating a safe environment.

Second, regarding the pandemic and climate crisis demands, we find new ways to continue sustainable international artistic work. One way to develop online participation could be structured group work in which participants would not be alone but would work together in small groups in the same location and interact with other groups in other locations.

1 *PoN* showed how art could develop and enhance an empathic and loving relationship towards nature from the perspective of pluriversal experience in a participatory project.
2 We find this action of empathy topical, as we live in a period in which human actions have caused widespread problems worldwide.
3 Third, motivation to be actively involved in participatory artistic action is enhanced through utilising digital channels to remediate the embodied interaction in sound-or image-based artwork cocreated with audience members or participants. This impacts the feeling of togetherness and projective empathic connections among all in the performative space.

Last, during participatory art events, when the interconnections between the artist and participants are remediated into the artistic outcome in real time, bodily or online, the artist or curator should aim to focus the attention first on developing emotional empathy among the group, and second on playfulness in interhuman connectedness. When discussing the importance of digital channels for communication – whether from online participation in an art symposium or a live performance event – connections between people are visible while using all the senses the real-life, non-digital contact between the involved individuals are of value. When the senses are in focus, there is a shift towards valuing moments of real contact. According to discussions in research and development towards process innovations (Trott, 2017), culture and context in organisations directly influence the implementation of novel processes, led by face-to-face interactions between individuals. In other words, innovation happens between people, not between organisations as institutions. Therefore, moments of real contact drive the innovation processes in art, and for these moments to be frequent and beneficial, participation must be designed as a positive experience. This was especially evident in the *PoN* workshops that occurred in Lapland Forests, where poor internet connections limited Moldovan's participation. However, participant feedback supports our claim to use empathy to increase connection with nature. It also confirms that while digital participation is possible, it requires empathy, tools and forward planning to be successful. It is explained in the two following extracts:

> My own experience with the workshop was that it was very revitalising and liberating. I received good advice from Francis' contribution both to strengthening my own nature connection and to guiding the client in finding their own nature connection. I found Hugo's dance rehearsals very invigorating. They took root for a moment, focused on the body and nurtured creativity. I would have liked Hugo's part to continue for longer. For me, Smaranda's role remains unclear, or I just do not remember it anymore.
>
> (Anonymous participant, July 2021)

> I remember that the workshop created an 'agreed' space for the group to spend time in the forest, rush free. The simple, clear instructions helped me to focus and be present, without thinking I had to do anything anywhere else. The exercise gave me the chance and the space to open up and connect to my experience, sensations, emotions and thoughts in a natural environment, which I found very beneficial regarding relaxation and gaining clarity. The workshop also made the group, I believe, come together by connecting with a common set of values.
>
> (Anonymous participant, July 2021)

The core goal of digital participation is to create a feeling of a united space and togetherness in the same process. Kester (2004) argued that the dialogical aesthetic is conversational art. The conversation can vary from a digital performance with an audience to non-verbal connections with trees. Lacy (2010) stated that performance also provides a sense of immediacy, feedback, boundary-blurring and direct communication from the empathic action between audience and performer. Schwarz (2002) highlighted the value of the non-judging environment for quality participant involvement. Therefore, motivation for active participation can be designed around clarity in communication and a safe, empathic and non-judging place.

When involving technology, the core issues are that the technology should be functioning (Trott, 2017) and that all should know how to interact using it. Salen and Zimmerman (2004) argued that interactive and playful activities are essential in adapting to a digital space. It is important not to lose optimism due to the complexity of actions or technological errors. When technology meets art, it needs to be contextualised. Fluency is required in the instruction part before participants enter the digital space of artwork and after participation. This enabled the clarification of how each individual experienced the participation.

The two cases discussed in this chapter suggest that empathic connectedness does not depend solely on technology, and the facilitator should strategise it regarding the narratives built into the invitations to interact (Hobye & Lowgren, 2011). These values are central to the concept of ISEAS and participatory performance environments, where playfulness and the motivation to engage actively are key. We recommend that the same practices be more widely adopted in different organisations. ISEAS can be considered a third-sector organisation, and as an output of this experiential development research, we can provide a broader understanding of how other third-sector organisations also benefit from our results. More research should be conducted on human and non-human relationships through art and aesthetic means.

Summary 1: Lessons learned that can contribute to the organisational or business context

This study showed the parts of online art and technology-based interactions in performance art that succeed in creating a sense of togetherness, although all the senses cannot be utilised within this format. Notably, highlighting empathy can partially mitigate this. The desire to participate is enhanced by creating a non-judging, communication-based environment. The empathic responses of all artists to the ABR methods (storytelling, conversational art, sharing images and videos) played a significant role by enhancing and communicating empathy in digital connections. Empathic connections by utilising technology can lessen creativity barriers for participants and communication barriers for artists.

Summary 2: Contribution to organisational or business knowledge or practices

Both case studies created a sense of togetherness using digital tools. Focusing participation on group work rather than solo tasks promotes community feelings, particularly in non-profit or voluntary organisations. Regarding art projects, community building through group-based activities can induce longitudinal connections and collaborations among all the members. Our recommendations include dialogue-based participation in art projects in GLAM (galleries, libraries, archives and museums) and NGO organisations, where the artist needs to remain flexible and ready to adjust and respond to participants' interactions. Also, we recommend involving artists in organisations so that the collaboration meets the expectations of both the artistic goals and the organisations.

References

Anderson, J. D., & Anderson, B. F. (Eds.). (2009). *Narration and spectatorship in moving images*. Cambridge Scholars Publishing.

Arslan-Ari, I., Ari, F., Grant, M. M., Vasconcelos, L., Tang, H., & Morris, W. S. (2020). Becoming action researchers: Crafting the curriculum and learning experiences for scholarly practitioners in educational technology. In E. Romero-Hall, E. Hsiao, & F. Gao (Eds.), *Research methods in learning design and technology* (pp. 78–93). Routledge.

Barone, T., & Eisner, E. (2012). *Arts based research*. Sage.

Bhabha, H., Jacob, M., & Brenson, M. (1998). Conversational art. In M. F. Brenson, E. Camara, R. Frank, W. Riedweg, & M. O'Connell (Eds.), *Conversations at the castle: Changing audiences and contemporary art*. The MIT Press.

Bishop, C. (2004). Antagonism and relational aesthetics. October, Fall, 51–79.

Bourriaud, N., Pleasance, S., & Woods, F. (2002). *Relational aesthetics*. Les presses du reél.

Dourish, P. (2001). *Where the action is: The foundations of embodied interaction*. The MIT Press.

Friesem, Y. (2016a). Developing digital empathy: A holistic approach to media literacy research methods. In M. Yildiz & J. Keengwe (Eds.), *Handbook of research on media literacy in the digital age* (pp. 145–160). IGI Global.

Friesem, Y. (2016b). Empathy for the digital age: Using video production to enhance social, emotional, and cognitive skills. In S. Tettegah & D. Espelega (Eds.), *Emotions, technology, and behaviors* (pp. 21–45). Academic Press.

Griniuk, M. (2020). Reflexive research on performance art documentation through EEG. A visual essay. Research in Arts and Education, 2/2020, 87–96.

Griniuk, M. (2021a). *Bridging the City: Connecting Art, Performance Design, Environment and Education*.Society. Integration. Education: Proceedings of the International Scientific Conference, 4: 528–538.

Griniuk, M., (2021b). Performing in an art fair: Inviting strangers into the artistic action. A visual essay. *Invisibilidades*, 15, 114–123.

Griniuk, M., (2021c). Arts-based action research on enhancing children's creativity by affect within participatory performance art and performance pedagogy. *Creativity Studies*, 14 (2).

Griniuk, M., (2021d). Performance art using biometric data. *Art History & Criticism/ MIK*.

Griniuk, M., & Mosich, T. B. (2021). Recorded bodily conditions as interpreted/ remediated documentation and as a score for performed communication. In R. Vella & M. Sarantou (Eds.), *Documents of socially engaged art*. InSea.

Hiltunen, M. (2008). Community-based art education: Contemporary art for schools and well-being for the community? In A. Ahonen, R. Rajala, E. Alerby, & I. Ryzhkova (Eds.), *Crystals of children's well-being: Cross border collaboration between schools in the Arctic* (pp. 151–159). University of Lapland.

Hobye, M., & Lowgren, J. (2011). Touching a stranger: Designing for engaging experience in embodied interaction. *International Journal of Design*, 5 (3).

Huhmarniemi, M., & Juhola, K. (forthcoming). International art symposium as a space of knowledge creation and creative engagement. In A. Sinner, C.-C. Lin, & R. L. Irwin (Eds.), *Transversalities: International perspectives on community art education.* Intellect.

Jokela, T. (2019). Arts-based action research in the north. In G. Noblit (Ed.), *Oxford research encyclopedia of education.* Oxford University.

Joy, F. (2018). *Sámi shamanism, cosmology and art: As systems of embedded knowledge* [Doctoral dissertation, University of Lapland]. Acta Universitatis Lapiensis, 367. Lapin yliopistokustannus.

Juhola, K. (Ed.). (2018). *ISEAS Finland 2017 International Socially Engaged Art Symposium.* Scholars' Press.

Juhola, K. (2019). Curating participatory art in the time of anthropocene. *Design & Art Papers*, 7 (1), 27–44. Eurostampa.

Juhola, K. (Ed.). (2020). *ISEAS international socially engaged art symposium 2018.* Scholars' Press.

Juhola, K. (2021). Ylisukupolvisia kohtaamisia: Kuinka kiertotaloustyöpaja leikittää [Intergenerational encounters: How the circular economy workshop plays]. In M. Huhmarniemi, S. Wallenius-Korkalo, & T. Jokela (Eds.), *Dialogista vaikuttamista— Yhteisöllistä taidekasvatusta pohjoisessa* [Dialogue Influence – Community Art Education in the North] (pp. 102–114). University of Lapland.

Juhola, K., Huhmarniemi, M., & Raatikainen, K. (2020). Artistic research on dialogical aesthetics: Ethics of gathering. *Ruukku Journal. Ecologies of practice special issue.*

Juhola, K., & Moldovan, S. (2020). International art symposium in focus on educational places and power relations. *Research in Art and Education, special issue.*

Kantonen, L. (2005). *Teltta, Kohtaamisia nuorten työpajoissa* [*Meetings in workshops for young people*]. LIKE.

Kantonen, L. (2010). *Ankaraa ja myötätuntoista kuuntelua: Keskustelevaa kirjoitusta paikkasidonnaisesta taiteesta* [Dialogical writings on place-specific art]. Kuvataideakatemia.

Kester, G. (2004). *Conversation pieces: Community and communication in modern art.* University of California Press.

Kim, J. H. (2015). Kinaesthetic empathy as aesthetic experience of music. *Les Cahiers philosophiques de Strasbourg* [Online], 38. http://journals.openedition.org/cps/446; https://doi.org/10.4000/cps.446.

Lacy, S. (2010). *Leaving art: Writings on performance, politics, and publics, 1974–2007.* Duke University Press.

Leavy, P. (2017). *Research design: Quantitative, qualitative, mixed methods, arts-based, and community-based participatory research approaches.* The Guilford Press.

Leavy, P. (2018). *Handbook of arts-based research.* The Guilford Press.

Lithoxoidou, L. S., Georgopoulos, A. D., Dimitriou, A. T., & Xenitidou, S. C. (2017). 'Trees have a soul too!' Developing empathy and environmental values in early Childhood. *International Journal of Early Childhood Environmental Education*, 5 (1), 68–88.

Mann, S. (1997). *An historical account of the 'WearComp' and 'WearCam' inventions developed for applications in 'personal imaging'.* Proceedings of the 1st International Symposium on Wearable Computers: Digest of Papers (pp. 66–73). IEEE Computer Society.

McKenzie, J. (2001). *Perform or else: From discipline to performance.* Routledge.

McNiff, S. (1998). *Art-based research.* Jessica Kingsley Publishers.

Miettinen, S. A., Akimenko, D., & Sarantou, M. (2016). Narrative-based art as means of dialogue and empowerment. In S. Golchehr, R. Ainley, A. Friend, C. Johns, & K. Raczynska (Eds.), *Mediations: Art & design agency and participation in public space* (pp. 137–149). Royal College of Art.

Peloquin, S. (1996). Art: An occupation with promise for developing empathy. *American Journal of Occupational Therapy*, 50 (8), 655–661. doi:10.5014/ajot.50.8.655.

Raatikainen, K. J., Juhola, K, Huhmarniemi, M., & Peña-Lagos, H. (2020) 'Face the cow': Reconnecting to nature and increasing capacities for pro-environmental agency. *Ecosystems and People*, 16 (1), 273–289. https://doi.org/10.1080/26395916.2020.1817151.

Rolling, J. H., Jr. (2013). *Arts-based research*. Peter Lang.

Salen, K., & Zimmerman, E. (2004). *Rules of play: Game design fundamentals*. MIT Press.

Sarantou, M. (2020). 'My piece of heaven': Explorations of resources in arts-based research and making environments. *Human, Culture, and Education*, 1 (35), 100–119. doi:10.34130/2233-1277-2020-1-100-119.

Schechner, R. (1977). *Essays on performance theory, 1970–1976*. Drama book specialists.

Schwarz, R. M. (2002). *The skilled facilitator: A comprehensive resource for consultants, facilitators, managers, trainers, and coaches*. John Wiley & Sons.

Snellman, M. (2018). *Echoes from the dark-dark forest: Affect on learning contemporary art and the ecology of subjectivity* [Doctoral dissertation, Aalto University]. Aalto University Learning Centre. https://aaltodoc.aalto.fi/handle/123456789/34807.

Thompson, N. (2012). *Living as form: Socially engaged art from 1991–2011*. Creative time books and The MIT Press.

Trott, P. (2017). *Innovation management and new product development*. Pearson.

Valera, L. (2014). Posthumanism: Beyond humanism? *Cuadernos de bioetica: revista oficial de la Asociacion Espanola de Bioetica y Etica Medica*, 25 (85), 481–491.

5 Collaborative art and storytelling as an empowering tool for social design

Daria Akimenko, Melanie Sarantou and Satu Miettinen

Introduction

This chapter draws on two workshops carried out with a group of Anangu Aboriginal artists and the Fibrespace Incorporated textile artist group in South Australia. The two workshops are part of a two-year project titled 'Women Living on the Edges of the World', which is also informally known as 'Margin to Margin' (2016–2017). The role of art, storytelling and narrative practice as a means for local empowerment is discussed in this chapter, here by focusing on the front end of social design processes, when artistic and social design methods are used to familiarise the participants, designers, artists or artist-researchers with one another.

The art and research explore the concepts of marginality, which, in this project, is defined by conditions of isolation and migration, for example, living in remote and extreme remote regions of South Australia in the far west coast and mid-north regions, while some of the artist-researchers, artists and designers who participated in the project were situated in locations removed from capital cities and centres in the same South Australian areas, Arctic Northern Lapland in Finland, Eastern Finland, the Kola Peninsula in Russia and Namibia. This cross-continental collaboration explored and presented the art and research processes of women working in different situations across various continents while facing challenges of isolation and marginality.

The objective of this chapter is to discuss the front end—or the initial stage—of social design processes, specifically the social innovation journey (Fassi et al., 2015), in using artistic and narrative tools to build empathy, capture the participants' experiences and create an understanding of the local context with the collaborating communities in remote areas of South Australia. The aim of the workshops was to discover, gain insights and explore local contexts with the participating communities. This chapter asks the following: 'How can empathy be created among the participants and facilitators of socially engaged interventions?' 'How can arts-based processes facilitate empathic social design processes?'

Empathy refers to the capacity to understand the elements that shape the realities and situations people face. One aspect of empathy is emotional

DOI: 10.4324/9781003227557-6

empathy, or the 'the vicarious sharing of emotion' (Smith, 2006, p. 3), a capacity that can facilitate one's understanding of emotions and feelings that underpin the associated meanings connected to one's circumstances. Another capacity—cognitive empathy—which is also referred to as 'mental perspective taking' (Smith, 2006, p. 3), was a key concept in the workshops' methodology; it is associated with understanding and contextualising the user's needs and experiences in social design through cognitive or more rational processes.

Empathic design recognises users as a rich resource for design, encouraging designers to immerse themselves in the user's experience, perspectives and emotional responses to products and services. Mattelmäki et al. (2014) revisited a concept of empathy deployed in design research in the 1990s. Experiences, emotions and meaningful everyday practices were studied to stimulate innovation and human-centred solutions. Here, empathic design for stimulation of empathetic processes is based on design practice because it is an interpretative approach in creating new solutions in users' lives.

Empowerment refers to the degree of self-determination and autonomy in groups or individuals and the ability to represent their interests responsibly and in the way they determine. Translocal empowerment is recognised as a strategy for building sustainable and autonomous communities, referring to 'being locally rooted as well as globally connected' (Flor et al., 2019; Loorbach et al., 2020; Van der Schoor, 2021, p. 3), which was one of the ways in which the Margin to Margin project helped create a sustainable impact. The social aspects that design can address in general, as well as in the specific context of marginalised communities, are exemplified in the South Australian project study, along with the role of empathy in stimulating cultural and contextual understanding, commitment and connection between facilitating artists, designers, artist-researchers and communities.

The narratives of empowerment and care that emerge through art- and craft-making practices offer a way to come to terms with marginal states. This approach enables a more balanced situation to emerge, one where the participants, as well as the artists, designers or artist-researchers, cope with the familiar and unfamiliar. In this chapter, the authors discuss the role of art as a medium for shaping identities in marginalised communities, as well as a tool to process and develop relationships within the communities (Miettinen et al., 2016). These art methods were used to explore the front end of a social design process underpinned by an empathic approach.

Workshop participants

In October 2016, the Margin to Margin research group carried out two art and storytelling workshops with a group of Anangu Aboriginal artists in South and Western Australia and the Fibrespace Incorporated textile artist group. It is an international research and art collaboration between various global artist communities with the goal of studying how art empowers women who are living in marginal conditions. Meeting women from the Edges of the World project was an empowering process for the group of artists, designers and artist-researchers who constituted the Margin to Margin research group. After one year of intense planning sessions facilitated through Skype over several continents, the anticipation came to an end when the artist-researchers met the communities in South Australia. The commonalities soon revealed between the women coming from diverse backgrounds and locations were the geographical remoteness and regionality of the communities and the important role of hands-on art and craft-making. Group work and the use of artistic tools for sharing personal stories were empowering narrative mechanisms incorporating the design approach for stimulating the empathetic shared processes adopted in both workshops.

Women artists and craft-makers predominantly participated in two intensive art-making and data collection workshops of less than one week each; the workshops had an emphasis on using narratives as a social design tool. Here, narratives refer to the representation of certain themes through oral and multimedia storytelling. The workshops aimed to build empathy with the participants by presenting a platform for dialogue to render audible stories and artistic processes. Central to this study were female artists who may move from one role to another, be it spouse, mother, researcher, professional, teacher, artist, designer, craftsperson, maker or friend. Therefore, they continuously had to manage their fluctuating identities (Lawler, 2007, 2015) to enable their becoming within communities while surviving their marginalities.

Social design

Social design is closely connected to other forms of design, such as service or experience design. Following from the perspective of design, the link between design and social element was constructed by Simon (1969, p. 111), who took up the argument in his book *The Sciences of the Artificial* that 'Everyone designs who devises courses of action aimed at changing existing situations into preferred ones'. In a similar vein, Escobar (2018) argued for 'design for everyone', which is what communities understand is the best for themselves while having the power to drive decision making towards *their* common goals. He explains that design was a project of modernity (Escobar, 2018) because of its historic positivistic outlook, connections to ideas of universality and progress and development discourse. In addition, to create a break from setting up binaries in the mind–body split that stems from cartesian and rationalist traditions, Escobar argued for an agenda in design that is closer to communities. Thus, Escobar's ideas promote an inherent social understanding of the role of design. However, caution is needed because although design is celebrated, it needs to be viewed critically to uncover its unsustainability. The need exists to critically reorient design towards relational modes of being/becoming and knowing/doing.

As theories in relation to social design have slowly emerged, these have been referred to as socially responsible design (Papanek, 1972; Whiteley, 1993), the 'social model of design' (Margolin & Margolin, 2002), design for social entrepreneurship (Tan et al., 2005), social innovation (Jégou & Manzini, 2008) and design for social impact (Resnick, 2019). Mulgan (2012) defined social innovation as the new ideas that can meet social needs and goals, while Manzini (2014) understood social innovation as creatively recombining existing and available resources to achieve collaboratively recognised needs in novel ways. The three reasons why a focus on social design is paramount, according to Manzini (2014), is that social initiatives need to tackle the manifold societal challenges faced by communities. In addition, social design can tackle these challenges and help transition towards sustainability not only collaboratively with communities, but also autonomously by communities seeking empowerment and self-determination. Finally, as societies change, the nature of social design continuously needs reinvention, new methods and collaborative action to uncover improbable potentials.

Social enterprises are essentially hybrid because they are built on business models and entrepreneurial components, for example, as organisational missions, target markets and supply chains, but they also aim to address social needs (Grassl, 2012). Wilson and Post (2013, p. 715) aptly defined social business as 'a form of organization and a practice that deliberately harnesses market dynamics to address deeply rooted social issues through the design and implementation of a core product or service'. Social enterprises are socially orientated, aiming at creating sustainable businesses that can create benevolence among the communities they serve; thus, they often address the needs of marginalised communities (Santos et al., 2015). New markets can be created when such needs are targeted, but social enterprises often remain fragile because they need to carefully balance the social needs they seek to address and those of the markets they serve (Santos et al., 2015). Because of their fragility, social enterprises depend on innovations, tools, novel approaches and skills such as empathy, all of which are suited for the delicate contexts and communities they target.

Methodology and research approach

Positive emotions can stimulate social and emotional well-being and personal growth (Um et al., 2012). Human-centred approaches can employ participatory design and ABMs to inspire and guide participants to reflect on their own lives, here with the aim of stimulating alternative strategies and ideas for their futures (Friedland & Yamauchi, 2011). There are several design tools that have been developed to create empathy and user insights; for example, Gaver et al. (1999) employed cultural probes that create empathy and help contextualise the user experience. This chapter disseminates the use of a cultural probe—the life story mandala—an art-based process that was used in South Australia to facilitate life span mapping, which is a tool deriving from life span psychology and based on a model that identifies and discusses triggers, modes, contexts, functions and outcomes (Webster et al., 2010). This human-centred design practice and process for reflection on life changes and future strategies involved the painting of life story mandalas, which represent a participant's life story or a section thereof

(Miettinen et al., 2016). Storytelling is used to process the expressions, content and symbolisms consciously and perhaps subconsciously portrayed in these artefacts, while collective empathy is created through verbalising the stories.

The methods used were workshops, arts-based methods (ABMs), storytelling and narrative analysis. Foster (2016, pp. 1–2) explained ABMs as enabling 'a diversity of experiences to be communicated in ways that disrupt "common sense" understandings and act as a reminder that there are possibilities for things to be otherwise'. ABMs involve sensory perceptions and emotion, as well as intellectual responses; they can assist in shaping different understandings and ways of knowing the world. ABMs have the potential to address subtle nuances such as difference, politics of gender and identity and power and justice, all of which are often overlooked by other approaches. These nuances emerge when the participants have the opportunity to express their personal narratives and lived experiences through art-making. The advantage of ABMs lies in their strong focus on 'visualisation', which is more democratic and inclusive, while the common mapping techniques used in these methods strengthen their communal focus (Mohan & Stokke, 2000).

With a strong focus on reflexivity that comes about through storytelling, the participants piece together their experiences into life stories that make sense to them, and through critical reflection on the world, art becomes an interruptive practice (Savin-Baden & Major, 2013; Baden & Wimpenny, 2014). The purpose of life span mapping is to overcome changes in life cycles and cope with lived experiences and change through making and reflection. Three different methods were used in the project study to create understanding and empathy: (a) life story mandalas as a collaborative artistic process and method applied in arts-based research that enabled women to share their life stories with participants, here by using textile art as an enabling medium; (b) participant interviews as a means to learn, document and analyse the participants' experiences of marginalisation coming through the narratives they shared; and (c) video and audio documentation as a means to digitally document and preserve the participants' life stories. The findings of two follow-up workshops, which were hosted after the South Australian workshops in December 2016 in Finnish Rovaniemi and Russian Murmansk with local artist communities, mirrored and complemented the data and outcomes of the South Australian research findings.

Life story mandalas as a tool for self-reflection and sharing

In the preparatory phase, the discussions centred on the importance of cultural exchange with the local Australian groups. Thus, the concept of life story mandalas, which were proposed for use as cultural probes, emerged as a means to share life histories and meaningful experiences. This tool was previously employed in a workshop context in Inari, Finnish Lapland, with a group of local women including Indigenous representatives. The use of this tool proved successful, enabling the group to map in individualistic and intuitive ways and share their life histories in meaningful and effective ways. This was the rationale behind employing the same artistic method in South Australia.

The South Australian women's life stories were captured through visualising important periods in their lives using different colours, symbols, drawings and text on cotton textile circles with acrylic paint (Figure 5.1). The visualisations signified important periods or single years in the women's lives. Many of the visualisations started in the middle of the cotton circle, typically from birth to the present moment. However, most participants used different ways of marking to interpret and express their life span mapping. Each participant's life story mandala was stitched together with the others in a continuous thread. The joined thread of the life story mandalas was then installed in a three-dimensional spiral that represented the women's life stories, creating an interconnected web of narratives (Figure 5.2).

The mandala-making enabled the women to process their life stories in two significant phases. The first phase consisted of the applied visual method of painting, which enabled conceptualising and representing the important events of their lives. The second consisted of verbal sharing, which focused on the participants' thinking and shaping of the stories they were to share. Some groups painted their mandalas while listening to others who told stories. Other participants worked more individually and shared their stories, either with the facilitating researcher or with the videographer–researcher of the group. This enabled two processes to occur simultaneously: painting and sharing in a group facilitated peer-to-peer learning, whereas individual self-reflective work enabled the processing of personal stories. The video and audio recordings of

Figure 5.1 Process of making life mandalas on cotton textile circles with acrylic paint. Photography by Daria Akimenko (2016).

Figure 5.2 Installation of the three-dimensional spiral made of the life mandalas stitched together. Photography by Daria Akimenko (2016).

the individual stories shared with others was an important tool in rendering the voices of the individuals to be heard.

The empowering effect of processing one's own life events and sharing stories facilitated listening to and learning from one another, while visualising a life story was a self-reflective tool to understand personal histories and circumstances. For example, one of the Aboriginal artists discussed her personal growth since the birth of her child, transforming her life from dealing with addictions towards becoming a successful artist and a caring and independent mother. Another artist discussed the tragedy of the Maralinga nuclear testing that harshly affected the lives of many Anangu Aboriginal people. The Aboriginal communities living in and around the Maralinga area in the 1950s were displaced from their homes to facilitate British nuclear testing.

Listening to these stories created both empathy and understanding of the communities positioned in these margins of South Australia. The life story mandala is a participatory and expressive artistic tool used for creating empathy and understanding of the historical, political and geographical contexts of individual participants. The mandalas were a medium to share life histories and the mutual empathetic response that the workshop participants facilitated in the creation of a safe environment for both the women who shared and those who listened.

The connections between the facilitating artist-researchers and participants supported the process of creating empathy, which is essential for the success of the front end of the social design journey. In addition, the life story mandalas contributed to the front-end social design process in a more direct and practical way. The overall process enabled the collection of a large body of data that now help engage in a more academic manner with the women living in marginal situations. This information is valuable for the social design process, which starts by establishing and learning about contextual or structural problems.

Project process description

In October 2016, the Margin to Margin research group carried out two art and storytelling workshops in South Australia. The first workshop was held together with the representatives of a group of Anangu Aboriginal artists of South and Western Australia and took place in a tent camp in Fowlers Bay, South Australia. During the second activity, the research group worked with the Fibrespace Incorporated textile artist group in Port Augusta, South Australia. The Fibrespace artists and researcher–artist group from Finland created the life story mandala installation in Port Augusta at the Platform Gallery, which also helped build an empathetic understanding among the group participants. Female artists and craft-makers predominantly participated in two intensive art-making and data collection workshops. Each of the workshops lasted less than one week. An emphasis was made on narrative processes and hands-on artistic practices and their use as social design tools.

The process of building researcher–participant empathy here is similar to the framework for empathy in design practice introduced by Kouprie and Visser (2009), who compared empathic design practices against long-existing psychological frameworks for empathy and introduced four comprehensive phases of empathic design: (1) discovery, (2) immersion, (3) connection and (4) detachment; They discussed how the relationship between the designer and user changes from phase to phase. Within this study, the above-mentioned phases of the framework for empathy in design practice translate in a similar way. However, these phases are less distinct but instead overlap and, at times, merge with one another. Because the current project study focused on the front end of social design, phases 1–3 are more prominent because empathy and understanding achieved during these phases help identify the challenges to be processed in a more long-term perspective.

Phase 1, discovery, occurred through receiving 'empathy probes' (Mattelmäki, 2003) from both participant groups and discussing these with the local host. Empathy probes included the artwork that facilitated learning from the local participants. The process of discovery went deeper upon the first face-to-face encounters with the groups, including informal introductions between the facilitating artist-researchers and participants. In this phase, the artist-researchers inhibited their roles as facilitators to allow the emergence of a bottom-up approach. This resulted in the Anangu Aboriginal women introducing the artist-researchers to a significant location and cultural ritual, while the Fibrespace artist group introduced the artist-researchers to their annual brainstorming process.

Phase 2, immersion, developed through individual and collaborative art-making processes, where mutual observing and sharing of artistic processes and techniques enabled a deeper familiarisation between the artist-researchers and participants. This took place through weaving baskets and felting. Learning these techniques enabled the group to work together and create personal relationships while also facilitating learning from one another.

Phase 3, connection, evolved through the participant interviews, storytelling processes and collaborative artistic work on life story mandalas, where the participants elaborated on their work and life challenges from the perspective of both artists and women, revealing very personal and sentimental narratives. During the process of sharing, the artist-researchers also placed themselves in the position of storyteller and shared their experiences, finding common ground with the participants. The storytelling took a multidimensional form, being documented in video, audio, photo, fieldnotes and physical artefacts. Clearly, the immersion and connection phases of the framework merge in the present project study.

Finally, phase 4, detachment, is partially seen in the process of writing this chapter. In various ways, this phase in the South Australian project study was experienced differently from the psychological framework for empathy proposed by Kouprie and Visser (2009). Detachment phases are complex, needing sensitive exit strategies to promote sustainability and avoid the negative impacts on the intervention. Facilitating artist-researchers often find themselves in positions of withdrawal for the purposes of reflection, analysis and monitoring. In the project the artist-researchers distanced themselves from the intense empathic experience, processing the body of research and artistic data and sharing the outcomes with broader academia and artistic communities through research chapters and exhibitions.

Participant interviews, storytelling and digital documentation as methods of fostering connection

In the current project study, the art- and craft-making and the tactility of materials, such as raffia, cotton, wool fibres, yarns and textiles, helped create a familiar situation that stimulated shared participation. According to the adopted ethnographic methodology approach, it also creates a space in which the behaviour of participating individuals could be observed within their own environments. Ethnographic practice is best suited to social design processes because it enables a holistic understanding of the research contexts. The artist-researchers aimed to learn from the participants so as to better understand their cultural and contextual environments while bringing their own personal cultural backgrounds, life experiences and narratives into the research and art activities.

By giving the participants an opportunity for input into the art-making processes to the front end of the social design journey, both the participants and the artist-researchers can be enabled to share on an equal footing. Through equal participation in art-making and shared storytelling, connectedness is also enabled. In this way, participants have the power to shape ongoing mapping processes through their narratives captured during the interviews conducted within familiar physical work environments.

The women who were interviewed during the two South Australian workshops were art- and craft-makers. Some of them identified as artists, while others identified as craftspeople. The duration of the interviews depended on the individual's narratives and their art- and craft-making processes because some participants found it easier to share their stories while staying engaged in art- and craft-making. Drawing on these processes instigated storytelling because many participants were confident in their art-making environments, which allowed storytelling to occur effortlessly.

In addition to these interviews and stories describing the life cycles depicted in the life story mandalas, video and audio documentation supported all the processes of making and storytelling throughout the two workshops. Additional stories were documented and supported by physical artefacts as a part of a storytelling intervention carried out by one of the artist-researchers. Some parts of the audio and video material were processed immediately, resulting in a series of 'visual journal' entries, while most of the documentation has yet to be engaged with both artistically and in the context of broader research.

The importance of documenting personal stories enables the expansion of temporal and spatial dimensions, but also the audiences of individual stories. This means that documented stories can be preserved in a specific time to then travel and reach out through space and to wider audiences with the help of digital technologies. The idea of having a conversation with other makers living in other parts of the world empowered the participants to share their stories and messages and engage in digital participation (Sarantou et al., 2018). The moment of capturing a story, also through smaller-scale engagements and documentary attempts by individuals, enables meaningful sharing because it is a personal process usually undertaken by only one person who documents the encounters and is therefore more intimate (Kalow, 2011). The mere action of dedicating time and space for documenting the story contributes significantly to building empathy. Documentation processes are at the core of art and design processes. At the front end of social design, one is engaged in different types of learning, such as peer-to-peer or practice-based learning. Such processes contribute to creating empathy and understanding through mutual or collective discovery, and to defining both the problem and innovation space of operation.

Process for creating empathy

The useful framework, discovery, immersion, connection and detachment of Kouprie and Visser (2009) are parallel to the process for creating empathy that the project artist-researchers experienced, yet with some variations. During the discovery phase, the first encounters with the South Australian groups included informal introductions between the artist-researchers and participants. In this phase, the artist-researchers inhibited their roles as facilitators to allow for the emergence of a bottom-up approach. This resulted in the Aboriginal women introducing the artist-researchers to a significant location and cultural ritual, while the Fibrespace artist group introduced the artist-researchers to their annual brainstorming process. With both initial introductions, traditional food and various forms of textile art played important roles in forging links within the groups. These further enabled the immersion phase, which came about by introducing the participants to cultural probes in the form of the life story mandalas.

Individual and collaborative art-making processes, where mutual observing and sharing artistic processes and techniques enabled deeper familiarisation between the artist-researchers and the participants, were guided through the narrative function, which facilitated immersion. This took place through traditional basket weaving and felting. Learning these techniques enabled the group to work together and create personal relationships with each other while also facilitating learning from one another. Art- and craft-making activities stimulated the discussion and sharing of skills and knowledge. The cultural probes, art- and craft-making, storytelling and participant interviews, in which the participants elaborated on their work and challenges in life from the perspective of being both an artist and woman, reinforced the personal narrative component.

Although the first three phases of this framework (discovery, immersion and connection) were similarly mapped by the artist-researchers in the South Australian project study, they were not distinct and separate but rather overlapping and merging one into the next (Figure 5.3).

The artist-researchers' involvement through an ethnographic approach led to an empathetic understanding, reflection, analysis and deeper involvement with the workshop participants, as opposed to a diametrical detachment, which is the final phase proposed by Kouprie and Visser (2009). Detachment processes are complex and require highly sensitive withdrawal strategies that promote sustainability and avoid negative impacts on the intervention. The artist-researchers facilitating social design journeys often enter the withdrawal phase with the aim of reflection, analysis and monitoring. In the current project, this took the form of the artist-researchers distancing themselves from the intense process as a way to create empathy to analyse the body of research and artistic data and share the outcomes with broader academic and artistic communities through research chapters and exhibitions. This analytical, rather than detachment, phase enabled the defining and sharing of contextual knowledge, as well as laying the ground for designing services relevant to the South Australian context. Because one of the research group members continuously works with Aboriginal artists and Fibrespace artists, the process does not end in detachment for her but rather starts more in-depth working phases with these communities.

Another difference in the mapping framework of the facilitating artist-researchers was that the process for creating empathy in the South Australian project study included a fifth phase of planning that bridged the first and final stages of Kouprie and Visser's (2009) framework (discovery and detachment). Planning permits the empathy process to adopt a cyclical nature. As a result, this process for creating empathy can be applied in all phases of the social design journey.

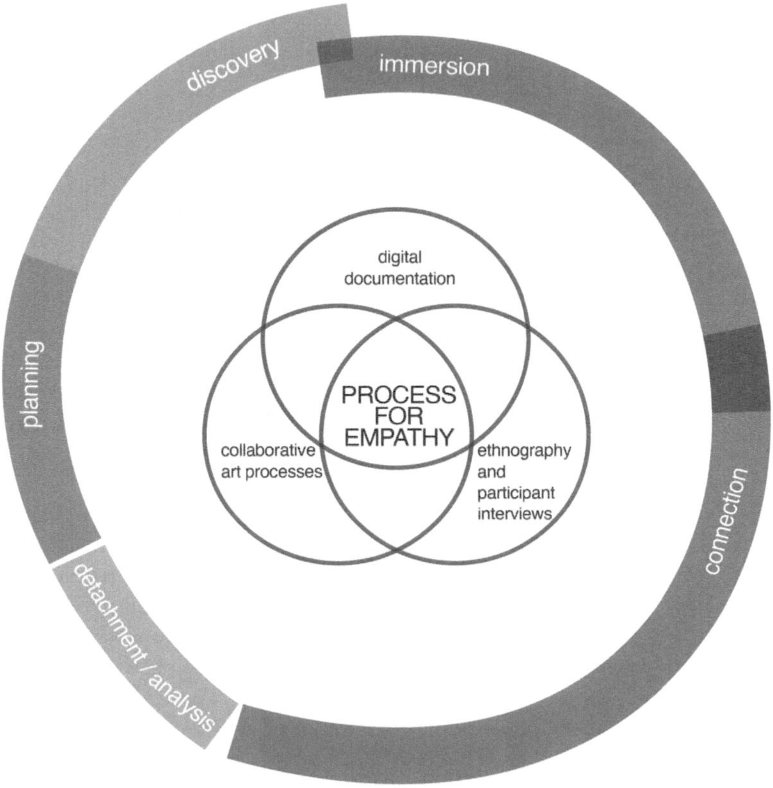

Figure 5.3 A process for creating empathy by Daria Akimenko (2016).

Conclusion

In this project study, empathy supported by the narrative function—namely storytelling practices—facilitates the planning for social design interventions. The value of the workshop processes is manifested through the collected data and documentation, which enables defining the challenges that can be further worked through the social design approach. Further, the impact of using artistic methods, such as the life story mandala and video journals, helps in creating a sense of community and commitment, both in situ and from a distance. Follow-up workshops, artefact-making and representation in Finnish and Russian communities mirrored and complemented the data and outcomes of the South Australian project study (Akimenko et al., 2017). During processes of sharing, the artist-researchers positioned themselves as storytellers by sharing their own experiences, thus finding common ground with the participants' life situations. Storytelling came about through multidimensional forms such as video, audio, photo, fieldnotes and physical artefacts. The narrative function is a crucial tool to facilitate and share empathetic processes at the front-end phase of design processes, for example, social or service design, when immersion into contexts is paramount in facilitating connections between people.

The process for creating empathy not only stimulated connection, but also provided a safe environment for the participants to feel comfortable and share their stories, while the capacity to understand the situations of others was also enhanced. Empathy influenced how the facilitating artist-researchers and participants communicated, learning about each other's challenges and, thus, shaping a contextual understanding and preparing the groundwork and mapping frameworks for potential social design events. The process for creating empathy is relevant for all social design activities that involve participants and different stakeholders to create a shared understanding of a given context. The process can be enriched with different methods and approaches, depending on the resources available within the given context. The researchers have, for example, used the process in different research cycles, in which various materials have been used to generate the life span maps (see Miettinen et al., 2019). In addition, the process may be repeated and revisited during the iterative social design journey of Fassi et al. (2015). The same applies to service design journeys.

The limitations of the life story method can be problematic in relation to past trauma because the participants often recollect and process difficult periods in their life spans. Therefore, facilitators need to be aware of and make clear to the participants that they do not have to share any information they do not want to. In case the participants do want to share sensitive information, appropriate support and counselling services should be available (Miettinen et al., 2019).

Summary 1: Lessons learned that can contribute to the organisational or business context

The process for creating empathy introduced in this chapter builds on the phases of mutual discovery, creative immersion, connection through storytelling, listening and learning and detachment to engage in autonomous action to tackle the identified challenges. These four phases are followed by planning and preparation for iterative action, continuous empathy building and ongoing engagement in social innovation journeys, whether in situ or virtually, between the stakeholders of any given organisational or business process in for-profit, public or NGO sector contexts. Narratives of empowerment stemming from such empathy processes can stimulate strategic and sustainable translocal empowerment for building sustainable and autonomous communities, organisations and businesses.

Summary 2: Contribution to organisational or business knowledge or practices

The life story mandala method is a life span mapping tool that can assist with practical empathy-building activities when social interventions and joint action are needed for the promotion of community agendas. The method can be applied creatively, which means that alternative resources and materials can be used for the life span mapping part of the process, here in combination with storytelling and reflection. Although empathy is usually considered an essential ingredient for the front end of design thinking processes, embedding opportunities for creating it throughout entire process, service or social innovation journey is paramount in creating a sustainable social impact. Organisations dealing with the many social needs and issues related to well-being within communities can use this practical method to stimulate empathic interactions between participants, users, consumers, process facilitators and researchers to drive sustainability, especially in social enterprises, the NGO and public sectors that engage with social well-being.

Acknowledgements

The Women Living on the Edges of the World project was funded by the Kone Foundation (Konen Säätio).

A part of this chapter appeared earlier in: Miettinen, S., Sarantou, M., & Akimenko, D. (2016b). Collaborative art and storytelling as an empowering tool for service design: South Australian case study. In P. Ryhtilahti & S. Miettinen (Eds.), *For profit, for good: Developing organizations through service design* (pp. 74–80). Faculty of Art and Design, University of Lapland.

References

Akimenko, D., Sarantou M., & Miettinen, S. (2017). Arctic identities: Knowledge transfer between communities through art-making and narrative processes. In L. Heininen, H. Exner-Pirot, & J. Plouffe (Eds.), *Arctic yearbook 2017* (pp. 1–15). Northern Research Forum. http://arcticyearbook.com.

Baden, M. S., & Wimpenny, K. (2014). *A practical guide to arts-related research*. Springer.

Escobar, A. (2018). *International Institute of Social Studies (IISS) lecture*. https://www.youtube.com/watch?v=Kl4TuUjoiU8.

Fassi, D., Meroni, A., & Simeone, G. (2015). Design for social innovation as a form of design activism: An action format. In A. Nicholls, J. Simon, & M. Gabriel (Eds.), *New frontiers in social innovation research* (pp. 14–15). Palgrave Macmillan. https://doi.org/10.1057/9781137506801.

Flor, A., Dumitru, A., Cipolla, C., Kunze, I., & Wittmayer, J. (2019). Translocal empowerment in transformative social innovation networks. *European Planning Studies*, 28, 1–23. https://doi.org/10.1080/09654313.2019.1578339.

Foster, V. (2016). *Collaborative arts-based research for social justice*. Routledge.

Friedland, B., & Yamauchi, Y. (2011). Reflexive design thinking: Putting more human in human-centered practices. *Interactions*, 18 (2), 66–71. https://doi.org/10.1145/1925820.1925835.

Gaver, W., Dunne, T., & Pacenti, E. (1999). Design: Cultural probes. *Interactions*, 6 (1), 21–29.

Grassl, W. (2012). Business models of social enterprise: A design approach to hybridity. *ACRN Journal of Entrepreneurship Perspectives*, 1 (1), 37–60.

Jégou, F., & Manzini, E. (2008). *Collaborative services. Social innovation and design for sustainability* (Vol. 1). Polidesign.
Kalow, N. (2011). *Visual storytelling: The digital video documentary*. CDS Publication.
Kouprie, M., & Visser, F. (2009). A framework for empathy in design: Stepping into and out of the user's life. *Journal of Engineering Design*, 20 (5), 437–448.
Lawler, S. (2007). *Identity: Sociological Perspectives*. Polity Press.
Lawler, S. (2015). *Identity: Sociological perspectives*. John Wiley & Sons.
Loorbach, D., Wittmayer, J., Avelino, F., von Wirth, T., & Frantzeskaki, N. (2020). Transformative innovation and translocal diffusion. *Environmental Innovation and Societal Transitions*, 35, 251–260. https://doi.org/10.1016/j.eist.2020.01.009.
Manzini, E. (2014). Making things happen: Social innovation and design. *Design Issues*, 30 (1), 57–66.
Margolin, V., & Margolin, S. (2002). A 'social model' of design: Issues of practice and research. *Design Issues*, 18 (4), 24–30.
Mattelmäki, T. (2003). *Probes: Studying experiences for design empathy*. In I. Koskinen, T. Mattelmäki, & K. Battarbee, (Eds.), *Empathic design: User experience in product design* (pp. 119–130). IT Press.
Mattelmäki, T., Vaajakallio, K., & Koskinen, I. (2014). What happened to empathic design? *Design Issues*, 30 (1), 67–77.
Miettinen, S. A., Akimenko, D., & Sarantou, M. (2016). Narrative-based art as means of dialogue and empowerment. In S. Golchehr, R. Ainley, A. Friend, C. Johns, & K. Raczynska (Eds.), *Proceedings of the Mediations: Art & Design Agency and Participation in Public Space conference* (pp. 137–149).. Royal College of Art.
Miettinen, S. A., Sarantou, M. A., & Kuure, E. (2019). Design for care in the peripheries: Arts-based research as an empowering process with communities. *Nordes*, 8. https://archive.nordes.org/index.php/n13/article/view/467/438.
Mohan, G., & Stokke, K. (2000). Participatory development and empowerment: The dangers of localism. *Third World Quarterly*, 21 (2), 247–268.
Mulgan, G. (2012). *Social innovation: What it is, why it matters, how it can be accelerated*. Basingstoke Press.
Papanek, V. (1972). *Design for the real world*. Thames and Hudson.
Resnick, E. (2019). *The social design reader*. Bloomsbury Visual Arts.
Santos, F., Pache, A. C., & Birkholz, C. (2015). Making hybrids work: Aligning business models and organizational design for social enterprises. *California Management Review*, 57 (3), 36–58.
Sarantou, M., Akimenko, D., & Escudeiro, N. (2018). Margin to margin: Arts-based research for digital outreach to marginalised communities. *The Journal of Community Informatics*, 14 (1), 139–159.
Savin-Baden, M., & Major, C. H. (2013). *Qualitative research: The essential guide to theory and practice*. Routledge.
Simon, H. A. (1969). *The sciences of the artificial*. Massachusetts Institute of Technology.
Smith, A. (2006). Cognitive empathy and emotional empathy in human behavior and evolution. *The Psychological Record*, 56 (1), 3–21.
Tan, W. L., Williams, J., & Tan, T. M. (2005). Defining the 'social' in 'social entrepreneurship': Altruism and entrepreneurship. *The International Entrepreneurship and Management Journal*, 1 (3), 353–365.
Um, E., Plass, J. L., Hayward, E. O., & Homer, B. D. (2012). Emotional design in multimedia learning. *Journal of Educational Psychology*, 104 (2), 485.

Van der Schoor, T. (2021). Grid governance; what new roles for the community energy movement? In S. Hielscher & J. Wittmayer (Eds.), *Proceedings of the 12th International Sustainability Transitions Conference: Mainstreaming sustainability transitions: From research towards impact* (pp. 1–8). Fraunhofer ISI. https://research.hanze.nl/ws/portalfiles/portal/36217013/2021_IST_panel_proposal.pdf.

Webster, J. D., Bohlmeijer, E. T., & Westerhof, G. J. (2010). Mapping the future of reminiscence: A conceptual guide for research and practice. *Research on Aging*, 32 (4), 527–564.

Whiteley, N. (1993). *Design for society*. Reaktion Books.

Wilson, F., & Post, J. E. (2013). Business models for people, planet (& profits): Exploring the phenomena of social business, a market-based approach to social value creation. *Small Business Economics*, 40 (3), 715–737.

Section B

The role of stories in creating empathy

Step 2: Create emotional insights

6 Building empathy in a digital business through Love and Break-up Letters

Rosana Vasques, Mikko Koria and Maria Cecilia Loschiavo dos Santos

Sharetribe: A digital platform for the sharing economy

This chapter aims to present a narrative on how the Love and Break-up Letters method was used to build empathy with the Sharetribe users to develop the service into a global marketplace platform. The first version of Sharetribe was published in 2009 by Juho Makkonen and Antti Virolainen, who were then students at Aalto University (in Espoo, Finland). Operating as a start-up in the sharing economy context, the platform went through several phases of developing its services, and as it did so, it rapidly reached global markets. Originally called *Kassi* (a bag in Finnish), the platform initially offered the possibility of sharing, selling and exchanging products among students through the Aalto University Community Marketplace, reaching over 4,000 members by 2013. In developing their offering, they interviewed students, coming to understand that many would like to borrow things and get help for services such as fixing a guitar, walking a dog or moving to another house. Although their first launch focused on lending goods and exchanging services, the founders soon realised that students also wanted to sell course books and look for apartments, so additional functionalities were implemented (Makkonen, 2013; A. Virolainen & J. Makkonen, personal communication, 14 June 2013).

The start-up soon expanded its market to the cities of Helsinki—with a similar marketplace for the Kallio neighbourhood—and Vantaa in the metropolitan region (Makkonen, 2013). In this growth phase, they also changed the venture's name to Sharetribe as a way to portray the emerging global nature of the digital platform, hence enabling local users to create their own marketplaces (A. Virolainen & J. Makkonen, personal communication, 14 June 2013). From the official launch in 2011 until 2013, the core business was to build communities by selling, renting, swapping and sharing goods and services. However, already in 2012, the founders realised it was difficult to grow their customer base using the initial approach. Thus, a pivoting was needed, as explained by Antti Virolainen (personal communication, 15 September 2021):

> Our tool was a nice to have product for existing companies and cities and universities. However, we were contacted by few entrepreneurs who

DOI: 10.4324/9781003227557-8

> planned to start an online marketplace and they asked if our tool could be customised for their needs. This led us to understand that for this segment we have a really needed tool (after we do some changes). In 2013 we sought funding with the new story and got some. The first internationally available version for this purpose was launched in 2014 although we did pilot in 2013 already.

From 2014 onwards, Sharetribe has focused on helping to build business marketplaces for all the stages of their clients' life cycles. As a result, the company retains a portfolio of over 1,000 marketplaces 'from first-time entrepreneurs to Fortune 500 companies' (Sharetribe, 2021).

During this process, it was essential to develop the platform empathically, in addition to putting in technical programming. A key need was to understand what was working for its users and enable the pivoting of the business when necessary. This chapter describes the development of the digital platform that took place while enhancing the experience initially provided back in 2013. The underpinning research question is framed as follows: 'How can we quickly capture positive and negative feelings from Sharetribe users?'

Empathy and design in the digital era

The word empathy has its origins in the Greek word *Empatheia* (meaning 'em' = 'into', and 'pathos' = 'feeling'). Before being translated into English, the word was used in German as *Einfühlung* = 'feeling into' (Kouprie & Visser,

Figure 6.1 Name and logo change from Kassi to Sharetribe and Kassi website and user's feedback page.
Sources: A. Virolainen and J. Makkonen (personal communication, 14 June 2013); Lampinen et al. (2013).

2009). Krznaric (2014) defines empathy as 'the act of putting yourself in the other's shoes through imagination, understanding their thoughts, perspectives and using this understanding to guide your own actions' (p. 10). Hence, empathy is an essential skill for designers. For example, in 1979, the designer Patricia Moore challenged her colleagues at Raymond Loewy Consultancy to develop a fridge that was easy to open by a person with arthrosis. The idea was not taken forward but led Patricia to conduct an empathic experiment between 1979 and 1982, dressing up like an older person to deeply understand the challenges of being an 85-year-old woman. This immersion led international product design into a new direction regarding the understanding of the user needs, allowing Patricia to develop numerous products that could be used by the elderly (Hanington & Martin, 2012; Krznaric 2014).

According to Battarbee et al. (2014), who are designers from IDEO, empathy is 'the ability to be aware of, understanding of, and sensitive to another person's feelings and thoughts without having had the same experience' (p. 1). Furthermore, they pointed out that empathic design is highly connected with creativity and innovation because it can generate functional and emotionally meaningful products and services for people by drawing on real-world user experiences.

As proposed by Tuomala and Baxter (2019), empathy can be associated with design either as *empathy for design*, when it is a research approach in the design process (e.g., human-centred design, generative research, inclusive design), or as its output—*design for empathy*, which means the goal of the project is to enhance sociocultural empathy.

Over time, several techniques and tools have been developed to ensure that user-centred design processes are empathetic (Kouprie & Visser, 2009). For instance, design ethnography is a technique carried out 'to deeply experience and understand the user's world for design empathy and insight' (Hanington & Martin, 2012, Chapter 27, para. 1). Unlike anthropology and the other social sciences, in which researchers engage with their target groups for long periods of time, design ethnography usually takes place to get 'good enough' information about the behaviours and experiences related to products and services.

Kouprie and Visser (2009) also draw attention to the need to apply the concept of empathy to its origins in psychology. The types of empathy include cognitive and emotional (or affective) empathy. Affective experiences can embrace empathic distress and concern because of feeling for the other, while cognitive processes include imagining from one's own and other perspectives (Hess & Fila, 2016).

Thus, empathy is directly related to feeling how the other feels, which can be extremely challenging given the complexity of a person's experiences. It is especially problematic to place someone else in an empathetic position when this person does not experience the situation from the actual users' points of view or from their cultural and life backgrounds. This might include the fears and frustrations that designers and researchers cannot understand when just performing or simulating someone else's experience. Here, empathy can serve as a projection of what we can capture as others' feelings. Zatorre (2016) proposes that we should have an empathic approach and look to better understand the reasons behind these feelings and experiences through alterity (otherness); this means we recognise ourselves as being in a different position than the user. This implies that only going through interactions with the product or service would not provide enough of an understanding from the users' perspectives and experiences. Hence, it is essential to interact and observe while learning from the users' own reasoning, feelings, and experiences.

It is worth mentioning that the main research methods and techniques for empathic design (e.g., observations, diary and photo studies, cultural probes, contextual inquiry and design ethnography) have in-person meetings as one of the fundamental ways of building trust at the beginning of the field research. Nonetheless, Miller (2020) argues that we can engage with others remotely by discussing our *routines and feelings*; he highlights this process as essential for conducting ethnographic research online.

With the digitalisation of the social world, Kozinets (2009) proposes netnography as an ethnographic method that can be adapted when following the interactions and activities mediated by technology through learning, doing and leading discussions in online communities. Another example of building empathy using digital media is described in the paper from Sljivic et al. (2021) on how digital storytelling can evoke empathy through narratives, tone of voice and story content; they prepared an exhibition (the Listening Lounge) that presents ten digital stories encompassing narratives from older adults. The young adults reported that they empathised with the narratives and changed their generalisations about older adults after watching the storytelling exhibition.

In this sense, Terry and Cain (2016) offer a construct for *digital empathy* as the 'traditional empathic characteristics such as concern and caring for others expressed through computer-mediated communications' (p. 1). Consequently, digital empathy embraces sharing thoughts, feelings and behaviours, here with the advantage of easy access while avoiding the awkwardness of talking about emotions with a stranger or even when it is not possible to meet in person. However, the disadvantage is the lack of emotional clues that we can observe in face-to-face meetings (Walther, 2011).

Love and Break-up Letters to Sharetribe

After performing netnography and experiencing the Sharetribe service at first hand by sharing a room on a trip to another country, we recognised the need to take a radical position of alterity to develop deeper insights and to learn from the users' feelings and fears related to the digital platform instead of just trying to simulate their experiences by using the platform.

Nonetheless, conducting a qualitative investigation to empathise with users can be challenging for a service that is delivered by a digital platform because its primary touchpoint is its website. Sharetribe promotes encounters between people who want to share, sell, swap, lend or borrow items and services. As a digital platform, there is no physical space where the service is delivered. In setting up our study, we noted that there was no place where we could perform observations without intervening with the users' experiences. We could only know about the encounter by agreeing with those who would exchange things or services. Although questionnaires could be easily distributed in a digital format to the users registered on the platform, we also noted that questionnaires tend to have low return rates (around 10 per cent) if there are open questions.

To address the complex setting, we combined a questionnaire to evaluate specific touchpoints building on the 'love and break-up letters' (Smart Design, 2010) approach, which is a tool used to investigate how emotions and feelings are associated with using products and services. We aimed to understand the main frustrations with the Sharetribe service, as well as how it brought meaning to the user experience. The Smart Design method proposes that the respondent write a letter for the product or service as if they were in a romantic relationship. Thus, people are invited to openly express their feelings in a known way. The letters work as a narrative revealing why they love, hate, or even want to break up with the product or service (Hanington & Martin, 2012; Vasques et al., 2017).

The questionnaire was distributed to 100 platform users. In total, 53 valid letters to Sharetribe were collected from 58 respondents. The letters express the main difficulties and what users liked the most about the platform, rapidly allowing designers and developers to empathise with the users by understanding their pains and gains and identifying points for service improvement.

By analysing the content of the letters with a bubble graph produced by the Voyant tool (Figure 6.2), it is evident that most of the letters express positive feelings, as shown by the number of citations of words such as 'good' (mentioned 14 times), 'like' (12), 'thanks' (11), 'nice' (9), 'easy' (8), 'happy' (6) and 'love' (7). The word 'people' was also one of the most cited (17), reinforcing the power of the community. The terms 'service' (25) and 'Sharetribe' (19) also appeared frequently.

Going through the letters in detail, we can group them into three types: 'Sorry, our relationship does not work for me' (4 letters, or 7.5% of the valid letters); 'I like you, but our relationship could be better' (19, or 35.9%); and 'I love you Sharetribe' (30, or 56.6%). In this chapter, we present the comments from Antti Virolainen (one of Sharetribe's founders) next to the subcategories

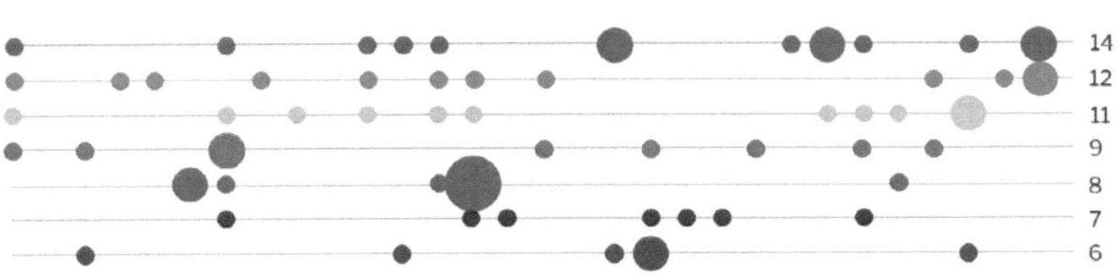

Figure 6.2 Bubble graph evidencing users' positive feelings for Sharetribe.

of letters that mentioned the same kind of issues on the break-up letters. His comments shed light on how Sharetribe improved its service by responding to many of these emerging issues.

Sorry, our relationship does not work for me

Among the 53 valid letters, only four expressed deep frustration. In these cases, the users would potentially leave the community/service if the problem was not fixed.

The Sharetribe interface presented the offers and requests in a list, and the main frustrations were concerned with both the need to browse through many posts and the lack of information about whether the offer/request was still valid.

> I didn't find the possibility to look after particular items or kinds of service. So, **I had to browse through everything**. (n. 17)
>
> I tried to touch base with the Nat/Gat in Kalamazoo, MI but **ran into dead-ends and no shows**. (n. 43)
>
> There should be even more people involved (= more stuff). **There should also be a 'best before' day for every item that is sold/wanted.** A simple reminder in email could be used to elongate the offer. (n. 22)

It is worth mentioning that even though the letter n. 22 suggests how to improve the service, there were no comments regarding the good points about Sharetribe. Hence, it was classified as a break-up letter.

Regarding the improvements from the user's pains that came up with this group of letters, Antti Virolainen (personal communication, 15 September 2021) explains that Sharetribe developers added the possibility for more specific subcategories to be browsed and a better search function. In addition, it is possible for listings to now have a 'due to date' when they close automatically. Also, listing authors were more clearly prompted to close their listing when answering to people if the listing did not need to remain open, which helped reduce 'outdated' listings.

I like you, but our relationship could be better

Although these letters present issues that should be improved, the relationship was unlikely to be broken because they also offer advice for improving the issues. Additionally, these letters included compliments about Sharetribe regarding how nice, easy to use and helpful the service was.

As well as in the break-up letters, the problems mentioned in this category also included the difficulties in figuring out if an item was still available and the methods for searching for these items.

> **It is a nice service, but it could have some improvements.** For example, showing if an item already has been requested or how many

people have contacted the owner asking about that item and, therefore, avoiding useless messages asking about the status of the item …

> **Also, there should be some more clear methods to search for items**, one listing after the other is too confusing … (n. 4)
>
> **It's nice when you can find something that you need.** However, **finding it can be quite difficult** because there aren't really that many categories and **it's not always clear if the older stuff is still available**. (n. 8)
>
> Your service is basically as I would expect it to be and working well. However, **there still are some ways you could develop the service**. For example, I would like to be able to **search items by categories**. (n. 16)

Other problems were presented in letters n. 32 and 33, such as the number of notifications sent by email and the lack of advanced filters for searching offers/requests nearby.

> I think Sharetribe is very nice and convenient to use. At some point, I got frustrated with getting too many emails, so I shut down some of those. (n. 32)
>
> Love: fit the niche to offer a service that's useful for students and community people to share or dispose of something. Hate: search is coarse. no advanced filter functions. no the 'near my location' search. picture uploads limits. limited contents or activity. The picking-up of an item sometimes is more trouble than the value of the item. (n. 33)

As commented by Antti Virolainen (personal communication, 15 September 2021), the problems concerning excessive notifications and localisation were fixed with the implementation of the marketplace approach after 2014: 'These days there are possibilities for marketplace owners to bring any type of filters they want to help users browse the content. Also map view helps to find nearby things and can be combined with search and filters'.

Problems in searching for items and the lack of filters were mentioned many times. Letters n. 15 and 38 presented very interesting suggestions on how to promote offers and requests. This could be a paid functionality, or the user could use their 'points' as a good community member or by increasing the number of members/offers through advertising.

> **I have found your service so useful over the years.** At first, it helped me acquire my first coffee machine for a very reasonable price. Then, I gained some cash and met some interesting people while selling some old things that I wasn't using anymore (making extra room in my apartment). I found out some information on where to find composting worms (not easy to find in Finland!) thanks to a helpful tribe member, and now, I'm waiting for someone to request my dog walking services. I got some interest when I first posted it (not to walk with dogs, but with another person, so not quite what I was looking for). **Because the post is now**

> **older and has moved way down into the search results, I haven't had a lot of interest lately. Unless the words in my post are searched for, I suspect it will never be discovered. It would be nice if Sharetribe offered functionality to help promote posts that are still very relevant but are not so recent anymore. I would like the opportunity to have my post on the homepage for a period of time. I'm not sure I would pay any money for that (since I'm not asking money for my service), but perhaps if I earned enough 'goodwill points' for being a good community member, I could use those to 'buy' time on the homepage. It's just a suggestion.**
>
> Overall, **Sharetribe fits in with my values of not being wasteful and recycling as much as possible**. Some things that I thought were rubbish for me were able to find new homes, so that makes me happy. Thanks, Sharetribe! (n. 38)
>
> Overall, I love that you've made a very user-friendly interface. Creating an account, messaging, browsing other tribes – extremely easy. **What I missed was a lack of filters to properly search for things with more efficiency, but then again, as there weren't that many offers in my tribe, that wasn't much of a problem.**
>
> Great work though, you've created a wonderful thing. **You just need to advertise more.** (n. 15)

Paid functionalities were implemented after 2014. Nowadays, 'it is possible for a marketplace admin to lift a listing to the top position. Some marketplaces have used that as a paid feature' (A. Virolainen, personal communication, 15 September 2021). Nonetheless, this feature was not implemented in the Aalto marketplace because the focus in this marketplace was on free exchanges.

Trust and reciprocity are critical points in the sharing economy (Bostman & Rogers, 2011). The indebtedness and feelings of reciprocity and how they shape behaviours in the Sharetribe service was previously studied[1] by Lampinen et al. (2013). Hence, Sharetribe adopted a feature to give feedback after any transaction. Still, there were some concerns about how the reviewing process worked, and room for improvement still existed, as mentioned in letters n. 51 and 30. An easier way of giving feedback and replying to negative feedback was seen as a way to increase users' satisfaction with the service.

> I bought something from someone, and **it was a successful experience, but I have no idea how to give him positive points?? Please try to simplify the reviewing process** so that it doesn't require much effort, finding out how to do it or anything from the subject of the review. Thx. (n. 51)
>
> I want to start off by saying that this is truly a genius concept that you got here! **I really love the idea of a place where a bunch of people living in the same area can sell, buy and trade stuff and services.**

> I have also noticed some things that might need some improving. At least in Otaniemi, **there are a lot of announcements about wanting to rent an apartment. Those kinds of announcements would deserve their own category in the announcements (yes, there is the 'living category' but that covers also furniture, etc.).**
>
> I also have been thinking about the feedback giving feature of Sharetribe. **Usually (in Finland), people don't like to give and get feedback cause they cannot handle it quite well. If people need to give feedback, they usually just say something nice (even if they would have something bad to say). That's just the way it goes.**
>
> Also, **I myself had a quite troubling incident with the feedback. I was selling an item that I wrote was old and in poor condition but still works (and that's why it is so cheap of course). Some girl bought it, and after that, she gave me feedback that said that everything went well except that the item was old and in poor condition. She knew that already but posted it to my profile, and now, other people get the impression that I lied and sold some rubbish to the girl. That is not right in my opinion.**
>
> That is all I can think of right now. Keep up the good work! :). (n. 30)

The feedback system was given to both parties. The seller and buyer are clearly requested by email to write a review. However, public responses to feedback were not implemented (A. Virolainen, personal communication, 15 September 2021).

It is interesting to note that even some people who had never used the service followed it because Sharetribe might provide a helpful way to solve future needs. Following the emails was also pointed out as funny (letter n. 40) and may be related to a FOMO (fear of missing out) feeling.

> I have now been your user for about 3 years. I have to admit that during that time, I have not bought anything via your service. However, **I think that the concept is great, and that is the biggest reason that I am answering this survey and writing this letter. I think that there is a real need for Sharetribe, and my gut feeling is that you are doing a good job. Many of my friends have found what they have been looking for** (moving help, a band etc.) via Sharetribe, and **I have never heard anyone say a bad thing about your service**. Even for me, 'a not so active user', **it is sometimes fun to read the email with the latest announcements** – even if I would have no intentions of buying anything. Nevertheless, I am quite confident that the time will come, when I, too, will find something that I need on Sharetribe, or be helping another person by announcing that I have, e.g., spare furniture. So, **thank you for being there and waiting for me! :)**. (n. 40)
>
> Your purpose has been good, and you have probably provided happy moments to lots of people, but **unfortunately, you haven't been able**

> **to satisfy my needs yet. Maybe it is that we have different needs that do not match**, e.g., I am a stuff member and most people using your service are students. **You are not the right one for me, but I don't mind following you and maybe trying my luck when in need. Maybe someday, there will be a real match, and you can make me happy.** Maybe I could do something and try right now as it came to my mind how you could help me. **I wish you lots of success and happy moments!** (n. 31)

I love you Sharetribe

For those who declared they loved Sharetribe, the reasons were the easy, convenient and pleasant website (user friendly) and the business fit to users' values, such as helping other people and concern over environmental issues (less consumption and second-hand use).

> **I am perfectly happy with the services provided** by Sharetribe. (n. 7)
>
> I always forget my password since I'm not a regular user. Thanks for making it easy to gain it again! (n. 26)
>
> I like that your website is very easy to use. (n. 28)

The perfect fit with the community's needs was one of the most significant reasons to love Sharetribe, as letters 11, 29 and 39 reveal. The service made the students' lives easier, helping them find and sell things or services while saving or making money through a free service.

> **The guy who fixed my guitar for a bottle of wine** (compared with €100 at a shop) **was awesome.** (n. 11)
>
> **I love Sharetribe because I can easily find if there is something I am looking for, and I can trust on these people** because they are all from this campus area, and it is easy to get contact with them. And **Sharetribe is free of charge!** (n. 29)
>
> You've got **very nice website that helps lots of students save money and recycle items. Thank you!!!** (n. 39)

Feelings of love and gratitude for the Sharetribe idea, as well as missing a similar service in other countries as expressed in letter 34, suggested there would be room for internationally expanding the service, which had already been in the cofounders' plans since 2011.

> I don't use the service anymore because **I'm not in Finland anymore, but I love the idea of offering and requesting of things you need. I miss something similar to Sharetribe at Aalto in my country.** (n. 34)

Conclusions

Start-ups are companies founded by entrepreneurs who believe an idea has potential demand. In its first stages of operations, it is essential to deliver a product or service that is aligned to their clients' needs to grow and expand their business. However, with a limited budget and revenue, it is impossible to invest in market studies with methods that demand long-term research to build empathy and understand the positive and negative aspects of the product or service delivered. Design methods can help put the user at the centre of the development process, adjusting its process to understand the constraints and users' needs while rapidly testing ideas.

Digital empathy is built by sharing feelings and emotions within computer-mediated communications. Without personal encounters, it was possible to take a deep dive into Sharetribe users' feelings and emotions regarding its service, here by applying the Love and Break-up Letters design research method in a digital questionnaire. We used this method to quickly obtain meaningful digital narratives that expressed the main frustrations and motivations of using Sharetribe.

Because the sharing economy was mainly based on exchanges and trust among strangers, forming 'tribes' around a common place or interest (such as the Aalto student's community or Kallio neighbourhood) and matching them to what was seen as valuable to users (e.g., sports equipment sharing) were fundamental approaches for starting and developing the Sharetribe service. The letters offered many additional opportunities to improve the service beyond aligning with the users' needs.

Hate and break-up letters usually point out problems that need urgent attention. If the relationship is broken or about to fall apart for some right now, others may give up in the future because of the same reasons. For instance, the letters indicated the need to improve on how one could check the availability of product and service offers and requests. Still, the letters that expressed love and pointed out improvements are the most inspiring because they clearly show the user cares enough, offering suggestions and recommendations on enhancing the relationship or hinting at what needs to change. These letters highlight the relevance of the rich insights that may emerge. Bringing one of the founders' comments on how they improved their service right next to the hate and break-up letters shows how the research method can help deliver better services and experiences.

The total number of love letters (30/53) showed that many of Sharetribe's users were satisfied with the service. These users not only supported Sharetribe by sending messages of gratitude, but they potentially brought in new users by saying positive things about the service to friends and family, both in-person and on social media. Furthermore, this group of letters also reminds the service what brings meaning to the user experience, such as creating a service that fits into individuals' values, saves money and is free to access. Therefore, these letters expressed positive feelings that emerge in the relationship between the user and Sharetribe.

Summary 1: Lessons learned that can contribute to the organisational or business context

Building digital empathy is challenging—but not impossible—when using methods and techniques closer to the users' daily lives. The Love and Break-up Letters method brought an insightful and joyful experience for both the users and company. The feedback provided by the company on how they improved their service to deliver a better experience shows the relevance of the method.

Summary 2: Contribution to organisational or business knowledge or practices

Using the Love and Break-up Letters method as part of a questionnaire to better understand the user experience with a digital service offered an easy, cheap, funny and valid method to obtain insights from users rather than using a numeric evaluation such as the Net Promoter Score (NPS) that does not express the reasons behind one's emotions. People become involved and express their real feelings when writing the letters because they understand the service as it really is: a relationship with a company.

Acknowledgements

The authors are thankful to Antti Virolainen and Juho Makkonen (Sharetribe founders) for their comments regarding and support of this research. The authors also acknowledge the financial support from CAPES (Proc. 18925/12–0) as part of Rosana Vasques' PhD degree, as well as the International Design Business Management Programme, Aalto University School of Business.

Note

1 The service was still called Kassi when Lampinen et al.'s research was performed in April 2012.

References

Battarbee, K., Suri, J. F., & Howard, S. G. (2014). *Empathy on the edge*. IDEO. https://www.ideo.com/news/empathy-on-the-edge.

Bostman, R., & Rogers, B. (2011). *What is mine is yours*. Harper Collins.

Hanington, B., & Martin, B. (2012). *Universal methods of design: 100 ways to research complex problems, develop innovative ideas, and design effective solutions*. Creative Publishing International. [Kindle for PC version]. Retrieved from Amazon.com.

Hess, J. L., & Fila, N. D. (2016). The manifestation of empathy within design: Findings from a service-learning course. *CoDesign*, 12 (1–2), 93–111. doi:10.1080/15710882.2015.1135243.

Kouprie, M., & Visser, F. S. (2009). A framework for empathy in design: Stepping into and out of the user's life. *Journal of Engineering Design*, 20 (5), 437–448.

Kozinets, R. V. (2009). *Doing ethnographic research online*. SAGE Publications.

Krznaric, R. (2014). *Empathy: why it matters, and how to get it*. Perigee Books.

Lampinen, A., Lehtinen, V., Cheshire, C., & Suhonen, E. (2013). *Indebtedness and reciprocity in local online exchange*. In ACM Conference on Computer Supported Cooperative Work, San Antonio, Teksas, Yhdysvallat, 23–27 February 2013 (pp. 661–671). ACM.

Makkonen, J. (2013). *How to create a lively peer-to-peer marketplace*. https://www.shareable.net/how-to-kick-off-a-shareable-spring/.

Miller, D. (2020). *How to conduct an ethnography during social isolation*. https://www.youtube.com/watch?time_continue=5&v=NSiTrYB-0so&feature=emb_logo.

Sharetribe. (2021). Retrieved from: https://www.sharetribe.com/.

Sljivic, H., Sutherland, I., Stannard, C., Ioppolo, C., & Morrisby, C. (2021): Changing attitudes towards older adults: Eliciting empathy through digital storytelling. *Gerontology & Geriatrics Education*. doi:10.1080/02701960.2021.1900838.

Smart Design. (2010). *Smart design: The breakup letter*. https://vimeo.com/11854531.

Terry, C., & Cain, J. (2016). The emerging issue of digital empathy. *American Journal of Pharmaceutical Education*, 80 (4), 58.

Tuomala, E., & Baxter, W. (2019). Design for empathy: A co-design case study with the Finnish parliament. *Proceedings of the Design Society: International Conference on Engineering Design*, 1 (1), 99–108. doi:10.1017/dsi.2019.13.

Vasques, R. A., Koria, M., & Santos, M. C. L. (2017). Why do I love you Vaatelainaamo? Analysis of motivations, barriers and opportunities in a Finnish service for sharing clothes. *The Design Journal*, 20 (S1), S721–S731. doi:10.1080/14606925.2017.1353018.

Walther, J. B. (2011). Theories of computer-mediated communication and interpersonal relations. In M. L. Knapp & J. A. Daly (Eds.), *The SAGE handbook of interpersonal communication* (pp. 443–479). SAGE Publications.

Zatorre, C. (2016). *Empatia e Alteridade. Como a alteridade pode trazer qualidade para a pesquisa em design* [*Empathy and Alterity: How alterity can bring quality to design research*]. https://medium.com/@carolzatorre/empatia-e-alteridade-2644a4fa8c80.

7 Comprehending the lenience on academic assessment regulations through university students' emotional insights in Tanzania

Albert Tibaijuka and Ludovick Myumbo

Introduction

The academic assessment regulations (AARs) in universities are purported to be instrumental in promoting quality education, as well as students' commitment to studying (Gibbs & Dunbar-Goddet, 2007; Yorke, 2008). Universities in Tanzania also have similar AARs. As they attempt to provide quality education, universities set a number of measures used for assessing students' academic performance before awarding them different academic titles (certificates, diplomas, degrees, etc). Over the course of administering these AARs, however, instructors in Tanzania have been attacked for being lenient, which is a major issue considering their professionalism is crucial to the education system of the country (Ishengoma, 2007; Mgaiwa & Ishengoma, 2017; Peter, 2014).

The exercise of administering AARs, among other things, considers measures such as compulsory class attendance; adherence to submission deadlines; the production of original assignments/projects; and injunctions on all sorts of cheatings (see Agolla & Ongori, 2009; Hong, 2009). University instructors consider the observance of these conditions as a prerequisite for students to pass the assessments. Failure to adhere to one (or some) of the conditions had on many occasions been a punishable fault (Hong, 2009).

Present practices in academic assessment, however, as experienced by the authors' long-time involvement in serving universities in Tanzania, are no longer uniform. University instructors in the country and beyond—depending on different circumstances—are increasingly becoming more lenient when dealing with the students' faults (see, e.g., Ashwin, 2008). In a number of incidents, university instructors have been observed waiving AARs after listening to students' reasons for their failures to meet the conditions. In other words, the university dons are becoming empathetic towards students' stories/experiences that led to their failure in meeting the AARs. Though it is argued that such tendencies are compromising the quality of university education, they are also considered pragmatic, intelligible and true to life given the socio-economic realities against the demands and rigours of the higher education system in Tanzania (Ishengoma, 2007).

This state of affairs has been little studied, especially for understanding the factors behind the instructors' empathetic responses to students' stories during

DOI: 10.4324/9781003227557-9

the enforcement of AARs. Therefore, the current study set out to discover what transpires between university instructors and students in a course of observing the AARs. The intriguing question, therefore, was as follows: In which ways are students' empathic stories compelling the instructors to reconsider the AARs? Responding to this, the study went through the university students' emotional insights, which were drawn from semistructured interviews, to spell out part of what is behind the so-called instructors' lenience in observing the AARs. In more particular terms, the study drew from the students' stories and experiences to demonstrate how feelings and emotions may serve as powerful analytical lenses to speak about empathic actions.

Empathy: A conceptual reflection

Empathy refers to the capacity of understanding the situation of another person—that is, understanding that person's definition of the situation and the symbolic universe in which the elements of the situation become meaningful and shape actions (Rughinis & Huma, 2014, as cited in Miettinen et al., 2016). This is understood as a skill that humans employ to understand each other's emotions, and institutions such as universities can use it to engage their students and academic staff in identifying the challenges and opportunities in academic assessment processes (Wetter-Edman, 2013). By being empathetic, instructors have a chance to think about the needs of their students and act on them (De Lille et al., 2012). Far from academic requirements, they attempt to understand the elements that underpin the realities and situations that are experienced by their students (Ashworth & Lucas, 2000; Rumble et al., 2010; Saarikivi, 2018), eventually responding to their inner and emotional states (Patnaik, 2009).

By being empathetic to students, university instructors are, arguably, considered wiser, particularly by demonstrating their abilities in understanding and sharing students' inner lives (Brink et al., 2011, p. 1). This implies that instructors are revealing levels of understanding that are beyond conventional practices in universities and are thoughtful to students' emotions and feelings, which inform them about the associated meanings connected to students' actions and inactions.

These empathetic actions and decisions from the university dons are considered to be part of the well-known approaches towards empathy, namely cognitive, affective and compassionate. By being able to recognise what students feel, instructors are said to be applying cognitive empathy because they are understanding the intentions of their students (Baron-Cohen & Wheelwright, 2004; Bloom, 2017; Brink et al., 2011; Shamay-Tsoory et al., 2005). When they share emotions with their students, that is, they are able to imagine and experience a certain situation, from a student's point of view, the instructors are applying affective empathy (Brink et al., 2011, p. 2). More so, when they assist students in coping with their emotions and circumstances as a way of alleviating their suffering, compassionate empathy is being applied (Bloom, 2017; Riess & Neporent, 2018; Ekman & Ekman, 2017, p. 41).

Narratives and empathic processes

Narratives can facilitate empathic actions. They also serve as a process for the same. When a person speaks, he or she tries to build a specific identity for him- or herself and for others. As Gee (2011) elaborates, narrators ascribe meanings to other people, to relationships, to systems of knowledge and so forth. Through storytelling, people construe the world they live in. This is likely to be the same when university students share their empathic stories with instructors. Possibly, they talk in a way that they want to be recognised as a particular sort of individuals (aggrieved, ill-treated, disadvantaged, desperate, etc.) and as people who seek help/advise from instructors. In all likelihood, their narrations will insinuate a quest for assistance, and chances are the instructors will recognise them as such.

In the course of narrating an empathic story, a speaker is likely to use a particular language; show certain actions and interactions; refer to some commonly shared values; and even use certain signs and symbols (Gee & Handford, 2013) as a process of placing issues together in a certain order for a listener to understand his or her intentions or respond to his or her innermost emotions or feelings. Therefore, narratives can be used as a tool to process and overcome challenges for individuals and communities (see Miettinen et al., 2016, p. 138).

Methodology

The need to know more than facts to understand how instructors and students felt about the AARs in universities in Tanzania was very critical in the current research. We imagined that without feelings, it would become difficult to gain an in-depth understanding of the lived experiences of both instructors and students. In this respect, we targeted stories that were graphic, containing explicit and vivid descriptions of the dire circumstances that the instructors and students go through during academic assessments in universities in Tanzania.

As instructors ourselves, we were aware that many students have emotions that are strongly felt but are given expression only in the private sphere and remain confined to offices, corridors, telephones and homes. When academic assessment reaches the public sphere, in policy forums, decision-making meetings, classrooms or in the literature, the emotions around it are seldom mentioned and hardly ever taken seriously or explored (Steinberg, 2008, p. 42). In other words, the process of AARs is treated as an emotionless and objective reality at the public and policy levels of educational interactions, whereas in the lives of the people involved, assessment appears to be a highly emotional experience. In this context, therefore, our research design was framed to facilitate the expressions of emotions involved in the process of AARs in universities in Tanzania.

From the above perspective, therefore, narrative enquiry appealed to us for several reasons. Among other things, narrative enquiry is sensitive to the 'subtle textures of thought and feeling' (Webster & Mertova, 2007, p. 7) at play in an account of lived experiences, allowing for the events that have been of most significance to be brought forth in the stories told by the participants. Clandinin and Rosiek (2007, pp. 42–43) wrote that a narrative enquiry focuses not only on individuals' experiences, but also on the social, cultural and institutional fabrics within which individuals' experiences are constituted, shaped, expressed and enacted. In addition, a narrative enquiry helps a researcher or inquirer to 'de-experience' and 'de-world' the world of the participants with the hope of gaining an in-depth understanding of their lived experiences (Safranski, 1998, p. 146).

For the sample of the present study, we used a snowball sampling technique to reach out to students who had experienced strong emotions of anxiety, irritation, despair and even joy during their academic assessment at St. Augustine University of Tanzania (SAUT). We initially made contact with those instructors who providentially helped us establish contact with the potential participants in our research. The technique was possible thanks to the solidarity that exists between the instructors and students who had gone through the above experiences. Indeed, some instructors knew the students very well and would meet them regularly for social and psychological support. Through these instructors, therefore, we had a rare and important opportunity to 'enter' the wider community of students who had experienced strong emotions during their academic assessment, in which we became members of the 'landscape', as suggested by Clandinin and Connelly (2000, p. 63).

As soon as rapport had been built between us and the potential participants, we purposefully recruited only four participants for several reasons. First, a relatively small number of participants would foster trust more easily during our sessions of storytelling. Second, a few participants would keep the process personal and active and would make our contact more direct and consistent (Ospina, 2004). Third, with a few participants, we could access thick and rich data, which is an important aspect of qualitative research (Langdridge, 2007). In selecting the four participants, we ensured that different programmes and categories of students were represented. We targeted students aged between 18 and 25 years, an age group that we thought would articulate well their lived experiences of academic assessment.

At this stage, we sought the informed consent of the participants. We and the participants agreed on the use of pseudonyms to protect their confidentiality and prevent harm. We also agreed on how to store the data in a protected way. In this vein, we agreed on the importance of having a field diary, where we would document and keep everything observed, heard and found. In addition, we carefully selected the time and locations for our meetings for safety reasons. The participants possessed knowledge of safer and better sites—often in the offices of instructors who were considered peaceful and understanding, including our own offices. In addition, a process of reflexivity was included not only to account for any power imbalances, but also out of consideration for the validity and reliability of the data (Hertz, 1997). With reflexivity, we (inquirers) were made aware of the existing stereotypes and biases, and we were often reminded to act only as a catalyst to promote enquiry into issues that affected the participants. This enabled us to also document our personal biases and frustrations and to think critically about the entire process. Through narrative analysis, the study used SAUT students' stories to capture empathic processes, which helped make sense of the instructors' lenience on the AARs.

Findings

The students were urged to narrate emotional stories that could inform us about their instructors' lenience in adhering to the AARs. Although it is the students' authentic experiences that we aim to bring out in this section, we are also aware that we carry our own personal baggage and perspectives, which might influence how we infer meanings from their narratives—there indeed is a temptation for researchers to intrude and take over the participants for their own purposes (DeVault, 1999, p. 34). With this in mind, we made a deliberate effort to refrain from overriding the participants. In other words, we assumed only the role of a passenger rather than a driver behind the steering wheel to allow the students' authentic experiences of AARs to take the lead.

Some of the stories represented in the participants' own words, lives that had been shattered by incomprehensible acts of violence and neglect, required an empathic instructor to listen to and respond to their needs. From the stories narrated, an array of situations was revealed, ranging from being late to lectures because of a long queue in getting antiretroviral drugs (ARVs) to pregnancy complications, death of parents and sexual assault, to mention but a few situations. These issues are presented and discussed in greater detail here.

John Kamishije is a second-year student pursuing a Bachelor of Arts in Public Relations and Marketing. He did not attend a lecture where the instructor issued a quiz, which had 10 out of 40 points for the semester course work. The following day, he approached the instructor, who at first refused to listen to his excuses. Then, after pleading with the instructor for some time, John was given a chance to explain himself. The following is John's dreadful and distressing situation:

> I was very sorry to miss the lecture. I plainly told the instructor that it was not my intention to miss his lecture. I came late to the lecture hall and found the door closed, so I could not get in. I was late because there was a very long queue at the hospital, where I had gone to take ARVs. I am HIV positive.
>
> My candidness to the matter caught the instructor by surprise; he was completely astonished, shocked and somehow in disbelief as soon as he heard my story. He never imagined hearing such a story in the manner I said it, so he became more curious, wanting to know what exactly had happened to me. I told him it is a sad sorry but real. I am an orphan. My parents died of HIV/AIDS at my age. I contracted HIV/AIDS at birth and

> never knew about it until when I was 12. During my childhood, I was sick most of the time without knowing what troubled me. With support from my brother, I visited many hospitals for medical check-ups and treatments but never got well. Given my age, the medical experts never imagined I could be HIV positive and, therefore, did not bother to test my HIV/AIDS status. It was until when I turned 12 that I visited a medical expert who was a friend to my brother and was aware of what happened to my parents. It is him who advised my brother and later checked my HIV/AIDS status and found out that I was positive. After several consultations between the two friends, I was later taken to a counsellor and started using ARVs. I continued well and successfully completed the ordinary and advanced levels of secondary education and now am at the university.

Jamila Ishebabi is a fourth-year student of Bachelor of Laws (LLB). She missed almost 30% of the semester's lectures, including assignments and tests. Given the circumstances and according to the assessment regulations, Jamila was not supposed to sit for the final exams of her last year in the university. It was the instructor's decision to listen empathetically that changed Jamila's fate, as implied in the following story:

> I was impregnated by my fellow student, who later abandoned me. My parents were mad at me when I told them about the pregnancy and refused to support me. So I struggled on my own to take care of the pregnancy. The only source of income I relied upon was a loan I received from the government as a student. This was not enough, as it had to still help me in paying for meals and accommodation, meeting house bills and other academic requirements.
>
> Unfortunately, I had pregnancy complications when in labour, and I required caesarean section. This made me spend so much time in the hospital, and when I returned to my hostel, no one was there to assist me and the baby. In this sense, I had to take all responsibilities alone while at the same time required to attend the lectures, something which was not possible. As I could not afford a babysitter, I was forced to choose between staying with my baby or going to attend the lectures. I was bound to choose the former, except for a few instances when a woman (a cleaner of the hostel where I stayed) accepted to stay with my baby for a few hours. These were the days I afforded to attend classes, but it was not sufficient enough to meet the academic assessment regulations.

The story of Jackson Mwambola, who had just finished writing his final exam for a Bachelor of Law and had defended his research project, is very touching. He was waiting for an oral exam that would have made him complete all academic assessment requirements before graduation. Two days before the oral exam, at night, he received a call from his father, who wanted to send him bus fare so that he could travel back home after completing his university studies.

Jackson told his father that there was still one more (oral) exam to be done and advised him to send the money after the exam. After a brief conversation, they agreed on the arrangement, and Jackson asked his father why he was still awake so late that evening. The parent answered in short that he was busy writing something. Here is what followed after that:

> The following morning, I received a call from a close relative informing me about the passing on of my father—a person I had talked to a couple of hours before. Out of shock, disbelief and grief, I left the university premises without following proper procedures and went to attend my father's burial. While away, the oral exams proceeded, and the panellists went on assessing other students without knowing the reasons for my absence and, therefore, cancelled my candidacy. This meant that I was to appear for the oral exam at the end of the following academic year. As desperate and sorrowful as I was, I travelled back to the university after burying my father and went to meet one of my lecturers, who was a member of the panel for my oral exam. This was a couple of days after the end of all oral exams. The lecturer was kind enough to listen to my story. The lecturer was anguished with my revelation that my father was writing a will that very night when we talked over the phone when I questioned him why he was still awake in those late hours. He died a few hours after he had written the will.
>
> As weak as I was, full of tears and with so much grief, I pleaded with the lecturer for a special oral exam.

As for another story, Atupele Masumbuko was raped, missed lectures, but found sympathy and a positive response from her instructor, as narrated below:

> It was my first social event at the university, and it had been a fun night. We danced until we were ready for sleep. As I was leaving, a guy offered to walk me home. Walking home alone at night and in the dark was something I wanted to avoid, so I gladly accepted his offer.
>
> When we got to the steps of my hostel, the guy politely asked me if he could come in for a glass of water. I let him in, and after he had finished drinking the water, he demanded that I go to my room. I refused and even attempted to get him to leave, but he was relentless: 'You wouldn't let me in if you didn't want something to happen', he argued. Suddenly, there was someone physically stronger than me, refusing to leave. It became instantly clear to me that his intention had never been to get me home safely. Suddenly, he grabbed my arm so fiercely and took off my tights. When he was done, he finally left. I was left overwhelmed with disbelief, disgust, self-blame and guilt. I thought if I reported what had happened to me, I would not be believed—I was the one who let him in into my room. I didn't physically try to fight him off.
>
> What happened didn't fit any label that I recognised: he wasn't a stranger, and there was no dark alley. I was also worried of going to the police

> as I thought the process for sexual assault would take ages—How would my studies be affected by a serious criminal investigation and trial? I told myself that I should not tell no one.
>
> Days passed and I would try to forget as I didn't want the incident to define me. I worked hard on it, but I would still come back to the same reality: 'I was raped'. This affected me so much that I couldn't concentrate on my studies anymore. I felt lonely and ashamed because of my experience. I was gripped by fear, which made me miss almost all the lectures and didn't do assignments or meet deadlines.
>
> One day, I decided that I needed to speak to someone for help. I gathered up my courage and requested an urgent five-minute appointment with my instructor, as I believed he would understand my situation. I told him that I was a victim of sexual assault and that I wanted to discuss the possibility of extending my assignments. Although clearly sympathetic, the instructor explained that the university required instructors not to extend their students' assignments. However, he offered himself to explain my situation to the head of the department for help. A note was then sent to other instructors to help me, without necessarily giving the reason. Weeks passed, and the majority of the instructors were understanding and helpful.

If you were to put yourself in the instructors' shoes, what would have been your decision in relation to the quiz missed by John because of a long queue in getting ARVs, Jamila's skipping of some lectures because of pregnancy complications, Jackson's failure to show up for an oral exam because of his parents' death or Atupele's inability to meet deadlines because of a sexual assault? Surely, in such situations, no one's arm would be too short to render help, nor his/her ear too dull to hear and listen empathetically. Certainly, upon hearing such touching stories, one will be compelled to go far beyond by simply being compassionate and treating such students the way they would want to be treated themselves—the golden rule.

Conclusion

The current study has shown that students' empathetic stories influence their instructors' lenience in applying AARs for several reasons. First, instructors are human beings, and one of the fundamental aspects of being human is the capacity to feel, show and express emotions, but also to emphasise and build a considerate and sympathetic relationship of trust with those in need (Karnieli-Miller et al., 2009, p. 283). In this respect, instructors are not expected to be in a value-free position of neutrality in their application of AARs for the sake of objectivity, which might lead to what Shacklock and Smyth (1998, pp. 6–7) called an 'obscene and dishonest position'. Second, as facilitators of learning, instructors are called to pertain to the essential attitudinal qualities of a good facilitator in their application of AARs, including being 'real' and 'genuine' to their students' situations, as Rogers (1983, p. 106) explained:

> Perhaps the most basic of these essential attitudes is realness or genuineness. When the facilitator is a real person being what he is entering into a relationship with the learner without presenting a front or facade, he is much more likely to be effective. This means that the feelings that he is experiencing are available to him, available to his awareness, that he is able to live these feelings, be them, and able to communicate them if appropriate. It means that he comes into a direct personal encounter with the learner, meeting him on a person-to-person basis. It means that he is being himself, not denying himself.

Seen from the above point of view, an instructor can be a real person in their relationship with their students. They can be enthusiastic, can be bored, can be interested in students, can be angry, can be sensitive and can be sympathetic, which may influence their application of AARs. Because the instructor accepts these feelings as their own, they have no need to impose them on their students. The instructor can like or dislike a student product without implying that it is objectively good or bad or that the student is good or bad (Rogers, 1983, p. 106). The instructor is simply expressing a feeling for the product, a feeling that exists within him- or herself. Thus, they are a person to their students, not a faceless embodiment of a curricular or AAR requirements, nor a sterile tube through which knowledge or academic assessment is passed from one generation to another (Rogers, 1983, p. 106). In this respect, instructors are bound to practice AARs not only as an intellectual exercise, but also as a process that is felt deeply.

It makes sense to say that instructors' lenience in AARs is not a weakness, as some scholars have suggested (Ishengoma, 2007; Mgaiwa & Ishengoma, 2017). On the contrary, it is an indispensable attitude that stands out in those who are successful in facilitating learning. Rogers (1983, p. 109) thought of it as an attitude of 'prizing' the learner's feelings and opinions. It is about caring for the learner, but a nonpossessive caring. 'It is an acceptance of this other individual as a separate person, having worth in his own right' (Rogers, 1983, p. 109). It is a basic trust, a belief that this other person is somehow fundamentally trustworthy. When the instructor has the ability to understand the student's reaction from the inside and has a sensitive awareness of the way the process of AARs appears to the student, then the likelihood of significant learning increases (Rogers, 1983, pp. 111–112). This kind of understanding of AARs is sharply different than the usual evaluative understanding, which follows the pattern of 'I understand what is wrong with you'. When there is a sensitive empathy, the reaction in the students follows something of this pattern: 'At last someone understands how it feels and seems to be me without wanting to analyse me or judge me. Now I can blossom and grow and learn' (Rogers, 1983, p. 112). This attitude of standing in the other's shoes, of viewing the world through the student's eyes, has a tremendously releasing effect when it occurs.

Summary 1: Lessons learned that can contribute to the organisational or business context

This study informs organisations about the importance of stretching the limits of their operational rules and regulations in order to embrace stakeholders' life realities. This can be done by being open to flexibility, accepting that an objective approach to the decrees is necessary but not a sufficient condition. The incorporation of subjectivity in administering the rules and regulations, here in a sense of considering the emotional insights of the employees and other immediate stakeholders, will not only facilitate business operations, but also enable organisations to gain trust and a positive image.

Summary 2: Contribution to organisational or business knowledge or practices

The study's findings refute criticism that flexibility in the governing statues of organisations is detrimental to the good performances of the entities. Instead, it argues that being empathic to problems or the life challenges facing employees and other stakeholders are stimulants to better organisational performances. As data attest, empathic action to people's (e.g., employees) emotional experiences can revive working spirits, particularly of those who would have otherwise quit their jobs. The way empathic actions are pursued demonstrates a true meaning of a sense of care, teamwork and mutual understanding, which are the underlying foundations of the success of any business.

References

Agolla, J. E., & Ongori, H. (2009). An assessment of academic stress among undergraduate students. *Educational Research and Review*, 4 (2), 63–70.

Ashwin, P. (2008). Accounting for structure and agency in 'close-up' research on teaching, learning and assessment in higher education. *International Journal of Educational Research*, 47 (3), 151–158.

Ashworth, P., & Lucas, U. (2000). Achieving empathy and engagement: A practical approach to the design, conduct and reporting of phenomenographic research. *Studies in Higher Education*, 25 (3), 295–308.

Baron-Cohen, S., & Wheelwright, S. (2004). The empathy quotient: An investigation of adults with Asperger syndrome or high functioning autism, and normal sex differences. *Journal of Autism Development and Disorders*, 34 (2), 163–175. https://doi.org/10.1023/B:JADD.0000022607.19833.00.

Bloom, P. (2017). Empathy and its discontents. *Trends in Cognitive Sciences*, 21 (1), 24–31.

Brink, T. T., Urton, K., Held, D., Kirilina, E., Hofmann, M., Klann-Delius, G., Jacobs, M. A., & Kuchinke, L. (2011). The role of orbitofrontal cortex in processing empathy stories in 4-to 8-year-old children. *Frontiers in Psychology*, 2, 80.

Clandinin, D. J., & Rosiek, J. (2007). Mapping a landscape of narrative inquiry: Borderland spaces and tensions. In D. J. Clandinin (Ed.), *Handbook of narrative inquiry: Mapping a methodology* (pp. 35–75). SAGE Publications.

Clandinin, J., & Connelly, M. (2000). *Narrative inquiry: Experience and story in qualitative research*. Jossey-Bass.
De Lille, C., Roscam Abbing, E., & Kleinsmann, M. (2012). *A designerly approach to enable organizations to deliver product-service systems*. International Design Management Research Conference, Boston, MA.
DeVault, M. L. (1999). *Liberating method: Feminism and social research*. University of Chicago Press.
Ekman, P., & Ekman, E. (2017). Is global compassion achievable? In E. M. Seppälä, E. Simon Thomas, S. L. Brown, M. C. Worline, C. D. Cameron, & J. R. Doty (Eds.), *The Oxford handbook of compassion science* (pp. 41–49). Oxford University Press.
Gee, J. P. (2011). *An introduction to discourse analysis: Theory and method*. Routledge.
Gee, J. P., & Handford, M. (2013). *The Routledge handbook of discourse analysis*. Routledge.
Gibbs, G., & Dunbar-Goddet, H. (2007). *The effects of programme assessment environments on student learning*. The Higher Education Academy.
Hertz, R. (1997). *Reflexivity and voice*. SAGE Publications.
Hong, D. R. (2009). A critical study on the university and academic assessment system in Korea. *Inter-Asia Cultural Studies*, 10 (2), 292–302.
Ishengoma, J. M. (2007). The debate on quality and the private surge: A status review of private universities and colleges in Tanzania. *Journal of Higher Education in Africa/Revue de l'enseignement supérieur en Afrique*, 5 (2–3), 85–109.
Karnieli-Miller, O., Strier, R., & Pessach, L. (2009). Power relations in qualitative research. *Qualitative Health Research*, 19 (2), 279–289.
Langdridge, D. (2007). *Phenomenological psychology: Theory, research and method*. Pearson Education.
Miettinen, S., Sarantou, M., & Akimenko, D. (2016). Art and storytelling as an empowering tool for service design: South Australian case study. *For Profit, for Good: Developing Organizations through Service Design*, 74–80.
Mgaiwa, S. J., & Ishengoma, J. M. (2017). Institutional constraints affecting quality assurance processes in Tanzania's private universities. *Journal of Higher Education in Africa/Revue de l'enseignement supérieur en Afrique*, 15 (1), 57–67.
Ospina, S. (2004). Qualitative research. In G. Goethals, G. Sorenson, & J. Burns (Eds.), *Encyclopaedia of leadership* (pp. 1279–1284). SAGE Publications.
Patnaik, D. (2009). *Wired to care: How companies prosper when they create widespread empathy*. FT Press.
Peter, S. (2014). Academic staff capacity in private universities in Tanzania. *Papers in Education and Development*, 32, 53–73.
Riess, H., & Neporent, L. (2018). *The empathy effect: Seven neuroscience-based keys for transforming the way we live, love, work, and connect across differences*. Sounds True.
Rogers, C. R. (1983). *Freedom to learn for the 80s*. Charles E. Merrill.
Rumble, A. C., Van Lange, P. A., & Parks, C. D. (2010). The benefits of empathy: When empathy may sustain co-operation in social dilemmas. *European Journal of Social Psychology*, 40 (5), 856–866.
Saarikivi, K. (2018). Empathy, emotion, technologies and human experience. *The Evolving Role of Service Design*, HKISDNC18. https://www.bing.com/videos/search?q=Saarikivi+Katri+2017+youtube+empathy&view=detail&mid=2CAA151A10E26A4ABBFB2CAA151A10E26A4ABBFB&FORM=VIRE.
Safranski, R. (1998). *Martin Heidegger: Between good and evil*. Harvard University Press.

Shacklock, G., & Smyth, J. (1998). *Being reflexive in critical educational and social research*. Falmer Press.

Shamay-Tsoory, S. G., Tomer, R., Berger, B. D., Goldsher, D., & Aharon-Peretz, J. (2005). Impaired 'affective theory of mind' is associated with right ventromedial prefrontal damage. *Cognitive Behavioural Neurology Sciences*, 18, 55–67.

Steinberg, C. (2008). Assessment as an 'emotional practice'. *English Teaching: Practice and Critique*, 7 (3), 42–46.

Webster, L., & Mertova, P. (2007). *Using narrative inquiry as a research method: An introduction to using critical event narrative analysis in research on learning and teaching*. Routledge.

Wetter-Edman, K. (2013). Relations and rationales of user's involvement in service design and service management. In S. Miettinen & A. Valtonen (Eds.), *Service design with theory: Discussions on change, value and methods*. Lapland University Press.

Yorke, M. (2008). *Grading student achievement in higher education*. Routledge.

8 Building trust with storytelling

Dialogues and encounters in the Arctic

Caoimhe Isha Beaulé and Mari Viinikainen

Introduction

Engaging in cooperative work can be both rewarding and challenging in terms of innovation and project outcomes. Such activities, whether they occur in business, organisational or research settings, require a high level of interpersonal and emotional ability for actors in leadership positions, for all members of a team and for the group as a whole. The notion that 'two heads are better than one' is only true if the group reflects emotional intelligence or 'the collective equivalent of empathy' (Goleman et al., 2002, p. 61). Among the elements that constitute the perfect recipe for effective cooperation and teamwork processes in complex projects, trust has been identified as an indispensable ingredient (Avenier, 2000; Le Cardinal et al., 1997). This is no surprise, given that trust underlies most aspects of society as it is a fundamental part of human cooperation at large (see Rothstein, 2005). The topic has been studied extensively in fields, such as psychology, economics, management, organisation studies and sociology, and is described as a dynamic, complex and multi-level phenomenon (Rousseau et al., 1998). Although there is no universally accepted definition of trust within scientific fields, a cross-disciplinary study describes its common understanding as a 'psychological state comprising the intention to accept vulnerability based upon positive expectations of the intentions or behaviour of another' (Rousseau et al., 1998, p. 395). Therefore, when trusting someone or something, one decides to take on a certain level of risk.

In this chapter, we discuss how stories have potential in enabling trust building and fostering an environment that supports cooperation when projects involve a diverse set of team members. To do so, we delve into the many roles that stories can play in transdisciplinary, interorganisational and intercultural cooperative projects, particularly those that involve working with Indigenous knowledge. We present Dialogues and Encounters in the Arctic (DEA), a two-year project whose aim is to develop a model for cooperation between communities and researchers in the Arctic regions based on Indigenous Sámi knowledge and know-how. The Sámi are the only acknowledged Indigenous peoples in Europe, and their land, Sápmi, overlaps the borders of four different countries: Finland, Norway, Sweden and Russia. DEA was initiated by the Sámi Education Institute

DOI: 10.4324/9781003227557-10

(*Sogsakk*) and involves partners from the University of Lapland's Faculty of Art and Design and Social Sciences and Umeå University (Várdduo – Centre for Sámi Research). This transdisciplinary project brings together actors in Sámi education, Sámi handicrafts and design, Indigenous knowledge, storytelling and research, including art and design, health and social sciences.

Although many of the actors involved are Sámi, this project has also included many that are not, including ourselves. It is important to acknowledge that the views and reflections shared in this chapter stem primarily from our experience as part of the University of Lapland's team, which was in charge of organising workshops and coordinating activities for the project. This required sensitivity and care regarding how the Indigenous knowledge with which we were engaging was being treated and used, and what role it would play in the project. While challenging, this intercultural characteristic of the project reflects the reality of many Arctic cooperative projects, and it has allowed partners to engage in discussions about issues faced by different parties involved in such activities. We see our reflections as a contribution within this broader discussion. As such, DEA is not a research project per se; thus, the activities presented below stem from the collaborative work conducted as part of the general project goals and unexpected outcomes due to adapting to the COVID-19 pandemic context. This exploratory chapter is a discussion opener on a topic that has emerged from the initial stages of doctoral research conducted by one of the authors (C. I. Beaulé), who is investigating the process of building trust in collective design practices.

The questions guiding this chapter ask: How did storytelling play a role in building trust in the DEA project? and: How do storytelling and discussions about trust and empathy contribute to making collective practices in organisational contexts more effective? In approaching these questions, we will first give a broad overview of the connection between empathy and trust in cooperative contexts and teamwork. Next, to contextualise the DEA project, we will provide a general description of what we mean by Indigenous knowledge and stories. We will continue with reflections on the roles of stories in DEA, mainly discussing *stories as knowledge* and *stories as dialogue* in the project. We will conclude with a discussion on how relational exchanges such as storytelling can support the creation of a trusting environment for cooperation based on our experience of coordinating activities in this project. Although we acknowledge that the audience for this topic might be more niched, we do think it is an important part of the broader discussion about storytelling and empathy in organisational contexts. Moreover, we view this chapter as being insightful for businesses and organisations that are orientated towards social responsibility and engage with groups, cultures or knowledge systems that have been historically marginalised and perhaps also designers working with communities and within intercultural teams.

The connection between trust and empathy is accompaniment

There is a direct link between trust and empathy when working in teams. Our understanding of trust draws on the cross-disciplinary findings of practitioners who have researched the mechanics of 'collective practices' (see Avenier, 2000). In Avenier (2000), the process of collective work, including what happens within organisations and businesses, is discussed as having three core elements: *trust, collective cognition* and *accompaniment*. Here, trust is seen as 'a complex facilitator, both an indispensable ingredient and peripheral result of processes developed to reach specific ends' (loose translation from French; Avenier, 2000, p. 29) and is also described as a foundational competence to acquire. Collective cognition can be understood as a driving force and motivating factor during collaborative processes but also as a result, as project outcomes and new knowledge emerge from collective action (Avenier, 2000). In addition, the author presents accompaniment (from the French word *accompagnement*) as connected to the roles actors play in supporting and navigating the process of cooperation and explains how it relates to both being the 'accompanied' or 'companion' depending on the situation. Although distinguishable, these three elements are constantly in flux and inseparable entities in cooperative processes.

In turn, empathy can be broadly understood as 'an emotional response that stems from another's emotional state or condition and that is congruent with the other's emotional state or situation' (Eisenberg & Strayer, 1987, p. 5). In other words, it is feeling what another is feeling or the ability to put oneself in another person's shoes. Having empathy skills enhances one's ability to understand others and to communicate and adapt to an individual or a group's emotional state, and this is essential in helping to find sustainable solutions to challenges when working collectively towards common goals. Working in the field of marketing, Batat (2019) highlighted how empathy can be strongly connected to common activities and experience:

> Empathy is what makes one recognize others not as a single object, but as an alter ego that, despite its persistent difference, aims at the same world as us. Inter-subjectivity is then the starting point of an understanding of empathy … An important part of it lies in the common experience of action. This shared experience then turns out to be the pillar of shared identity.
>
> (p. 169)

In cooperative projects, empathy and emotional abilities are seen as the invisible mediators that make collective projects successful and innovative by creating a foundation that enables intersubjectivity and relational exchanges among team members or collaborators. We view these intersubjective exchanges as being highly connected to the notion of accompaniment. This common experience in action, such as cooperating in mutual projects or tasks, means that having empathy can support the decision-making process and agility of project leaders and team members. Such soft skills enable individuals to fit into their social environments. According to Goleman et al. (2002), emotional intelligence – both in individuals and groups – requires four main capabilities: self-awareness, self-management, social awareness and relationship management. The authors add that 'at the team level, social awareness – especially empathy – is the foundation that enables a team to build and maintain effective relationships with the rest of the organization' (p. 59). For instance, according to the authors, we can recognise self-awareness within a group by acknowledging the general mood of a group and of the emotions of the individuals within that group and by listening to everyone's perspective: 'That caring attitude builds a sense of trust and belonging that underscores the shared mission: We're all in this together' (p. 59). Moreover, when looking at ways to create optimal settings for team performance in creative activities, relationships among actors are seen as being entirely mediated by trust (Gong et al., 2012). This has been exemplified by Google's approach to their psychological safety strategies for optimal teamwork: 'There is no team without trust' (Delizonna, 2017, p. 2). The connections between trust and empathy in collective action take place, among other things, through an accompaniment process involving the group members.

Given the wide audience targeted by this book, before discussing the role of stories in creating a trustful environment in DEA, the following section will provide background on how stories and storytelling can be viewed when working with Indigenous knowledge.

Stories and Indigenous knowledge

As a basic concept, storytelling is a natural human activity. Most of us engage in and with stories on a daily basis. Stories can be told for entertainment, knowledge sharing and education and are closely connected to societies, cultures, practices and values. In the DEA project, the primary way stories that we used originated from sharing and documenting Sámi knowledge and know-how and from dialogue during the project activities. Attempting to summarise views on Indigenous knowledge is a challenge as Indigenous nations and communities across the globe are not one homogenous whole; they have their own specific knowledge systems and ways of knowing that are rooted in place and land. Nonetheless, Indigenous knowledge systems can be described as:

> the complex arrays of knowledge, know-how, practices and representations that guide human societies in their innumerable interactions with the natural milieu: agriculture and animal husbandry; hunting, fishing and gathering; struggles against disease and injury; naming and explaining natural phenomena; and strategies for coping with changing environments.
>
> (Nakashima & Roué, 2002, p. 2)

Nakashina and Roué (2002) reinforced the idea that Indigenous knowledge combines both knowledge and know-how, which is not common in Western worldviews whose disciplines are highly compartmentalised. This is reflected in the way it is transmitted orally but also through *doing*. Indigenous knowledge is therefore directly tied to place and land as it was developed over thousands of years by people living in their native territories, passed down through generations, primarily through oral histories (Williams, 2018). Kovach (2012) and Thomas (2005) emphasised that stories and oral traditions have crucial functions for Indigenous peoples and communities; they hold within them knowledge: historical and mythological stories provide teachings and knowledge, but also serve as reminders of belonging and relationships. They also noted that stories can be personal narratives of experiences, happenings and places. Stories address the relationships between people, but also make visible the connections and kinships to flora and fauna, addressing the interconnectedness of everything and how everything is related (Williams, 2018). Indigenous storytelling, or 'storywork', is a research methodology of its own (see Archibald Q'um Q'um Xiiem et al., 2019).

The relationship between the storyteller and the story is similar: stories cannot be isolated from the teller (Kovach, 2012; Thomas, 2005; Williams, 2018). Kovach (2012) described storytelling as a relationship-based approach; the relationship is in the centre within the Indigenous research frameworks that hold inside them certain responsibilities, protocols and ethical considerations. When using such methodologies, the primary relationship is between the researcher/listener and the research participant/storyteller (Kovach, 2012). The author adds that for the story to surface, there must be trust. Earning trust is critical, and it might take time; thus, a pre-existing relationship between the researcher/listener and the research participants/storyteller is invaluable. If the relationship is not there, it must be built (Kovach, 2012). Moreover, transparency and reflection are at the core of the process and the base for the relationship; these are created by locating the position of the researcher/listener (Kovach, 2012).

In the following section, we present a selection of activities and work that were conducted as part of DEA. In particular, we discuss the role of stories in engaging and documenting Indigenous knowledge and in initiating dialogues between collaborators and across borders.

Storytelling in the DEA project: Knowledge and dialogue

Stories as knowledge: Documenting Sámi know-how through video

As mentioned earlier, the reflections and discussions presented in the following sections were primarily conducted as part of the broader DEA activities and the general experiential knowledge accumulated through productive work in the project. Although DEA does involve some research activities, the films and workshops used for discussion were not conducted as part of them. The overarching themes *stories as knowledge* and *stories as dialogue* were selected as they are the two main ways stories and storytelling have been used in the project activities and workshops.

When the DEA project started in the spring of 2020, the original plan was to have the activities and workshops involve real-life encounters in settings that were favourable to encounters and dialogues within the project themes (e.g., sustainable Sámi food cultures, local environmental observations and Indigenous design and innovation) as we explored the use of storytelling methodologies. These themes were primarily chosen by the leading partner, the Sogsakk, during the funding application process. The activities, organised as workshops, were each planned to take place over a couple of days in outdoor settings, such as around a fire in a Sámi *lavvu* (a type of temporary dwelling). In April 2020, the Sogsakk collaborators were trying to think of ways to start some project work despite the COVID-19 pandemic limitations. Quickly enough, two collaborators from their institution, an experienced and skilled *duojár* (Sámi craftsman) Arto Saijets and coordinator Marina Falevitch, were equipped with a small portable camera with the idea of seeing how they could start documenting Sámi know-how. As they are also life partners, the two managed to start filming Arto's different activities even as the pandemic restrictions persisted. In this storytelling relationship, Marina was behind the camera as the documentarist, and Arto the teacher and teller, explaining what, why and how he was doing his work, all in the North Sámi language. These activities included going into the woods to choose the right birch tree to make a *guksi* (a wooden cup made from a burl), the making of a sledge pulled by reindeer in the winter, the welding and making of a knife and also discussing with their son-in-law – a young reindeer herder – about the challenges brought on by the heavier-than-usual snowfall. Topics were wide-ranging, including documenting visits to historical Sámi museums, Arto's homeland, fishing and preparing fish soup, the process of drying and smoking reindeer and elk meat in the *lavvu*, hay cutting, project activities and meetings with collaborators (when they were possible) and more. Although their approach was initially exploratory and experimental, over time, Marina and Arto further developed and perfected their method and habit of filming regularly, capturing what they thought would be of value to document and record. Through this process, they accumulated hundreds of hours of footage featuring Arto, but also various relatives and knowledge keepers from the community (for a glimpse of this footage, see Figure 8.1).

The limitations brought on by the pandemic, making most physical contact and collaboration impossible, led to the DEA project collaborators seeing the value and relevance of putting the camera into the hands of community members. The personal and trustful relationship between the storyteller (Arto) and the documenter (Marina) set the groundwork for a process that was smooth, natural and highly accessible, ultimately enabling them to collect all this material. The films, owing to Arto's body of knowledge acquired during his lifetime, allowed the documentation of knowledge about Sámi livelihoods and ways of doing. Their contents reveal the interconnections of knowledge, stories, land and life. In parallel, we were actively developing ideas on how these films could be used to meet the project goals within the limits set by the pandemic. This led to a series of brainstorms, discussions and tests with the project collaborators, thus leading to the development of new ideas.

Figure 8.1 Snippets from Arto and Marina's footage were used in one of the workshops on Sámi food culture that covered smoking meat in the *lavvu*, lake fishing, and making fish and potato soup. Footage by Marina Falevitch for the DEA project (2020–2021).

Stories as dialogue: Using film stories for cross-border exchanges

A few months into the project, Marina and Arto presented some of their footage in a general meeting and work session online with the main DEA collaborators. However, it was unclear how these could and would be actively used in the project and contribute to meeting the project goals. When the first footage was made available, we agreed to make a first 15-minute film with Marina that would be edited for the purpose of a small online workshop on storytelling. That film was edited in close cooperation with Marina and Arto, who provided the Finnish subtitles, as most of the film was in the Sámi language. We proceeded to do the same for the English subtitles. The workshop structure plan was discussed during a meeting in a *lavvu* with a few of the collaborators from the University of Lapland and the Sogsakk who could meet in person. The idea was to explore how films could be used as part of a workshop to initiate discussions among participants, again focusing on the themes of the DEA project. A smaller 'test' workshop was organised first to see how we could use the films in an online setting.

Over the course of the year, more footage was collected. We narrowed down what would be selected as part of the next online workshop on Sámi food cultures in which a greater number of participants would be invited. The footage was selected mainly by Marina, and our suggestions were based on what we felt would work the best in the online workshop we were coordinating. The films deemed the most relevant to the workshop were about lake fishing with nets, making fish and potato soup and smoking and drying reindeer and elk meat in the *lavvu*. Editing was a somewhat lengthy process as it was done remotely under the direction of Marina, who knew the material very well and the order in which films should appear. It was also crucial to work closely with Marina and Arto, given that the language was foreign to the person editing the film. This also allowed us to ensure that the production respected the participants' voice, preferences and participation for ethical and mutual knowledge production.

The online workshop gathered participants from the broader Sámi community, including reindeer herders, project collaborators, scholars and activists, as well as researchers and students. The participants were primarily from Finland, Sweden and Norway. Four short films, totalling about 30 minutes, were made available exclusively via a private link to all participants a few days before the workshop. The workshop lasted an entire day, which included presentations from panellists, including Arto and Marina. The films functioned as the red thread that served as a basis for discussions during the entire day.

Storytelling, trust and empathy: A relational process

The importance of building trust in cooperative projects in the Arctic

When discussing trust building, the specific context of a project is central and directly related to the process (Le Cardinal et al., 1997). The DEA setting involved many elements: it took place in the European Arctic, it involved Indigenous and non-Indigenous actors, universities and community organisations and representatives with multiple cultural backgrounds and nationalities, and it involved working with highly sensitive cultural knowledge and material. The pandemic context was also highly influential, as it added unforeseen limits that impacted communication. Thus, finding ways to develop a relational base to meet the common goals was crucial in order to create a trustful environment for cooperation. When working with Indigenous knowledge and peoples, there are many reasons for distrust towards researchers and universities, because of a long history of unethical and unidirectional research practices, racism and colonialism (see Kuokkanen, 2004; Smith, 2012). Kovach (2012) noted that 'For story to surface, there must be trust. Given the egregious past research practices in Indigenous communities, earning trust is critical and may take time, upsetting the efficiency variable of research timelines' (p. 98). Similar to Avenier (2000), Kovach suggests that trust is something constructed and facilitated by the interactions between the actors involved. In Finland, the tensions and distrust between the Sámi society and the state are rooted in the history and continuation of settler colonialism (Kuokkanen, 2020) and being left out and unacknowledged in decision-making processes that are affecting the Sámi society, traditional livelihoods and self-determination (Lehtola, 2015). Moreover, according to Lehtola (2015), there is a lack of awareness and a prevalence of inaccurate information about Sámi people and Sámi society and their history within the general population. Given the intercultural context of the project, working and actively using Indigenous knowledge necessitated constant attention. This strengthens the relevance of projects such as DEA, but also points out the need to adopt approaches that are based on cooperation, reciprocity and dialogue. There is a strong need to change the paradigm when working on a project of such a nature.

Accompaniment as an underlying process

Here, we need return to the first question guiding this chapter: How did storytelling play a role in building trust in the DEA project? As discussed in the previous section, storytelling and stories, embodied through the film footage, played a central role in allowing collaborators to start working together, discussing challenging topics such as intellectual property, privacy, informed consent and appropriate documentation methods. In fact, since the whole project revolved around 'dialogues' and 'encounters', this set a strong basis to start developing relationships that would be crucial for the work to be done. As illustrated in Figure 8.2, dialogues and the development of relationships were seen as initiators of empathy and trust among collaborators. Small in-person encounters organised in settings favourable to discussion and ease, for instance, with food around a fire, were central to the initial idea. When made possible, these meetings were the most informative and effective. Moreover, having a few key collaborators who have strong relations with members of the community can support a smoother process in the early stages. In this sense, the project leader from Sogsakk, who has known Arto and Marina for two decades, acted as a mediator and translator in the first encounters. Later on, we continued work with Marina and Arto independently. As mentioned by Kovach (2012), trustful relations are essential for stories to emerge. Similarly, as stories are shared through this dialogical process, more trust and empathy can emerge.

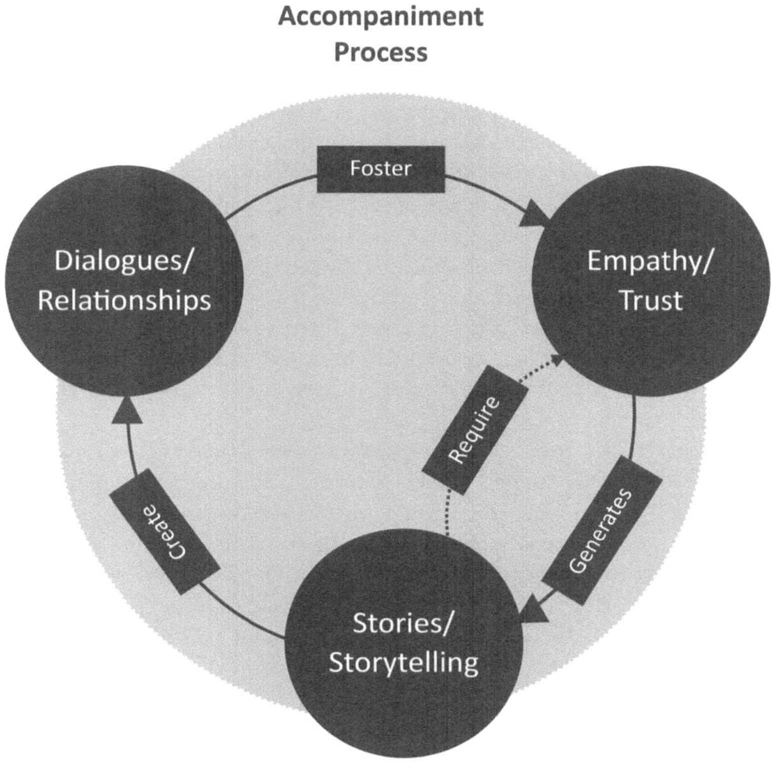

Figure 8.2. Optimal cooperation through accompaniment: dialogues, relationships, empathy, trust and storytelling. Figure by the authors, 2021.

At first, the pandemic created new challenges for the project, and everyone needed to adapt and learn how to manage in the new situation. Trust and empathy were needed in order to navigate in this new situation in order to gain an understanding of individual contexts during the process. From the start, the atmosphere involved a lot of uncertainty and improvisation. Nonetheless, since every collaborator and partner was being affected by this world event, the underlying mindset was that 'We are all in this together'. Thus, we worked collectively to try to do something interesting with our limited means. This required group emotional intelligence, or 'collective empathy' (Goleman et al., 2002). We theorise that stories and storytelling have played a crucial role in this project, primarily through the relational and dialogical process in which they emerged, as described in the previous sections. We see storytelling, in this case, the films, as a tangible mediator in these interactions.

Given the sensitive cultural setting of the project, it would not have been possible to do this work without building trust among new collaborators. In the DEA activities described in the previous section, looking through the lens of trust allows us to see more clearly the value of the ideas of Avenier (2000), particularly the notion of accompaniment. As noted at the beginning of this chapter, the ability to build trust in cooperative work is viewed as being directly related to our abilities to support and be supported by peers in the project's journey (i.e., accompaniment). Accompaniment proved to be a process in which we were unknowingly engaged. When conceptualising accompaniment, an analogy is made between collective practices and a string quartet (Avenier, 2000). In a quartet, there is no conductor. Each member's role is different yet equally important, and they must simultaneously be attentive to others' non-verbal cues, both adjusting their part and supporting the other members in order to create the desired harmonies. The necessity of trust is evident here. We see this image as a powerful one when conceptualising optimal teamwork and cooperation, where the aim is to find a moment of flow and harmony and collectively make a project happen.

In the descriptions provided in the *stories as knowledge* and *stories as dialogue sections*, some examples suggest there was accompaniment at play. Kovach (2012) reminded us that the relationships in storytelling methods are based on active listening and reflexivity. Storytelling methodology might evoke extremely personal responses that might demand sensitivity from the researcher to be available to hear stories when the participant is ready to share them (Kovach, 2012; Thomas, 2005). Here, as the coordinating and recording of the stories and knowledge was done collaboratively between Marina and Arto, their strong and pre-existing relationship played a key role in the process of making the filming process as large and extensive as it became. Although Marina is not Sámi herself (she holds an obvious place of respect within the local community, partly through her decades of work at Sogsakk), it seemed like an innovative, intimate and personal way to collect stories. This led to a fluid documentation process that would most likely not have occurred with an outsider. By working together with Arto, Marina developed her own skills and style in filming. The person behind the camera, the one listening to the stories, alongside the person telling them (Arto), engaged in a dialogical process, constructing the stories together through the means of the film. This valuable footage was made possible through trust, but equally importantly, through the process of accompaniment they both engaged in as they developed their documentation approach. Moreover, regarding the films, we had to engage in the accompaniment process. In some instances, we needed to take the lead on matters that went beyond Marina and Arto's knowledge or responsibilities, such as technical limitations with the editing, or needs from other collaborators for a workshop or project goals. By the same token, we had to be guided by them when matters exceeded our areas of knowledge, for instance, selecting the footage to be included in a film or the documentation process itself, which we scarcely took part in. Accompaniment was also at play when finding ways to use the films to meet the project general aims and augment the workshop programmes, which we managed to do through a series of tests with project collaborators, finally including them as central parts of the digital workshops. These processes went hand in hand with building trust with our collaborators throughout the project.

Trust and emotional ability for effective cooperation

A primary aim of our study was to determine how storytelling and discussions about trust and empathy contribute to making collective practices in organisational contexts more effective. As coordinators and planners in the project, it was essential to have emotional abilities – including empathy and emotional intelligence – in order to progress and adapt to the needs that would emerge, which suggested that we were engaging in an accompaniment process. The roles of listener and learner, one being the accompanied and the other the companion, have proven to be invaluable in having open dialogues and building trust through relational exchanges. That process, involving both accompaniment and trust building, happens during all dialogues and developments that occur during a project. We also felt that our previous experiences (both through work and education) relating to engaging with Indigenous people and knowledge helped us have a basic understanding of why dialogue and trust would be crucial to our development as non-Indigenous collaborators as well as inform our actions. For instance, understanding why Indigenous people might distrust certain things given the history of research misuse and abuse regarding Indigenous cultures and knowledge, one can act in a way that supports the development of trust, but also apply this knowledge in most aspects of the projects to work in a respectful way. This required us to constantly be self-aware and to self-manage, have social awareness, and manage our relationships within the team. As new ways of collaborating in Indigenous contexts are still being developed across disciplines and fields, these skills were essential to simply start 'doing the work' and prioritise dialogue and transparency with collaborators to inform our actions. The way in which this process works in action, however, must be further studied in the next steps of the research on trust. Accompaniment and all the elements that constitute its mechanisms present themselves as a compelling topic for collaborators involved in projects such as DEA, but also for professionals working in businesses and organisations that have social purposes. Since designers working in co-creation settings often take on leadership roles, the connection between building trust and accompaniment should be further developed. A profusion of literature on the positive impact of emotionally skilled leaders within businesses and organisations exists; however, looking at this topic from the perspective of trust building highlights the need to focus not only on the leaders themselves but also on the interactions and roles all actors play in collective action.

Conclusion

In this exploratory chapter, we have reflected on the roles storytelling and stories can play in intercultural, interorganisational and transdisciplinary projects like DEA, as part of the first stages of a doctoral research project on the topic of building trust in collective practices involving designers. Based on our experience as coordinators and planners, we reflected on the relevance of storytelling in the broader discussion about trust and empathy in collective practices. The DEA project shed light on the role of stories, which emerge in an inherently relational process and help to build trust based on having constant dialogue, building relationships, and requiring empathy between individual members but also within the group, thus leading to successful outcomes. Accompaniment processes seem to underly and connect all these elements and should be studied in the next phases of the research. These elements are interconnected and seem to strengthen each other as they are developed during a project. We have also highlighted how emotional abilities and empathy were essential skills for us, as non-Indigenous collaborators, to have and actively use as they allowed us to be sensitive and aware of tensions and areas that required more dialogue.

We conclude by stating that storytelling as a methodology to build trust and empathy is broad, and there are many ways in which it could be developed. We hope that the examples presented in this chapter can inspire professionals and researchers actively working with sensitive cultural material to explore how stories could play distinct roles in their respective projects and lead to more emotionally intelligent teams. These reflections are of particular relevance for businesses and organisations that are orientated towards social responsibility and engage with groups, cultures or knowledge systems that have been historically marginalised, and perhaps also designers collaborating with communities and within intercultural teams. Increasing knowledge and awareness of the importance of these emotional abilities can lay the groundwork for an environment that is favourable to cooperation, creative flow and participatory engagement. To do so, individuals must be willing to take a leap into the void and trust one another and the process if the best outcomes are to be achieved.

Summary 1: Lessons learned that can contribute to the organisational or business context

This exploratory chapter discusses the strong connection between empathy and trust when engaging in cooperative action, particularly in projects involving sensitive cultural contexts. The authors present the Dialogues and Encounters in the Arctic (DEA) project as an example of how stories can support the development of a trusting environment between new collaborators in transdisciplinary, intercultural and inter-organisational contexts.

Summary 2: Contribution to organisational or business knowledge or practices

The chapter highlights how further research into the processes of trust building in collective work could benefit organisations and businesses, particularly those that are orientated towards social responsibility and engage with groups, cultures or knowledge systems that have been historically marginalised. Although this chapter focuses on Indigenous knowledge and stories, the authors believe the process and unexpected outcomes generated by personal film footage could inspire other professionals and researchers who work in teams to explore stories as mediators to support innovation, relationship development and effectiveness. Finally, as design is increasingly being used as a strategic tool for innovation within various businesses and organisational settings, the chapter strengthens how increasing knowledge on the role designers play in trust-building processes would be beneficial.

Acknowledgements

The authors would like to thank all project collaborators and workshop participants from the DEA project, particularly Arto Saijets and Marina Falevitch, who have been generous with their time, energy and knowledge and whose general enthusiasm for project activities has been contagious. We would also like to thank Pierre De Coninck (Université de Montréal) for inspiration and his insightful comments and suggestions on the topic of trust. The Dialogues and Encounters in the Arctic project is EU funded by Interreg Nord and has received funding from Lapin Liitto (official decision no. NYPS 20203486). This work has also been supported by the Fonds de Recherches du Québec – Société et Culture (FRQSC) through the doctoral scholarship.

References

Avenier, M. J. (2000). *Ingénierie des pratiques collectives: La cordée et le quatuor [The engineering of collective practices: The climbing group and the quartet]*. Éditions L'Harmattan.

Archibald Q'um Q'um Xiiem, J. A., Lee-Morgan, J. B. J., & De Santolo, J. (2019). *Decolonizing research: Indigenous storywork as methodology*. Zed Books.

Batat, W. (2019). *Experiential marketing: Consumer behavior, customer experience and the 7Es.* Routledge.

Delizonna, L. (2017). High-performing teams need psychological safety. Here's how to create it. *Harvard Business Review*, 24 (2).

Eisenberg, N., & Strayer, J. (1987). *Empathy and its development.* CUP Archive.

Goleman, D., Boyatzis, R., & McKee, A. (2002). The emotional reality of teams. *Journal of Organizational Excellence*, 21 (2), 55–65. https://doi.org/10.1002/npr.10020.

Gong, Y., Cheung, S. Y., Wang, M., & Huang, J. C. (2012). Unfolding the proactive process for creativity: Integration of the employee proactivity, information exchange, and psychological safety perspectives. *Journal of Management*, 38 (5), 1611–1633. https://doi.org/10.1177/0149206310380250.

Kovach, M. (2012). *Story as Indigenous methodology. Indigenous methodologies: Characteristics, conversations, and contexts.* Toronto University Press.

Kuokkanen, R. J. (2004). *Toward the hospitality of the academy: The (im)possible gift of indigenous epistemes* [Doctoral dissertation, University of British Columbia]. University of British Columbia Library. https://dx.doi.org/10.14288/1.0055119.

Kuokkanen, R. J. (2020). The Deatnu Agreement: A contemporary wall of settler colonialism. *Settler Colonial Studies*, 10 (4), 508–528. https://doi.org/10.1080/2201473X.2020.1794211.

Le Cardinal, G., Guyonnet, J. F., & Pouzoullic, B. (1997). *La dynamique de la confiance: Construire la coopération dans les projets complexes* [*The dynamic of trust: Building cooperation in complex projects*]. Dunod.

Lehtola, V. (2015). *Saamelaiskiista: Sortaako Suomi alkuperäiskansaansa?* [*The Sámi dispute: Is Finland oppressing its Indigenous peoples?*]. Into Kustannus.

Nakashima, D., & Roué, M. (2002). Indigenous knowledge, peoples and sustainable practice. *Encyclopedia of Global Environmental Change*, 5, 314–324.

Mayer, R., Davis, J., & Schoorman, F. (1995). An integrative model of organizational trust. *Academy of Management Review*, 20 (3), 709–734. https://doi.org/10.2307/258792.

Rothstein, B. (2005). *Social traps and the problem of trust.* Cambridge University Press.

Rousseau, D. M., Sitkin, S. B., Burt, R. S., & Camerer, C. (1998). Not so different after all: A cross-discipline view of trust. *Academy of Management Review*, 23 (3), 393–404. https://doi.org/10.5465/amr.1998.926617.

Smith, L. T. (2012). *Decolonizing methodologies: Research and indigenous peoples.* Zed Books.

Thomas, R. (2005). Honouring the oral traditions of my ancestors through storytelling. In L. Brown & S. Strega (Eds.), *Research as Resistance: Critical, Indigenous and Anti-Oppressive Approaches* (pp. 237–254). Canadian Scholars Press.

Williams, L. (2018). Ti wa7 szwatenem. What we know: Indigenous knowledge and learning. *BC Studies*, 200, 31–44. https://doi.org/10.14288/bcs.v0i200.191456.

9 Imagine this!

Storytelling, places and empathy

Juha Iso-Aho, Nina Luostarinen and Pekka Vartiainen

Introduction

Implemented in 2017–2020 in South-east Finland with the aim of producing storytelling material linked to fascinating yet little-known sites—primarily for the purposes of tourism businesses in rural areas—Rural Explorer was a joint project initiated by the Humak and LAB Universities of Applied Sciences.

South-east Finland is a region at the eastern frontier zone facing Russia; it is rich in waterways and cultural history. Throughout its history, the region has been sparsely populated, but also ravaged by several wars and redefinitions of the national border. However, there is little material cultural heritage, such as buildings or monuments, to be found.

The colourful history has given rise to a multitude of stories, but many of the physical scenes of the intriguing events that have occurred here are rather modest in appearance or difficult to reach. For these reasons, in many areas, the attitudes of the local people towards their own history has been dismissive, and local tourism businesses have also neglected to highlight the stories found in their own areas.

The Rural Explorer project produced 51 stories based on historical facts and oral tradition, linking them to geographical coordinates from the regions of South Karelia and Kymenlaakso (Figure 9.1) in South-east Finland. The stories were published in the form of a book entitled *River of Stories* (Vartiainen et al., 2020), which also included translations of the stories in English. These stories were further developed to produce dozens of example productions (videos, images, animations, songs and a comic strip). A practical guide (Iso-Aho et al., 2020) aimed at the primary target group, that is, tourism businesses, was published on the tools and methods utilised in the project and their application in tourist products and services. Information regarding the project was shared with the target groups on the project's Facebook page and in newsletters. All of the sites included as scenes of the stories were marked on maps and linked with electronic geographical data on the Google Maps platform.

The project sought to raise local residents' awareness of their own history while offering tools for making the history related to local sites visible through the means of storytelling. In contrast to some similar projects, Rural Explorer

DOI: 10.4324/9781003227557-11

Figure 9.1 Screenshot from Google Maps to demonstrate the number and location of all the Rural Explorer stories. The Finnish–Russian border is visible diagonally in the lower right-hand corner. To view the map in detail, please visit the Rural Explorer map at https://urly.fi/1DYW.

paid special attention to both the experiential nature of the stories and linking them with the specific sites. For example, a vast number of treasure stories told across the centuries in the Kainuu region have been collected into a book entitled *Maaginen aarrekartta* (*Magic Treasure Map*) and linked with location data that are expressed as geographical coordinates. The genre of these stories follows the straightforward and factual style of narrating that is familiar from our recorded folklore (Myllyniemi, 2016).

In contrast, the selected point of view in the stories included in the Rural Explorer project almost invariably became that of a person experiencing the events first-hand, here being the central character of the story or the one witnessing the events as they unfolded. In this method of storytelling, different narrative strategies (see Tjupa, 2014) like free indirect speech and interior monologue were widely used. Very soon after the first stories were written, it was realised that the emotional power of the text was coming not solely from the outset of a story but from the reader's possibility of finding an identified subject in the narrative. See the examples of this below ('To the Pyre!' versions 1 and 2).

In Rural Explorer, the events in which we already have plenty of historical documentation settle into a narrative framework; they are about the fates of individuals and the situations and moments they have been driven to as if to remind us of the unchanging fundamentals of being human. People in love, those disappointed in life, the happy and the unhappy and those people who are afraid or galvanised with bravery do not change—only the times in which they live do.

The aim of the stories that were collected and edited during the Rural Explorer project was to infuse them with a touch of the elusive experience residing between reality and imagination, the present and past. The stories were close to what we interpret as reality. The brief moment in time that comes across from the stories—a fleeting sense of something that may be difficult to reach and that is not quite the same story as the one you are actually reading—could be exactly the element that many of the stories in the project are reaching for. Stories can lead us to a moment of insight—a transient understanding that filters through from between the lines.

On stories and the mechanisms of recognition

In the project, all the stories came from the past, sometimes from the very beginning of time when the first people settled in South-east Finland. However, because stories have their roots in history, the same also goes to the very act of storytelling. It has been suggested that a story is the most original form of human communication, that a human is, by nature, a 'homo narrans' (Fisher, 1984 p. 1), a narrating human who uses the devising and reiteration of stories to situate oneself in time and place, to seek and find a connection with other human beings and to find a shared history and future. Thus, stories serve to construct our identity—the self that has echoes of both our own special consciousness and a shared one. This kind of constructive element of narratives—listening and creating stories—can already be seen in an early stage of childhood, where practical and learned skills and expectations of others are mediated through stories. According to Gallagher, narratives provide us with 'a massive hermeneutical background', helping us cope with different kinds of social situations (Gallagher, 2012, pp. 371–372).

As a concept, the story is multifaceted and changes with history. According to one definition, it is a 'form that a person distinguishes within the current of events and that gives that person pleasure' (Torkki, 2014, p. 59.). Or, alternatively, it is 'a four-dimensional shape detected by a person' (Torkki, 2014, p. 37.) or, in slightly more concrete terms, 'a way of speaking that includes the elements of emotion and meaning, magic and fairy tale, as well as lies and seduction' (Torkki, 2014, 130.). The latter definition suggests that a story may also seduce the listener. Some researchers have referred to stories as an obsession of the brain (see, e.g., Paavonheimo, 2020), even going so far as to suggest that stories were a prerequisite for the development of language as the medium of human communication.

All things considered, therefore, stories constitute a form of human interaction that affects us on the levels of both emotion and reason—whether they are shared orally or reproduced literally or non-verbally with the aid of imagery. As such, stories tempt us to empathise with situations and events and with those things happening to other people. Thus, stories can be considered as aiding us in recognising emotions and feeling empathy, which is 'the ability to share someone else's feelings or experiences by imagining what it would be like to be in that person's situation' (Cambridge University Press, n.d.).

These mechanisms of recognising emotions have often been associated with reading fictional literature. A very common perception is that reading high-quality fiction can develop one's ability to empathise. Written stories, therefore, train us to grow as people. Recently, however, this view of literature that highlights its utilitarian value has been criticised and regarded as part of a wider phenomenon in contemporary culture that emphasises storytelling—to an even precarious extent—and that is governed by an 'experiential conception of narrative' (Mäkelä et al., 2018). A typical element in such a perception is emotional influence because stories evoke compassion and intensify the sense of identification.

Discussions of fictional stories, reading and their predicted positive capability to awake emotions has been recently part of public debate. In his essay in Finland's biggest newspaper *Helsingin Sanomat*, Jari Paavonheimo, who has been awarded a Finnish honorary title for his work in library services, regards the discussion on the mutual interaction of empathy, reading and literature as problematic precisely because of this view of literature that emphasises a utilitarian, practical viewpoint (Paavonheimo, 2020). Such views, albeit well-intentioned and educationally motivated, seem to overlook the deeper impact of literature and art. Several studies have also arrived at a similar conclusion when examining the connections of storytelling with, for instance, therapy implemented with the aid of stories. As useful and individually applicable as stories may be in evoking positive emotional experiences, employing them for the development of empathy and ability to understand and relate to the emotions and feelings experienced by others should be viewed with caution (see Gair & Moloney, 2013).

Journalist Jussi Ahlroth recently discussed the effect of stories as instruments of power (Ahlroth, 2020); his position is that we need to be careful with stories in these times, when stories and storytelling have been reborn, as it were, with more and more snags of lies swimming below the surface in the current of information. Stories are used to influence us, whether the case concerns pushing products, artistic experiences or political motivations. Indeed, stories are used to hide or gloss over the actual message that the teller is trying to get across.

As stated by Ahlroth (2020), however, our relationship with stories is quite multifaceted and difficult to verify. One might say that stories take us deep into the core of humanity, where our relationship with time—and with remembering or memories—becomes visible. We are not always even able to specify the effect of stories—why does a story make us cry, laugh or feel disgust, fear or anger and hatred? Why do some stories cause physical symptoms, making us sweat or giving us goosebumps (see Ahlroth, 2020)?

A story is a tool that aids us in analysing our experiences. A story enables us to move from one time and space to another, to journey into ourselves or to already forgotten moments in the past—yet, as emphasised by Ahlroth (2020), all of this occurs in the present. This entails that our experience of time is also narrative in nature. This is to say, we devise a story for ourselves about a past that helps us function in the present. It is a story about ourselves telling a story.

However, we will never be able to access this moment in time without a story. All that we are inevitably left with is a story, a narrative, a handwritten or typed account of the moment. This is why a story relates and, at the same time, leaves out something that cannot be told. That is also why examples of stories ('A Jump off the Rock', 'To the Pyre!' or 'Story of the Cave'), that you can read in the current article are not 'just stories' but metaphorical bridges from the past to the present.

From story to narrative and storytelling

A Finnish dictionary of literary terminology defines the Finnish word *tarina* for story as 'a relatively brief verbal or written account, tale or report of a series of events' (Hosiaisluoma, 2003, pp. 909–910). A closely related word, *kertomus*, that is, tale or narrative, then refers to a short-form, typically prosaic, fictional or nonfictional work that 'describes a specific event or series of events' (Hosiaisluoma, 2003, pp. 414–415). Both definitions can be said to emphasise the methodical nature of a narrated representation or storytelling—a structure that relies on the specific elements (like plot, time, place, narrator, etc.) inherent in a story. To work or be convincing, a story must meet the listener's or reader's expectations, which researchers also refer to with the concept 'horizon of expectation'. Very strange, alienating stories shift the horizon of expectation and, thus, may bring about a collective change in expectations (Hosiaisluoma, 2003). All stories may fundamentally be largely the same, but this is not to say that they are all similar.

However, if a story is a tool to help us navigate through the riptide of our shared history, we should dare to look deeper beyond the surface to where and how stories are born. In the Rural Explorer project, the journey towards this bottom was made by studying the structures of narration, by seeking a means through which stories become stories—the kind which we may only tell each other or to ourselves.

These structures were accessed through the factual and historical material collected during the project. This material was processed further to 'enliven' history to make it more easily accessible, interesting and suitable for commercial purposes. The latter aspect refers to the use of storytelling in business development, where it has rapidly become a key tool for marketing, strategising and branding (see Choy, 2017). In our case, this entailed the development of the tourism business.

Based on this premise, we began to process the collected material in the direction of storytelling. Various narrative methods were employed (e.g., Martinheimo, 2000), the external and internal features of the characters were elaborated on, and conventional narration was combined with a certain point of view technique, one in which the 'gaze' in different stories was sometimes that of the protagonist and sometimes that of a character observing the events from the side lines or from above (see Faherty, 2019). The direct link between historical material and time and place was enhanced by the construction of internal conflicts within various events, and the cause-and-effect relationships were focused on by varying the order of events, without losing their attachment with historical authenticity. In a way, we were using a kind of 'Ricoeurian' view on history, memory and narration where our 'refusal of time' (Remodo, 2021, p. 10), as being part of our narrative technique, helped lead to combining historical facts with fiction.

Stories are made of details that allow the reader or listener to become immersed in the mood of the story. Details provide narration with a rhythm and can be used to create suspense or slow down or speed up the progression of the plot. The details also bring the story to life at the sensory level. How something feels and sounds like and what it smells or looks like are all significant.

The ending of the story is naturally also not insignificant—is it an open ending or a clear resolution where closure is provided. Does the story end with a happy moment or a gripping sorrow that stays with the reader or listener for a long time? Perhaps, the far-sighted gaze of the narrator, reaching to us from beyond a historical distance, also infuses the ending with a particular tone.

Certain liberties regarding the material used were no doubt taken in the Rural Explorer project. If a story is about the first settlers of an area and offers a fictional description of what they thought and how they experienced specific situations or behaved in them, we have, admittedly, moved far beyond the line of imagined reality. However, for an occasional traveller reiterating the story on site, the story may awaken an interest in the place, its history and the people who used to live there, perhaps even provoking empathy towards them (regarding the importance of spatial narrative and imagined places, see also Grahn, 2021, pp. 11–12). This is the case with the story of 'Jumping Rock', from which, centuries ago, captives were forced to jump down onto sharp metal spikes. The story gains a new experiential meaning because the events are depicted through a fictitious character. A young man ascends the rocky hill, takes a final look at his destroyed village and hurls himself off the cliff and down to his death.

The story is based on descriptions of the cruel treatment of prisoners, whose stories have been preserved in the form of oral tradition. There is no knowledge of who the jumpers were, who made them jump or how common this type of practice was.

A Jump off the Rock

They forced me to jump. Not once, but twice.

The first time, I managed to avoid the sharp spikes. At the final stage of the long drop I aimed my bare feet at the empty space between the metal spikes. I thudded down on the hard earth and the spikes just brushed my skin. My left calf got a scrape with a bleeding flap of skin hanging down.

My brother was not so lucky. Crying and screaming, he flopped right onto the spikes. There was silence while the soldiers picked up my brother's lifeless body and flung it on a cart, like a worthless piece of waste, among the other dead and wounded.

The commanding officer told me to climb to the top of the rock again. In a powerless rage and fury, I began the arduous journey to the heights. The soldiers watched my progress, harangued and poked at me with their bayonets, laughing at my desperate attempts to shake them off. When I finally reached the spot from where I was to throw myself off for a second time, I raised my eyes to where our village was burning like an inferno. The crackle of the flames was mixed with monotonous drumming and people's screams of horror.

Hurtling down, I still heard the sound of the broken tune. Then nothing.

(Vartiainen et al., 2020, p. 17, transl. Annira Silver)

Another story, 'To the Pyre!', is about a young woman condemned to be burnt at the stake for infanticide. The first version of the story introduces a neutral narrator, a modern-day annalist, who reveals the documented facts behind the incident to the reader. In the second version, the point of view shifts to that of the convict's beloved as he witnesses the implementation of the woman's sentence. With the latter of the two versions of the story, the reader is transported to the centre of the depicted events, which augments an identifying experiential interpretation of the events.

To the Pyre! [Version 1]

There is a spot on the church hill of Iitti, where the life of 21-year-old Maria Simontytär ended on the pyre.

The daughter of a landed peasant had been married in the summer but had hidden the fact that she was already pregnant by a farmhand. Her intention was to kill the child once born, which happened later in November. Maria gave birth secretly in the cowshed, killed the child and hid its body under a pile of logs. A few days later, she moved it into the sheep pen and then on into a newly dug grave in the Iitti cemetery. But the crime was found out and Maria sentenced to death and burning on the pyre. The sentence was implemented in the autumn of 1784. A crowd of people watched as the young mistress of a prosperous house walked behind two priests, her black betrothal silk covering her face, towards the executioner's axe and her cruel fate.

(Vartiainen et al., 2020, p. 118, transl. Annira Silver)

To the Pyre! [Version 2]

The monotonous, disharmonious chanting of priests carries far. Your sweet face is hidden under a black kerchief. The chill autumn wind makes many of us pull our coats tighter together. I am holding back tears brought forth

> by rage. All that we had a year ago is gone, vanished like it was only a dream. The walks hidden from other eyes, the shy seeking of hands for the other, the smiles fixed on the eyes. And the moment when you told me that our time together is soon to end.
>
> Now you walk, eyes cast down, slowly behind those shuffling ahead of you. Many people stare at you solemnly, some find a word or two even on this occasion. There, away from the others, you are watched by your husband, serious, shivering from the cold or something else. Maybe you are also watched from some place by the infant whose life you ended so suddenly and violently.
>
> I follow your broken, sobbing form. I heard that after your deed you had returned to the tiny corpse again and again. Like one demented, you moved the grey bundle from one hiding place to another. You told me nothing of this. Nor about the final resting place of our child. I wonder where it is now.
>
> I turn away. I do not need to see the rest. Soon you will be no more. My own life ended a long time ago.
>
> (Vartiainen et al., 2020, p. 118, transl. Annira Silver)

In the story entitled 'Karhusaari', a dance pavilion that has already vanished is brought back to life as the first encounter of a married couple is imagined to have occurred there. In the story, an old woman is reminiscing about her late husband, their first meeting and the heady atmosphere of youthful expectation in summer. The present and past come together in memories that give the narrator at least a momentary glimpse of happiness.

The story production process

The objective in Rural Explorer was to lay the foundation for the construction of an empathetic relationship among a present-day individual, the characters in a story and the scene of the events. The functionality of the stories was tested during the project by visiting the scenes of the stories with groups of customers. The stories were also published in newsletters and on a Facebook page, enabling the inclusion of audio and video material. For example, a video was also produced for the story 'A Jump off the Rock'; the story in the video was also told from the point of view of the narrator by means of 'voice-overing' and the so-called subjective camera technique.

The materials for the stories were collected from various sources, such as the Finnish Literature Society (SKS) archives, previously published books, research materials and newspaper and magazine articles. In addition, we conducted interviews in the regions of South Karelia and Kymenlaakso.

A typical story might have originated from an archived extract of a few lines or a suggestive sentence uttered during an interview. The final stories are a combination of historical facts, geographic data and a fictional description of what might have occurred at a specific location or how an actual recorded event might have transpired.

In Rural Explorer, the story production process did not end with the drawing up of the written narrative. The core story can be developed further by using various modes and media of expression, which may bring added experiential and sensory value to the story, on the one hand, and, on the other hand, broaden the range of possibilities for utilising the story in tourist products. Varied examples and models of products for further use were also developed from several of the stories, such as the videos, in addition to illustrations, songs and animations, as well as a comic strip and soundscape. Ample photographic material of all of the sites was also produced.

The story production process implemented in the project is described in the chart (Figure 9.2), in which the original reason for telling the story—the source of the idea—is given on the left-hand side. This may have entailed a place, person, event, period or combination thereof that was regarded as something necessary to talk about. The next phase consisted of a survey of sources that could provide more material for the story. These may have included various literary sources, such as archives, books or articles, as well as oral sources, such as interviews or lore known to the writer of the story. In addition to these, the producers of the stories availed themselves of their imagination to fill in the gaps left by the sources to rework the text into dialogue or to bring in new characters, for example, to serve as witnesses to the events recorded in other materials.

This source material gave rise to the core story that, in the case of Rural Explorer, was presented in the form of a short narrative. This is, in itself, already a usable product that can be published in printed or electronic form or read aloud at the scene of the events. The latter format was tested during the project, with two bus tours arranged in May and August of 2020. On these two themed story tours of sites related to rocks and cliffs, the audience on one tour comprised tourism industry professionals and, on the other, participants of varying ages in a private event. One of the destinations included in the bus tours was a cave on the face of a hill at a height of about ten metres and running right through the hill, with a related story about the times of the Russian occupation known as the Great Wrath during the Great Northern War in the early eighteenth century.

The 'Story of the Cave' is the tale of the people of Lassila village amidst the devastation of war. The village is located in Ruokolahti near the present-day border between Finland and Russia. In Ruokolahti's local chronicles edited by Sulo Siitonen, the events are recounted as follows:

> The hill got its name from the cave running inside it. During the years of Russian persecution, the villagers used to run to the cave to escape the enemy. Pekka Huhtanen had recounted that 40 villagers had been hiding in the cave during the Great Wrath. Armed guardsmen stood watch by both mouths of the cavern. When the enemy could not force the Finns to come out of the cave, they boiled some water and poured the scalding liquid through cracks in the rock onto the people in the cave. This did not

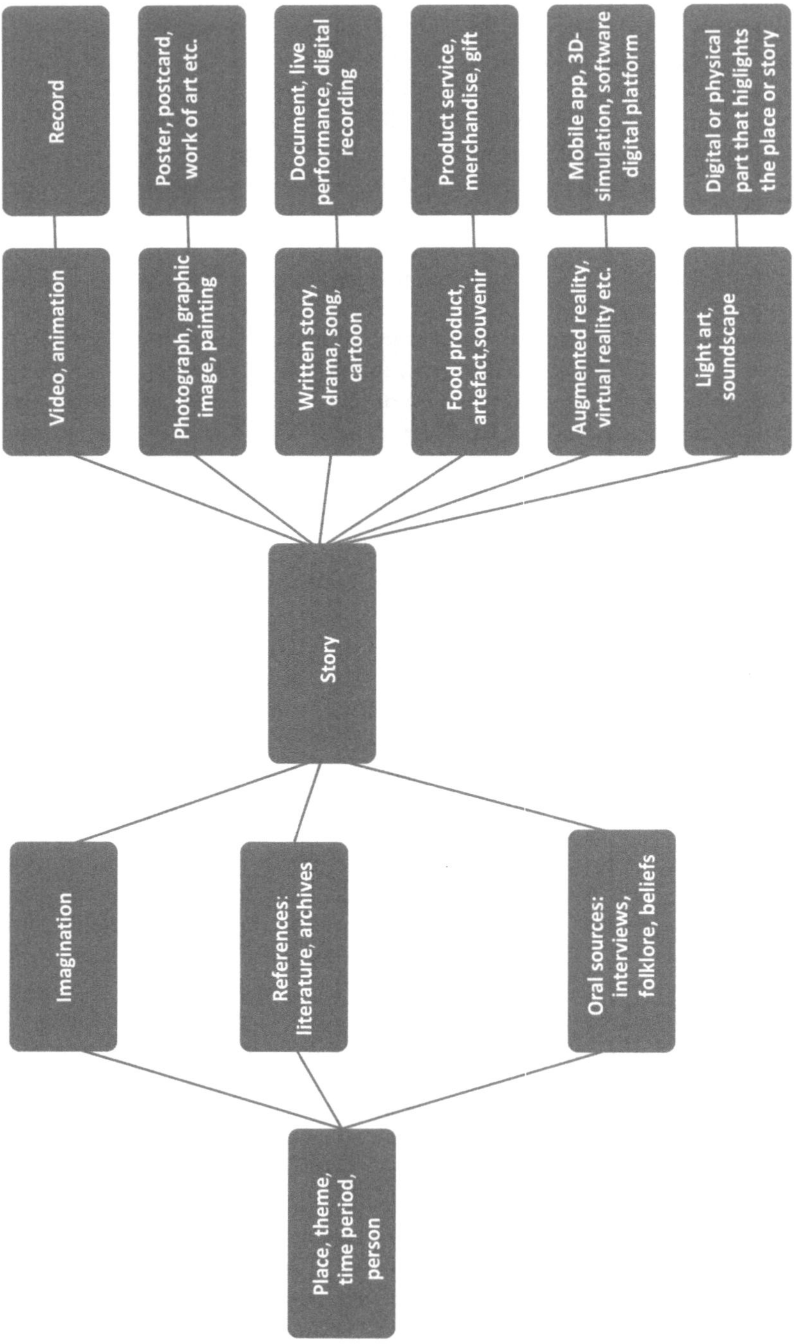

Figure 9.2 The story production process (Iso-Aho, 2020, p. 7).

cause any harm, however, as the water had cooled down by the time it reached the cavern.

(Siitonen, 1983, p. 109)

When written into a story, the account of the siege of the cave takes the following form:

Story of the Cave

Dad said we must hold this place. Call out if they come. Mustn't let them through, come hell or high water. I nodded, although I'd have liked to just vanish into thin air. Or back to the time before this yelling, screaming, children crying and all the fear.

There were three of us, kind of leaning on one another and each holding on to our weapons. Burning bits of tree branches dropped at our feet, the smoke stung our eyes. But the worst were the voices bouncing off the rock wall, the angry orders with a frightening echo. There was a rumble above us that made the ground tremble as it came closer. My knees gave way, and I thought that this is the end of everything. Until someone grabbed my arm, pulled me up, and soon I was with the others, prodding and using sharp spears to repel the arms, dark faces with unfamiliar smells, strange voices, attempting to gain entry.

There was a large wound on my shoulder. Then water started to drip into the narrow crevice where we were standing guard. Blood ran in a rivulet down my side. One of my comrades bandaged my wound with a thick piece of cloth. It hurt. Someone shouted to watch out. I guessed that the water that felt warm on the skin was something other than what God had created.

When I looked up, I saw some dark bird fly over the narrow gap.

(Vartiainen et al., 2020, p. 32, transl. Annira Silver)

Because the cave depicted in the story is very tight and an entire tour group of 30 visitors, for example, could not be taken into the cavern all at once, the story was read aloud for the group on the bus while they parked at a small turnaround by the destination. Afterwards, the participants were able to visit the cave with the story fresh in their minds. The objective was that the story, when read aloud in advance, would set the mood for the visit and aid the visitors in empathising with the tragic events and circumstances of the villagers who had sought refuge in the cave. Based on the feedback received, the stories heightened the experience for the visitors and revealed the emotional layers of the events more than mere facts would have been able to do.

In the case of the 'Story of the Cave', the tightness and darkness of the cavern sparked the idea of further intensifying the experience with a soundscape. A two-minute recording that combines the calls and scuffle of soldiers outside the cave and crackling of burning branches, as well as the sounds of panic and anxiety among those huddled in the cave, was completed just before the conclusion of the project, and it has since been tested in practice by at least one local adventure activity business with its own test customer group. The soundscape is available for listening via the following YouTube link: Luolan tarina Lassilan linnavuori, www.youtube.com/watch?v=8kSN-thKN7w&t=55s.

For some of the stories, a video offered the best opportunity to visualise something that could not otherwise be seen. The Stone Age site of Kuurmanpohja in Joutseno, which dates back to the post-Ice Age era 11,000 years ago, is historically significant but visually modest. Archaeological excavations have left an open field of sand that is a few dozen square metres in size and bordered by young forest, all resting on top of a ridge. The excavations revealed that the site is among the oldest permanent settlements discovered in Finland. It was also known that the ancient settlers had quarried for quartz to build their tools and that they kept dogs. A dramatic story 'The Wolves Came at Midnight' was set on the site, describing the approaching winter, the scarceness of food and the threat of wolves. This written story was used in a video as voice-over combined with video material of the site as a visitor will see it today; it also included an interview of a specialist of Stone Age culture. These three elements together offer not only a chance to *see* the site from a different perspective, but also to *feel* the anxiety of those ancient settlers and *know* more about the conditions they lived in.

The role of places in stimulating empathy

Rural Explorer sought to turn unknown points on the map into meaningful places by means of 'deep mapping'. Mullen (2015) defined the concept as follows:

> A deep map is a map of a place rather than a space. Geographers often distinguish between place and space. Space is the grid of reference that we use in making maps: 31.7833° N, 35.2167° E is a pointer in space. Place, on the other hand, is the meaning that we make out of space.

This is also quite close to Flatley's notion of 'affective mapping'. According to Flatley (2008), 'affective mapping indicates the affective aspects of the maps that guide us, in conjunction with our cognitive maps, through our spatial environment' (p. 77). He explained that our spatial environments are inevitably imbued with the feelings we have about the places we are going, the things that happen to us along the way and these emotional valences affect how we create itineraries (Flatley, 2008, pp. 77–78).

The objective of the project was also to feed the geographical imagination. In terms of definitions, the activities were guided by Massey's (2006) idea that '[a] lot of our "geography" is in the mind. We carry around with us mental images of the world, of the country in which we live in. The layer of geographical imagination which focuses on images of places' (p. 48). The philosophical basis was provided by Harris's (2015) view that '[m]aps are more than pieces of paper. They are stories, conversations, lives and songs lived out in a place and are inseparable from the political and cultural contexts in which they are used' (p. 28).

The aim was to provoke empathy with the aid of stories. As Bertling concluded, 'empathy has close ties to aesthetic experience and is able to facilitate connections to environment' (2012, p. 1). Brown et al. (2019) also referred to several recent studies stating that 'emerging evidence across disciplines and suggest a new model exploring interactions between place, identity and empathy' (p. 11). In her study, Sinquefield-Kangas combined imagination and empathy, suggesting that '[i]maginative behaviors play a central role in nourishing empathetic understandings for culture, people, and ideas. Imagination provides a gateway through which meanings and values become interwoven as our consciousness works to create understanding of the old and the new' (2019, p. 23).

The objective of the Rural Explorer project was to determine whether deep mapping, storytelling and the feeding of the imagination could be employed to bring about local empathy that transforms the way in which a place is experienced and that shapes people's activities related to the place. This is to say, we sought to examine rural placemaking and transform the rural sites in question into essential destinations to visit: '[p]lacemaking is about turning a place from somewhere you can't wait to go through to somewhere you never want to leave' (Placemaking in the Nordics, 2020, p. 8). Empathetic emotions and experiences between people (or protagonists) can be enhanced by stories that are based on bits of facts related to specific places. At the same time, those places become animated and alive, thus enabling empathy for and attachment to them. By revealing the narrative levels of places, they can even be liberated from modern and rational notions of places, moving towards ancient animistic worldview of Finns (Mikita, 2018; Pulkkinen, 2014), where places were believed to have forces and spirits.

Conclusion

In this project, parallels can be drawn between the development of the project and processes of biological origin. A prerequisite for launching a project is the fruitful coupling of a project idea with a financer. This induces the period of gestation, that is, the development project itself. As the end result of the project, a new operational model, innovation, product or service is born. It is not until this point that we can begin to determine whether the offspring are viable or whether the life of the new innovation will be cut short in its infancy. If the product is viable and shows potential for advancement, we must either find genuine demand for it in the market or attract further financing to allow the methods to be further developed and made more usable.

Regarding future development, the results of the Rural Explorer project face two significant challenges. The first is getting tourism and adventure businesses to actively use these storytelling methods. In this regard, we have already seen some positive signs with specific businesses in the area, and on the other hand, there has been interest in the methods applied in the project in designing the content of other tourism projects aimed at businesses and service providers. The project's secondary target group, namely tourists, has also found the destinations, at least to some extent. By September 2021, over a period three years, there had been 1,839,551 viewings of images added to Google Maps under the Rural Explorer hashtag.

The second challenge involves studying the effectiveness of stories and storytelling methods. To achieve a systematic utilisation of stories through the means experimented with during the project, we should collect information on how the stories affect the experiencer's relationship with a specific site. How can stories be used to arouse empathy, and how can this be measured?

Even though there are no exact ways for measuring the experience of empathy, it seems that the Rural Explorer case demonstrates both Gallagher's and Ricour's ideas of how narrativity provides a means to identity construction and empathy. We can give a deeper meaning to a place via creating a subjective experience when combining history, the past and memories.

There is a potential in how these narrative elements could be put in use for developing tourist products in a manner that enhances the value received by the travelling customer while also generating value for the target region and the business operations therein.

Summary 1: Lessons learned that can contribute to the organisational or business context

In the project Rural Explorer, there were significant challenges in getting tourism businesses to actively use the storytelling methods. Feelings of uncertainty in competencies and the need for more practical support for creating stories were the main reasons behind this. At the same time, few businesses were ready to invest financially to overcome these kinds of problems. Although there were many difficulties for entrepreneurs to solve, many of those who joined the project also started using the storytelling method in a very successful way. However, from a research and development point of view, a systematic method of measuring the impact of stories is still needed.

Summary 2: Contribution to organisational or business knowledge or practices

Imagine this! examines empathy and the use of storytelling in the project Rural Explorer. The aim of the project was to collect stories from different historical and remote sites in South-east Finland and to test how different narrative techniques might help make these sites more attractive. The material for stories was collected from different sources and was modified to written and other forms of stories by using narrative strategies that awoke the readers' capability of empathising with the protagonist's point of view. The response from the clients showed that storytelling can be an asset in developing tourist products and enhancing local residents' awareness of their histories.

References

Ahlroth, J. (2020, 21 November). Tarinoita kritisoidaan todellisuuden etäännyttämisestä, mutta ehkä taide voi näyttää todellisuuden [Stories are criticised for distancing us from reality, but perhaps art can show us reality]. *Helsingin Sanomat*. https://www.hs.fi/kulttuuri/art-2000007631487.html?share=514a4f3bcf7d48a07074c97e0d478ff1.

Bertling, J. (2012). *The art of empathy: A mixed methods case study of a critical place-based art education program*. The University of Georgia.

Brown, K., Adger, W. N., Devine-Wright, P., Anderies, J. M., Barr, S., Bousquet, F., Butler, C., Evans, L., Marshall, N., & Quinn, T. (2019). Empathy, place and identity interactions for sustainability. *Global Environmental Change*, 56, 11–17.

Cambridge University Press. (n.d.). Empathy. In *Cambridge dictionary*. https://dictionary.cambridge.org/dictionary/english/empathy.

Choy, E. K. (2017). *Let the story do the work. The art of storytelling for business success*. AMACOM (American Management Association).

Faherty, A. (2019). *Why do stories matter to museums and how can museums become better storytellers?*https://www.museumnext.com/article/why-do-stories-matter-to-museums-and-how-can-museums-become-better-storytellers/.

Fisher, W. R. (1984). Narration as a human communication paradigm: The case of public moral argument. *Communication Monographs*, 51 (1), 1–22. doi:10.1080/03637758409390180.

Flatley, J. (2008). *Affective mapping: Melancholia and the politics of modernism*. Harvard University Press.

Gair, S., & Moloney, S. (2013). Unspeakable stories: When counter narratives are deemed unacceptable. *Qualitative Research Journal*, 13 (1). https://www.emerald.com/insight/content/doi/10.1108/14439881311314568/full/html?skipTracking=true.

Gallagher, S. (2012). Empathy, simulation, and narrative. *Science in Context*, 25 (3), 355–381. doi:10.1017/S0269889712000117.

Grahn, M. (2021). Kulttuuriperintöyrittäjyys maaseudun voimavarana [Cultural heritage entrepreneurship as a resource in rural areas]. *Matkailututkimus*, 17 (1). https://doi.org/10.33351/mt.107796.

Harris, T. (2015). Deep geography – Deep mapping: Spatial storytelling and a sense of place. In D. J. Bodenhamer, J. Corrigan, & T. M. Harris (Eds.), *Deep maps and spatial narratives* (pp. 28–53). Indiana University Press.

Hosiaisluoma, Y. (2003). *Kirjallisuuden sanakirja [Dictionary of literary terms]*. WSOY.

Iso-Aho, J. (2020). Tarinan toiset ulottuvuudet eli miten tarina tuotteistetaan? [The other dimensions of a story: How to productize it?] In J. Iso-Aho, A. Nuutinen, & P. Vartiainen (Eds.), *Tarinareitti: Hyödyntämis- ja aktivointiopas yrityksille [Trail of stories: Utilisation and activation guide for businesses]*. Humanistinen ammattikorkeakoulu. https://www.humak.fi/julkaisut/tarinareitti-hyodyntamis-ja-aktivointiopas-yrittajalle/.

Iso-Aho, J., Nuutinen, A., & Vartiainen, P. (Eds.). (2020). *Tarinareitti: Hyödyntämis- ja aktivointiopas yrityksille [Trail of stories: Utilisation and activation guide for businesses]*. Humanistinen ammattikorkeakoulu. https://www.humak.fi/julkaisut/tarinareitti-hyodyntamis-ja-aktivointiopas-yrittajalle/.

Mäkelä, M., Björninen, S., Karttunen, L., Nurminen, M., Raipola, J., & Rantanen, T. (2018). Kertomuksen vaarat. Kokemuspuhe, eksemplumin paluu ja aikalaiskriittinen narratologia [The dangers of a narrative: Experience discourse, the return of the exemplum and critical contemporary narratology]. *Avain*, 1. https://journal.fi/avain/article/view/70012.

Martinheimo, A. (2000). *Parempi lause. Uusia vir(I)kkeitä luovaan kirjoittamiseen* [*A better phrase: New sentences/stimuli for creative writing*]. WSOY.

Massey, D. (2006). The geographical mind. In D. Balderstone (Ed.), *Secondary geography handbook* (pp. 46–51). Geographical Association.

Mikita, V. (2018). *Kantarellin kuuntelun taito: Itämerensuomalaista maailmankuvaa etsimässä. kirjoittamiseen* [*The skill of listening to a chanterelle: In search of a Baltic-Finnish worldview*]. Kustannusosakeyhtiö Sammakko.

Mullen, L. (2015). *Deep maps*. https://lincolnmullen.com/projects/spatial-workshop/deep-maps.html.

Myllyniemi, S. (2016). *Maaginen aarrekartta. Eräretki 200 kainuulaiseen tarinapaikkaan* [*Magic treasure map: A wilderness trek to 200 scenes of stories in Kainuu*]. Salakirjat.

Paavonheimo, J. (2020, 28 November). Kirjallisuus voi paitsi lisätä empatiaa, myös vähentää sitä, ja siksi puhe lukemisen hyödyistä on ongelma [Literature can not only increase empathy but also decrease it, which is why discourse on the benefits of reading is a problem]. *Helsingin Sanomat*. https://www.hs.fi/kulttuuri/art-2000007646685.html?share=b4c72c8af6b0f627361f911f808e9ee1.

Pulkkinen, R. (2014). *Suomalainen kansanusko: Samaaneista saunatonttuihin* [*Finnish folk belief: From shamans to sauna elves*]. Gaudeamus.

Remodo, A. (2021). *The narrative identity in Paul Ricoeur's hermeneutics of the self*. https://www.academia.edu/18073338/The_Narrative_Identity_in_Paul_Ricoeurs_Hermeneutics_of_the_Self.

Siitonen, S. (Ed.). (1983). *Ruokolahti. Kotiseutulukemisto II. Historiaa – kuvauksia – tapahtumia ja tarinoita* [Ruokolahti. Regional chronicles II: History – depictions – events and stories]. Ruokolahti-seura.

Sinquefield-Kangas, R. (2019). Looking for empathy in visual encounters. *International Journal of Education & the Arts*, 20 (21). http://doi.org/10.26209/ijea20n21.

Tjupa, V. (2014). *Narrative strategies. The living handbook of narratology*. https://www.lhn.uni-hamburg.de/node/119.html.

Torkki, J. (2014). *Tarinan valta: Kertomus luolamiehen paluusta* [The power of a story: Tale of the return of the caveman]. Otava.

Vartiainen, P., Iso-Aho, J., & Nuutinen, A. (Eds.). (2020). *River of stories. Legends to guide tourists in South-east Finland*. https://www.humak.fi/wp-content/uploads/2020/05/TARINAJOKI-2020.pdf.

10 Telling the story

How arts-based methods can create space for empathy in students and teachers in the postcolonial university design context

Michelle Olga van Wyk

Introduction

Over the past few decades, there has been an increased focus on decoloniality in educational institutions, including the way teachers and students experience the learning journey and the opportunities offered within this environment. The limitations created by the pandemic mirror many past and present challenges experienced in African universities. The stark difference that is seen in the ability of the Global North and South to respond and adapt to the 'new normal' has been an echo of the growing pre-pandemic crises in the African design classroom. These crises have been seen in the desperate-turned-violent cry from students for a change in the university's approach towards the learning experience of African students, and to move away from a solely Eurocentric focus towards a more inclusive African-focused approach to learning (Hendricks, 2018). In response to the COVID-19 pandemic, the World Health Organization (WHO, 2021) issued guidelines for the public on taking preventative measures. Many of these guidelines are based on a standardised norm, where space and running water are assumed (WHO, 2020). However, this is not the case for many families living in the Global South. In an attempt to curb rising infections, many countries implemented national lockdown initiatives, causing most of the world's workforce to work from home (Corpuz, 2021). This was true for employees in various organisations and students at all levels, including those studying at universities. Within all these globally compulsory changes, lay a conversation related to empathy, waiting to unfold. Empathy has several definitions and has generally been described as a positive pathway to connect to and understand the experience of another with sensitivity and care (Levin, 2016; Pedwell, 2013, p. 19). In this chapter, empathy is framed with a hybrid definition. Drawing from Smeenk et al. (2018), who defined empathy as 'people's intuitive ability to identify with others' lived experiences such as thoughts and feelings, motivations, emotional and mental models, values, priorities, preferences, and inner conflicts' (p. 1), the current study stitches their definition to the perspective of Köppen and Meinel (2014, p. 16), which positions empathy as insights that present as a form of knowledge. This stance is taken to draw attention to the connection that can be created through the

DOI: 10.4324/9781003227557-12

digital storytelling of the human experiences, values and inner conflicts found in the university design student. By enabling an understanding of the emotional state of someone, it can be used as an effective connecting tool in contexts where tension exists.

This chapter looks at empathy's role in the process of decolonising learning experiences from the student's perspective through the use of creative writing and digital storytelling as an arts-based method (ABM). The methodology draws on my own lived experiences and uses digital storytelling to navigate complex experiences within colonial university structures. I position the method as a possible framework that can be used as a tool to help students explore their own experiences and needs within the design classroom in the larger context of universities. The aim is to use empathy, here presented as knowledge, to identify potential pathways to enhance the creative learning journey for both students and learning facilitators alike, encouraging connections and healing through creativity. In re-centring the student experience as the starting point for empathy, this method aligns itself with the aims of decolonial design approaches that value knowledge systems previously disregarded by a Eurocentric approach to learning. Through storytelling, which is an age-old, universal practice, I frame creative writing and digital storytelling (DST) as a two-prong resilient approach to learning, teaching and creative practice that can be used in the traditional university classroom or even the 'new norm' created by the pandemic. The concluding thought of this chapter is that an intentional decision to explore empathy through technology may just offer universities and other business arenas the opportunity to harness the wealth of creativity that is wrapped up in their most precious resource: their human capital.

Context: How in the world did we get here?

The need for increased proximity in the workplace and classroom during the pandemic added additional strain to already struggling public universities in the Global South. Many students from marginalised communities found themselves back home with limited resources at their disposal and the need to engage a curriculum that was built on the foundations of face-to-face engagement. The design courses in most African higher education institutions (HEIs) consist of a hybrid curriculum that includes practical and theory subjects, but with a historical legacy anchored in vocational training, there is an unspoken emphasis on the practical component—the making of products within specific disciplines. This can be seen in the title one attributes to a graduate; for example, a jewellery designer designs jewellery. The emphasis is on practice, not so much experience. During the pandemic, the teaching of theoretical subjects moved online almost seamlessly, while practical subjects suffered as teachers and students had no access to workshops because of lockdown regulations and the indefinite closing of universities. The strategies adopted in crises—which then became the norm—often resulted in exclusion and the marginalisation of communities that do not fit the 'standard' or norm. This has been—and continues to be—a growing dilemma in the classroom, too. Students have entered into an academic pandemic of colonial knowledge and physical structures and have had to comply with 'norms' that negate their social circumstances and cultural identities. Although technology as a tool could be perceived as a great facilitator of connectivity during the pandemic, access to educational platforms remains a challenge for many, creating varied experiences that are nuanced depending on the participants.

This one-size-fits-all approach to learning has caused both harm and frustration in the learning environment, further stretching the thin veil of empathy shielding the privileged methods of teaching from the critical overhaul they require. Methods include teaching Eurocentric content in English to students whose first language and origin stem from Africa (Ortley, 2005). In this way, an additional degree of separation is introduced for students who are located in physical contexts where they have no direct link to the Eurocentric knowledge and practices that are recognised in academic contexts. Already tasked with the quest of navigating design content and practices from foreign origins, the African design students' cultural perspective and way of being is almost always overshadowed. Students in the Global South have begun to resist the oppressive academic practices that have been accepted by the modern world for so long, and the pandemic has brought with it a magnifying glass with which to see the need for re-evaluation (Keikelame & Swartz, 2019; Hendricks, 2018, pp. 839–840). This weariness, coupled with the need for finding alternative ways to learn, provides the culture bed and opportunity to reframe these challenges into opportunities, if explored from a local, grassroot perspective and not towards it (Rautiainen et al., 2021). However, the move towards understanding what these alternative, empathic and decolonised approaches could look like needs to start at home, with Africa. As Clapham (2020) noted, 'A genuine decolonisation of knowledge production for Africa must rest on a return to its roots within the continent itself' (p. 137). I believe this return to self—through empathy—needs to start with the student, and I write this chapter from this stance.

Method: Exploring by telling the story

The methodological approach in this chapter examines the application, experiences and outcomes of the use of creative writing and DST as a two-part ABM to cultivate empathy in my own practice as I reimagine the classroom experience of the student maker in the midst of crises (Leavy, 2015; Ohler, 2013). I do this by positioning the lived experience of learning, as presented through story, as equal to the skill that is learned/practised in an educational context. In a world that attributes value to ability, it is important to pause and consider what role the student experiences and how teaching plays a part in this phenomenon of attribution (McLeod, 1995). This exploration forms part of my practice-led doctoral studies in the field of art and design, drawing on self-reflection as the main data collection tool and method of analysis (Kolko, 2010). The main research question underpinning this particular exploration is as follows: 'How can experience and storytelling permeate aspects of the traditional classroom to increase empathy and cater to creative learning and working in unfamiliar spaces?' I propose a framework informed by the work of Ohler (2013) and personal reflections on a past experience of participating in a workshop, where the goal was to create a five-minute digital story. The probe, reflecting on one or a few significant moments that served as points of tension and were related to your identity (specifically as experienced through the lens of race), served as the starting point for unlocking what was to be told.

The goal was to capture this experience in a digital narrative by using the digital storytelling process of identifying the challenge that the main character experienced, the change the main character had to undergo and the response and solution that resulted in the tension being resolved (Ohler, 2013, pp. 96–97). The story unfolds, as Ohler (2013) has explained, when the student 'transverses from inquiry to discovery' (p. 100). Taking an empathic approach in DST anchors itself in the five factors that foster empathy, as defined by Smeenk et al. (2018). These factors are emotional interest (EI), sensitivity (SE), self-awareness (SA), personal experience (PE) and mixed perspectives (MP), which are a combination of EI, SE, SA and PE. When students transversely use this tool, their starting point is that of SA, taking on a 'neutral, receptive and open stance' with the self (Smeenk et al., 2018 p. 5). The next step was to plot the story through writing and the chosen images, generating EI in their own experiences. These could be sourced from personal photographs, drawings or generic open-source stock photos or videos that would help convey the story to the audience in a rich and vibrant manner. In addition to these layers, a story could be supported by background music and, most importantly, a narration recorded by the storyteller.

The enigmatic power of the story almost rests completely in the voice of the storyteller. All stories were limited to two to five minutes (Ohler, 2013, p. 95). Although Ohler (2013) pointed out that storytelling can never truly have rules, he offered guidelines that are given to help retain the essence of the story and the attention of the listener through the 'storytelling covenant' (pp. 93–94), which honours the act of telling and listening. The framework proposed uses DST in the classroom as a tool for empathy generation used by the student, for the student and for the lecturer, drawing on MP to bring forth empathy as knowledge that can transform future experiences. I produced a short digital story titled, 'Colours, Numbers and Names' (van Wyk, 2014; see Figure 10.1) that documents three selected experiences and the numbers that are irrevocably linked to them.

'Colours, Numbers and Names': A short story

Figure 10.1 shows my story based on lived experiences linked to identity contextualised by race while living in southern Africa. The short story is centred around the six stages of the story from the hero's journey, as defined by Joseph Campbell in 1973 (Ohler, 2013, p. 96). The form (see Figure 10.2) is offered as

Figure 10.1 The six stages of the story from the hero's journey, as defined by Joseph Campbell in 1973 (Ohler, 2013, p. 96). Diagram by the author, 2021.

a scaffold within which to build story using the six stages: the call to adventure, denying the call, accepting a guide to help to navigate the journey, passing tests, personal transformation and returning to the beginning.

My story starts off with a brief summary of the facts related to temperatures and the physical properties of certain elements such as water, gold and hair. My hair led me to my first encounter with race. Having been born with naturally curly hair, I questioned why my mother's (straight) hair was different than mine. In fact, most hair products were advertised by women with straight hair. My teacher, even those who had naturally curly hair, had straight(ened) their hair. In this sphere of influence, I embarked on a journey of altering my hair texture with heat so that I could mirror what I perceived the correct way to be. When I moved to a city with humid weather, my curls were a point of contention. I lost the battle and surrendered to the texture of hair I was born with yet had fought for so long against. In this defeat, I found a new sense of beauty. The next encounter with race was through what I believed to be discrimination based on the colour of my skin and the perception that I was somehow deserving of injury because of my not complying with the expectation of being a subordinate. This memory documents the moment that I injured myself and

Figure 10.2 'Colours, Numbers and Names'—Digital story by Michelle van Wyk. Photograph supplied by the author, 2014.[1]

did not receive help because of previous events that had been informed by what I believed were racially charged. And now when I hear water boil, I can clearly recall the sensation of scalding on my tan-coloured skin, and how in that moment, I could understand how colour influences my reality. The last section of my DST speaks to the lessons I have learned from teaching my students about the properties of gold. These physical properties—the colour and malleability—in many ways reflected who I wanted to be. Who I was. And am. These crossroads changed me, and the nature of heat transformed in my eyes. I transversed by starting with SA. I also now know how powerful DST is as a tool for generating empathy both in the storyteller and audience.

By using DST, I was able to unpack and reframe confusing experiences that impacted my perception of self. The aim of using DST in the context of personal creative practice is that it would uncover submerged beliefs, how they impact practice and how they open up the possibilities for creating solutions.

Discussion

Reflecting on my own educational journey has remained a complex place for me; despite knowing that I felt excluded I could not find practical tools to help myself to express this experience, consequently this has muted my experience of making and innovating jewellery. This type of creative existence is painful in that in creative practice, freedom becomes a haunting longing whose fulfilment is both out of reach and inescapable. In examining these creative liminal spaces, such as classrooms or working/studying from home during a pandemic, which exist as thresholds between the familiar and unfamiliar—I've attempted to explore the agency found in DST to transform these lacunas into places of emergence for myself.

The aim of the method was to explore the tender points of learning from the perspective of the learner enrolled in universities and assess the pockets of need for empathy that the pandemic has so vividly made visible. By probing the discomfort in learning through ABM to facilitate empathy, it is the heart that is brought to the fore, the chamber that holds inherent creative knowledge but that often is overshadowed by the knowledge of the mind because of it being the site of many colonial wounds and consequent confusion. My experience as a doctoral student within the field of art and design creates an atmosphere of possibility for me, one where I hope to restore all the tangled experiences of my undergraduate career as a student enrolled in jewellery design and manufacture. The wound created by engaging in creative practice within the overarching pervasive subtleties of colonial structures in a university causes an identity numbness that brings with it layers of guilt and shame because it is difficult to articulate the nuanced experience of non-belonging. With no visible empathy in the classroom for cultural experiences—ones that require words of encouragement and invitations to show up as yourself—the student learns that in places and processes of learning, they can be many things, as long as they are not themselves.

The strength of this ABM was that it paces the unpacking of experience by using creative writing as the first of a two-step storytelling approach, or as Ohler termed it, the 'story core' (2013, p. 96), which aligns with the African oral tradition of conveying value through spoken words. This pace acknowledges that there is something of value to be heard that might not have been said before. The second step—weaving technology with story—refines the story even further to a visual art form that nurtures empathy. Student-generated empathy creates room for voice, hence making hidden needs (i.e., the need to release shame and guilt) explicit to themselves and their teachers (Pedwell, 2013). The hope is that these recorded accounts of experienced creative reflection in practice through the lens of digitalisation would elevate the human experience of creativity and frame it in value through the eyes of the student. This, in turn, can generate the metaphorical bricks and mortar with which to build a pathway towards emotional capacity to navigate the plurality of experience, allowing teachers and facilitators to engage with. The expected outcome of the method is to find ways to strengthen empathic teaching and learning in creative practice (jewellery making) during times of crises and offer lecturers insights into their responsibility towards empathy. Therefore, this helps in positioning empathic decolonised design approaches as a strategic practice of resilience. Lecturers may have a desire to practise empathy with students but do not know how to best go about this precarious task. It is for this reason that I believe that a student-led focus is the most effective approach.

I acknowledge that the tools that are needed for digital storytelling require the knowledge of how to use each tool, software, and devices that capture images and/or voice recordings. These tools can be used individually or collectively. However, most students have experienced digital storytelling in some format because they form one of many key pillars of social media platforms, such as the Stories/Reels function on Instagram. The knowledge of story creation is pervasive, with most social platforms boasting a wide range of technological tools that are easy to explore and understand. Consequently, the digital story has become even more accessible through the use of applications on mobile devices. The ability to access and generate visual and audio content on one single device has provided students with a powerful tool with which to bring to life that which they wish to bring to the world's attention. It is the practice of writing and reflection on learning that facilitates the understanding of *what* story to tell and how telling these stories can create a bridge between where we are and where we want to be.

By documenting reimagined learning journeys and making practice from a personal context as a case study, this explorative work has suggested that the urgent need to reframe creative education should ideally start with the student. This is a step towards the future in a Global South context that explores decolonising design practices and acknowledges the necessity for empathy and inclusivity in design education. In positioning the student as the main character, digital storytelling can be used as a vehicle for students to engage in difficulties that they may experience at an emotional or mental level, while developing their practical skills, but do not know how to navigate. By facilitating personal reflection and understanding through experience and story, empathy is made possible on an internal level because the digital story helps make explicit experiences that might otherwise have remained dormant. The second layer of this experience is that it offers the teacher insights into how the student experiences their learning journey and where there is room for additional support.

The novelty of the approach responds to the research gap of finding ways to support creativity for design students in times of crises that disrupt traditional creative teaching and learning within the product-making environment. This is important because despite many teachers acknowledging the need to decolonise the curriculum in design courses, it is done so amid a fog of confusion. This confirmation is needed for the student to see practical decisions taken in the classroom that translate to the re-centring of the learner to the heart of education. This intentional focus on the student experience need not be draining to the teacher, as is usually the case when universities require a paper or electronic trail to evidence the engagement of students on online learning platforms.

Presenting students with the tools to generate empathy with themselves might help lead lecturers along a path of understanding the student experience of learning in a kaleidoscope environment coloured with different knowledge systems, traditions and explicit and intangible expectations.

Conclusion

Empathy is perceived as a bridge and, as Pedwell (2013) stated, 'is framed as that which can heal past wounds and move us forward into a more peaceful, harmonious and equitable future' (p. 19). Smeenk et al. (2018) positioned empathy as an understanding of human experiences and all that this encompasses, while Köppen and Meinel (2015) argued that the empathic understanding of these experiences is knowledge. This knowledge births stories waiting to be told from a personal stance. Kolko argued that design helps tame or organise chaos (2010, p. 15). In this way, the use of storytelling acts as an ally through the often-chaotic experience of the story of learning a new skill and, in this instance, of finding a new and emotionally safer way to learn. Storytelling has been positioned as a decolonising design methodology (Keikelame & Swartz, 2019, p. 1) in my creative practice as I explore how to find a path that encompasses rather than annihilates the cultural experiences, understanding and wealth embedded in identity. ABMs—and in this case creative writing and DST—serve a dual purpose in that they both work as tools and guidelines for increasing the presence of empathy in the learning process and the classroom. The road to the decolonial classroom is not yet clear, but students and teachers need one another to discover the possible routes to this empathic space. The two creative methods in this chapter are by no means complete, but they are resilient, which means they can be kneaded into the shapes they need to rise into. They can be practised in an individual or small group setting, within or outside the traditional classroom, lending themselves to the lived experiences of students and teachers alike who want to find their way back. An intentional decision to explore empathy through technology may just offer universities the opportunity to heal the disconnect that a colonial past and challenging pandemic has laid at the table of education while making progress towards harnessing the wealth of creativity that is wrapped up in their most precious resource—their students.

Summary 1: Lessons learned that can contribute to the organisational or business context

Digital storytelling (DST) is a powerful communication tool. However, it is the positioning of the storyteller as a narrator who is self-aware (SA) that makes this a particularly effective approach for fostering empathy within organisations on a micro or macro level. This allows empathy to present itself as new knowledge that can shape the strategic decisions taken by management and that will impact those within an organisation. The use of the DST approach within educational organisations offers all stakeholders a framework to help navigate their way into unchartered territories of negotiations, where change is needed and needs to be mapped out through empathic approaches. These outcomes can shape the learning experiences and identities of future stakeholders and organisations themselves.

Summary 2: Contribution to organisational or business knowledge or practices

Using the two-prong method of creative writing and digital storytelling as a tool in organisations can help build empathy and connections within small or large organisations. The accessibility of the method lends itself to easy adoption by stakeholders at varying levels within an organisation. The tool is both easily adapted and scaled to suit the needs of the organisation and, therefore, is easily translated into different types of organisations. In making every voice in organisations heard, this tool is both empowering and effective.

Note

1 Retrievable at: *Colours, Numbers and Names* (2014). https://drive.google.com/file/d/0B4Xg00_zVb7yLW5nX1pfelo3VWc/view?usp=sharing&resourcekey=0-WM0Z8gxJsC83Qaq9ZLnvHA

References

Clapham, C. (2020). Decolonising African studies? *The Journal of Modern African Studies*, 58 (1), 137–153. https://doi.org/10.1017/S0022278X19000612.

Corpuz, J.C.G. (2021). Adapting to the culture of 'new normal': An emerging response to COVID-19. *Journal of Public Health*, 43 (2), 334–335. https://doi.org/10.1093/pubmed/fdab057.

Gair, S. (2011). Exploring empathy embedded in ethics curricula: A classroom inquiry. *Advances in Social Work*, 12 (2), 329–344. https://doi.org/10.18060/1949.

Hendricks, D. (2018). *Decolonisation in tertiary design education. Redesigning the content, structure and space of design disciplines for an inclusive pedagogy*. To get there: Designing Together. Cumulus Conference Proceedings Paris, hosted by CÉSAAP Conférence des écoles supérieures d'Arts appliqués de Paris, France in 11–13 April. https://www.academia.edu/37640718/Decolonisation_in_Tertiary_Design_Education_Redesigning_the_Content_Structure_and_Space_of_Design_Disciplines_for_an_Inclusive_Pedagogy.

Keikelame, M. J., & Swartz, L. (2019). Decolonising research methodologies: Lessons from a qualitative research project, Cape Town, South Africa. *Global Health Action*, 12, 1561175. https://doi.org/10.1080/16549716.2018.1561175.

Kolko, J. (2010). Abductive thinking and sensemaking: The drivers of design synthesis. *Design Issues*, 26 (1), 15–18. https://doi.org/10.1162/desi.2010.26.1.15.

Köppen, E., & Meinel, C. (2015). Empathy via design thinking: Creation of sense and knowledge. *Design Thinking Research*, 15–28. http://doi.org/10.1007/978-3-319-06823-7_2.

Leavy, P. (2015). *Method meets art: Arts-based research practice* (2nd ed.). The Guilford Press.

Levin, J. (2016). Review: Productive dialogues across disciplines: Literature and empathy studies reviewed work(s): Rethinking empathy through literature. *Journal of Modern Literature*, 39 (4), 187–193. https://doi.org/10.2979/jmodelite.39.4.14.

McLeod, S. H. (1995). Pygmalion or golem? Teacher affect and efficacy. *College Composition and Communication*, 46 (3), 369–386. https://www.jstor.org/stable/358711.

Ohler, J. B. (2013). *Digital storytelling in the classroom: New media pathways to literacy, learning, and creativity* (2nd ed.). Corwin. https://r3.vlereader.com/Reader?ean=9781452277462.

Ortley, J. (2005). Decolonizing methodologies: Research and indigenous peoples (review). *The American Indian Quarterly*, 29 (1), 285–288. http://doi.org:10.1353/aiq.2005.0061.

Pedwell, C. (2013). Affect at the margins: Alternative empathies in a small place. *Emotion, Space & Society*, 8, 18–26. http://dx.doi.org/10.1016/j.emospa.2012.07.001.

Rautiainen, M., van Wyk, M., & Miettinen, S. (2021). Navigating uncertainty: Developing the facilitator's role through participatory service design workshops. In T. Seppälä, M. Sarantou, & S. Miettinen (Eds.), *Arts-based methods for decolonising participatory research* (pp. 164–181). Routledge.

Smeenk, W., Sturm, J., Terken, J., & Eggen, B. (2018). A systematic validation of the Empathic Handover approach guided by five factors that foster empathy in design. *CoDesign: International Journal of CoCreation in Design and the Arts*, 1–21. https://doi.org/10.1080/15710882.2018.1484490.

van Wyk, M. (2014). *Colours, numbers and names.* https://drive.google.com/file/d/0B4Xg00_zVb7yLW5nX1pfelo3VWc/view?usp=sharing&resourcekey=0-WM0Z8gxJsC83Qaq9ZLnvHA.

WHO. (2020). *New PSA campaign from WHO and YouTube is a playbook for a safe holiday season.* https://www.who.int/news/item/17-12-2020-new-psa-campaign-from-who-and-youtube-is-a-playbook-for-a-safe-holiday-season.

WHO. (2021). *Advice for the public: Coronavirus disease (COVID-19).* https://www.who.int/emergencies/diseases/novel-coronavirus-2019/advice-for-public.

Section C

The role of design in creating empathy

Step 3: Wayfinding and initiating action with beneficiaries

11 Empathic perspective to understand people's experiences in the service prototyping context in Chile

Mira Alhonsuo and Mariluz Soto Hormazábal

Introduction

Service prototyping is a commonly used method in design practice, especially in the service design field. The values of service prototyping are not only found in concretising abstract services, but also in the fact that it is a method that supports internal and external communication (Blomkvist, 2014) and enabling the exploration of new behaviours (Coughlan et al., 2007). In service prototyping, peoples' stories and experiences play a vital role. However, the design community has increasingly put effort into exploring how to get closer to the experiences and needs of people (e.g., Kouprie & Visser, 2009; Mattelmäki et al., 2014). In Chapter 1, the editors of this book illustrate that the concept of empathy has been widely studied in different disciplines, which means that numerous definitions for this concept exists. Hence, there is a potential to explore an approach where empathy is defined specifically with the needs of service prototyping in mind and, hence, can also bring clarity to its adoption, practices and application as an approach and method for organisations.

This chapter reflects part of a research project carried out in Chile. The focus of the project was to identify the different aspects that could be transferred from Service Innovation Corner (SINCO) in Finland to the Chilean culture. SINCO laboratory, which is located at the University of Lapland, is a prototyping environment based on role playing and offers technology-aided tools for the visualisation and concretisation of service situations (Rontti et al., 2012). Because Chilean and Finnish cultures are different, we planned workshops to collaborate with design students, researchers and professionals to ask them directly about their experiences. With COVID-19 starting during the project, we adapted the workshops to an online format, where the challenge was the highest. After an intense process of thinking and discussing how to connect with the participants to better understand their emotions and expectations about service prototyping, we found empathy to be the core of this part of the project. The participants' good and bad experiences and knowledge about the practice of service prototyping were shared through storytelling and were reflected by their evaluations and expectations of the future. We selected the trilogy of 3C (in Spanish, the initials '*cabeza*' is head, '*corazón*' is heart, and

DOI: 10.4324/9781003227557-14

'*cuerpo*' is body), where the three emphases are the precision of rational thoughts, the identification of emotions and the definition of behaviours or actions (Tolosa, 2008). This trilogy helps us understand the situation and cultural expectations and the context of prototyping in Finland. These three levels of head, heart and body have a strong link to the experience of services so they should be more prominently considered as part of service development and also more strongly integrated into service prototyping. When people are involved in service prototyping with their lived experiences, assumptions can be dispelled and colonial practices avoided (Vink & Oertzen, 2018).

This chapter asks the following research questions: 1) How can service prototyping be analysed from personal and collective experiences? 2) How can the connection between empathy and service prototyping be learned through personal experiences and work towards building an understanding of their significance as part of the development of an organisation's services? As one of the practical outcomes, a framework named 'Prototyping through Empathic Insights' was produced, which can be used in two ways: as a way to introduce empathy and service prototyping for an audience that does not yet understand the topics and as a tool to utilise during the practical and hands-on prototyping sessions for increasing the importance of empathic levels. The framework utilises and follows a collaborative autoethnography (CAE) approach, which is also the methodological approach used for the whole study.

Service prototyping as a way to share and experience stories

Prototypes are the core elements in design practices; they represent abstract ideas in a more concrete, tangible and experiential way (Coughlan et al., 2007). In a product design framework, prototypes are the physical representations of artefacts, but for services, we often understand them more as intangible, heterogeneous features (Zeithaml et al., 1985) and as having a 'relational and interactional nature' (Rodrigues & Holmlid, 2017, p. S2248). Thus, services are more challenging to prototype. Service prototyping is a commonly used method in the service design field. It is an activity in which a future situation is explored and evaluated through concrete ideas, concepts or hunches (Blomkvist, 2014). Hence, it is used to learn about and implement transformative changes (Kuure et al., 2014). Prototypes have been investigated not only to speed up the development of a new idea, product, service, environment or experience, but also to encourage behavioural change within an organisation (Coughlan et al., 2007). Coughlan et al. (2007) highlight three primary ways of prototyping organisational change: building to think, learning faster by failing early and giving permission to explore new behaviours.

In service prototyping, services are concretised through a 'service walkthrough', which helps the participants better understand the different experiences of individuals. It also helps designers feel empathy (Blomkvist, 2016). According to Blomkvist (2014, p. 25), prototyping supports internal and external communication, thus affecting the participants' mindsets. People describe their actions, feelings, thoughts and behaviours through stories, creating a view for other people about the experience (Hunsucker & Siegel, 2015). Stories and narratives are a 'natural way of beginning dialogue with users' (Erikson, 1995, p. N/A) and play an important role in design practices when information is created, generated and shared within an organisation (Bailey et al., 2019), but they might also lead to misinterpretations when listeners create their own thoughts of the experience. Hence, service design uses a variety of visualisation and concretisation tools and methods (Koh et al., 2011) to help visualise user experiences (Prendiville et al., 2017; Segelström, 2013) and create a common understanding of the experience or service. Nevertheless, the analysis of stories told by people remains very superficial and only emphasises the emotional curve of the service user, for example, how an individual feels at a certain moment, omitting an exploration of the activities and behaviour in more detail.

Empathic insights

Over the past few decades, the design community has increasingly put more effort into exploring how designers can get closer to the experiences and needs of 'putative, potential, or future users' (Kouprie & Visser, 2009, p. 437; Koskinen et al., 2003; Mattelmäki et al., 2014). Especially in service design, empathy plays a central role (Koskinen et al., 2003; New & Kimbell, 2013). However, empathy is a widely studied and discussed field with many different and more or less detailed definitions (Vignemont & Singer, 2006). The typical way of understanding empathy is to step 'in someone else's shoes' (e.g., Bloom, 2016, p. 15; Battarbee et al., 2014, p. 3; Fulton Suri, 2003), in which an action well describes service prototyping. Thomas and McDonagh (2013) define empathy as 'our intuitive ability to identify with other people's thoughts and feelings—their motivations, emotional and mental models, values, priorities, preferences, and inner conflicts' (p. 3). Nevertheless, empathy has been investigated in many fields, such as psychology, philosophy, education and science, and the definitions within each field greatly vary (Riess & Neporent, 2018). Hence, empathy needs to be defined from a prototyping action perspective.

It is important to understand the different levels of empathy. Kouprie and Visser (2009) divide empathy into two areas: first, there is the affective dimension, which is associated with feelings and emotions; second, there is the cognitive dimension, which is the capacity for understanding and perspective. Similarly, but more broadly, Riess and Neporent (2018) divides empathy into three aspects: emotional, cognitive and motivation. The major capacity of people is emotional empathy, which signifies the feeling of how others feel. For example, this can be linked to physical pain when someone is cutting a deep wound through the skin. Cognitive empathy, also known as the 'theory of mind', is when one understands others' minds, thoughts and feelings; this includes a component called 'perspective taking', when others give their 'attention, imagination, and curiosity' to understand 'physical, psychological, social, and spiritual perspectives' of the person (Riess & Neporent, 2018, p. 23). The third aspect is the motivation for action and compassion, which has two sides: action for doing something or personal distress for not doing anything about it. The shared experiences can impact the brain as emotional and physical pain, which can lead to empathic concern and create the willingness and motivation to help others (Goleman, 2017).

The above-mentioned emotional, cognitive and motivational aspects of empathy by Riess and Neporent (2018) can be reflected through the trilogy of 3C by Tolosa (2008). The trilogy of 3C was selected as a base for the empathic framework for the current study because it is widely used in many Latin American communities and provides a definition of emotions in a broader picture rather than simplifying feelings during any kind of experience. Also, the three levels of head, heart and body in the trilogy of 3C can be clearly visualised as a framework and be utilised during the service prototyping sessions. The trilogy of 3C focuses on the understanding of a person or community by using three aspects: mental representations, emotions and behaviours or actions; these three aspects give a deep and wide perspective about each person, not necessarily with more detailed information but with more connected information. The link between the different aspects of people's lives brings clear knowledge to another with the possibility to better understand other realities.

Several sources have fed into the critical discussion about (experience) prototyping and its empathic aims. According to Buchenau and Fulton Suri (2000), we must focus our concerns on the fact that the audience might be focusing more on improvisational theatre rather than how someone is really experiencing something. The interest towards personal experience increases when it resonates with personal experiences, and thus, it is easier to understand and feel greater empathy (Buchenau & Fulton Suri, 2000, p. 425). There is also a risk for colonial practices in service design, which use empathic methods, such as service prototyping, without the people having lived experiences of it (Vink & Oertzen, 2018). Vink and Oertzen (2018, p. 474) refer to Tunstall (2013) by emphasising colonialism as 'undermining the self-definition of people'. The risk is that people assume that they know how others feel through their own actions without real lived experiences. This empathic colonialism also resonates with Bloom's (2016) definition in which empathy is 'the act of coming to experience the world as you think someone else does' (p. 16).

Methodology

The present study used collaborative autoethnography (CAE) as its basis throughout the process, and its elements have been utilised in the research process of this study, in the structure of five online workshops and in the 'Prototyping through Empathic Insights' framework. CAE is ideal when researchers can share a rich amount of data, which can be personal narratives from the researchers' memory or collected data by interviewing, observing and analysing each other. Autoethnography as a design inquiry focuses on the researchers' personal experiences (Leavy, 2017), but it also incorporates cultural aspects of the individual narrative (Glesne, 2011). Adding the collaborative aspect into autoethnography, the researchers are both the instrument and data source (Chang et al., 2013, p. 22), where they gather their insightful knowledge and experiences (Ellis & Adams, 2014).

CAE in the research process

The CAE approach was appropriate for the study because it combined both the authors' own observations from the five workshops and their previous experiences related to service prototyping. The workshop planning phase was based on the personal experiences of service prototyping by the authors, such as what challenges researchers have faced in service prototyping as a method, what elements need to be added to service prototyping to achieve a deeper empathic level and how to make shared experiences and service prototyping visible and be more effectively structured, especially in situations where more people share their experiences, for example, from the same service. In addition, the authors shared their experiences of how to bring and consider an empathic understanding into prototyping.

The authors created an online workshop structure, which enabled the participants to collaborate in the CAE approach. During the workshops, the authors observed both the clarity of the workshop structure and the discussions and notes produced. After the workshops, the authors organised a meeting with each other, where the workshop observation notes, workshop data and researchers' own experiences were reflected. The relevance of the shared knowledge was created by the fact that both of the researchers looked at their experiences through their own cultures. In Finland, prototyping is a well-known and widely used method in the service design field, while in Chile, prototyping is mainly used as a mock-up technique in the design process.

CAE in the five online workshops

Shared experiences can have an influence when it comes to transformative learning and connect people around a commonality (Blalock & Akehi, 2018); hence, it can bring value for the organisational settings. Here, the workshops enable people to share their experiences based on their own or heard stories while allowing them to produce data out of it. In a collaborative format, whether in an in-situ or remote workshop, the participants could take the role of researcher and be both the instrument and data source (Chang et al., 2013).

When aiming for transformative learning, two approaches are referred to. First, critical reflection rests at the centre of the process (Mezirow, 2000); and second, the roles of imagination and emotions during transformative learning experiences can be used (Dirkx, 2014). In the five online workshops, the schedule and tasks were planned so that there was enough time for reflecting the prototyping method through a critical lens and sharing the individuals' own experiences fostering their imagination and emotions.

Online workshops

This study was conducted through five online workshops in five different regions in Chile. Each workshop lasted for approximately two hours. Figure 11.1 summarises the workshop participation of each region and gives a description of the profiles of the participants in each workshop. Service prototyping is at a less-developed stage in Chile, and, hence, the workshops aimed to introduce the topic to the audience, who were either not familiar with prototyping or who had some experience in developing services of organisations, for example, as a design student. Originally, the workshops were aimed to be in-situ and more practice-based, but because of the COVID-19 pandemic, the workshops were held remotely. The situation also challenged the facilitators, who are also the authors of this chapter, to plan the workshop

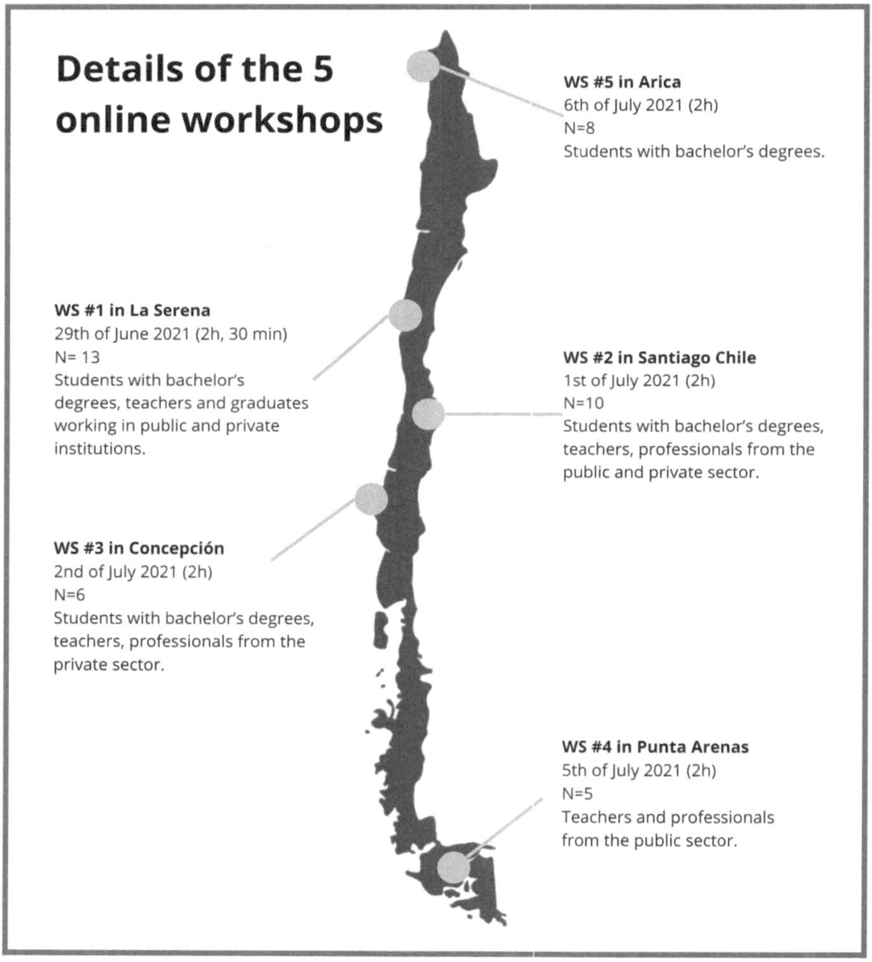

Figure 11.1 Details of the five online workshops. Figure by Mira Alhonsuo, 2021.

so that the theory of empathy and service prototyping would be clearly linked and introduced more from a practical point of view. The workshops had two objectives: first, they sought to build an understanding of how service prototyping would work and be implemented as a method in an organisation, along with what benefits and values service prototyping can have for organisations. Second, the structure of the workshops helped outline the importance of different levels of storytelling and empathy as part of collaborative practices, the importance of dialogue and interactions as part of sharing experiences and producing them into material where each participant's experience is made visible.

The data comprised five recorded workshops, Post-it Notes produced during the workshop, the authors' own observations and reflective notes during the workshops and the authors' reflective discussions after the workshops (Figure 11.1). The data were analysed through a thematic analysis method as a part of the reflective discussions. Being a flexible approach, a thematic analysis aims to modify the needs of studies and provide a rich, detailed and complex account of data (Braun & Clarke, 2006). It is a qualitative research method for identifying, analysing, organising, defining and describing the different themes found in the data (Nowell et al., 2017). A thematic analysis is an ideal method when making sense of a large number of sticky notes and field notes, so it visually parses the data as part of the CAE.

The authors of this chapter facilitated the five online workshops on the Miro platform, which is a platform for visual and remote collaboration and discussion. Figure 11.2 illustrates the structure of the workshop and its layout in Miro. The workshop started with a short introduction round and the workshop aims, which was followed by a PowerPoint presentation of the trilogy of 3C. Thereafter, the participants were asked to freely share their bad service experiences (Exercise 1: Share your experience in Figure 11.2). The aim was to create emotional insights through stories between the participants and to help them understand a person's inner life (Brink et al., 2011). The participants were then asked as a team to select one bad experience and pick a picture that illustrates the service. The picture of the service aimed to remind the participants to keep the conversation with the situation. Then, the participants analysed the service further through the trilogy of 3C, aiming to perceive and recognise the shared experiences through the emotional (heart), cognitive (head) and motivation (body) capacities, here holistically understanding the person's different feelings and behaviours while experiencing the bad service.

After the first exercise, a 15-minute PowerPoint presentation of service prototyping was presented by the author. The presentation included, for example, the value of service prototyping in service design practices, how service prototyping could be done through roleplaying, a desktop walkthrough and paper-based prototyping and how the SINCO laboratory is utilised as a holistic service prototyping environment. After the presentation, the participants understood what service prototyping is and how it can be implemented in different ways as part of the formation of experience.

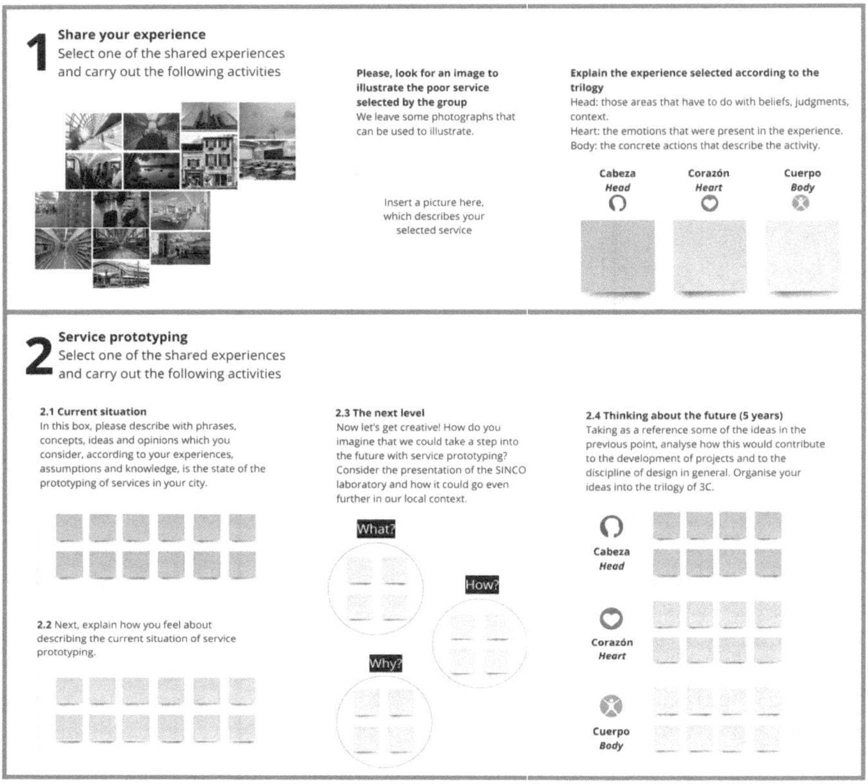

Figure 11.2 The workshop template in an online Miro board, which introduces the exercises. Figure by Mariluz Soto and Mira Alhonsuo, 2021.

The following exercises (Exercise 2: Service prototyping in Figure 11.2) took the initial steps further and were done in one or two groups. One of the aims was to introduce, develop and implement service prototyping in Chile. Therefore, the current situation of prototyping in the region was discussed in Exercise 2.1. The main question was formulated as follows: 'In this box, please describe with phrases, concepts, ideas and opinions which you consider, according to your experiences, assumptions and knowledge, is the state of the prototyping of services in your city'. Afterwards, the participants briefly discussed their feelings when describing the current situation of service prototyping in Exercise 2.2. After obtaining a consensus of the current situation of prototyping and how the participants felt about it, a brainstorming session started in Exercise 2.3 (sticky notes in three circles in Figure 11.2). The task was described as follows: 'Now let's get creative! How do you imagine that we could take a step into the future with service prototyping? Consider the presentation of the SINCO laboratory and how it could go even further in our local context'. The topic was divided into what, how and why. The participants freely ideated how prototyping could be done and implemented in Chile, especially in the region in which the participants lived. The last task—Exercise 2.4, 'Thinking about the future'—focused on defining some of the ideas from the previous exercise based on the following task description: 'Taking as a reference some of the ideas in the previous point, analyse how this would contribute to the development of projects and to the discipline of design in general. Organise your ideas into the trilogy of 3C.'

Results

The first task in the workshop where the participants had an opportunity to share their bad service experiences created an atmosphere of trust and confidence in which everyone had an opportunity to be heard. The participants were very open to sharing their experiences, and different stories, for example, from the waiting room of a hospital to online shopping, were discussed. Stories in which one or some of the other participants identified with the experience garnered much discussion, and through these stories, many other situations or details emerged among the participants. After sharing their experiences and selecting one bad service for the empathic analyses, more participants joined in the discussions. It was noteworthy that the matrix of the trilogy of 3C, here when based on the selected service, helped focus the conversation with the situation, and the participants began to fill out the matrix from different levels. When one found it easier to complete the service experience through the cognitive (head, mental representation) level, the other started, for instance, to fill it out from the action point of view (body).

In Exercises 2.1 and 2.2, the criticism of prototyping was discussed in every workshop, and one of the most questioned themes was the culture itself. Service prototyping in Chile was not seen as rigorous, and many companies are not focusing on the people's experiences at all but instead trusting their own assumptions on how companies think their end users are experiencing their services. Overall, these companies were criticised for being very result-oriented and as just 'thinking about the solution without understanding the problem' (participant's note). Another participant stated, 'There is no testing of the service', which refers to the fact that companies only want solutions without evidence or user testing. However, several participants specified that many companies are collecting the feedback from their end users, but 'no visible feedback of customer satisfaction' (participant's note) indicated that the feedback was not utilised for developing the services—or such an image some of the participants had. The discussion was conducted in a group where the participants saw great value in utilising the feedback in collaborative prototyping, and the end users or even communities could play a more active part in the service prototyping actions and service development. Nonetheless, this was seen as a significant change in culture.

There were several discussions and comments regarding the 'need to integrate the community into the design' (participant's note). Collaboration could already be found in the work between design students, but there is potential for stronger and more active collaboration. Service prototyping was seen as 'necessary to design' (participant's note) and well suited to the culture, as shown in the following comment: 'I think that culturally, Latinos like role playing; therefore, I think it would be a good way to prototype' (participant's note). Also, the possibility of failure through prototyping was seen as a valuable element for service development in Chilean culture. After the service prototyping presentation, there was a comment, 'The result [overall quality of the local services] would have been different if it had been prototyped with these parameters', which refers to the presented prototyping approaches and methods. The empathic aspects of what can be achieved through prototyping were discussed as being very valuable and rich in the culture and region of the participants.

From the participants' comments, we can conclude there is not a deep and wide knowledge about prototyping. It is mostly understood as a mock-up building moment. Therefore, the workshop helped the participants see beyond the technique or method, seeing the SINCO experience as an inspiration to think about how far prototyping can be understood and the multiple opportunities it has to improve Chilean service experiences.

The trilogy of 3C, which is usually used to understand people, was a great tool to understand and clarify the different aspects of an experience. The collaborative process of delving into the specifications organised on the trilogy of 3C helped paint a panoramic, detailed and integrated vision of the experience. During the process of experience, characterisation and specification contributed to understanding how the service is perceived and, therefore, which considerations to design a service experience is given and how helpful the prototyping environment is when it comes to including all the aspects related with the experience.

Discussion

Scaling the experiences through the CAE approach and 'Prototyping through Empathic insights' framework

The workshop structure as an online format was an easily approachable and inclusive review of both service prototyping and the levels of empathy, here as discovered through people's experiences. The workshop followed a collaborative autoethnography approach, starting with the experiences of the individual and then scaling it further through collaborative storytelling before concluding the stories for the framework. The value and impact of the framework lies in its practice-based analysis, which emphasises the multilevel nature of empathy. It can be used as a tool for fieldwork analysis or as a template for documenting the service prototyping sessions. However, some critical reflections can be discussed based on the atmosphere of the workshop, in which the role of the facilitator is especially emphasised. The tool itself does not guarantee success, but the facilitator must be able to read situations and feelings and give people space to talk and be heard. This is especially challenging in an online environment where it is often challenging to read the signs of body language, for example.

In the current study, the role of sharing one's own experiences or heard stories is essential. The 'Prototyping through Empathic Insights' framework (Figure 11.3) structures and makes visible the stories while allowing others to add their own thoughts and experiences. The framework helps participants step into the shoes of an observer and interviewer, view others' stories as researchers, reflect on their own similar experiences as part of the narrative and bind together both the step-by-step story of an individual and a more detailed analysis of the three different emotional levels of these steps. Then, the participants can investigate the stories, which can be—and are often—added with other participants' experiences. This approach has similarities with the CAE approach, where a rich number of peoples' insightful knowledge and experiences (Ellis & Adams, 2014) are shared. When the participants produce and analyse the stories, they are both the instrument of the data and the data source (Chang et al., 2013).

The most significant value of the framework is in highlighting multilevel experiences that can be utilised in, among other things, understanding people's behaviours and articulating experiences and feelings aloud; thus, it serves as a framework for moving concretely to prototyping services. Insights can be highlighted from the framework, which can play a major role in experiencing a holistic service. The framework also seeks to dispel assumptions that may lead to colonial practices (Bloom, 2016; Tunstall, 2013; Vink & Oertzen, 2018).

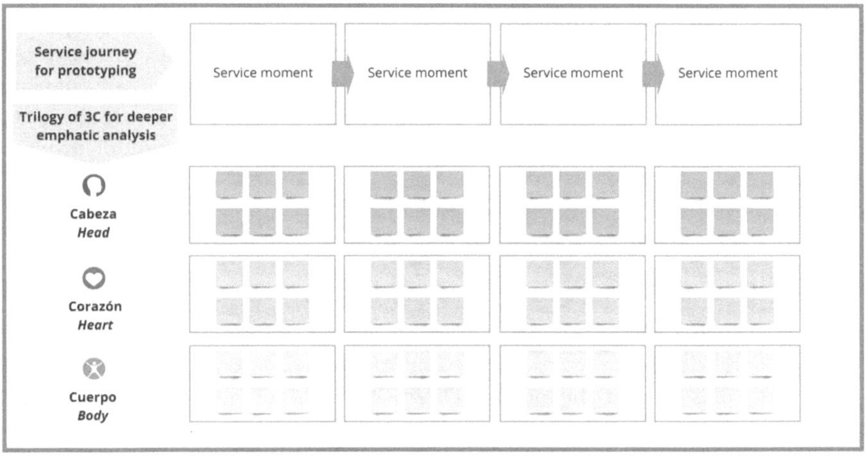

Figure 11.3 'Prototyping through Empathic Insights' framework. Figure by Mira Alhonsuo, 2021.

Transformative learning and change in adapting empathy and service prototyping in an organisation

The transformative learning and change highlighted in this article are seen as a continuum of two phases. The 'Prototyping through Empathic Insights' framework supports transformative learning approaches, which are the critical reflection (Mezirow, 2000) and roles of imagination and emotions during transformative learning experiences (Dirkx, 2014). According to Blalock and Akehi (2018), shared experiences can have an influence on transformative learning and connect people around a commonality (Blalock & Akehi, 2018); hence, service prototyping can bring value within organisational settings. Still, the critical reflection should give more space and support, hence emphasising the interactions between both the facilitator and participants. At the beginning of the five workshops, the participants were specifically asked to share bad service experiences to allow for critical thinking as well. According to Coughlan et al. (2007), prototypes not only speed up the development of a new service, but they also encourage transformative change within an organisation. Starting from the learning and then creating the change within the practical service prototyping session would be an ideal combination in an organisational setting.

The workshop structure aimed to create an understanding of the importance and knowledge of empathy and service prototyping as a part of a service development culture in an organisation. Although the current study lacks a hands-on prototyping workshop organised in the organisation on site, the online workshops specifically helped to understand the importance of shared experiences and broke down empathy into three different levels. Utilising this lesson, a possible prototyping session can also be more rewarding.

However, the ambiguities of empathy theories do not build a clear bridge to support the multilevel nature of the experiences highlighted in service prototyping. Integrating empathy and service prototyping into a clear and easy-to-analyse framework can provide a tool for developing services that will open up the experiences of service end users more broadly. However, this framework does not remove the role of the designer in the service development process. Designers often investigate services from a neutral position and, thus, are a communication link between service end users and the organisation.

Conclusion

In summary, the present paper has argued that there is the potential of exploring and adapting a practice-based approach where empathy is defined in a way that helps further the needs of service prototyping. As the chapter has shown, organisations have very different perceptions of what prototyping is, so using this approach can offer new benefits, for example, in the context of service development or in the context of implementing new developing practices as a part of an organisation's culture. Importantly, the results provide a basis for understanding the following key points: 1) The template utilised in scaling experiences helps participants, both as individuals and as a group, understand the different levels of empathy and their meanings as part of a holistic picture. 2) Transformative learning and change are needed when introducing new methods as a part of an organisational culture. However, the framework introduced in this chapter is only an initial attempt to explore the role of service prototyping and empathy, and it does not consider, for instance, the size of the organisation or what their offered product or service is. This can also affect how prototyping and empathy will be seen value-wise in an organisation.

Summary 1: Lessons learned that can contribute to the organisational or business context

The chapter provides an insightful approach to build an understanding of empathy and service prototyping through a practical tool for embedding empathy into prototyping activities by using the trilogy of 3C. Using this tool, the chapter highlights the values of personal, shared experiences that are integrated as a collaborative thinking and sharing. The lessons learned for organisations are that experiences consist of different levels, which together are important to understand and consider while investigating and developing service experiences. Also, the levels help discuss the experiences and better clarify the meaning of behaviours and feelings. The practical tool can be transferred directly to an organisational context, for instance, in workshops to embed empathy in prototyping activities or even to find a way to implement prototyping activities into an organisation.

Summary 2: Contribution to organisational or business knowledge or practices

As a practical outcome, the paper provides the 'Prototyping through Empathic Insights' framework. As a tool, this framework highlights experiences from a perspective of empathy and can be utilised in, among other things, understanding people's behaviours and articulating experiences and feelings aloud. Thus, it serves as a frame for concretely moving to prototyping services. The framework helps to gather and analyse people's experiences and interpret them through different emotional levels by using the trilogy of 3C. As a process, the paper introduces a way to adapt and implement service prototyping and its empathic perspective to an organisational practice, here considering transformative learning and change.

Acknowledgement

This chapter is part of the dissemination of the progress and results from research project number 494113 called 'Valor y contribución del Prototipado de Diseño de Servicios para el fortalecimiento de la industria. Desde la experiencia Finlandesa al contexto Chileno', which was funded by Fondart Nacional, Convocatoria 2019, Ministerio de las Culturas, las Artes y el Patrimonio, Chile.

References

Battarbee, K., Fulton Suri, J., & Gibbs Howard, S. (2014). *Empathy on the edge: Scaling and sustaining a human-centered approach in the evolving practice of design, 2014*. https://new-ideo-com.s3.amazonaws.com/assets/files/pdfs/news/Empathy_on_the_Edge.pdf.

Bailey S. G., Bell, K. L., & Hartung, H. (2019). Service design empowering innovative communities within healthcare. In M. Pfannstiel & C. Rasche (Eds.), *Service design and service thinking in healthcare and hospital management* (pp. 137–153). Springer. https://doi.org/10.1007/978-3-030-00749-2_9.

Blalock, A. E., & Akehi, M. (2018). Collaborative autoethnography as a pathway for transformative learning. *Journal of Transformative Education*, 16 (2), 89–107.

Blomkvist, J. (2014). *Representing future situations of service: Prototyping in service design* [Doctoral dissertation, Linköping University]. https://www.diva-portal.org/smash/get/diva2:712357/FULLTEXT02.pdf.

Blomkvist, J. (2016). Benefits of service level prototyping. *The Design Journal*, 19 (4), 545–564.

Bloom, P. (2016). *Against empathy: The case for rational compassion*. Harper Collins.

Braun, V., & Clarke, V. (2006). Using thematic analysis in psychology. *Qualitative Research in Psychology*, 3, 77–101. doi:10.1191/1478088706qp063oa.

Brink, T. T., Urton, K., Held, D., Kirilina, E., Hofmann, M., Klann-Delius, G., Jacobs, M.A., & Kuchinke, L. (2011). The role of orbitofrontal cortex in processing empathy stories in 4- to 8-year-old children. *Frontiers in Psychology*, 2, 80.

Buchenau, M., & Fulton Suri, J. (2000). *Experience prototyping*. In Proceedings of the 3rd Conference on Designing Interactive Systems: Processes, Practices, Methods, and Techniques (pp. 424–433). ACM.

Chang, H., Ngunjiri, F., & Hernandez, K. C. (2013). *Collaborative autoethnography*. Left Coast Press.

Coughlan, P., Suri, J. F., & Canales, K. (2007). Prototypes as (design) tools for behavioral and organizational change: A design-based approach to help organizations change work behaviors. *The Journal of Applied Behavioral Science*, 43 (1), 122–134. https://doi.org/10.1177/0021886306297722.

Dirkx, J. M. (2014). *Extension education: A context for transformative learning presentation*. Michigan State University.

Ellis, C., & Adams, T. E. (2014). The purposes, practices, and principles of autoethnographic research. In *The Oxford handbook of qualitative research* (pp. 254–276). Oxford University Press.

Erikson, T. (1995). Notes on design practice: Stories and prototypes as catalysts for communication. In J. Carroll (Ed.), *Envisioning technology: The scenario as a framework for the system development lifecycle* (pp. 37–58). John Wiley.

Fulton Suri, J. (2003). The experience evolution: Developments in design practice. *The Design Journal*, 6 (2), 39–48.

Glesne, C. (2011). *Becoming qualitative researchers: An introduction* (4th ed.). Pearson.

Goleman, D. (2017). *What is empathy? In the HBR emotional intelligence series*. Harvard Business Review Press.

Hunsucker, A., & Siegel, M. (2015). *Once upon a time: Storytelling in the design process*. In Proceedings of the 3rd International Conference for Design Education Researcher (pp. 443–454).

Koh, L. C., Slingsby, A., Dykes, J., & Kam, T. S. (2011). *Developing and applying a user-centered model for the design and implementation of information visualization tools*. In

Proceedings from ICIV'11: 15th International Conference on Information Visualisation (IV) (pp. 90–95). IEEE.

Koskinen, I., Battarbee, K., & Mattelmäki, T. (2003). *Empathic design, user experience in product design*. IT Press.

Kouprie, M., & Visser, F. (2009). A framework for empathy in design: Stepping into and out of the user's life. *Journal of Engineering Design*, 20, 437–448.

Kuure, E., Miettinen, S., & Alhonsuo, M. (2014). *Change through service design: Service prototyping as a tool for transformation and learning* (Conference paper). http://www.drs2014.org/en/presentations/243/.

Leavy, P. (2017). *Research design: Quantitative, qualitative, mixed methods, arts-based, and community-based participatory research approaches*. The Guilford Press.

Mattelmäki, T., Vaajakallio, K., & Koskinen, I. (2014). What happened to empathic design? *Design Issues*, 30 (1), 67–77.

Mezirow, J. (2000). *Learning as transformation: Critical perspectives on a theory in progress*. Jossey-Bass.

New, S., & Kimbell, L. (2013). *Chimps, designers, consultants and empathy: A 'theory of mind' for service design*. Paper presented at the 2nd Cambridge Academic Design Management Conference, 3–4 September.

Nowell, L. S., Norris, J. M., White, D. E., & Moules, N. J. (2017). Thematic analysis: Striving to meet the trustworthiness criteria. *International Journal of Qualitative Methods*, 16 (1), 1–13. https://doi.org/10.1177/1609406917733847.

Prendiville, A., Gwilt, I., & Mitchell, V. (2017). Making sense of data through service design – opportunities and reflections. In D. Sangiorgi & A. Prendiville (Eds.), *Designing for service: Key issues and new directions* (pp. 225–236). Bloomsbury Publishing.

Riess, H. & Neporent, L. (2018). *The empathy effect: Seven neuroscience-based keys for transforming the way we live, love, work, and connect across differences*. Sounds True.

Rodrigues, V., & Holmlid, S. (2017). Discovering service variations through service prototyping. *The Design Journal*, 20 (S1), S2247–S2257. doi:10.1080/14606925.2017.1352741.

Rontti, S., Miettinen, S., Kuure, E., & Lindström, A. (2012). *A laboratory concept for service prototyping – service innovation corner (SINCO)*. In ServDes2012 (Service Design and Innovation Conference), 8–10 February, Laurea University of Applied Sciences, Espoo, Finland.

Segelström, F. (2013). *Stakeholder engagement for service design: How service designers identify and communicate insights*. Linköping University Electronic Press.

Thomas, J., & McDonagh, D. (2013). Empathic design: Research strategies. *The Australasian Medical Journal*, 6 (1), 1–6.

Tolosa, M. (2008). *A twist in communication the power of the oasis (Social Science Research Network SSRN Scholarly Paper ID 1310227)*. https://doi.org/10.2139/ssrn.1310227.

Tunstall, E. (2013). Decolonizing design innovation: Design anthropology, critical anthropology and indigenous knowledge. In W. Gunn, T. Otto, & R. C. Smith (Eds.), *Design anthropology: Theory and practice* (pp. 232–250). Bloomsbury.

Vignemont, F., & Singer, T. (2006). The empathic brain: How, when and why? *Trends in Cognitive Sciences*, 10, 435–441.

Vink, J., & Oertzen, A. S. (2018). *Integrating empathy and lived experience through co-creation in service design*. In Proceedings of the Conference on Service Design (pp. 471–483). Linköping University Electronic.

Zeithaml, V., Parasuraman, A., & Berry, L. (1985). Problems and strategies in services marketing. *Journal of Marketing*, 49 (2), 33–46.

12 Benefits and challenges of designer empathy work in multidisciplinary collaboration

Tarja Pääkkönen and Marina Bos-de Vos

Introduction

Design research has shown the importance of empathy when it comes to understanding the social contexts of users (Postma et al., 2012) and when trying to make projects more participatory, human-centred and cocreative (Steen, 2013). Reflection on how empathy might influence designers' work enhances the understanding of increasingly social multidisciplinary design-related situations. Currently, much like in participatory design, there is often no prefixed context; it rather emerges during actors' constant adjustments in their decisions and actions in cocreation (Botero et al., 2020). This chapter positions designers as actors in multidisciplinary collaboration within municipal, commercial or educational settings. Its aim is to support designers and those working with designers by triggering reflection on empathy as a work-related yet subjective issue in such contexts.

The level and understandings of empathising are context dependent (cf. Kouprie & Sleeswijk Visser, 2009). This chapter considers empathy as being a social construction emerging through human interactions (Hirschfield & Underman, 2016), incorporating cognitive, affective and other dimensions (cf. Heylighen & Dong, 2019). A pluralistic view of *designer empathy* is developed both from design literature such as codesign (cf. Steen, 2013), design thinking (Liedtka, 2020) and empathic design (cf. Heylighen & Dong, 2019; Koskinen et al., 2003; Mattelmäki et al., 2014), and from insights into empathy from the areas of psychology and organisation studies. Less-bounded work contexts (Light & Akama, 2012; cf. Carvalho, 2012) relate to a 'turn to work' in organisation research that is studying the forms of work and how actors reconstruct their identities and the social world around them (Phillips & Lawrence, 2012).

The concept *designer empathy work* is suggested, here relating to the kind of work that a designer does when empathising, be it with end users or other stakeholders. From the perspective of social constructionism (Berger & Luckmann, 1966), designers, in interaction with others, make sense of complex multi-stakeholder situations and themselves; the participants draw cues from each other and their contextual settings, partly leaning on their education,

DOI: 10.4324/9781003227557-15

professional norms, their peers and assumptions (cf. Weick, 2011; Helms-Mills et al., 2010).

The key objective of the chapter is to broaden the interpretations on empathy as a part of designers' work.

The chapter asks the following question:

> What are the potential benefits and challenges of empathy work for the professional designer who empathises with others in multidisciplinary collaboration?

Beyond the beneficial aspects, the chapter discusses challenges of designer empathy work and suggests linking designer empathy work with identity work and boundary work (Phillips & Lawrence, 2012).

Methodology

Interpretations of the suggested concept, *designer empathy work*, have been drawn from an iteratively scoped literature review (Schultze, 2015) on relevant representative design, psychology and organisation research. New insights emerged during the iterative cycles and influenced the search for, selection of and analysis of prior research (Schultze, 2015, pp. 182–183), enabling beneficial and challenging aspects to be discovered. The iteration cycles informed each other (Table 12.1). Several keywords, abstracts, articles and references in the articles were used for moving from a preunderstanding to broader understanding (cf. Alvesson & Sköldberg, 2018). Thus, connections between designer's subjective empathy work and forms of work (Waring & Bishop, 2018; Phillips & Lawrence, 2012) are suggested.

Understanding the multidisciplinary settings of designers requires broad scholarship (Alvesson & Sköldberg, 2018). The authors used reflexivity by combining the literature with experiences from designers in multidisciplinary collaborations or from working in such contexts. Methodologically, reflexivity (Alvesson & Sköldberg, 2018) studies the key assumptions and reveals or even challenges ideas of empathy work in design situations.

Table 12.1 Literature review.

Iteration cycles: example key words	*Focus and related concepts*
1. Design/er +/ empathy/empathising	Empathy, designer empathy
2. Design/er + facilitation/ multidisciplinary	Designers' work contexts
3. Design/er + identity/identity work	Connection to 1,2,4
4. Design/er + boundary work/emotion/al	Connection to 1,2,3
Iterations between 1 to 4	See the discussion section

Designer empathy work in multidisciplinary collaboration

New work contexts, identity work and boundary work

People have become reflexive while making efforts to reconstruct their identities and the social world around them (Phillips & Lawrence, 2012). Managerialism is suggested to threaten professionals' self-regulation; new norms, values and management language have replaced the ethos of public services, leading to new professional contexts (Carvalho, 2012; cf. Waring & Bishop, 2018). New forms of work influence professional role boundaries and identities (cf. Phillips & Lawrence, 2012; Waring & Bishop, 2018). Boundary work often occurs when an occupational community or profession's claim over a task area or jurisdiction is threatened (Koppman, 2014).

Actors with different backgrounds and power influence emerging designs, depending on the organisation, profession and projects (Levina, 2005; Light & Akama, 2012). Design facilitation has been suggested to play an important role (Aguirre et al., 2017; Light & Akama, 2012). Because other actors may not always recognise the benefits of such design facilitation or leadership, negotiating roles and values from diverse perspectives is often needed (Bos-de Vos, 2020; cf. van Onselen et al., 2020b). Designers may carry out empathy work as facilitators or in various participant roles.

Designers' roles and identities are shaped and shape multidisciplinary collaboration through socialisation processes. Here, backstage work with multiple agendas is at play (Light & Akama, 2012; Hyysalo & Hyysalo, 2018). Designers' work contexts with diverse participants form social constructions in flux, and it is within these contexts that participants make sense of (design) situations (Berger & Luckmann, 1966). These situations stretch beyond the organisation and involve actors in the broader context: the design space (cf. Pääkkönen et al., 2020; van Amstel et al., 2016) or 'hybrid space' (Waring & Bishop, 2018).

Empathy is socially constructed through human interactions (cf. Hirschfield & Underman, 2016). Those perceived as significant others influence one's self-image and role (Gerth & Mills, 1953). Identity construction is ongoing and social as individuals clarify the meanings of uncertain situations (Helms-Mills et al., 2010).

Identity work occurs in the processes of 'forming, repairing, maintaining, strengthening or revising the constructions … productive of a sense of coherence and distinctiveness' (Sveningsson & Alvesson, 2003, p. 1165). Identity work can be conscious, involving self-doubt and self-openness during encounters with others, and dynamic and fragmentary (Beech et al., 2008; Sveningsson & Alvesson, 2003), with contradictions and role expectations (cf. Sveningsson & Alvesson, 2003). A group might use its technical or professional discourse to reinforce boundaries (Beech et al., 2008). Designers, for example, might identify themselves as advocates for users. A professional designer might attune to situations (Light & Akama, 2012) and embrace, reject or negotiate roles, through which multiple identities constantly form (cf. Sveningsson & Alvesson, 2003). Empathy work fluctuates with both identity work (who am

I?) and boundary work (what is my role?) involving subjective, professional and collective considerations.

Human beings are born with a predisposition to experience empathy, which is cultivated in socialisation processes (Hoffman, 2000). A connection between empathy and moral reasoning has been suggested (Bloom, 2017). However, Heylighen and Dong (2019) were concerned about empathy having become a design ideology rather than being sometimes appropriate. To elaborate on this, the beneficial and challenging aspects of designer empathy work will be considered in the next two sections: 'Possible benefits of designer empathy work' and 'Possible challenges of designer empathy work'.

Possible benefits of designer empathy work

Improving stakeholder relations and collaboration

Designers' actions and decisions related to value creation can be strongly influenced by their professional beliefs (Bos-de Vos, 2020, p. 47). One such belief is that designers 'need to be interested and empathic towards all stakeholders and other design team members, and aware of the influence of their own positive or negative role on empathy in these processes' (Smeenk et al., 2019, p. 53). Empathising might improve stakeholders' inclusion or empowerment. Enabling more open discussion on values that are important for diverse stakeholders might mitigate value conflicts (Bos-de Vos, 2020), helping overcome psychological barriers (Liedtka, 2020). An agreement about the central role of users exists, for example, in codesign (cf. Steen, 2013), design thinking (Liedtka, 2020), empathic design (Koskinen et al., 2003; Mattelmäki et al., 2014) and human–computer interaction (HCI) development (Wright & McCarthy, 2008). Many design scholars find empathising with users to be important (Kouprie & Sleeswijk Visser, 2009; Suri, 2000). Reciprocal empathy could connect stakeholders on a deeper level (Smeenk et al., 2019). Empathising might involve tacit emotions, intuition, latent aspirations and feelings, creating shared experiences and reference points (cf. Mattelmäki et al., 2014; Smeenk et al., 2019, p. 54). Empathic and communicative coping strategies are suggested to be relevant for designers' professional development (van Onselen et al., 2020b).

Supporting broader goals

Devecchi and Guerrini (2017) link socially responsible design (Cipolla & Bartholo, 2014) to design for empathic experiences, going beyond psychological and cognitive approaches (Kouprie & Sleeswijk Visser, 2009). In a phenomenological approach (Devecchi & Guerrini, 2017), designers relate empathically with participants in codesign processes for establishing a dialogic design culture (Manzini, 2016).

Empathy might trigger pro-environmental moral reasoning (see Berenguer, 2010) or environmental empathy. Alternatively, designers might encourage businesses to work towards diverse United Nations (n.d.) sustainability goals (cf. Lemus-Aguilar et al., 2019).

Supporting value negotiations

When people do not sacrifice their own needs and interests while simultaneously maintaining positive concern for others, negotiation outcomes can be enhanced by adopting long-term perspectives (De Dreu, 2014). An empathic approach might encourage actors' reflection on divergent values by raising awareness of different standpoints (cf. De Dreu, 2014; Steen, 2013). Emotions generally influence the understanding of values and goals (Batson et al., 1995) by supplementing rationality (see Berenguer, 2010).

Designer empathy work could enhance the understandings of values in multidisciplinary settings, here with the help of tangible objects offering a common ground (cf. Bechky, 2003) for mutual conversations. If designer empathy work could uncover the values and discrepancies that guide actors' sensemaking in collaboration, this could benefit all actors.

Supporting creation or reframing of roles and boundaries

Holism is connected to empathising: service designers, for example, constructed their occupational mandate by expanding their role boundaries through holism, empathy and cocreation (cf. Fayard et al., 2016). In innovation contexts, immersion in users' lives has supported building empathy and emotional commitment (Liedtka, 2020). Blurred temporary boundaries (Bos-de Vos et al., 2019) between occupational roles and values can enable and constrain designers in pursuing personal, professional or other values. Just like architects who are multiskilled practitioners with a high level of advocacy and who use negotiating skills to achieve the integrity of the design (Ahuja et al., 2017, p.12), empathising designers undergo practical adjustments and boundary work (cf. McGivern et al., 2015), such as adopting new skills, languages (cf. Carvalho, 2012; Pääkkönen et al., 2020), tasks and roles. Empathy might be helpful, for example, in negotiating new roles (cf. Bos-de Vos et al., 2019).

Supporting identities and prosocial behaviour

Empathy, curiosity and optimism (cf. Liedtka, 2020; Michlewski, 2008) as a design mindset might support designers' identities. Because empathising motivates prosocial behaviour (Bloom, 2017) designers might succeed in multistakeholder negotiations that can support their identities as facilitators. Liedtka (2020) describes design thinking as a social technology enabling trust and psychological safety among stakeholders and users. However, it has been suggested that designers should consciously sense their own feelings for being able to understand others (cf. Smeenk et al., 2019).

In sum, evoking, feeling and showing empathy—or empathy work—forms a part of designers' currently expected professional mindsets and behaviours (cf. Postma, Zwartkruis-Pelgrim et al., 2012; Heylighen & Dong, 2019). Professional boundaries might stretch past empathy work to align with emerging contexts and interests; these include the possibilities for successful boundary spanning with new designer identities involving identity work.

Possible challenges of designer empathy work

Empathy remains a vague concept

Empathising blurs with reactions and emotions in unpredictable ways. The concept of empathy is vague (Cuff et al., 2016; Zaki, 2017). Despite connections to prosocial (Singer & Lamm, 2009, p. 84) other-regarding altruistic behaviour, empathising can be self-serving when it aims at reaching personal goals (Singer & Fehr, 2005). The level of empathy varies contextually and is influenced by interactions with others over time (Singer & Fehr, 2005). Spontaneous imitation enhances the interaction and liking of others, hence fostering empathy (Iacoboni, 2009). Yet empathising with one's own (professional) group is easier than doing so with others (Bloom, 2017); designers might prefer something familiar to themselves (cf. Elsbach, 2020; Steen, 2013). The spotlight nature of empathy implies selective attention, causing potential negative reactions (Bloom, 2017). Moreover, the distinction between the self and others remains blurred (see Kirman & Teschl, 2010).

Helping one person can lead to greater suffering for another (Bloom, 2017); empathy can be felt for one or two individuals but seldom for unidentified people. Empathy as a professional norm can lead to distress.

Conflicting professional values and boundaries

Although empathy work may help in involving others in collaboration, value discrepancies may emerge (Bos de-Vos et al., 2019). Values strike at the core of identity and are more likely to be taken personally (Harinck & De Dreu, 2004). For example, architects have experienced a mismatch between their professional education and actual practice (Ahuja et al., 2017), and the idealistic values from design schools may conflict with the commercial ones at work (van Onselen et al., 2020a), causing identity threats. Empathising with end users in reaching an optimal design outcome may not be prioritised in multidisciplinary collaboration, leading to limited budgets and mandates. Power relations may cause actors to ignore the work of others as a way to reaffirm professional, organisational or project involvement-based identities (Levina, 2005; cf. Light & Akama, 2012).

Designers in large technology companies may experience friction with engineers and managers. The designers' goal might aim 'to enable redesigning roles and power structures, as well as debate the ethical judgement calls inherent in design work' (Björklund et al., 2020, p. 113.) Value conflicts exist among junior design professionals (van Onselen et al., 2020a). Designers may try to 'sell' design horizontally in the organisation to create the collaboration needed for effective design (Björklund et al., 2020), thus translating between professional groups (Botero et al., 2020; Pääkkönen et al., 2020) and adjusting their roles through boundary work.

The desire to follow a design ethos (supporting identity) is present in striving for ideal designs, which becomes an almost sacred value. This might lead to boundary work; orchestration and convincing others whom designers need for accomplishing the best design outcome, forming an essential part of their identities.

Diverse goals of empathy work

Value discrepancies may often remain tacit rather than explicit (Bos-de Vos, 2020). Designers may also 'empathise' silently to avoid conflict if voicing value discrepancies forms a risk for the collaboration. Group decisions may result from an illusion of unanimity at the expense of fully exploring divergences (Janis, 1972). Understanding others' views remains limited to one's personal assumptions unless the participants explore mutual assumptions (De Dreu, 2014). So-called sacred values such as justice are very difficult to compromise on (Hanselmann & Tanner, 2008).

Powerful or significant people may influence others' behaviours. Participants draw from previously adopted norms and rules (cf. Helms-Mills et al., 2010) and develop joint feeling rules (Hochschild, 2003). In a business context, feeling rules may favour rationality (cf. Levina, 2005) or a customer-driven attitude, such as tapping into user emotions to shape strategic brands (cf. Straker & Wrigley, 2016) by utilising emotions (Hochschild, 2003). Emotional labour (Hochschild, 2003) occurs when designers do empathy work, such as mitigating value differences or empathising with users. However, when expected to provide profitable customer experiences, such work can become *instrumental*. This blurs *genuine* and *displayed* empathising on a personal level, leading to subjective confusion about oneself and one's role. A designer may ask the following: 'Who is the real me?' (cf. Hochschild, 2003).

Possible burnout or guilt

Drawing from designers' own experiences may have a psychological cost or can lead to misinterpreting users' situations. Disclosing personal experiences can be overwhelming and lead to withdrawal (Singer & Lamm, 2009).

Although excessive empathising risks leading to distress and burnout (Bloom, 2017; Hochschild, 2003), displaying empathy can be considered a skill to be learned (Heylighen & Dong, 2019). Because not all displays among actors are genuine, this leads to social situations and interactions becoming displays that distort interactions (Hochschild, 2003), in which the values and desired outcomes—but also identities and role boundaries—are at stake. Designers as advocates for the user may feel as though they are misunderstood.

People can disengage from empathy; empathy regulation enables selective control and the inhibition of sensory cues (such as facial expressions), triggering unpleasant reactions (Kirman & Teschl, 2010). Whether more empathetic persons feel guilt easier than others is not known (Bloom, 2017). Should this be the case, the designer might feel guilty when compromising on design or, alternatively, might be unable to refuse other stakeholder demands, leading to self-doubt (cf. van Onselen et al., 2020a).

Remote empathy work

There are stakeholders other than the immediate users (Björgvinsson et al., 2012) and end users can be imagined as such (Steen, 2013). Earlier HCI design often maintained a third-person perspective on users without extended, deep and direct contact, suggesting this as sufficient when it comes to empathic understanding (Wright & McCarthy, 2008). Designers may not interact with users as they often obtain user data collected by other researchers (Postma, Lauche et al., 2012). Moreover, users can be visually presented in ways that promote or hinder empathic understanding (Kouprie & Sleeswijk Visser, 2009).

Through designer empathy work, digital data utilisation in customer relationship (CR) activities may aim at shaping digital consumer identities for increased consumption (Beckett & Nayak, 2008), hence neglecting true human needs. Empathy is felt for one or few persons rather than for unidentified people in data (Bloom, 2017). By contrast, following real patient needs may lead to rejecting software, as Liedtka (2020, p. 71) exemplifies. Remote empathy, especially in digital contexts, deserves more attention beyond the scope of this chapter because of how it entails the danger of a lack of human empathy.

Empathy work with time constraints

Empathy is constrained to momentary situations. People appropriate designs later; envisioned use differs from actual use (Björgvinsson et al., 2012).

Hyysalo and Hyysalo (2018) point to mundane work behind long-term design collaboration projects; here, involving participants is time-consuming. People join and leave projects over time (Postma, Lauche et al., 2012), challenging empathy work. Empathising requires time (Kouprie & Sleeswijk Visser, 2009), and some designers may work without remuneration (Bos-de Vos et al., 2019) for optimal design outcomes. Many professionals feel their work is being compromised by time constraints (Knight, 2017; Levina, 2005).

In business contexts, agile methods may lead to compromising on empathy for the user. The pace of work generally limits designers' power; the speed of delivery can favour productivity at the expense of quality, hence threatening design authority (Knight, 2017). Design ideas may become reconfigured or neglected to meet commercial demands, costs or technical issues (Ahuja et al., 2017, p. 13; Koppman, 2014).

Time constraints may push designers towards the quick adoption of dominant values and frames through empathy for non-user stakeholders, hence, at the cost of neglecting values that are important for end users or the designer self.

In sum, empathy work can become challenging for the empathising designer, collaboration and the outcomes. As a form of emotional labour (cf. Hochschild, 2013), empathy work mixes genuine and instrumental empathy, causing identity work. Designers often do not provide outcomes independently, instead making efforts to holistically balance the voices of end users with commercial partnerships. These tensions remain problematic for designers' identities and roles, which are further limited by time and distance.

Discussion: Designer empathy work in multidisciplinary collaboration

New managerialism transforms the social practices of professionals and service users (Waring & Bishop, 2018), influencing multidisciplinary collaboration. Designer empathy work as a concept has been suggested as a way to intertwine identity work and boundary work (cf. Phillips & Lawrence, 2012).

Designer empathy work, identity work and boundary work

Designer empathy work in fluid multidisciplinary collaboration co-evolves with designers' professional role boundaries, identities and understandings of self. For example, the tensions related to creative, professional and managerial identities in city-building projects emerged when architects' creative identities were not understood by others (Ahuja et al., 2017). Knight (2017) observes a hybridisation of practitioners (cf. Adams & Sawchuk, 2021) when business analysts replaced designers in agile projects. A 'business designer' without design education, however, is likely to understand collaboration differently. Designers stress non-linear explorative approaches, while projects require rationality or technical solutions (Levina, 2005; Postma, Lauche et al., 2012). Boundary work may aim at changing the mindset or defending artistic logic (Koppman, 2014). Different forms of architects' boundary work have been observed (Bos-de Vos et al., 2019). Although some have defended original professional designer roles, others may acquire new roles. Designers might, for example, identify themselves by their strategic or managerial roles or frames (cf. Carvalho, 2012; Pääkkönen et al., 2020), thus expanding previously internalised roles as 'pure' designers (cf. McGivern et al., 2015).

Designer empathy work, identity work and boundary work fluctuate: identities continuously flow through empathy work to boundary work and back again (Figure 12.1).

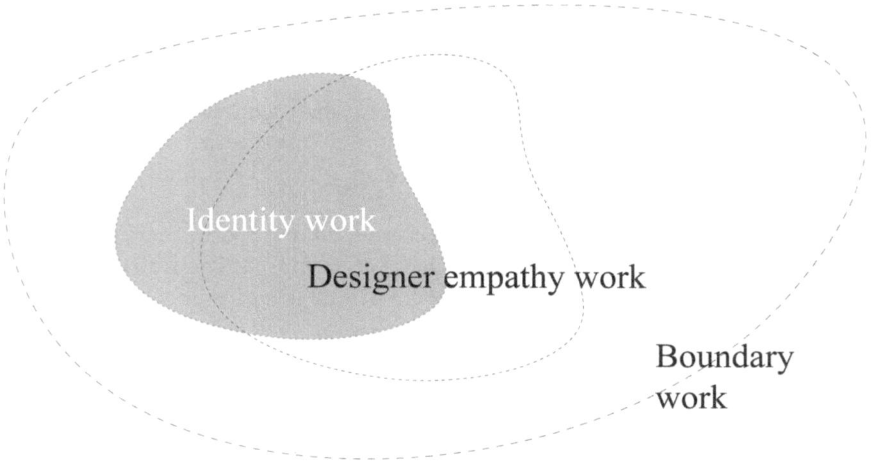

Figure 12.1 Designer empathy work co-evolves with identity work and boundary work.

Hybrid designers may adopt managerial values

Some designers, perhaps with technical specialties, may adopt new skills in existing and other areas (cf. Carvalho, 2012). This may lead to becoming a hybrid flexible designer (Ahuja et al., 2017) or a customer expert who can connect customer emotions to branding strategies (cf. Straker & Wrigley, 2016). Some might merge professionalism and managerialism to legitimate hybrid professionalism if they manage to reconcile internal contradictions between design professionalism and managerialism (cf. McGivern et al., 2015).

Power disparities undermine negotiators' ability and motivation to seek compromises (De Dreu, 2014). Could empathic designers prone to conflict avoidance favour the adoption of dominant frames or defend designerly values from their education? A designer might enable participants' awareness of discrepant understandings yet also adjust one's own identity or professional values. Negotiating values requires all the participants' willingness and efforts; mutual understandings benefit from seeing the bigger picture and the other party's situation next to one's own (De Dreu, 2014).

Identities are at stake

Empathy work involves the internal struggles between personal and professional beliefs, values and norms and can be related to feeling rules (Hochschild, 2003). Identity paradox (Ahuja et al., 2017) or identity work (Brown, 2015) in situations with tensions and surprises prompts 'feelings of confusion, contradiction and self-doubt, which in turn tend to lead to examination of the self' (Brown, 2015, p. 25). Following Hochschild (2003), one can become alienated from an aspect of self, 'either the body or the margins of the soul' (p. 7) that is *used* to do the work, thus much in the way a factory boy's arm or a service worker's smile becomes a piece of production or paid service. Genuine empathy work by designers may be utilised for building loyal customer relationships (cf. Straker & Wrigley, 2016); some designers may gain professional success through empathy work, while *genuine* empathy may turn into *instrumental empathy* for business purposes. End users may be 'reduced' into being customers rather than human beings (cf. Carvalho, 2012).

Identity work has been suggested to be intensive particularly in the creative industries (see Ahuja et al., 2017; Elsbach & Flynn, 2013; Elsbach, 2020). Empathy work balances between personal and design ethos and commercially tuned contexts. Tensions play a role in how a project develops along with the personal psychological adjustments that are made. The struggle over control and autonomy resembles nurse managers facing new public management: some have strengthened their traditional role as care experts, yet others have started considering management as part of care practice. This transformed patients into consumers with a cost side (Carvalho, 2012). Waring and Bishop (2018) describe a new hospital as a factory maximising customer flow, not care. Although designers strive to take responsibility over optimal design outcomes they may, at times, end up not compromising for moral reasons (cf. Bos-de Vos et al., 2019) instead of focusing on profits.

Empathy work may enhance multidisciplinary collaboration

For the best multidisciplinary negotiation outcomes, both self-interest and others' interests require consideration; willingness to revise assumptions of the other party is beneficial (De Dreu, 2014), suggesting that empathy work might enhance joint exploration of value discrepancies; yet equal power conditions are required (De Dreu, 2014). This would elevate all the actors in multidisciplinary collaboration *above* the conflicting situation, moving them towards exploring mutual assumptions.

Here lies the opportunity of cultural transformation (Buchanan, 2015; cf. Liedtka, 2020); designers might manage to convey their genuine empathic concerns in the decision processes. Design professionals might bring human value issues into the discussion through empathy work, including facilitation and design approaches, enabling conversations on values that might be taken for granted. Designers often orchestrate between occupations by noticing the issues that reside in between.

Although multiple and conflicting identities can lead to marginalisation and alienation (Ahuja et al., 2017), Fayard et al. (2016) describe how service designers created their occupational mandate partly because of earlier feelings of marginalisation. However, Ahuja et al. (2017) find that architects' design ethos did not resonate with their practices in multi-organisational projects, eventually leading to negative self-concepts. Designers may differ in being more controlling (rigid) or enabling cocreators, depending on their personal identities (Elsbach & Flynn, 2013). If smooth collaboration and empathy work with non-user stakeholders become a priority—with limited time and budgets—end users risk being of secondary value to the design outcome, undermining the core (sacred) value of design for human well-being.

Empathising with non-user stakeholders may smooth multidisciplinary collaboration, yet it risks an optimal design outcome from the end users' perspective. Strong end user empathy, on the other hand, may conflict with non-user stakeholders and their primary goals, causing friction in collaboration.

New variants of design-related professions can emerge while the sole designer or architect seems to have become a threatened species (Bos-de Vos et al., 2019). Some designers might succeed in turning their organisations and networks into purpose-driven ones or transform professional cultures (cf. Buchanan, 2015; Lemus-Aguilar et al., 2019) supported by empathy work triggering joint sensemaking.

Strong support for designers and other professionals who are facing challenges between their identities, professional ethos and roles is needed, not only for their own well-being, but for a future society: design has long-term consequences. The idea of education producing empathic professionals with attitudes and practices deserves consideration from all those who are involved. Conversations are needed beyond diverse design fields.

Conclusion

In this chapter, the beneficial and challenging aspects of designer empathy work were considered in multidisciplinary contexts. Designer empathy work may enhance collaboration between stakeholders, yet, this may come with consequences. From the point of view of the designer's identity and role, as an individual and a professional, the situation involves psychological and practical adjustments and challenges that are related to identity work and boundary work.

A distinction between more *instrumental* empathy work with underlying commercial ends and *genuine* designer empathy work that emerges spontaneously is suggested. The latter is a more personal but a vulnerable dimension of designer empathy work that is also linked with professional ethos. Empathy work intertwines with the professional and personal, consciously or unconsciously, raising the need for identity work.

A distinction between designers' end user empathy and non-user stakeholder empathy is suggested for clarifying the differences in future research. Empathising with end users for reaching the best design outcome may lead to conflicting personal and project values and feelings of alienation. Empathising with non-user stakeholders might smooth multidisciplinary collaboration yet neglect the end user perspectives or values that are important for the designer.

Mediating between the dominant, often managerial values and frames and design perspectives through empathy work involves psychological adjustments and identity work. However, empathising may help in modifying role boundaries when designers (re)construct their multiple professional identities in flux. Role-extending empathy work may sometimes increase confidence, supporting new designer identities and roles.

Fractured work has led to professional role and personal identity struggles in various design fields. The mixed experiences of genuine and displayed empathy bear a risk of exhaustion and identity confusion.

Finally, a broader view of environmental and societal empathy could motivate designers towards new contexts, such as the United Nations 2030 Sustainable Development Goals, hence triggering multidisciplinary collaboration. This could be one opportunity for designers to expand their professional roles and involve others in contributing to meaningful goals in the coming decade. Within individual and multidisciplinary reflection on such issues lies the key to finding mutual understandings about empathy work and its multiple faces.

Summary 1: Lessons learned that can contribute to the organisational or business context

New fluid forms of work change designers' role boundaries and identities in multidisciplinary collaboration. As a concept, designer empathy work is suggested. Designer empathy work co-evolves with identity and boundary work. Next to the potential benefits in multidisciplinary collaboration, the risks related to designers' identities and roles were identified.

Suggested emerging research areas include environmental empathy, instrumental versus genuine empathy and remote empathy in digital contexts.

Summary 2: Contribution to organisational or business knowledge or practices

Empathy as an expected professional attitude or skill blends the images of personal and professional identities and roles. The chapter reflects on how designers might act or feel in multidisciplinary collaboration and the potential influence this may have on such collaboration. The role of education in producing professionals with empathic attitudes and practices deserves consideration from all those involved. The chapter offers novel insights into empathy as a form of emotional labour in modern fractured business and work settings.

Acknowledgements

We would like to express our gratitude to the peer reviewers who guided us in improving this chapter. We are grateful to PhD candidate Katri Konttinen who helped us with the visualisation.

References

Adams, T., & Sawchuk, P. H. (2021). Professional-organizational contradictions and hybridization of knowledge: Insights from the study of engineering and nursing in Canada. *Vocations and Learning*, 14 (1), 75–93. https://doi.org/10.1007/s12186-020-09253-1.

Aguirre, M., Agudelo, N., & Romm, J. (2017). Design facilitation as emerging practice: Analyzing how designers support multi-stakeholder co-creation. *She Ji: The Journal of Design Economics and Innovation*, 3 (3), 198–209. https://doi.org/10.1016/j.sheji.2017.11.003.

Ahuja, S., Nikolova, N., & Clegg, S. (2017). Paradoxical identity: The changing nature of architectural work and its relation to architects' identity. *Journal of Professions and Organization*, 4 (1), 2–19.

Alvesson, M., & Sköldberg, K. (2018). *Reflexive methodology: New vistas for qualitative research* (3rd ed.). SAGE Publications.

Batson, C. D., Turk, C. L., Shaw, L. L., & Klein, T. R. (1995). Information function of empathy emotion: Learning that we value the other's welfare. *Journal of Personality and Social Psychology*, 68, 300–313.

Bechky, B. A. (2003). Sharing meaning across occupational communities: The transformation of understanding on a production floor. *Organization Science*, 14 (3), 312–330.

Beckett, A., & Nayak, A. (2008). The reflexive consumer. *Marketing Theory*, 8 (3), 299–317.

Beech, N., MacIntosh, R., & McInnese, P. (2008). Identity work: Processes and dynamics of identity formation. *International Journal of Public Administration*, 31 (9), 957–964.

Berenguer, J. (2010). The effect of empathy in environmental moral reasoning. *Environment and Behavior*, 42 (1), 110–134. doi:10.1177/0013916508325892.

Berger, P. L., & Luckmann, T. (1966). *The social construction of reality*. Penguin Books.

Björklund, T., Maula, H., Soule, S., & Maula, J. (2020). Integrating design into organizations: The co-evolution of design capabilities. *California Management Review*, 62 (2), 100–124. https://doi.org/10.1177/0008125619898245.

Björgvinsson, E., Ehn, P., & Hillgren, P.-A. (2012). Design things and design thinking: Contemporary participatory design challenges. *Design Issues*, 28 (3), 101–116. https://www.jstor.org/stable/23273842.

Bloom, P. (2017). Empathy and its discontents. *Trends in Cognitive Sciences*, 21 (1), 24–31. https://doi.org/10.1016/j.tics.2016.11.004.

Bos-de Vos, M. (2020). A framework for designing for divergent values. In S. Boess, M. Cheung, & R. Cain (Eds.), *Proceedings of DRS2020: Volume 1 Synergy Situations* (Vol. 1, pp. 39–53). Design Research Society. https://doi.org/10.21606/drs.2020.374.

Bos-de Vos, M., Lieftink, B. M., & Lauche, K. (2019). How to claim what is mine: Negotiating professional roles in inter-organizational projects. *Journal of Professions and Organization*, 6 (2), 128–155. https://doi.org/10.1093/jpo/joz004.

Botero, A., Hyysalo, S., Kohtala, C., & Whalen, J. (2020). Getting participatory design done: From methods and choices to translation work across constituent domains. *International Journal of Design*, 14 (2), 17–34.

Brown, A. D. (2015). Identities and identity work in organizations. *International Journal of Management Reviews*, 17 (1), 20–40.

Buchanan, R. (2015). Worlds in the making: Design, management, and the reform of organizational culture. *She Ji: The Journal of Design, Economics, and Innovation*, 1 (1), 5–21. https://doi.org/10.1016/j.sheji.2015.09.003.

Carvalho, T. (2012). Managerialism and professional strategies: A case from nurses in Portugal. *Journal of Health Organization and Management*, 26 (4), 524–541. http://dx.doi.org/10.1108/14777261211251562.

Cipolla, C., & Bartholo, R. (2014). Empathy or inclusion: A dialogical approach to socially responsible design. *International Journal of Design*, 8 (2), 87–100.

Cuff, B., Brown, S. J., Taylor, L., & Howat, D. (2016). Empathy: A review of the concept, *Emotion Review*, 8 (2), 144–153. http://emr.sagepub.com/content/early/2014/12/01/1754073914558466.

De Dreu, C. K. W. (2014). Negotiating deals and settling conflict can create value for both sides. *Policy Insights from the Behavioral and Brain Sciences*, 1 (1), 156–163. https://doi.org/10.1177/2372732214549016.

Devecchi, A., & Guerrini, L. (2017). Empathy and design. A new perspective. *The Design Journal*, 20 (S1), 4357–4364. doi:10.1080/14606925.2017.1352932.

Elsbach, K. (2020). Giving ideas that won't get rejected: How personal identity relates to idea-taking in creative collaboration. *Innovation: Organization and management*, 22 (1),12–38. https://doi.org/10.1080/14479338.2019.1626239.

Elsbach, K. D., & Flynn, F. J. (2013). Creative collaboration and the self-concept: A study of toy designers. *Journal of Management Studies*, 50 (4), 514–544.

Fayard, A. L., Stigliani, I., & Bechky, B. A. (2016). How nascent occupations construct a mandate: The case of service designers' ethos. *Administrative Science Quarterly*, 62, 270–303.

Gerth, H., & Mills, C. W. (1953). *Character and social structure: The psychology of social institutions*. Harcourt, Brace and Company.

Hanselmann, M., & Tanner, C. (2008). Taboos and conflicts in decision making: Sacred values, decision difficulty, and emotions. *Judgment and Decision Making*, 3 (1), 51–63.

Harinck, F., & De Dreu, C. K. W. (2004). Negotiating interests or values and reaching integrative agreements: The importance of time pressure and temporary impasses. *European Journal of Social Psychology*, 34 (5), 595–611.

Helms-Mills, J., Thurlow, A., & Mills, A. J. (2010). Making sense of sensemaking: The critical sensemaking approach. *Qualitative Research in Organizations and Management: An International Journal*, 5 (2), 182–195.

Heylighen, A., & Dong, A. (2019). To empathise or not to empathise? Empathy and its limits in design. *Design Studies*, 65C, 107–124.

Hirschfield, L. E., & Underman, K. (2016). Empathy in medical education: A case for social construction. *Patient Education and Counseling*, 100 (4), 785–787.

Hochschild, A. R. (2003). *The managed heart: Commercialization of human feeling*. University of California Press.

Hoffman, M. L. (2000). *Empathy and moral development: Implications for caring and justice*. Cambridge University Press.

Hyysalo, V., & Hyysalo, S. (2018). The mundane and strategic work in collaborative design. *Design Issues*, 34 (3), 42–58.

Iacoboni, M. (2009). Imitation, empathy, and mirror neurons. *Annual Review of Psychology*, 60, 653–670.

Janis, I. L. (1972). *Victims of groupthink*. Houghton Mifflin.

Kirman, A., & Teschl, M. (2010). Selfish or selfless? The role of empathy in economics. *Philosophical Transactions: Biological Sciences, Rationality and Emotions*, 365 (1538), 303–317.

Knight, J. (2017). Go with the flow: Accelerated digital design in the age of post-agility. *The Design Journal*, 20 (sup1), 2700–2715.

Koppman, S. (2014). Making art work: Creative assessment as boundary work. *Poetics*, 46, 1–21.

Koskinen, I., Mattelmäki, T., & Battarbee, K. (Eds.). (2003). *Empathic design: User experience in product design*. Edita IT Press.

Kouprie, M., & Sleeswijk Visser, F. (2009). A framework for empathy in design: Stepping into and out of the user's life. *Journal of Engineering Design*, 20 (5), 437–448.

Lemus-Aguilar, I., Ramirez-Portilla, G., Morales, A., & Hidalgo, A. (2019). Sustainable business models through the lens of organizational design: A systematic literature review. *Sustainability*, 11, 53–79.

Levina, N. (2005). Collaborating on multi-party information systems development projects: A collective reflection-in-action view. *Information Systems Research*, 16 (2), 109–130.

Liedtka, J. (2020). Putting technology in its place: Design thinking's social technology at work. *California Management Review*, 62 (2), 53–83.

Light, A., & Akama, Y. (2012). *The human touch: Participatory practice and the role of facilitation in designing with communities*. In Proceedings of the 12th Participatory Design Conference. Research Papers (Vol. 1, pp. 61–70). Association for Computing Machinery. https://doi.org/10.1145/2347635.2347645.

Manzini, E. (2016). Design culture and dialogic design. *Design Issues*, 32 (1), 52–56.

Mattelmäki, T., Vaajakallio, K., & Koskinen, I. (2014). What happened to empathic design? *Design Issues*, 30 (1), 67–77. https://doi.org/10.1162/DESI_a_00249.

McGivern, G., Currie, G., Ferlie, E., Fitzgerald, L., & Waring, J. (2015). Hybrid manager-professionals' identity work: The maintenance and hybridization of medical professionalism in managerial contexts. *Public Administration*, 93 (2), 412–432.

Michlewski, K. (2008). Uncovering design attitude: Inside the culture of designers. *Organization Studies*, 29 (3), 373–392.

Pääkkönen, T., Sarantou, M., & Miettinen, S. (2020). Design languages in the design space: Silicon Valley. In S. Boess, M. Cheung, & R. Cain (Eds.), *Proceedings of DRS2020: Synergy Situations* (Vol. 1, pp. 4–22). Design Research Society. https://doi.org/10.21606/drs.2020.148.

Phillips, N., & Lawrence, T. B. (2012). The turn to work in organization and management theory: Some implications for strategic organization. *Strategic Organization*, 10 (3), 223–230.

Postma, C., Lauche, K., & Stappers, P.J. (2012). Social theory as a thinking tool for empathic design. *Design Issues*, 28(1), 30–49. https://www.jstor.org/stable/4142780.

Postma, C. E., Zwartkruis-Pelgrim, E., Daemen, E., & Du, J. (2012). Challenges of doing empathic design: Experiences from industry. *International Journal of Design*, 6 (1), 59–70.

Schultze, U. (2015). Skirting SLR's language trap: Reframing the 'systematic' vs 'traditional' literature review opposition as a continuum. *Journal of Information Technology*, 30, 180–184.

Singer, T., & Fehr, E. (2005). The neuroeconomics of mind reading and empathy. *American Economic Review*, 95 (2), 340–345. doi:10.1257/000282805774670103.

Singer, T., & Lamm, C. (2009). The social neuroscience of empathy. *Annals of the New York Academy of Science*, 1156, 81–96.

Smeenk, W., Sturm, J., & Eggen, B. (2019). A comparison of existing frameworks leading to an empathic formation compass for co-design. *International Journal of Design*, 13 (3), 53–68.

Steen, M. (2013). Co-design as a process of joint inquiry and imagination. *Design Issues*, 29 (2), 16–28.

Straker, K., & Wrigley, C. (2016). Emotionally engaging customers in the digital age: The case study of 'Burberry love'. *Journal of Fashion Marketing and Management: An International Journal*, 20 (3), 276–299. https://doi.org/10.1108/JFMM-10-2015-0077.

Suri, J. F. (2000). Communicating with designers: The role of empathy, evidence and inspiration. *Proceedings of the Human Factors and Ergonomics Society Annual Meeting*, 44 (38), 795–798. https://doi.org/10.1177/154193120004403830.

Sveningsson, S., & Alvesson, M. (2003). Managing managerial identities: Organizational fragmentation, discourse and identity struggle. *Human Relations*, 56 (10), 1163–1193.

United Nations. (n.d.). *Department of Economic and Social Affairs. Sustainable development goals (SDGs).* https://sdgs.un.org/goals.

van Amstel, F. M. C., Hartmann, T., van der Voort, M., & Dewulf, G. P. M. R. (2016). The social production of design space. *Design Studies*, 46, 199–225.

van Onselen, L., Valkenburg, R., & Snelders, D. (2020a). Value-based conflicts experienced by junior design professionals in collaborative practice. *CoDesign*, 1–17. doi:10.1080/15710882.2020.1854314.

van Onselen, L., Valkenburg, R., & Snelders, D. (2020b). Exploring how junior design professionals cope with and learn from value-based conflicts. *CoDesign*, 1–23. doi:10.1080/15710882.2020.1834584.

Waring, J., & Bishop, S. (2018). Transforming professional and service user identities in the heterotopian 'hybrid spaces' of public–private partnerships. *Policy & Politics*, 46 (4), 663–679.

Weick, K. E. (2011). *Making sense of the organization.* Blackwell Publishing.

Wright, P., & McCarthy, J. (2008). *Empathy and experience in HCI.* Proceedings of the SIGCHI Conference on Human Factors in Computing. Dignity in design (pp. 637–646). Association for Computer Machinery.

Zaki, J. (2017). Moving beyond stereotypes of empathy. *Trends in Cognitive Sciences*, 21 (259), 59–60.

13 Towards a more empathic organization

An exploratory case study of a multinational manufacturing corporation

Krista Korpikoski

Introduction

Service design has been a growing trend in the last decade. It serves as a practical and concrete approach towards more customer- and user-centric ways to develop products and services (Stickdorn & Schneider, 2011). This is natural due to its holism that builds on the philosophy of design thinking, empathy, cocreation, human-centred processes, and customer-centric tools and methods (Sangiorgi & Prendiville, 2017). In this regard, service design serves as an empathic, holistic and multidisciplinary approach and practice (Prestes Joly et al., 2019; Yu & Sangiorgi, 2018) when executing customer-centric outside-in development strategies in the areas of new service and product development. An empathic design approach seeks to focus on the needs of end users by narrowing the gap between the designer and user in ways that are intrinsically user-based (Koskinen & Battarbee, 2007).

There are numerous discussions related to empathy (Heyes, 2018; Kalisch, 1973; Snow, 2000), its relation to design and empathic design (Fulton Suri, 2007; Koskinen & Battarbee, 2007; Koskinen, 2007; Kouprie & Sleeswijk Visser, 2009; Leonard & Rayport, 1997; Mattelmäki et al., 2014; Smeenk et al., 2019), empathic leadership (Badea & Pan☒, 2010; Deliu, 2019; Dewey, 2020; Sanchez, 2018; Tzouramani, 2017), and empathic listening in management (Gearhart & Maben, 2019; Marques et al., 2011; Parks, 2015). Despite this, the nature of an empathic organization and the way in which organizations can become more receptive to empathic development approaches remain to be studied in more detail.

The objective of this paper is to understand what an empathic organization means and how an organization should evolve to be able to use service design as an empathic development approach. In discussing the empathic development approach in this research paper, the author refers to service design as an empathic practice and development methodology that enables one to design with the customer, internal stakeholders and external stakeholders. The research question addressed in this chapter is: How can an organization evolve into being more receptive to service design as an empathic development approach?

DOI: 10.4324/9781003227557-16

The organization discussed in this case study is a multinational manufacturing corporation with approximately 60,000 employees across the globe. The corporation structure is similar to that of other manufacturing businesses and matrix organizations. Prior to the use of service design, the innovation and development strategies of the corporation had been mostly product-related. In that sense, end users had been the main source of information for designers. In addition, sales staff had given feedback to product development as reactive responses to customer requests from the field. Service design entered the corporation in 2014, and it became officially a part of research and development (R&D) in 2016. Owing to service design, business customers became more systematically involved in the early phases of service development.

The participating corporation is studied through events that occurred during 2005–2014 before the launch of service design in September 2014. The major events are reviewed by means of event listing, which was chronologically assembled based on 12 semi-structured qualitative interviews selected from the code group Organization Readiness for Service Design that consists of 119 codes. In addition, explanation building has been used to get a broader understanding of the phenomenon.

The findings presented in this paper suggest that in order for an organization to become more empathic, the following is required: (a) customer-centric project initiatives and active people enabling a change of mindset from non-customer-centric thinking to designing with customers, (b) organizational learning and strong support from the top-level management, and (c) a top-level vision. When all this is in order, the change can be implemented through management and other practicalities. In addition, societal changes may affect changes within organizations based on the direction where society is headed.

Organizational empathy: An empathic/empathetic organization

According to the *Oxford English Dictionary*, the word *empathic* derives from the word *empathy*. The word empathic is an adjective referring to sensing or feeling affection or passion. The word *empathetic* is a later form and synonymous with the previous one. The word empathetic is used occasionally when referring to situations where a person relates to, involves or is characterized by empathy; demonstrates empathy; or shows empathy towards another (*Oxford English Dictionary*). In this research paper, the word empathic is used by the author unless she is referring to a source where the word empathetic is used. It should also be noted that the sources used in this study have not made any distinction between the two words.

Empathy in literature is mostly handled as an individual trait of a person. As argued in Chapter 1 of this book, the dimensions of empathy are classified as cognitive, affective, compassionate and kinaesthetic (Baron-Cohen & Wheelwright, 2004; Brink et al., 2011; Bloom, 2017; Riess & Neporent, 2018; Reynolds & Reason, 2012; Cuykendall et al., 2015). There is not much research on the topics of organizational empathy and empathic/empathetic organizations. Up to this point, Lei and Greer (2003) have done the most in this regard.

According to Lei and Greer (2003, p. 142), organizational empathy is a process where the organization learns and grows alongside the customer. They highlight that an empathetic organization learns from customers in close, personal interactions, and in that sense discovers or generates new ideas, concepts and designs for future offerings. Thus, every customer is seen as a source of knowledge and insights, and customers are seen as an integral part of value creation (Lei & Greer, 2003).

The author also brings forward knowing organizations and learning organizations. Knowing organizations place high emphasis on consistent, replicable and standardised practices. Customers are distant from development and the offering is dependent on the organization's worldview. Learning organizations, instead, savour knowledge-sharing, experimentation culture and continuous improvement. In these organizations customer involvement and input are encouraged in development activities. Lei and Greer (2003, p. 161) argue that knowing organizations can evolve into learning organizations, but empathetic organizations can only evolve independently due to their sophisticated services or special skills required to create unique experiences (Lei & Greer, 2003).

Nussbaum (2005, para. 5) brings forward "the empathy economy" and argues that we are moving from a knowledge economy to experience economy where understanding, empathy and problem-solving are essential skills. Goleman (1998, p. 3) discusses empathy as part of a leader's emotional leadership skillset among four other components of emotional intelligence: self-awareness, self-regulation, motivation and social skill. Hence, we can see Nussbaum and Goleman associating empathy with one's emotional leadership skills in the context of organizational work.

New and Kimbell (2013, p. 8) ask an interesting question: "Can the capacity for (different sorts of) empathy be embodied in (different sorts of) organizational 'equipment', which might be reflected at the level of processes, techniques and capabilities?" This idea of empathy as machinery within organizations gets support from Villari (2021, pp. 193–194). She highlights the need for new conceptual spaces for innovation due to the COVID-19 pandemic. According to her (Villari, 2021, pp. 193–194), designers could play an important role in organizations' personal growth by integrating empathic components so as to break internal and external silos, encourage innovation and bring in new languages, management models and practices.

Empathic maturity of an organization

There is a limited amount of literature on empathic maturity, especially from the organizational point of view. Olsen (2001, p. 37) discusses empathy in the area of nursing as a cognitive structure of an individual: "Empathetic maturity is the basis on which the feeling of empathy, as a perception of mutuality, develops." Silverman (2018, p. 297) brings up empathy in the area of social work. Practising organizational assessment helps the worker to achieve a better understanding of organizational awareness regarding organizational empathy, which enables the worker to better influence, collaborate and lead work (Silverman, 2018). When assessing an organization, one must focus on the following areas: mission and vision; organizational values; current strategic and operational plan; fiscal challenges; and leadership style of the executives (Silverman, 2018, p. 300).

Design maturity is a common term that has been in use since the Danish Design Centre developed the Design Ladder model in 2001. The Design Ladder model consists of four steps: (1) non-design; (2) design as form giving; (3) design as process; and (4) design as strategy (Danish Design Centre, 2015). The purpose of the model is to work as a tool that enables companies to illustrate and rate their use of design. Hoedemaeckers (2016) has extended the ladder with two stages: (5) Systemic change and (6) Culture. Systemic changes refer to design helping to solve complex social issues and massive industry problems, and to streamline complex ecosystems. Culture is the sixth step, as design in these days is being used to create extensive cultures in organizations while shifting the mindsets of people towards more innovation-centric thinking and leading through design (Hoedemaeckers, 2016).

Sanders (2009) discusses the transition of the organization from designing *for* the customers and users to designing *with* them. She wonders why it is so hard for organizations to accomplish and why it takes so long. To find an answer, she explores co-creation on a large scale in terms of culture, mindsets, methodology, methods, tools and techniques. By culture she refers to learnt beliefs, values and behaviours, while a mindset is more of an attitude held by a person. She argues that mindset is the most critical element, because in an organization, designing with the customer requires people who think it makes sense to do so. Once this mindset is there, processes and culture can start to change (Sanders, 2009).

Junginger and Sangiorgi's (2009) argumentation is in line with that of Sanders (2009). According to Junginger and Sangiorgi (2009), transformative insights are needed in the areas of assumptions, values, norms and behaviours to generate genuine interest and commitment and thereby a link between design efforts and the organization. To achieve this, building trust is required throughout the process of co-creating potential visions based on external rewards and the internal positive traits of an organization. According to the authors, this happens through a reflective process that enables learning as the main result (Junginger & Sangiorgi, 2009, p. 7). In addition, Pruitt and Adlin (2006) argue that an organization is more likely to succeed with empathic design efforts if there is some previous experience of design activities, if the people in the organization are user-focused and if the people think about and communicate with customers and users.

Research design

The author of this chapter has worked as a service designer in the organization under discussion, and the methodology of this research is mainly based on an exploratory case study. According to Yin (2009), there are exploratory, explanatory and descriptive case studies in addition to comparative, single- and multiple-case studies. A case study is applicable when attempting to answer the research questions *who*, what, *where, how* and *why* (Yin, 2009, p. 9).

Yin (2009, p. 4) states that case study is a method that allows the researcher to retain the holistic and meaningful features of real-life events, and he does not make any distinction between the phenomenon and its real-life context. Instead, Yin (2009, p. 18) highlights the mutual dependency between the context and the phenomenon: "the boundaries between phenomenon and context are not clearly evident."

Merriam and Tisdell (2015, p. 37) refer to case study as "an in-depth description of a bounded system". They argue that the most important feature of a case study is the delimitation of the subject of the study, the case (Merriam & Tisdell, 2015, p. 38). The unit of analysis determines if a study is a case study, not the topic under investigation (Merriam & Tisdell, 2015, pp. 38–39). On the other hand, Stake (2005, p. 443) argues that a case study means choosing what is to be studied instead of making a methodological choice. In a case study the focus is on the individual case, and on the experiential knowledge related to its social context (Stake, 2005, pp. 443–444).

The results of this research follow Yin's (2009) and Stake's (2005) descriptions of context dependency, since the topic under study is seen as socially constructed in its context, time and place, and as natural and unique for the participating organization. The study discussed in this paper has no pre-determined outcome, which is why an extensive and in-depth understanding about the topic is needed to build causal links. Thus, the research follows the inductive research approach.

Data collection

Altogether 33 semi-structured interviews were conducted during the summer of 2018: 23 individual interviews, eight pair interviews and two group interviews with three interviewees in each. The interviews involved a total of 45 participants from various departments and from all organizational levels, excluding the company CEO. The aim of the interviews was to get a holistic understanding of the evolvement and impacts of service design in the participating organization. The findings presented in this paper are based on 12 semi-structured interviews. They were selected from the code group Organization Readiness for Service Design, which was examined as the main unit of analysis.

Participants

The 12 interviews had 15 participants. There were ten individual interviews, one group interview with three interviewees and one pair interview. Seven of the participants came from the R&D department: two design directors, three design managers and two design specialists. The rest of the interviewees represented various departments of the organization: two executive board members, a head of service transformation, two chiefs of business development, an information technology (IT) director and two customer experience specialists. All of the interviewees were chosen based on their involvement in service design-led projects.

Data analysis

The data analysis was carried out in two phases. During the first phase, all 33 interviews went through two coding rounds, Descriptive Coding and Concept Coding. The aim was to use computer-assisted qualitative data analysis software (Atlas.ti) to find out the conceptual themes that arise from the data. As a result, 24 code groups were formed. In the second phase, the conceptual code theme Organization Readiness for Service Design was chosen as the main unit of analysis for further investigation. Event listing and explanation building were used as analysis techniques to compile the findings.

The first phase: Coding

According to Harding (2013, p. 82), codes are important tools when conducting a thematic analysis. The first round of coding followed the rules of Descriptive Coding. Saldaña (2016, p. 102) notes that "Descriptive Coding summarizes in a word or short phrase – most often a noun – the basic topic of a passage of qualitative data." The aim in this study was to stay open for the empirical data and to see what themes and topics arise, although the interviews were semi-structured. In the end of the first coding round, the number of codes was 1,207. The codes were either words or short phrases representing the topics under discussion.

There also exists critique against Descriptive Coding: "[T]he noun-based codes of this method will not reveal very much insight into participants' minds" (Saldaña, 2016, p. 102). For this reason, the second coding round followed the rules of Concept Coding. According to Saldaña (2016, p. 119), Concept Coding is "analytic coding", which assigns meanings at the meso and macro levels. The concepts were described using short phrases or words to denote broader meanings, as is typically done in concept coding (Saldaña, 2016, p. 119).

After the second coding round, altogether 24 code groups emerged based on the concepts that emerged from the Concept Coding. Once the direction of the research became clear, the code group Organization Readiness for Service Design was chosen for further analysis as the main unit of analysis. Thus, the second phase of the analysis could start.

The second phase: Event listing and explanation building

During the second round of analysis, 119 codes from the main unit of analysis, Organization Readiness for Service Design, were reviewed and restructured.

This phase of the coding process is critical when searching for commonalities. "The researcher needs to look for connections between codes which were not initially obvious" (Harding, 2013, p. 92). In doing so, a clear narrative began to take shape. Categories of codes started to emerge as embedded units of analysis.

Myers (2009, p. 211) discusses a narrative analysis: "Traditionally, a narrative requires a plot, as well as some coherence. It has some sort of ordered sequence, often in linear form, with a beginning, middle, and end." This is what occurred when reviewing the 119 codes. Clear divisions of codes emerged based on how service design as a phenomenon has evolved in the corporation:

1 the time before service design was a part of the corporation;
2 how the corporation starts to evolve once service design has been introduced (early use of service design);
3 how the corporation continues to evolve in terms of leadership practices, management practices and culture after the service design approach has been used for some time (use of service design).

The first code category, *the time before service design was a part of the corporation*, was placed under further analysis. Twelve of the 33 interviews provided data for this category. Event listing was used as an analysis technique to track sequences of the organization's events. According to Miles and Huberman (1994, p. 111), concrete happenings are arranged chronologically into a series of events in event listing. The chronological order of events took shape based on the narrative of the interview data in the first code category. This was done to form an understanding of the major events of the organization that induced it to choose service design as an empathic development approach.

The explanation building method was used in the second analysis to build a broader understanding of the material. Explanation building is an iterative process where causal links are searched in the empirical data (Yin, 2009, p. 141). The same interview data as was used in the event listing of the first code category provided the basis for explanation building. These two techniques have formed the basis for the findings that are presented next.

Maturing towards an empathic organization

In this chapter, the motivations that led the participating organization to become more empathic and to take service design as an empathic development approach are viewed through events and stages of evolvement that the organization has undergone during the period 2005–2014. Figure 13.1 presents the major events and customer-centric actions of the organization during the ten years.

Below, the themes discovered in the narrative of the interview material are discussed in further detail. Explanation building was used as the technique of analysis. The order of the themes correlates with the chronology of the event

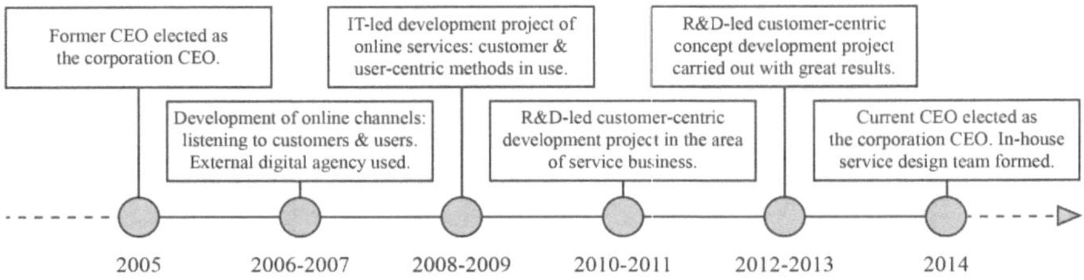

Figure 13.1 Event listing of the major events and customer-centric development actions of the organization during 2005–2014.

listing. In addition, the themes are addressed in relation to the theory that was discussed in Chapter 1. The aim is that the findings provide us a better understanding of the research gap referred to in the research question of this paper: How can an organization evolve into being more receptive to service design as an empathic development approach?

Sanders (2009) argues that in designing with customers, the mindset and attitude of those who support it are the most critical elements. The findings of this study support this notion. **In order for an organisation to become more empathic, a change of mindset is critical**, but before the mindset can be changed, organizational learning and trust building with the top-level management must occur first. Once the attitude and mindset are there, processes and culture can start to change (Sanders, 2009). Next, the stages through which a change of mindset occurs in the organization under study are discussed more closely under the following themes that have emerged from the empirical data.

In order for an organisation to become more empathic, customer-centric project initiatives and active people are required to facilitate learning that enables a change of mindset from non-customer-centric thinking to designing with customers. Sanders (2009) discusses the required change of mindset regarding the transition from a non-customer-centric organization to designing with the customer. This study claims that in order to achieve a change of mindset, organizational learning – especially in top-level management – must be enabled first. This can be done with the help of customer-centric project initiatives made by active personnel and potential partner organizations.

In the participating organization, user-centric development approaches had been applied in product development since the beginning of 2000, but customers had not been systematically involved. The first projects in which customer-centric service development methods were used concerned the development of online channels and services during 2006–2009. These projects were IT-led, and a digital agency brought in customer-centric methods in 2006–2007 when the channels were being developed. At that time, the term *customer experience* (CX) was introduced in the organization in the development of IT services. As a consequence, the digital platform director became a proponent of customer-centric development.

> We were working with an external digital agency who brought that approach to us. [...] at that point we were exposed to, [...] what wasn't necessarily called service design but user-centred design, and the idea that you start by listening to [...] users and customers, and then you work back from that. [...] After that I was a true believer.
>
> (n44)

After IT-led projects, an R&D-led service business development project was executed in 2010–2011 by in-house industrial designers, managers and directors. The project did not receive much attention from the top-level management, but the methods were considered valuable.

> By that time, we presented with [*name of the former design manager*] the work that was done for the UK market [...] They [*referring to top-level management*] saw the surface of it, as design is often seen as such, that design is the surface. Then we were in that category. Can we [*referring to top-level management*] get these development tools and methods, these are what we want to show for inspiration. Then they [*referring to top-level management*] said goodbye, and that was it.
>
> (n12)

Moving on to the period 2012–2013, a new customer-centric R&D-led project was executed by a design manager and a design director with a *customers and users* team to ideate new concepts based on customer needs. The idea was to test customer-centric development methods more thoroughly in order to see where they can lead. At that time there was no prior knowledge of service design in the organization. The project had to be carried out in secret, and once completed with the results available, permission had to be asked from the unit leaders to show it to the executive board. The project ended up being a huge success.

> [*Name of the executive board member*] said that this was not great, this was very great. Then he began to praise it. He had talked about it with [*name of the CEO*], saying that he cannot explain what he saw, and suggested that the CEO go and see it. Well, [*name of the CEO*] rearranged his schedules so that he could come and see it [...] Everybody came. Then we kept 70 presentations of it.
>
> (n12)

In order for an organisation to become more empathic, organizational learning and strong support from the top management are required. As highlighted in connection with the previous theme, organizational learning must be enabled first in order to achieve further support from the top management. Referring to Junginger and Sangiorgi (2009), in developing transformative insights in an organization, learning must occur as the main output. Especially learning in the top-level management is crucial, and this indeed was the result of the completed R&D-led customer-centric project experiments in the participating organization during 2010–2014.

> It stuck in [*name of the executive board member*] mind that when he had to start this new offering, he became acquainted with the matter in complete silence and then said, "This is how we will do it."
>
> (n12)

> It starts with the management. That they understand and internalize that this is the right way to go.
>
> (n27)

> [*Name of the executive board member*] was the driving force, and [*name of the CEO*] of course, too, because [*name of the CEO*] wanted differentiation in the area of services, but it concretely came through that [*name of the executive board member*] wanted this. [...] He created those conditions in a certain way.
>
> (n34)

The findings above are in line with those of Pruitt and Adlin (2006), who claimed that an organization is more likely to succeed with empathic design efforts if there is some previous experience of design activities. In addition, the successful projects facilitated the building of trust (Junginger & Sangiorgi, 2009) between the design specialists, managers and top-level management. Top-level organizational learning through project experimentation supported trust building, and hence value- and norm-related insights typically found in the management of knowing organizations started to emerge. Thus, the lessons learnt from the executed customer-centric projects started to strengthen a trust in customer-centric development. This, in turn, increased a readiness for approaching service design from the viewpoint of empathic development.

In order for an organization to become more empathic, a top-level vision is needed, after which the change can be implemented through management and other practicalities. As discussed, trust is needed throughout the process to enable a change of mindset, but co-creating visions based on external rewards and internal positive traits are also needed in the generation of transformative insights (Junginger & Sangiorgi, 2009). The empirical data support this notion. New visions of what can be achieved through service design as an empathic and customer-centric approach had formed in the mind of an executive board member based on the lessons learnt from the executed project experiments. Once the visions had emerged and a change of mindset occurred in the top management, organizational practicalities and decision making came into play in terms of investments, teams, expertise, collaboration and practical facilitation of customer-centric projects.

> Changing the operating model must start from the management, but once the willingness has emerged […], it requires a lot of facilitation. […] Both are needed, willingness and a direction and then practical facilitation.
>
> (n34)

> I guess if we want to have it widespread, and not in one single project, it requires leadership, clarity about the direction where we want to go with it. And then, of course, it requires thinking how you build the teams and expertise and […] how you make them collaborate with the rest of the organization.
>
> (n30)

All in all, after ten years and after accruing knowledge from four customer-centric project experiments, the situation reached a point in 2014 where more empathic development approaches started to be favoured within the organization under study: (a) the current CEO had just been elected, and he was driven to differentiate the services from those of other producers; (b) the executive board member had become acquainted with customer-centric ways of working and had the willingness to engage in it; and (c) two leaders of service business had a strong desire to do things differently. The executive board member in question was the leaders' superior, so he was able to clear the path for them.

> It happened at that point because [*name of the CEO*] was adamant, [*name of the executive board member*] had the willingness and we were maybe the only few people […] who had an urge to do things, like in principle, a bit differently. Goddamn it, let's do things differently than what the dinosaurs here have done the last 30 years, […]. This kind of mentality.
>
> (n34)

Looking at the ten-year time span, one might agree with the leader who stated: "As good things always are, it's a sum of many things, sometimes the stars get aligned in history" (n34). Organizational learning had occurred, new visions had been created and a former design manager had thereby been given a mandate to form an in-house service design team that kicked off their pilot project on 1 September 2014. Hence, the people and abilities were in place to start the implementation of customer-centric development.

> Then there was [*name of the former design manager*] and all the others there, and that group fit in the picture really well, in my opinion. Maybe that was the key to the solution, really. That the chain went from necessity to hard will, a will to do things differently, and there was a group of people who were capable of starting to play the game with us real fast.
>
> (n34)

Still, it was not until the first pilot project was finished that the corporation management was convinced about service design as an empathic development approach.

> In our case [*the project name*] was a successful pilot, and there was a board-level sponsor, [*name of the executive board member*], and on account of him, the other board members were convinced that this was the right way to act.
>
> (n27)

In addition to the themes discussed above, the empirical data set shows that **based on the direction where society is headed, societal changes affect the changes taking place in organizations by reforming their business from selling products to selling data**. The market share and significance of digital services have grown. The shift is also visible in the participating organization, since it is evolving into the direction of software business. Instead of selling products, they are starting to sell data. There is a need for customer-centric and holistically empathic development approaches that consider the organization as whole, understand the needs and values of customers, and construe those needs and values as new service opportunities, processes and systems.

> The share of the service is growing and its importance is growing and it is also easier to increase profitability.
>
> (n1)

> We are becoming more of a software company, and the services are also more abstract. What has been done now, service design has helped us.
>
> (n27)

> We started to think in the company about the voice of the customer, how we measure the [...] input and feedback from the customers constantly, and how it flows back into our processes and systems.
>
> (n44)

The societal transformation from product- to service-centricity and, eventually, competition have driven the participating organization to find new growth opportunities in the area of services to reinforce differentiation: "There was a necessity in services to find new growth, new competitiveness and differentiation. [...] We may not have been looking for service design per se, but [...] that's where it started from" (n34).

Conclusions

A change of mindset is critical in order to enable an organization to evolve towards empathy, especially if the organization is a traditional knowing organization. This research paper follows the argument of Lei and Greer (2003) that an organization can evolve from a traditional knowing organization to a learning organization. What remains unclear, and needs further research, is whether knowing and learning organizations can evolve into being truly empathic instead of an empathic organization only being able to evolve independently, as Lei and Greer (2003) argue.

A change of attitude and mindset is only the starting point on a path towards an empathic organization. Management and practicalities also need to be addressed in order to implement the change. Overall, more research is required to understand how an organization evolves once empathic development approaches, such as service design, have been adopted. It is also worth studying how an organization-wide alignment can be carried out in a large matrix organization in terms of its culture, management models, practices, operational processes and systems, project management, human resources (HR) and training to enable a transition into an empathic organization.

Summary 1: Lessons learned that can contribute to the organisational or business context

In order for an organization to evolve into an empathic one, it is crucial to effect a change of mindset among the top-level management. This enables a transition to designing *with* customers instead of designing *for* them. These notions are in line with the findings of Sanders (2009). To enable a change of mindset, first, customer-centric project initiatives and active people are required. Second, organizational learning and strong support from the top-level management are needed to advance customer-centric development. Third, a top-level vision is necessary. And finally, management, practicalities and the implementation of customer-centric development must be addressed. In addition to these, societal changes may affect the changes taking place in an organization.

Summary 2: Contribution to organisational or business knowledge or practices

This exploratory case study of a multinational manufacturing corporation increases our understanding of how an organization can evolve into being more receptive to service design as an empathic development approach. The results of the study suggest that in order for an organization to become more empathic, organizational learning of what empathic development approaches mean in terms of internal traits and external rewards (Junginger & Sangiorgi, 2009) must occur first. This enables the creation of potential visions and transformative insights. Once this is understood, a change of mindset into understanding why it is sensible to design with customers can take place.

References

Badea, L., & Pană, N. A. (2010). The role of empathy in developing the leader's emotional intelligence. *Theoretical & Applied Economics*, 17 (2), 69–78.

Baron-Cohen, S., & Wheelwright, S. (2004). The empathy quotient: An investigation of adults with Asperger syndrome or high functioning autism, and normal sex differences. *Journal of Autism Development and Disorders*, 34 (2), 163–175. https://doi.org/10.1023/B:JADD.0000022607.19833.00.

Bloom, P. (2017). *Against empathy: The case for rational compassion*. Random House.

Brink, T. T., Urton, K., Held, D., Kirilina, E., Hofmann, M., Klann-Delius, G., Jacobs, M. A., & Kuchinke, L. (2011). The role of orbitofrontal cortex in processing empathy stories in 4- to 8-year-old children. *Frontiers in Psychology*, 2, 80.

Cuykendall, S., Soutar-Rau, E., Cochrane, K., Freiberg, J., & Schiphorst, T. (2015). *Simply spinning: Extending current design frameworks for kinesthetic empathy*. In Proceedings of the Ninth International Conference on Tangible, Embedded, and Embodied Interaction (pp. 305–312).

Danish Design Centre (2015). *The design ladder: Four steps of design use*. https://danskdesigncenter.dk/en/design-ladder-four-steps-design-use.

Deliu, D. (2019). Empathetic leadership – Key element for inspiring strategic management and a visionary effective corporate governance. *Journal of Emerging Trends in Marketing and Management*, 1 (1). http://www.etimm.ase.ro/?p=364.

Dewey, B. (2020). The Power of empathetic and collaborative leadership. *Library Leadership and Management*, 34 (2), 1–6. https://journals.tdl.org/llm/index.php/llm/article/view/7427.

Fulton Suri, J. (2007). Empathic design: Informed and inspired by other people's experience. In I. Koskinen, K. Battarbee, & T. Mattelmäki (Eds.), *Empathic design: User experience in product design* (pp. 51–58). Edita IT Press.

Gearhart, C. C., & Maben, S. K. (2019) Active and empathic listening in social media: What do stakeholders really expect. *International Journal of Listening*. doi:10.1080/10904018.2019.1602046.

Goleman, D. (1998). What makes a leader? *Harvard Business Review*, 76 (6), 93–102.

Harding, J. (2013). *Qualitative data analysis from start to finish*. SAGE Publishing.

Heyes, C. (2018). Empathy is not in our genes. *Neuroscience & Biobehavioral Reviews*, 95, 499–507. https://doi-org.ezproxy.ulapland.fi/10.1016/j.neubiorev.2018.11.001.

Hoedemaeckers, B. (2016). Are you getting the most out of design? *Design for Business*. https://medium.com/design-for-business/are-you-getting-the-most-out-of-design-f2f47caf2339.

Junginger, S., & Sangiorgi, D. (2009). *Service design and organizational change. Bridging the gap between rigour and relevance*. IASDR09 conference, Seoul.

Kalisch, B. (1973). What is empathy? *The American Journal of Nursing*, 73 (9), 1548–1552. doi:10.2307/3422614.

Koskinen, I. (2007). Empathic design in methodic terms. In I. Koskinen, K. Battarbee, & T. Mattelmäki (Eds.), *Empathic design: User experience in product design* (pp. 59–65). Edita IT Press.

Koskinen, I., & Battarbee, K. (2007). Introduction to user experience and empathic design. In I. Koskinen, K. Battarbee, & T. Mattelmäki (Eds.), *Empathic design: User experience in product design* (pp. 37–50). Edita IT Press.

Kouprie, M., & Sleeswijk Visser, F. (2009). A framework for empathy in design: Stepping into and out of the user's life. *Journal of Engineering Design*, 20 (5), 437–448. doi:10.1080/09544820902875033.

Lei, D., & Greer, C. R. (2003). The empathetic organization. *Organizational Dynamics*, 32 (2), 142–164. https://doi-org.ezproxy.ulapland.fi/10.1016/S0090-2616(03)00015-9.

Leonard, D., & Rayport, J. F. (1997). Spark innovation through empathic design. *Harvard Business Review*, 75 (6), 102–113.

Marques, J., Dhiman, S., & King, R. (2011). Empathetic listening as a management tool. *Business Renaissance Quarterly*, 6 (1), 15–20, 65–66.

Mattelmäki, T., Vaajakallio, K. and Koskinen I. (2014). What happened to empathic design? *Design Issues*, 30 (1), 67–77.

Merriam, S. B., & Tisdell, E. J. (2015). *Qualitative research: A guide to design and implementation*. ProQuest Ebook Central. https://ebookcentral-proquest-com.ezproxy.ulapland.fi.

Miles, M. B., & Huberman, A. M. (1994). *Qualitative data analysis: An expanded sourcebook* (2nd ed.). SAGE Publications.

Myers, M. D. (2009). *Qualitative research in business and management*. SAGE Publications.

New, S., & Kimbell, L. (2013). *Chimps, designers, consultants and empathy: A 'theory of mind' for service design*. 2nd Cambridge Academic Design Management Conference, 4–5 September.

Nussbaum, B. (2005). The empathy economy. *Business Week Online*. https://bengin.net/paperse/empathy_economy.htm.

Olsen, D. P. (2001). Empathetic maturity: Theory of moral point of view in clinical relations. *Advances in Nursing Science*, 24 (1), 36–46. https://doi-org.ezproxy.ulapland.fi/10.1097/00012272-200109000-00006.

Oxford University Press. *Oxford English Dictionary OED*. Oxford University Press.

Parks, E. S. (2015). Listening with empathy in organizational communication. *Organization Development Journal*, 33 (3), 9–22.

Prestes Joly, M., Teixeira, J. G., Patrício, L., & Sangiorgi, D. (2019). Leveraging service design as a multidisciplinary approach to service innovation. *Journal of Service Management*, 30 (6), 681–715. https://doi-org.ezproxy.ulapland.fi/10.1108/JOSM-07-2017-0178.

Pruitt, J., & Adlin, T. (2006). *The persona lifecycle: Keeping people in mind throughout product design*. ProQuest Ebook Central. https://ebookcentral-proquest-com.ezproxy.ulapland.fi.

Reynolds, D., & Reason, M. (Eds.). (2012). *Kinesthetic empathy in creative and cultural practices*. Intellect Books.

Riess, H., & Neporent, L. (2018). *The empathy effect: Seven neuroscience-based keys for transforming the way we live, love, work, and connect across differences*. Sounds True.

Saldaña, J. (2016). *The coding manual for qualitative researchers* (3rd ed.). SAGE Publications.

Sanchez, P. (2018). The secret to leading organizational change is empathy. *Harvard Business Review*. https://hbr.org/2018/12/the-secret-to-leading-organizational-change-is-empathy.

Sanders, E. (2009). Exploring co-creation on a large scale: Designing for new healthcare environments. In P. J. Stappers (Ed.), *Designing for, with and from user experiences*. Symposium, Faculty of Industrial Design Engineering, TU/Delft, Delft, The Netherlands.

Sangiorgi, D. & Prendiville, A. (2017). *Designing for service: Key issues and new directions*. Bloomsbury Academic.

Silverman, E. (2018). Moving beyond collaboration: A model for enhancing social work's organizational empathy. *Social Work*, 63 (4), 297–304. https://doi-org.ezproxy.ulapland.fi/10.1093/sw/swy034.

Smeenk, W., Sturm, J., Terken, J., & Eggen, B. (2019). A systematic validation of the Empathic Handover approach guided by five factors that foster empathy in design. *CoDesign*, 15 (4), 308–328. doi:10.1080/15710882.2018.1484490.
Snow, N. (2000). Empathy. *American Philosophical Quarterly*, 37 (1), 65–78.
Stake, R. E. (2005). Qualitative Case Studies. In N. K. Denzin & Y. S. Lincoln (Eds.), *The SAGE handbook of qualitative research* (3rd ed., pp. 443–466). SAGE Publications.
Stickdorn, M., & Schneider, J. (2011). *This is service design thinking: Basics-tools-cases*. BIS.
Tzouramani, E. (2017). Leadership and empathy. In J. Marques & S. Dhiman (Eds.), *Leadership Today* (pp. 197–216). Springer.
Villari, B. (2021). The empathic (r)evolution. Lessons learned from Covid-19 to design at the community, organization, and governmental levels. *Strategic Design Research Journal*, 14 (1), 187–198. https://doi-org.ezproxy.ulapland.fi/10.4013/sdrj.2021.141.16.
Yin, R. K. (2009). *Case study research: Design and methods* (4th ed.). SAGE Publications.
Yu, E., & Sangiorgi, D. (2018). Service design as an approach to implement the value cocreation perspective in new service development. *Journal of Service Research*, 21 (1), 40–58. https://doi-org.ezproxy.ulapland.fi/10.1177/1094670517709356.

14 Design, empathy and autonomy

Reflections on theory and practice

Bruna Montuori, Maria Luiza Viana, Rosana Vasques and Maria Cecilia Loschiavo dos Santos

Introduction

For decades, empathy has been investigated in the social sciences and related fields dealing with social relations (Bednarek-Gilland, 2015) while also being brought to design to amplify the perspectives of researchers and practitioners when designing for a specific public or user. In a broad understanding, empathy, as defined by the dictionary, refers to 'the psychological identification with or vicarious experiencing of the feelings, thoughts or attitudes of another'.[1] The idea of seeing yourself in someone else's shoes[2] has been absorbed by design theory and practice with the aim to expand the imagination boundaries of practitioners, making them closer to the lived experiences of the subjects they design for and with (Fulton Suri, 2003).

In the institutionalised spaces where designers address problems or issues requiring solutions, empathy is helpful in supporting the understanding of how users are feeling and how they are experiencing the material world (see Battarbee et al., 2018). Design researcher Jane Fulton Suri (2003, p. 53) argued that as much as people come from different cultures and environments 'with different worldviews and lifestyles', their experiences and behaviours might show similar patterns, providing useful insights to designers. Fulton Suri (2003, p. 54) explored empathy as a method for design practice, unveiling what observation alone cannot provide—a human connection that allows practitioners 'to imagine new and better possibilities for people'.

Envisioning empathy as intuitive and interpretive abilities that open the space for imagination in design, Fulton Suri (2003) spoke of the topic from North American and European conceptions of life and society. As we bring these conceptions to a South American context, we observed that certain methodological approaches cannot be prescribed as formulas. Doing so ends in enforcing worldviews and social practices on subjects who have carried trauma throughout generations. Through these case studies, we depart from decolonial perspectives to reflect on empathy as a method and practice, considering its implications in design research. By decolonial perspectives, we refer to the ideas encompassing ontologies and epistemologies beyond Western boundaries that have been historically erased and excluded (Escobar, 2018).

DOI: 10.4324/9781003227557-17

With these concerns at the centre of the debate, in this chapter, we discuss empathy based on two case studies held in the urban contexts of Brazilian peripheries that are known for their legacies of social exclusion. These spaces are on the edge of capitalism, where people have been obliged to project their own lives as a form of survival (Loschiavo, 2014). Because many design researchers are educated under Eurocentric perspectives outside of Europe, we argue for another understanding of empathy in collective design processes and research. Focusing on participatory research practices, we have observed the need to incorporate a more critical account of empathy in our practices and research activities. We argue that empathy alone is not an accurate method for understanding the lived experiences of subjects; it overlooks the ways life trajectories shape and affect the perspectives of subjects, which, without a critical gaze, might lead to a naive and alienated design process.

Considering these thoughts, we ask the following: In which ways could our research practices as designers embrace ongoing collective community experiences and coproduce knowledge with them? Where would empathy sit in these terms? Is it possible to forge dialogical and empathetic design actions to support the issues affecting the basic rights of these populations? The chapter emerges from Maria Luiza and Bruna's doctoral investigations, which focus on the collective action of marginalised communities transforming their spaces of dwelling through art, culture, knowledge production and the recognition of identities and memories. One case is Morro do Papagaio, a favela[3] located in Belo Horizonte, where residents work collectively to support community demands. In this case, we explore the project 'Rua do Livro' (Book's Street), which started through in-person activities and later moved to digital engagement. The other case is Maré, a set of 16 favelas located in Rio de Janeiro, where the local organisation Redes da Maré works to guarantee the rights of its residents. For this case, we focus on the project 'Posters for the Right to Public Security and Access to Justice', which emerged from year-long research carried out by members of the NGO on the quality of public security in Maré.

Both cases illustrate experiences of participation in person that transitioned to virtual community networks, here focusing on the processes of local engagement. Our exchange with these groups was held prior to the COVID-19 pandemic, allowing in-person interactions that are less constrained compared with digital communication. It is worth noting that the authors of this chapter are not originally from the favelas mentioned, and this text reflects our perspective based on years of collaboration with the residents and local organisations of these sites.

This chapter is structured into three main parts. In the first part, we draw a brief reflection on the notion of empathy in design, here considering decolonial perspectives that are seeking design as a relational, critical and autonomous practice (Escobar, 2018; Quijano, 2005; Lugones, 2008). In the second part, we bring the two cases of study through two narratives—one from Maria Luiza and another from Bruna—that highlight the stories, relationships and learning exchanged in our practice with the groups. These narratives offer entry points for discussing empathy in our research practice according to the processes of design collectively established. In the third part, we bring reflections upon our experiences working with these groups, supporting our interpretation of empathy in design. These reflections are based on fieldwork experiences considering the ideas discussed in the first part of the chapter, focusing on empathy in design towards autonomy and emancipation (Freire, 2020; Escobar, 2018).

Our research methodology was based on participant observation, a technique used in ethnography in which researchers are particularly interested in understanding a specific organisation, group or community and their dynamics and challenges. In our work, we followed Caroline Gatt and Tim Ingold's (2013) approach to participant observation as a practice of ethnography that sets researchers free from the descriptive role, allowing them to deeply engage with the reality of the subjects. This notion of participant observation entails an attitude not based on the objectivity of describing the fieldwork, collecting data and then leaving. It entails a practice focused on engagement and correspondences between the anthropologist and subjects here brought to the design research practice. Ingold (2017) touched upon this practice when describing anthropology as not interpreting or explaining others' behaviours. Rather, it is about sharing presence and seeking future possibilities of correspondence with participants, 'researching with' rather than 'about' them (Ingold, 2017).

Pain et al. (2007) also supported these ideas when they posited that participatory engagements could go beyond the researcher trying to give visibility to the groups they are working within. They refer to a research practice based on knowledge coproduction in which new practices emerge from the encounter of researchers and subjects. Within our research processes, we sought to embrace methodologies that were not rigid, attaining these theoretical observations that could support a more organic and fluid research practice.

Brief reflection on empathy in design considering decolonial perspectives

This chapter focuses on empathy in design according to our experiences as design researchers working in the urban peripheries of Brazil. To bring our perspective to this topic—from the Anglo-Eurocentric gaze to a Latin American view—we depart from those theories reflecting other worldviews outside the canon. In Latin America, Western domination has resonated in our historical constitution, based on the control of bodies and subjectivities through classifications of race, gender, sexuality and labour. This control is based on an extractivist logic of capital accumulation that perpetuates the power relations embedded in colonisation, what Aníbal Quijano (2005) coined 'coloniality'. The latter is still present in our knowledge production, subjectivities, social, cultural, economic and labour relations, foremost in the ways we design our processes and products.

Walter Mignolo and Madina Tlostanova (2016) reminded us that modernity underpinned the ideas of universality, scientificism, progress and development as part of capitalist production. The authors from decolonial studies[4] have argued the knowledge, worldviews, subjectivities and experiences of those outside of this inscription have been obliterated as subjects and knowledge holders. Such ideas reveal the supremacy of Europe—after World War II—of North America, hence defining the social geography of capitalism (Quijano, 2005).

Given that the current geopolitical scenario is defined by these categorical differences, Global North nations sustain their hegemonic power through globalisation and neoliberal strategies, maintaining the relations of violence and appropriation inherited from colonisation (Escobar, 2018). As these strategies deepen social inequality, they reinforce segregation and binarism (of rich and poor, developed and underdeveloped, and what is and is not knowledge), as discussed by Ahmed Ansari (2019), by means of design, underpinning the practice to Anglo-European worldviews and ontologies. The authors' perspectives explored above confirm the growing need to recognise different forms of acting, living and relating to the world as well as how these are accounted by design.

Design and empathy within and beyond Western thought

In this context, we understand design as a field of practice rooted in Western thought, which emerged from modern values to organise the material culture of an industrialised society (Ansari, 2019). One may point to the implications of importing design practice and education to a country marked by a legacy of slavery and centuries of colonisation. Because design shapes our material culture, it endorses the dominant social values through our uses and experiences and through the ways the design process is carried out.

Arturo Escobar (2018) highlighted that design is based on the social values that do not encompass the myriad worldviews and ontologies within the Global South. Addressing design as an ontological practice based on our way of being in the world and how we perceive and relate to it, Escobar (2018) argued for a pluriversal view in the field; he stressed the urgency to support autonomous forms of living and networks of care that protect marginalised groups whose histories have been consistently erased.

Thus, we propose a change in perspective that breaks with the logic of universality, repositioning our research practice and focusing it on relationships. It is a perspective that acknowledges memories, histories, habits, rituals, forms of care and affect beyond materiality and the logics of production and consumption. It is a way of understanding design as a relational, dialogical, critical and autonomous practice that concerns collective forms of living, moving, gathering, expressing and connecting. At the same time, we refer to a practice that goes beyond the production of the material world, supporting other ways of living to keep them alive throughout time. Such a design practice is pervaded by interpersonal relations guided by a dialogical construction between subjects, including designers.

Without prescribed and ready-made methodologies, we start from the idea of building collective processes with groups already engaged in actions and projects that correspond to the needs and potentialities of their contexts. We argue that a nonhegemonic perspective in design is only possible through deep engagement with the social realities of these communities, where people project their lives through forms of cooperation and resistance against top-down violations.

We understand that design is not only able to contribute through products and production processes, but also that it is aligned to the political demands and visions of these groups. Thus, we investigate design as a process that can give shape to these collective experiences as a way of cogenerating knowledges, concepts and values in territories historically invisible. Our perspective dialogues with Escobar's (2018) reasoning, which supports the idea of design as an autonomous field, one that is independent from its shackles to the aspects of productivity, functionality, industry and market driven. Escobar (2018) suggested a turn in design, focusing on matters of political and cultural autonomy, whether in theory or practice, as a creative way of coping with the contemporary civilisational crisis.

According to Escobar's (2018) perspective, design stems from rationalist and cartesian traditions in which the ethics of reason is the predominant one. He seeks to break with these legacies by means of an ontological design, which is conceived of as autonomy and plural ways of living not determined by capitalist ideals. Along these lines, we seek to understand empathy and its role in the design processes embedded in the context of community engagement fighting for urban struggles.

With the aim to approximate designers to the lives and experiences of users, empathy supports the design process in making products and services meet consumers' needs. Designers have been using the tools and frameworks that promote more careful approaches in relation to the experience of the 'other'. As a tool, Merlijn Kouprie and Froukje Visser (2009) discussed how empathy can be applied to design through games, storytelling and communication techniques that stimulate ideation through imagination.

Drawing from these above-mentioned perspectives, we seek a perspective that moves the focus to the user, who is seen as a passive consumer or depository of ideas, to an active agent who has self-determination in their choices and decision making. Furthermore, we embrace empathy in design as a practice of self-reflection for designers in which they comprehend the differences and dissent throughout the design process. Still, it is worth noting that our experiences revolve around third-sector and informal community groups dealing directly with the needs of their communities outside market interests.

Carolyn Pedwell (2012), working on feminist theory and empathy, moved away from empathy centred on knowledge, accuracy and prediction, formatting another kind of imposition from the researcher towards research participants. Analysing empathy within the current political systems of transnationality and neoliberalism, which are based on systemic oppression, she highlighted the problems of applying empathy without considering the implications of power imbalances and cultural differences. In her words, she mentioned the following:

> When empathy, employed by those occupying positions of political and social privilege within transnational hierarchies of power, becomes a technology of access to cultural 'others' which, with increasing accuracy, can produce increasing powers of prediction, it is susceptible to functioning primarily as a technique of discipline, regulation and even annihilation.
> (Pedwell, 2012, p. 127)

One could question the implications of applying empathy in design. As a tool, we believe empathy is not enough to understand the complexity of oppression systems, legacies of exclusion and the everyday knowledge that residents carry through their lived experiences. Empathy within the dualist perspective, as discussed by Escobar (2018), can only provide a fragmented understanding of the realities that carry intergenerational traumas. Working only through fragments gives designers an incomplete understanding of subjects' lives and worldviews, risking addressing misconceptions that reinforce inequalities and impositions.

Kouprie and Visser (2009) affirmed that studies in psychology understand that the central mechanism of empathy operates from the emotional and cognitive components in highly interrelated and indivisible ways. In their approach, empathy involves a state of balance between affective and cognitive resonance. Other authors, such as Antje Bednarek-Gilland (2015), who looked at empathy within qualitative methods, also pointed out the role of emotion in research collaborations. She described empathy as 'an emotional practice' that requires 'an active, intentional and emotional intellectual endeavour' to 'feel the other person' and 'comprehend their current experience' (p. 33).

Kouprie and Visser's (2009) reflections on the emotional role of empathy are relevant to our approach because they open the space for another kind of rapport. Both cognitive and affective components are observed as a unity without looking at the research participants in compartmentalised ways. By adhering to the idea of empathy as an emotional practice and entangling both components, it unfolds as relationship forming based on dialogical relations between designers and participants (Escobar, 2018).

Akama et al. (2019) have discussed similar paths while doing participatory design with Australian Aboriginals, exploring artefacts to provoke conversations and emotion sharing. They highlighted that designers should be more engaged with subjects and their realities, not seeking to solve problems but seeking possibilities with people. Dori Tunstall (2013) also discussed empathy within decolonial thinking, questioning the consequences of design thinking and design innovation processes in communities outside of Western boundaries. She observed how categorisations and a false position of neutrality end up reinforcing hierarchies between designers and participants through an ontological imposition rebranded as innovation. Given this, Tunstall (2013) advocated for a design practice going beyond empathy, one anchored in compassion. From her perspective, compassion means the 'acceptance of the intrinsic worth of everything and the treatment of them with dignity and regard' (Tunstall, 2013, p. 245). Her ideas resonated with our aims because she has tried to break with Eurocentric conceptions of doing design, opening doors for a committed practice based on emotions and reciprocity.

Curiously, her ideas are aligned with Bednarek-Gilland's (2015) understanding of empathy as an emotional practice, providing us with potential paths for the interpretation we seek in this chapter. When we reflect on other ways of thinking about empathy in design, we position design side by side with the knowledge from the favelas, observing the multiple inequalities that appear on the surface. Design is a field that has historically tried to reach the masses through industrialisation and consumption; however, in the case of Brazil, it prioritised mainly privileged groups. At the same time, favelas can be understood as products of uneven modern urban planning that fragmented the experience of urban life, segregating people by race and income. How could designers empathise with favelas' residents when they access a range of resources and high connectivity but favela residents do not? These questions bring us to a concrete reality of what it means to act in contexts in which the state's action is repressive and racist.

Two cases of study with two community groups in Brazil

Design and engagement experience at Morro do Papagaio, Belo Horizonte

This narrative describes Maria Luiza Viana's[5] involvement in a local project named Rua do Livro Morro do Papagaio (Morro do Papagaio Street of book), an informal initiative of a group coordinated by a local community leader whose objective was to encourage reading among children and adults in the community. The proposal arose from the community leaders' observations about the lack of access to literature for the children in the community. The 'Rua do Livro' project started with the distribution of books in commercial establishments and expanded to hold itinerant events in Morro do Papagaio's public spaces. It consists of collecting books from publishers and making them available to residents. The choice of books is based on the participants' themes of interest, as previously identified within the community, including literature, cuisine, religion, gardening and health.

Maria Luiza's research began in 2018, adopting participant observation (Ingold, 2017) within all project phases. She engaged in the tasks of planning, organising and working as a graphic designer. Because of the COVID-19 outbreak in 2020, the challenge was to seek other ways of contributing with the community, here considering the context of the pandemic, and understanding that reading and sharing stories were important activities for those residents dealing with social isolation. Through a collective proposal, the project sent digital books for families to read at home and to be accessed through their phones, computers and tablets. The families without internet access received printed versions of the books in their homes.

The proposal was then directed at children, who, after reading, were encouraged to produce videos and drawings about the stories they had read. The families who participated and sent their children's contributions were gifted hardcover books. The project phases consisted of making virtual contact with the families, selecting digital books available on an online platform and sending them to the families. After their participation, the project organisers edited and disseminated the materials produced by the participants. Maria Luiza's role in the design involved planning and co-organising these phases to virtually guide the development of the project with the team, guiding the logistics and resources and activating the network of actors involved. They established direct communication with the families through virtual meetings, aiming to organise the tasks according to the schedule of the project.

Through their engagement, they were immersed in the social structure of the families and the conditions to which they were subjected in the pandemic. They identified the key people to take on the tasks by considering the literacy levels of the participants—adults and children—as well as the participants' profiles, age groups, preferences for reading, technical resources available and families' daily life dynamics. These aspects required a specific time organisation for the exchange of messages, allowing all participants to complete the stages of the project. It is worth noting the predominant participation of women in the reading activities and in the production of drawings and videos with the children. Maria Luiza supported the development of graphic pieces, videos and animations from the children's productions, supporting project dissemination.

The engagement with the participants was based on mutual trust and reciprocity that existed in the community because the participants asked neighbours, friends and relatives to join the project. As such, a solidarity network was created among the people who donated not only books, but also other care resources and hygiene kits (containing hand sanitiser and masks for COVID-19 prevention) to the families. Through reports, videos and photos, it was noticeable that reading meant a valuable moment of integration in families and was an important educational and playful activity for the children. Empathy was entangled in all stages of their collaboration, involving attentive listening to the social conditions of the participants and the modes of solidarity action, enabling the exercise of a flexible, open and sensitive design practice.

Acting in the fight for rights with Redes da Maré, Maré, Rio de Janeiro

The collaboration between Bruna Montuori[6] and the Redes da Maré organisation began in 2015, and since then, Montuori has been involved as a designer and researcher in different design activities, such as producing graphic materials, conducting workshops with members and residents, joining their events and proposing actions collectively. Since 2007, the NGO has worked to guarantee that residents' rights are attended to by authorities and to create a collective consciousness of rights through residents' lived experiences and stories. NGO members are mixed between residents and non-residents of various ages, working as social workers, geographers, educators, mobilisers and artists. Because of a legacy of stereotypes, many residents do not feel entitled to their rights as citizens. To create a critical perspective with residents, NGO members identify and produce counternarratives of rights based on testimonies and stories from the territory. As such, NGO members support residents in moments of trauma, fear and injustice, particularly when they are afraid of denouncing police brutality.

During her fieldwork, from September 2019 to January 2020, Montuori followed the daily activities of members working with public security. She participated in different occasions, such as placemaking in areas of trauma from police operations, film exhibitions, book launches and lectures on the impact of violence on residents' bodies and subjectivities. Their collaborations began through graphic materials, establishing a rapport beyond the limited client–designer relationship. Because she was following their work as a researcher and as a designer, they built a relationship of mutual respect in which they agreed that all materials would be produced collectively. It was an exercise of balancing the multiple tasks of the work in which they had the space to negotiate the role of design to support their goals. They invited her to coproduce a series of posters that highlighted the main information from their '2019 Bulletin of Public Security and Access to Justice'[7] (Redes da Maré, 2020). Although she did not produce the visual identity of the bulletin project, they invited her to do the posters because of her awareness of the territory dynamics and residents' gaze over violations.

As they began the process, she left the fieldwork and moved the collaboration to digital exchanges. One month before the COVID-19 outbreak, they collectively designed posters based on the residents' responses to the report that had been previously launched. They raised the main graphic points that could come up in the posters and the ways datasets could be presented in simple and visual elements. Because most members are from Maré, they had to deal with days in which their internet connections did not work, other days when police operations affected their working hours and other situations that impacted the collective process. These were very insightful moments because when members were affected by the uncertainty of things, their collaboration was also affected.

Their ways of collaborating depended on the daily occurrences of Maré, even though they were, at that stage, codesigning from a distance. At the same time, they relied on video conferencing because other digital tools for engagement were not common and reliable in terms of language, accessibility and financial access. After a few weeks of discussions, production of tests and final approval from the coordinators, the organisation members started spreading the posters throughout the territory, expecting the reactions and responses of the residents. Whenever they got feedback from the residents, they would communicate with Bruna, trying to update her on what would be better 'next time'. Knowing their collaboration would continue, she nurtured her empathetic experience as an open space for further exchange, here based on the learnings and challenges that emerged in this process.

Our interpretation of empathy as a relational and dialogical practice

The experiences with the groups reveal participatory perspectives that are embedded in dialogues and correspondences, requiring us to situate ourselves within the challenges and aspirations of the research participants. As we sought to understand the issues these communities were dealing with, relationships of trust were established in which the decisions were defined collectively. By exploring ways to revert the common logic of design, decisions, actions and solutions were not unilaterally defined from the expert's side. We explored ways to position the design knowledge and skills not as superior to the knowledge they were locally producing. At the same time, we could not rely on prescribed models and methods because both contexts are continuously dealing with uncertainty and unpredictable occasions.

Both cases show that the negotiations were more organic and fluid following the proposed projects of the group members, whose tasks and rules were established through partnerships. Such aspects were also revisited by Akama and Light (2012) when they pointed to the roles of timing and the rhythms of the different involved actors. Both cases illustrate design processes based on pre-existing demands, in which the design was articulated with local forces, their eminent issues and their modes of action. In the case of Morro do Papagaio, they were particularly concerned with the right of reading and learning for children not accessing schools during the pandemic; whereas in Maré, they were concerned with public security and access to justice within the context of police operations and conflicts.

We dealt with scenarios and peoples litigating for basic rights, which have been precluded for these populations for decades. Because we have never dealt with such experiences in our lives, we were challenged to adopt an autonomous perspective, as proposed by Escobar (2018). We sought to proactively collaborate in the construction of the residents' and members' social values—not imposing but embracing their ways of thinking—as well as cocreating the conditions that support members in achieving emancipatory and transformative practices with the residents living under precariousness and vulnerable conditions.

In the case of Morro do Papagaio, activities occurred through virtual meetings, here according to the contact established with each family and their daily lives. Together, the researcher and designer, the community leaders and families tried to understand the profile and availability of the families based on their life conditions, ages, gender and labour division, as well as access to the internet. Through reading, they aimed to gather families, propitiating that such activities are more present in the children and their parents' everyday lives. All project phases were defined from the feedback given by the families, their expectations, desires and choices and preferences in the literature.

In the case of Maré, a collective proposal emerged from an invitation from the members with the design researcher based on previous collaborations within fieldwork. Because there was an existing relationship, the client–designer relationship was challenged through another partnership based on knowledge sharing and mutual trust. To find the best language of data visualisation to inform the residents about violations, they embraced the design process, seeking ways to hold a dialogue with residents through other mediums. In this way, the design process was entirely built on territorial knowledge of how social dynamics unfold. The territory, its peoples and the evidence raised on the Bulletin of Public Security always informed the design process.

The cases highlighted the importance of active listening towards local leaders and agents regarding their experiences and strategies of identification, contact and communication with residents. As our focal points, NGO members in Maré and community leaders in Morro do Papagaio guided our collaborations because they carry a deeper understanding of the social reality of these contexts. Their commitment to support residents going through struggles reinforced our engagement, particularly when we had to move from in-person activities to virtual engagement. Although our experiences of collaboration were limited from the viewpoint of experience while dealing with members from a distance, we managed to craft collaborations on a personal level through trust and commitment, learning to respect their struggles and interpersonal dynamics.

Understanding issues such as a lack of internet connection, lack of time from participants or the unpredictability of these places showed us our position of privilege while working from our fully equipped homes. These aspects shed light on the problems of putting ourselves in the community residents' shoes, because in doing so, we would only be able to comprehend a fragment of their struggles. By embracing a perspective of otherness, we were able to harness members' and residents' strategies designed from the bottom up. These experiences provided insights into the roles of observation, dialogue and reflexivity as paths for an immersed practice informed by knowledge exchange that fosters autonomy and emancipation. They informed us that empathy requires a position of inter-relatedness (Kouprie and Visser, 2009) that does not act as a method but as an emotional practice, as suggested by Bednarek-Gilland (2015).

Empathy, here, has unfolded through personal engagement and attentive and sensitive listening that aims to hold a dialogue and share knowledge and experiences with residents according to the local dynamics, issues and everyday struggles. Thus, empathy unfolds through making and feeling with others, as posited by Freire (2020), guiding a practice that did not target objective solutions to complex social and political problems but that posited hope in the potentialities of residents, whether through reading books or through disseminating information about violations and access to rights. In these terms, empathy supported the engagement of different epistemologies that are aware of their differences, giving us the chance to understand these contexts through residents' lenses and critical awareness of social injustice, inequality and oppression, noting their personal journeys to self-determination and autonomy.

As an emotional practice, empathy fostered emancipatory ideas based on a collective set of skills, ongoing collective action and negotiations that required a conscious and critical response from subjects.

Embracing these perceptions of empathy in design, we seek to establish a relational approach with the subjects based on dialogic relationships, one that is attuned and embedded in the times and rhythms of subjects, fostering mutual respect and trust, refraining from extractivist research positions and recognising the multiple oppressions that shaped and still determine the experiences and ontologies of the subjects.

Conclusion

In this chapter, we have looked at the role of empathy in design in Global North countries and the implications of importing it as a method in contexts of the Global South. Through ideas of design beyond Western thought, we contested the imposed conceptions of design that ignore the exploitation of categories of race, gender, sexuality, labour division and home location. Looking at the work of decolonial authors in design, in particular of Escobar (2018), we highlighted his notion of autonomous design, which embraces a perspective of multiple ontologies and epistemologies breaking away from the profit-driven ideals that sustain dominant economic regimes.

As we looked in depth at the relations between empathy, design and decoloniality, we observed a potential path for our research practices that abandon empathy to achieve solutions. We noted from the works of Tunstall (2013), Bednarek-Gilland (2015) and Pedwell (2012) and the problems of applying empathy without concerning the above-mentioned categories and perspectives of fighting racism and oppression. These authors offered visions of empathy based on the emotional practices of sharing and compassion. Through our personal experiences with the residents and members from the groups of Morro do Papagaio and Maré, we unfolded such emotional practices within the limits and constraints of virtual collaborations.

From the reflections discussed from these two cases, we proposed empathy as a relational practice that can help in sustaining and giving strength to the collective action that is already flourishing within these groups. Seeking to revert the logics of profit gain and problem solution in design, we have argued for empathy as a practice enacted through context immersion and inter-relatedness, one that is deeply aware of the legacies of exclusion and how residents navigate and position themselves. Empathy as a practice refers to building relationships of mutual trust and respect, recognising the different ontologies and epistemologies entangled in design processes.

Summary 1: Lessons learned that can contribute to the organisational or business context

Empathy as a method in design research is not accurate enough to comprehend the lived experiences of people under conditions of vulnerability in the Global

South. While enacting empathy with NGOs and collectives within marginalised communities, design research requires critical revisions in terms of pedagogy and methodology, here considering the legacies of colonisation, oppression and social resistance. Drawing from collaborations in two Brazilian favelas, we interpret empathy in design as an approach based on relationship-making, mutual trust and otherness. As a practice it needs to recognise the ontologies and epistemologies entangled in research processes and in the life context of locals.

Summary 2: Contribution to organisational or business knowledge or practices

The chapter looks at participatory research experiences with third-sector organisations and self-organised groups that originated from bottom-up processes, fighting for better living conditions in their territories. Drawing from decolonial and feminist theories, our contribution reflects on empathy in design as an inaccurate method to grasp the lived experiences of people living under vulnerable circumstances in the Global South. From collaborations with two groups located in Brazilian favelas (informal settlements), we offer an interpretation for empathy in design research as an approach based on solidarity, respect and mutual trust with marginalised communities, reorienting the research practice for the autonomy of these groups.

Notes

1 Source from Dictionary.com. Retrieved from https://www.dictionary.com/browse/empathy?s=t.
2 A few authors in the area of design refers to this expression while referring to enacting empathy in design processes. See Fulton Suri (2003), Battarbee et al. (2018).
3 There are numerous ways to refer to settlements. Here, we choose to work with the term 'favela' because it is commonly used to define such spaces, particularly from the viewpoint of residents. The term has also been used by a range of scholars researching the topic. See Zaluar and Alvito (2006).
4 Here, we choose to work mainly with Latin American authors engaged with decolonial perspectives. The majority come from the research group modernity/coloniality, including names such as Arturo Escobar, Aníbal Quijano, Walter Mignolo, Maria Lugones, Ramon Grosfoguel and others. Additionally, ideas that question the legitimacy of knowledge production are also embraced, including references such as Boaventura de Sousa Santos and Silvia Federici, who also address the issues and consequences of modernity.
5 Maria Luiza Viana has been mentored by Professor Maria Cecilia Loschiavo in her current doctoral research carried out at Faculdade de Arquitetura e Urbanismo, Universidade de São Paulo. The following narrative reflects part of Maria Luiza's engagement and fieldwork with residents of Morro do Papagaio.
6 Since her master's in 2016 and being mentored by Maria Cecilia Loschiavo at FAU-USP, Bruna has been working in partnership with Redes da Maré. Her doctoral investigation derives from this collaboration, which is partly described in this narrative.

7 Redes da Maré members annually produce the Bulletin of Public Security and Access to Justice comprising data from police operations, detailing aspects such as the age groups, geolocation, ethnicity and financial conditions of the victims. See Redes da Maré (2020).

References

Akama, Y., & Light, A. (2012). *The human touch: Participatory practice and the role of facilitation in designing with communities*. https://www.researchgate.net/publication/23784285.

Akama, Y., Hagen, P., & Whaanga-Schollum, D. (2019). Problematizing replicable design to practice respectful, reciprocal, and relational co-designing with indigenous people. *Design and Culture*, 11 (4), 1–26.

Ansari, A. (2019). Decolonizing design through the perspectives of cosmological others: Arguing for an ontological turn in design research and practice. *Crossroads*, 26 (2), 16–19.

Battarbee, K., Fulton Suri, J., & Gibbs Howard, S. (2018). *Empathy on the edge: Scaling and sustaining a human-centered approach in the evolving practice of design*. https://pt.scribd.com/document/387932139/Empathy-on-the-edge.

Bednarek-Gilland, A. (2015). *Researching values with qualitative methods: Empathy, moral boundaries and the politics of research*. Ashgate.

Escobar, A. (2018). *Designs for the pluriverse: Radical interdependence, autonomy, and the making of worlds*. Duke University Press Books.

Freire, P. (2020). *Pedagogia do oprimido* (74th ed.). Paz e Terra.

Fulton Suri, J. (2003). Empathic design: Informed and inspired by other people's experience. In I. Koskinen, K. Battarbee, & T. Mattelmäki (Eds.), *Empathic design: User experience in product design* (pp. 51–58). IT Press.

Gatt, C., & Ingold, T. (2013). From description to correspondence: Anthropology in real time. In W. Gunn, T. Otto, & R. C. Smith (Eds.), *Design anthropology: Theory and practice* (pp. 139–158). Bloomsbury.

Ingold, T. (2017). On human correspondence. *Journal of the Royal Anthropological Institute*, 23 (1), 9–27.

Kouprie, M., & Visser, F. S. (2009). A framework for empathy in design: Stepping into and out of the user's life. *Journal of Engineering Design*, 20 (5), 437–448. https://www.tandfonline.com/doi/abs/10.1080/09544820902875033.

Loschiavo, M. C. (2014). A note from Brazil: Looking at the production of design knowledge in Brazil. In E. Kalantidou & T. Fry (Eds), *Design in the borderlands* (pp. 151–156). Routledge.

Lugones, M. (2008). The coloniality of gender. *Worlds & Knowledges Otherwise*, 2 (Spring), 1–17.

Mignolo, W., & Tlostanova, M. (2016). Theorizing from the borders shifting to geo- and body-politics of knowledge. *European Journal of Social Theory*, 9 (2), 205–221.

Pain, R., Kindon, S., & Kesby, M. (Eds.). (2007). *Participatory action research approaches and methods: Connecting people, participation and place*. Routledge.

Pedwell, C. (2012). *Affective (self-) transformations: Empathy, neoliberalism and international development*. http://fty.sagepub.com/content/13/2/163.

Quijano, A. (2005). Colonialidad del poder, Eurocentrismo, América Latina. In E. Lander (Ed.), *La colonialidad del saber: Eurocentrismo y ciencias sociales. Perspectivas latinoamericanas* (pp. 201–245). Clacso.

Redes da Maré. (2020). *Boletim Direito à Segurança Pública na Maré* (4th ed.). Redes da Maré.

Tunstall. E. (2013). Decolonizing design innovation: Design anthropology, critical anthropology. In G. Wendy, T. Otto, & R. C. Smith (Eds.), *Design anthropology, theory and practice* (pp. 232–250). Bloomsbury Academic.

Zaluar, A., & Alvito, M. (Eds.). (2006). *Um século de favela* (5th ed.). FGV.

15 Materiality as a mediator of empathy through culture-based product design for tourism

Heidi Pietarinen, Eija Timonen and Melanie Sarantou

Introduction

This chapter investigates the role of materiality as a mediator of empathy through culture-based design by exploring the meanings that are associated with reindeer in product design. We adopt a culture- and material-based approach (Karana, 2010), which involves reflecting on how interactions amongst cultures can be recast as a resource in product design, specifically in the context of tourism. Materiality is defined as the 'combination of material and form' and the way in which physical materials are 'arranged into particular forms that endure across differences in place and time' (Leonardi, 2012, p. 29). Socio-materiality assumes human interaction that can be mediated and visibilised through objects, tools or materials that are underpinned by invisible social realities (Huifen & Qiuhong, 2012). Objects and materials can improve well-being through satisfying functional and emotional needs for both user and designer (McDonagh & Thomas, 2010).

The use of materiality to facilitate empathy in culture-based design provides designers with tools to enhance self- and wider cultural understandings through their complex making and social environments. The call for design to be empathic has been made since the 1990s (see Mattelmäki et al., 2014), which may be a way product designers who work specifically for tourism can use materiality to mediate empathy amongst people in cross-cultural contexts. People can grasp one another through emotions, intentions and desires to 'feel with' others and so engage empathically with one another, and as Marchetti et al. (2020, p. 1) explain, empathy is 'a dance between two individuals whose steps move between cognition and affect'.

This chapter draws on methods such as workshops and participant observation. We ask: How can materials mediate empathy in multicultural contexts and in product design for tourism? and: How can we draw on the characteristics of materiality to foster empathy through tourist-focused products? The chapter first discusses the workshops, design and working methods used, and the new product ideas that were generated. These ideas and design processes that underpin our analysis are presented after a description of the workshops. A theoretical framework for empathic design in tourist-focused products is

DOI: 10.4324/9781003227557-18

presented, which is developed from concepts borrowed from culture-based product design (Hanquinet & Savage, 2016; Tilley et al., 2006; Walker et al., 2018), and Leonardi's (2012) concept of materiality that includes multisensory experiences of materials (Bacci & Melcher, 2011; Haverkamp, 2011).

Organisational context: Tourism

If there is one thing that appeals to travellers coming to Lapland, it is reindeer. Northern Finland boasts a wide variety of small businesses that make and sell products made from reindeer hides, antlers and bone, which include souvenirs, interior textiles and clothing as well as useful and decorative objects. Most of the tourism and design businesses in Lapland use reindeer-based materials either directly or indirectly. Products featuring reindeer are creations inspired by Finnish culture: reindeer hides commonly decorate Finnish homes much like traditional *rya* wall rugs; candlesticks and key fobs are crafted from horn and bone; shops sell a range of reindeer meat products; and live reindeer are a premier attraction provided for tourists by the experience industry. Even a quick look at souvenir shops in Finnish Lapland reveals that the products are sold to locals as well as tourists.

The importance of tourism in the north has grown annually (Luiro, 2013; Tilastokeskus, 2019), and the commercial value of products being sold to travellers has increased rapidly. This suggests it might be worthwhile looking at how Japanese and Chinese travellers feel about design products and how such products can better match the expectations of Asian visitors and the conventions governing how the products are used in Asian cultures. This thought then provided the impetus for organising Finnish–Japanese–Chinese workshops. After all, Asian tourists represent the fifth largest and fastest growing group of tourists in Finnish Lapland (Business, 2019). Given the existing well-established collaboration, the researchers from the University of Lapland in Rovaniemi opted for Shanghai and Sapporo, where first a two-week workshop at Tongi University in Shanghai (2016) and then a second four-day intensive workshop at Sapporo City University (2018) were conducted.

Review of empathy in the literature

Empathy is explained as an imaginary process (Orzulak, 2006). Peloquin (1996, p. 656) claims that empathy can be fostered through visual and tactile thinking processes of 'what is' and 'how things can be' scenarios that can be acted upon by moving outward from feelings to thoughts and actions. Using empathy, people can imagine or think of the needs of others and act upon them (De Lille et al., 2012). Due to people's mental abilities and skills, they can, through objects or other forms of materiality, mediate empathic processes amongst one another because a triadic relationship can be formed with two persons and an object (Marchetti et al., 2020, p. 3). Verducci (2000, p. 67) posits that empathy is the 'affective relation between aesthetic objects and human viewers', as pleasant feelings of harmony can bridge the gaps between people and what they perceive, which contributes to the projective and affective elements of empathy.

However, the connections between empathy and aesthetics are problematic (Depew, 2005), because 'aesthetic experiences include judgement, not just perceptual cognition and affect', says Verducci (2000, p. 69). This means that sympathy and empathy favour affect; hence, they draw on other people and their emotions (p. 69), while aesthetic empathy may be projective, shaping symbolic connections to objective forms through subjective emotions and feelings (p. 67). Morgan (1996, p. 321) notes that visual interpretations are constructive actions to project human feelings into forms. Further, Verducci (2000, p. 66) seeks to clarify the plural nature of empathy, illustrating how she organises empathy as different phenomena on an emotive–cognitive axis, without attempting to claim 'truth' but rather to illustrate this plurality.

Peloquin's (1996) theory presents a suitable theoretical outline for deriving deeper understandings about the role of materiality in mediating empathy amongst people in multicultural settings, which is important for the tourism context this chapter is addressing. First, her ideas about affective action that can materialise through visual and tactile thinking, which can result in empathic encounters from aesthetic experiences, whether they are embedded in enjoying an artefact as a user, or making and designing it (p. 656), is central to the aims of this chapter. Secondly, she posits that humans' reliance on their senses can foster empathy (p. 569); and thirdly, that 'sensing, imagining and understanding' structures empathy (p. 660). Finally, Peloquin (p. 659) argues that empathy can be fostered through art due to its ability to 'inhabit virtual worlds', which supports Verducci's (2000) claims on the projective nature of aesthetic empathy.

Materials and methods: Reindeer workshops

The aim of the workshops was to develop and design reindeer products for the Rovaniemi, Shanghai and Sapporo tourism markets. The focus of the workshops was on the local, international and cultural dimensions of collaborative design, and we wanted to understand how material interaction can mediate empathic experiences in multicultural contexts. Our main assumption was that materials and the products in which the material is embodied take on different expressive meanings in different cultural contexts. The inspiration for the design processes came from experimentation with the materials and our assumptions regarding cultural effects; the source of inspiration was multisensory material experiences. The workshops enabled 20 bachelors and Master of Art students to understand the cultural importance of reindeer in Finland and utilise reindeer-based materials in designing. The workshop groups developed ideas, possibilities and concepts, articulating how reindeer (hide, fur, horns) can be seen (visual), felt (haptic), heard (auditory) and tasted (taste and smell) in contemporary Japanese and Chinese culture. The outcomes consisted of a poster exhibition, rapid prototypes for tourist markets and digital representations of the design processes.

The workshops started with a presentation of the role of *poro, xùnlù, tonakai,* which all mean reindeer. Play is one possible way of experiencing materials in people's verbalisations, so we not only asked students to describe reindeer materials, but also to share experiences or tell stories about reindeer. We gave the students an opportunity to hear the soundscapes of reindeer (Paliskuntain yhdistys, 2019; Tikkanen, 2016). These methods brought a three-dimensional and tactile aspect to the sensory reading of materials (Karana, 2010, p. 193; Sonneveld & Schifferstein, 2008, pp. 41–67). The workshops dealt with multisensory aspects of reindeer – students familiarising themselves with reindeer through sensory modalities such as taste, smell and touch (Table 15.1). The third stage consisted of sketching with a variety of materials and colours to develop reindeer-based products for the market. The fourth and last activity comprised preparations for the poster exhibition and presentation. Table 15.1 shows the parameters that the sensory modalities encompassed.

The multisensory design process facilitated the production of empirical evidence and an overview of the dominant sensory modalities involved in experiencing reindeer as a material. Five modalities were distinguished: visual, auditory, taste, haptic and olfactory. Haptic refers to what one physically experiences through touch when interacting with reindeer-based materials such as fur, horn, meat and leather. The modality captures the experience of touching rather than touching as such (Karana, 2010, p. 112; Sonneveld & Schifferstein, 2008, pp. 41–67). Tactility includes sensations of texture, temperature, force and pressure, and it should be pointed out that roughness can also be evaluated visually (Karana, 2010, p. 112). It was difficult to draw clear-cut boundaries between some

Table 15.1 The basic sensory modalities and their parameters: light, sound, taste, temperature, pressure and smell.

Sensory modalities	*Parameters*
1. Visual sense	**Light** reflection: glossy–matte Colour: colourful–colourless Material: decorative–undecorated, modern–traditional, luxurious–plain
2. Auditory system	Reindeer **sounds**: 'Lowing and grunting' (Tikkanen, 2016) 'Clicking hooves' (Paliskuntain yhdistys, 2019)
3. Taste system	**Taste**: pleasant–unpleasant, appealing–offensive taste
4. Haptic (touch) system	Material texture: rough–smooth **Pressure**: hard–soft Force: weight (light–heavy), strength (low–high), elasticity (low–high) **Temperature**: warm–cold
5. Olfactory system	Smell: natural–odourless

sensory modalities. Inasmuch as the materials involved also convey meanings, one noteworthy challenge in documenting the process was getting students to describe their multisensory experiences. For example, whilst they talked about the smell, colour and softness or hardness of materials, they also mentioned associations with cosy environments and luxury products.

We sought evidence of the parameters presented in Table 15.1 by asking students to relate different aspects of their experience with reindeer materials and the products they later produced. Data were collected through photographs, unstructured group discussions and note-taking and by gathering visual, interview and notational data. Workshops were documented for further research, using photos as well as field diaries kept by the researchers. We worked collaboratively with the students, analysing their verbalisations and design processes, and we asked them to describe materials (sensory modalities), explore sources (e.g., design magazines, books and the internet) and sketch ideas in order to brainstorm items that could be used in this context. Students came up with 180 ideas (sketches), of which they selected 20 for refinement. They then chose five product ideas for the final presentation.

Results

The 180 product ideas comprised our research material. We grouped the ideas by themes, focusing on how frequently an idea occurred, the practical function envisioned for the product, the relevant contexts and the elements of design, such as colours, surface and form and distinctive cultural characteristics. On the basis of this analysis, we distinguished three product categories: 1) Small and well-finished; 2) Controlling personal space; 3) Special editions; and 4) Whimsical. In what follows, we present these groups in detail and conclude, through reflection, how multisensory elaboration of ideas might guide empathic product design. The boundaries amongst the categories were not always clear-cut; rather, the same product might fall into more than one group. For example, a 'small and finished' clothes hook could be a utility item as well as a luxury product.

Small and well-finished

The students at both universities came up with ideas for small but finished mundane objects, such as a pillow, a clothes hanger with a long hook, slippers, a coat rack, soup ladle, fork and an umbrella with a reindeer-horn handle. What these had in common was that they were designed for everyday use, and attention was paid to details as well as proportions. For example, in Finland at least, hangers with long hooks are rarely found in the home; they are more likely to be seen in clothing stores, where clothes are hung at many heights, sometimes up to the ceiling. What we found was that apartments in large Chinese cities are often very small and have little storage space, so that people store clothing at ceiling height. One student in Shanghai designed a long-hooked hanger with a hook made of reindeer bone. Here, we saw a product that was practical, something used every day, easy to transport and, at the same time, a memento of a trip to Finnish Lapland.

Recent years have seen research on the Chinese surveillance camera culture (see Pajari, 2017, 2019), which involves cameras being placed everywhere and people being aware that they are there. The cameras are equipped with face recognition software, making it possible to identify individuals even in large crowds. Some of the cameras are even disguised as birds. The presence of the surveillance culture seems to be so self-evident to Chinese students that one of the students in the Shanghai group designed a camera covered with reindeer fur. To us, the researchers, it seemed as though products for the surveillance culture were being offered not only as disguised products but also as design products. This gave us an ability to understand the users' own context and that everyday life experiences, individual desires and emotions may have an impact on their lives.

Comparable small and finished products designed in the Sapporo workshop for everyday use included a reindeer hair artist's paintbrush, a seat cover for a moped and a small Japanese men's *gamaguchi* (coin purse). The Finnish *Lumi* (snow) purse is a similar product for female consumers usually produced in a wide range of colours and designs. Moreover, the sophisticated Japanese packaging tradition can be seen as representing 'small and finished', as the most minute details of packaging have been meticulously designed, much like a *gamaguchi* or *Lumi* coin purse. However, small and finished cannot in and of itself be a sufficient criterion for designing or introducing products.

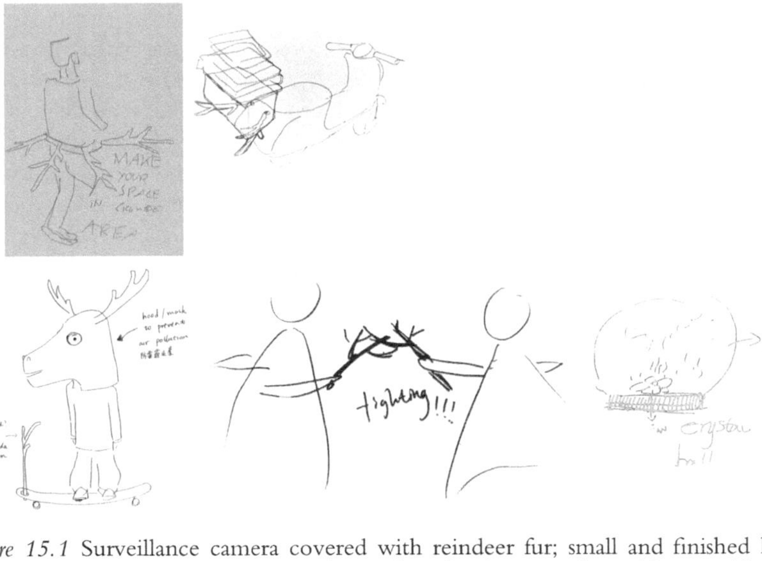

Figure 15.1 Surveillance camera covered with reindeer fur; small and finished hanger; headphones covered with reindeer fur; keeping the cold out with underwear or shoe insoles made of reindeer fur (stitched series of images).

An empathic approach provided an inspiring way to study the relationship between the students (users) and reindeer material (the object). Stepping into and out of users' lives helped us to understand their deeper values, needs and emotions: how to touch (kinaesthetic and tactile learning) and be touched (proximity, movement, emotion, affect and empathy). For example, unlike Finns, the students in Sapporo did not feel that a whole reindeer hide was a finished product suitable for interior decorating, but rather saw it as material that could be used as the basis for designing. When a hide was spread across a table in a Sapporo classroom, the reaction was more bewilderment than anything else. The students touched it and were intrigued by how rough it felt and by the structure of the fur. A multisensorial modality as an empathic tool or methodology can be applied to create a relationship with reindeer material at many levels. An extensively prepared reindeer hide can become a luxury product in an urban setting every bit as much as it is an everyday item in the reindeer-herding culture in the Arctic.

Controlling personal space

The students in Shanghai were particularly keen to design products made of reindeer antlers that would allow their users to stake out space for themselves in crowds or protect their privacy. Examples include antlers that could be mounted on the back of a scooter, an 'antler belt' that kept other passengers on the metro at a safe distance and a fence made of antlers. A striking feature of these designs is that they tap into the aggressive connotation of antlers. Reindeer antlers in an urban environment also manifest the boundary between nature and culture. This is bound to the particular culture and time. What to one person is a token of dangerous, wild nature might to another be part of a welcoming city park. Moreover, attitudes towards natural and synthetic materials vary depending on each individual's world of experience and the cultural codes they adhere to. Reindeer antlers in an urban environment also highlight the distinction between human beings and animals. The sharpness of this dichotomy also depends on the culture and time involved. Where product design is concerned, it was interesting that the students did not design products to protect people against animals; rather, reindeer-themed products were used to build barriers offering protection against groups of people and against the elements.

Physical, mental and social spaces are inseparable in people's world of experience. Space is defined in terms of a given time and culture and is produced in keeping with the social practices and codes of that time and culture (Laitinen, 2004, p. 4; Lefebvre & Nicholson-Smith, 1974/1991, pp. 17, 31). This observation is supported by our everyday perception that, in crowded cities, people's personal territories are smaller than in more sparsely populated areas. People are also accustomed to putting up with the unavoidable proximity of others in rush hour crowds without this causing panic or claustrophobia. On the other hand, studies have shown that people experience stress in cramped spaces and crowds, which involve a flood of auditory and visual signals (Ampuja, 2018, p. 85). This explains why those living in large cities have developed a wide range of ways to establish distance from others. They may immerse themselves in an auditory world of their own using headphones or focus on their mobile phone and the affordances it offers – the chance to communicate with friends. Here, we see headphones, books and mobile phones making it possible to carve out a mental space for oneself. But staking out a mental space is not always enough; physical distance is often necessary as well. It can be secured by taking up space on the adjacent seat, making noise or engaging in other behaviours that prompt others to keep their distance.

Such gestures for demarcating space as these are always aggressive to a certain extent, ones that challenge the norms of the community. This function can be seen in the antler belt or rear-mounted scooter antlers that the students designed. These products say 'stay away'. They can, or fail to, mediate empathy. The antlers could be repulsive or alarming in some cultural settings, as they might be perceived as a weapon in the fight for power and space. They are self-expressive products, generating or responding to emerging relationships through their own felt presence and individuality. In the case of antlers, the products can initiate users' understandings of their densely populated living spaces and everyday practices and activities in public and private spaces. The aggressive nature of the products is tempered or becomes more acceptable because the values they represent signal design and excitement. Yet, the acceptability of a product is ultimately determined by how it is used and its size against the backdrop of the cultural codes regarding touching and moving closer to others. This argument is borne out by the claim of cultural geographer Edward Malpas that a person's subjective space and movement in that space are related to the understanding of the public space where the subjective space is located (Laitinen, 2004, p. 5; Malpas, 1999, pp. 51–54). 'Public space' in this context can be seen as how a person moving around in a city understands their particular position within a given place, for example, the metro amidst the pulse of street traffic.

Special editions: Standing out from the crowd

Both groups of students generated ideas for products that would stand out through the choice of materials. These included headphones covered with reindeer fur, purses, pens and wallets made of reindeer leather. Using earphones covered in reindeer fur on the metro is a small and inconspicuous gesture aimed at standing out from the crowd, creating privacy and establishing presence in the commuter rush – but in a soft, private space. The effect of furry headphones or a leather wallet is to inject luxury into the everyday routine. Luxury, in turn, connotes limited availability and awareness of the materials used. It also means distinguishing oneself from the work-a-day world and an opportunity to focus on products and services that bring pleasure, as well as a chance, if only a brief one, to enjoy something that everyday life cannot offer (Nelskylä, 2018). This is what the reindeer-fur headphones had to offer in the present case.

In public spaces in Asia, particularly Japan, one sees a very elaborate toilet culture that entails a wide variety of sounds and washing features. One product that fit right in was a reindeer-skin toilet seat cover, designed by a student in Shanghai. One can even carry the furry seat around for personal use. Amid the hustle and bustle, one can pamper oneself and distinguish oneself with modest gestures. Here, we see a touch of luxury punctuating the daily routine.

The connection between distinguishing oneself from the crowd and luxury is an insightful one. Traditional luxury can easily be recognised by the choice of materials involved, but modern luxury plays down glitter and highlights tailored well-being services and individually selected materials and colours instead (Bevolo et al., 2011; Mattila, 2018). A toilet seat cover made of reindeer skin that one can carry around and a bold, red reindeer leather wallet represent this style of luxury at its purest. With the growth in tourism, the use of reindeer-based designs in tourism and aspects of culture associated with reindeer have become topical. Tourists expect design products to be compatible with their cultural conventions, yet at the same time, they want them to reflect the special character of the destination where they were bought.

Souvenirs and gifts made in Finland and designed to enable users to distinguish themselves from the crowd have to reconcile cultural as well as temporal differences in notions of luxury. At its best, a product that both distinguishes and links one to another culture could be such a novel product. Reindeer-skin headphones are an example of this: the user is associated with Chinese youth who wear headphones, but at the same time the headphones tell others that the user can afford to travel to Lapland and engage in exciting and unique experiences. This reminds us that there are many other ways to deepen our attachment to products. Personalisation symbolises both an achievement and expression of individuality for the users, an essential feature of luxury. It is no longer enough for the product to be a luxury item; rather, the entire production chain and the narratives associated with it (stories about reindeer in the present case) must signal luxury (Mattila 2018). Notably, luxury products also involve rivalry and social comparison, which may or may not mediate empathy amongst people. Little luxury items that serve to distinguish their users from the crowd can also reinforce users' identity and self-image, establishing who they are or expressing their status (Mattila, 2018). Materiality can represent our personality, social standing and wealth, but also our values, past, memories, history and relationships with others. Objects, such as reindeer-skin headphones, symbolise to us and to others who we are (see Niinimäki & Koskinen, 2015), but such significant objects can, or fail to, mediate connections or empathy amongst us and others.

Whimsical

Humour and having fun are essential ways to deal with cultural tensions. They also afford often surprising perspectives for analysing problems (Hietalahti, 2015). The Japanese students came up with product proposals that combined a serious social phenomenon and humour. Amongst other products, they designed a reindeer-fur mask that protects the wearer against air pollution. Such masks are used extensively in Asian cultures to prevent the flu and other airborne diseases from spreading, but in the COVID-19 pandemic, masks have become essential accessories. But a mask made of reindeer fur is not disposable; it is meant to be used for a long time. If designed to be something surprising – even impossible – a product takes on new meanings and uses.

In designing humorous products, the students took advantage not only of unique cultural and multinational features. Amongst other things, they recognised the use of crystal balls both in the global toy culture and as a means for fortune telling. In this spirit, one group designed a crystal ball that had reindeer hair floating in it. The position of the hair could be used to predict the future. The crystal ball also linked the idea of the product to the world of fairy tales and fantasies, including Disney animations, such as the *Wonderful Wizard of Oz* (1939), and Japanese animations, such as the character Yasuhiro Hagakure from *Danamronpa* (1989). The reindeer material was also entertaining, conveying a sense of playfulness, humour and fun.

Unfamiliar materials made it possible for students to detach themselves from designing conventions. When humour was chosen as the point of departure and interpretative context for design, the students managed to create a situation that highlighted a phenomenon and allowed for various interpretations. The cover of humour makes it possible to distance oneself from the phenomenon being examined and create an open interpretive frame. According to Knuutila (2018, p. 12), laughter reveals another side of an issue, makes the festive mundane, and the hopeful hopeless. Laughter makes things visible which cannot be presented using other means – at least not acceptably (p. 13). Humour can be based on comedy, black humour or nonsense humour (Hietalahti, 2018), but one thing the product proposals had in common, based on humour, was that in one way or another they all made a statement on social phenomena.

Meanings that point in different directions introduce conflicting elements into products, an example being the clash between reindeer living in harmony with nature and people having to live in polluted city air. Cases like these reveal the boundaries of conventions – on the one hand the meanings associated with reindeer, on the other Japanese culture. Perhaps, they also show which phenomena can be laughed at and which cannot. Connecting humour and fiction with product design also served to create an open atmosphere when the students were designing. This enabled rapid, freewheeling generation of ideas without any fear of being ridiculed. With humour framing their design moment, the students were able to laugh at themselves and each other without losing face. Other sources of inspiration besides humour were the unreserved joy and playfulness amongst the students. This could be seen in interactive reindeer-fur dice, swords made of reindeer bone, a fur-covered skateboard and fur mask. Rapid ideation and sketching (in a safe environment with like-minded product designers all presented with the same challenge) proved to be powerful innovative methods for generating empathy because the methods

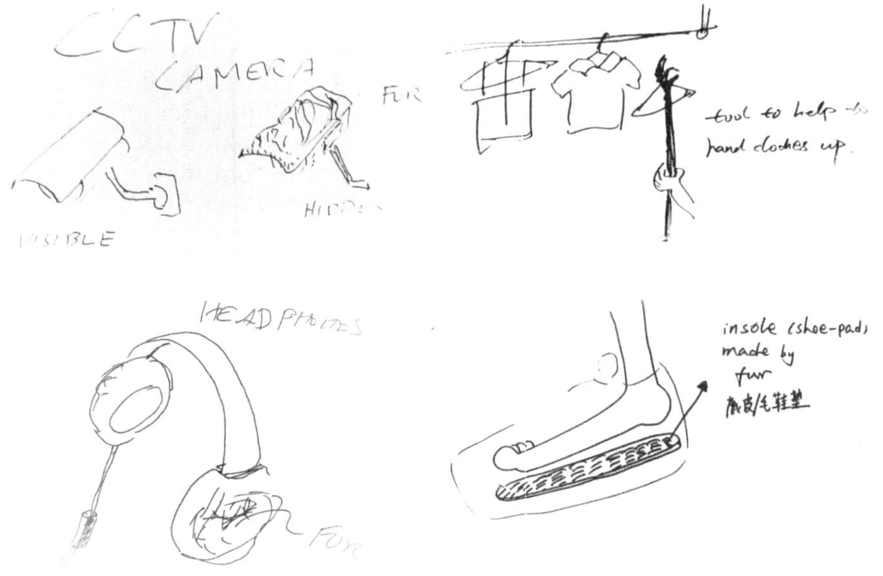

Figure 15.2 Taking control of one's personal space, for example, by mounting reindeer antlers on the back of a scooter ('Stay away!') or attaching antlers to one's waist ('Don't touch me!'); play and humour in product design: a crystal ball, boys' play swords, a skateboard, a mask and pogo stick.

enabled experimental ideas to be expressed, whether they were successful or not. Students could proactively seek and improve ideas, spurring one another on, without fear of being ridiculed. Exchanging ideations and sketches within a group that trusted one another without fear of failure or unconstructive critique unleashed creative energy and led to providing and sharing knowledge and emotional and practical support to one another.

Discussion

What prompted us to organise multisensory and material workshops was the idea of combining cultural and material product design, given that the interpretation of sensory experiences and observations is culture-bound. What we see is what we have learned to see. But familiarity with a culture is not enough in and of itself, for a product idea never gets off the drawing table if the idea does not reflect recognition of the material conditions essential to creating the final product. Even though the use of materials is culture-bound, the properties of a material, such as the nature of reindeer fur, the pliability of the skin, the hardness of antler bone and the range of colours, all play a decisive role in the manufacture of an artefact. We provided examples of socio-material approaches to mediating empathy amongst people. Next, a theoretical framework for empathic design in tourist-focused products is presented, which is inspired by Peloquin's (1996) outline for the role of empathy in creative contexts.

Affective action through visual and tactile thinking for empathic encounters

The empathic materiality workshops offered a different framework for us attending to the linguistic, cultural, visual, material and acoustic textures of participants' interactions. Workshops were in-between practices: they brought a three-dimensional and tactile aspect to the reading of materials, which can be understood as visual and tactile thinking. Exploring the experiential qualities of materials brought to everyone's attention the role of materials in affecting our ways of thinking, feeling and doing (Giaccardi & Karana, 2015, pp. 2447–2456; Karana, 2010; Veelaert et al., 2020). Materiality facilitated empathy in that it translated the participants' subjective experiences of materials into data. It evoked the discussion it corresponded to before giving the final form to an object (or material or immaterial form giving).

Reliance on senses for fostering empathy

When one runs one's hand over reindeer fur, the first thing the experience evokes is not the sensation of being in touch with some cool, sleek high-tech device, but rather a connection to something more natural that triggers a sense of mental and physical well-being. Associated with modern Asian culture is extensive digitalisation, as seen in the numerous Chinese and Japanese companies (e.g. Huawei, Alibaba, Kenzo, Muji, Nikon and Mazda). It was surprising that young students from Sapporo and Shanghai – city dwellers – combined little technology with the reindeer products they designed. Their ideas primarily centred on domestic aesthetics, interior decorating, well-being and free time. But it is still an open question to what extent our multisensory and materialist product design methods steered the students in this direction and to what extent their ideas derived from the images they associate with reindeer.

Sensing, imagining and understanding

The 180 product ideas and three product categories did not just fulfil functional or aesthetic roles; they played active roles in the unfolding of empathy. This was not experienced only at the *sensorial* (light, sound, taste, temperature, pressure and smell) level, but also at the *interpretive* (e.g., the evocative combination of the natural reindeer-derived material with playful, everyday life components), *affective* (e.g., promoting a feeling of speciality, nostalgia, modernity and luxury) and *performative* (e.g., inviting touching, developing a variety of ways to use the artefact and closely linking these to the material used) levels (see Giaccardi & Karana, 2015). These levels of dimensions, interrelated to each other, constituted participants' experiences, so the boundaries between the layers were not always clear-cut. For example, reindeer material looked soft but felt sharp or hard when touched (sensorial), which surprised or aroused curiosity (affective) and reminded others to stay away from you, like the user taking control of their personal space by wanting the opposite of empathy through repelling gestures and performativity. Reindeer antlers in this example confronted the senses to communicate that empathy is not asked for or needed.

Inhabiting virtual worlds through projection

The stretching of the imagination to see new perspectives and engage in creative occupations that enable understanding of the surrounding worlds through our senses, thereby transporting us into different possible worlds, describe how virtual worlds can be inhabited through projection. As design practitioners, materiality has the ability to transport the imagination so that knowledgeable designers can recognise, read, imagine and envisage new possibilities for giving new form and meaning to materiality. A significant role is played by materiality, form and the story of an artefact in product design for tourism, as cross-cultural understanding and new meanings need to be shaped by these elements within products to be sustainably produced and marketable in such competitive contexts.

Conclusion

Culture- and material-based product designs interact with one another: the materials are always interpreted in a particular cultural context, and the availability of the materials in turn shapes the culture. Nevertheless, the two design processes proceed from entirely different bases. Like humanistic, culture-based research, culture-based design takes as its starting point people, their values, the way they live and work as well as how they ascribe meaning to products; material-based design, in contrast, focuses on the physical properties of the materials envisaged as part of the design (Tilley et al., 2006; Walker et al., 2018). Products and materials take on meaning once they become interwoven with social contexts (Leonardi, 2012). Such materials and objects matter once they are interpreted by people for fulfilling certain functions, but at the same time, these materials and objects can be reinterpreted to transcend the contexts to which they are usually linked (p. 27). Culture-based design can facilitate such a transcendence as well as processes of mediation of empathy amongst people through materiality.

With the growth of tourism, the use of reindeer-based designs and cultural perspectives on reindeer have become topical. Tourists expect design products to be in accord with their cultural conventions whilst reflecting the special character of the destination. In other words, a product should have familiar elements but something extra as well, a touch of exotica. Souvenirs and gifts designed to help users distinguish themselves from the crowd have to accommodate and reconcile cultural differences. Product designers working for tourism markets need to be aware of how their souvenirs can mediate empathy in cross-cultural contexts. Products that serve to distinguish yet include – such as the reindeer-fur-covered headphones and bone coat hangers – represent such novel designs.

This project examined how culture-based design can create a sense of empathic materiality. Reindeer materials as empathic materiality derive from the communication amongst people and their surroundings, cultural settings and materiality. Our goal was to understand participants' distinctive cultural characteristics, by observing the users' own context: everyday life experiences, individual dreams and emotions, and how they were able to turn these into design inspiration. We examined and discussed how materiality can mediate empathy in product design for tourism and how it is experienced in designing and marketing products for tourism.

Summary 1: Lessons learned that can contribute to the organisational or business context

Sensory modalities can generate connections amongst people during design processes, but these modalities can also create connections amongst users. The use of methods for creating empathy, such as sensory modalities and their parameters, provides possibilities for designers to empathise, define, ideate, prototype and test during the course of the material production process (define, collect, analyse, develop, respond and improve). These sensory modalities enable expression in ways that may be characteristic of and pleasant for product designers. Sensory modalities and their parameters as methods for creating empathy amongst users illustrates the potential for qualitative and arts-based research to diversity and challenge ways of understanding cultural and social realities.

Summary 2: Contribution to organisational or business knowledge or practices

- Sensory modalities and their parameters: light, sound, taste, temperature, pressure and smell can be harnessed by souvenir and product designers working in cross-cultural tourism contexts to mediate empathy amongst people.
- In tourist contexts, sensory modalities can add value by creating empathy and potentially new cross-cultural connections amongst tourists, users and tourism service providers.
- Product and service designers working within organisational settings dealing with fragile and sensitive tourism contexts, for example Indigenous communities and environmental settings, can use sensory modalities and their parameters to enhance social, cultural and environmental sustainability by creating more empathic relationships and connections through (empathic) product and service design.

References

Ampuja, O. (2018). Tulkintoja hiljaisuuden merkityksestä. In H. Järviluoma & U. Piela (Eds.), *Äänimaisemissa* (pp. 73–98). Finnish Literature Society.

Bacci, F., & Melcher, D. (2011). *Art and the senses*. Oxford University Press.

Bevolo, M., Gofman, A., & Moskowitz, H. R. (2011). *Premium by design: How to understand, design and market high end products*. Ashgate.

Buchanan, R., & Margolin, V. (1995). *The idea of design: A design issues reader*. The MIT Press.

Business. (2019). *Lapland above ordinary*, industry brief: Tourism. https://www.lapland.fi/business/tourism-industry-in-lapland/#:~:text=Overall%2C%20Lapland's%20accommodation%20capacity%20is,largest%20tourist%20group%20in%20Lapland.

Danto, A. C. (1973). Artworks and real things. *Theoria*, 39 (1–3), 1–17.

De Lille, C., Roscam Abbing, E., & Kleinsmann, M. (2012, 8–9 August). *A designerly approach to enable organizations to deliver product-service systems*. 2012 International Design Management Research Conference, Boston, MA, United States.

Depew, D. (2005). Empathy, psychology, and aesthetics: Reflections on a repair concept. *Poroi*, 4 (1), 6.

Giaccardi, E., & Karana, E. (2015). *Foundations of materials experience*. Proceedings of the 33rd Annual ACM Conference of Human Factors in Computing Systems (pp. 2447–2456), CHI '15, ACM Press. https://www.researchgate.net/publication/270586693_Foundations_of_Materials_Experience_An_Approach_for_HCI.

Hanquinet, L., & Savage, M. (2016). *Routledge international handbook of the sociology of art and culture*. Routledge.

Haverkamp, M. (2011). *Synesthetic design: Handbook for a multi-sensory approach*. Birkhäuser.

Hietalahti, J. (2015). Laughing at oneself: On the new social character. *Studies in Social and Political Thought*, 25, 116–131. http://journals.sussex.ac.uk/index.php/sspt/article/view/30.

Hietalahti, J. (2018). Kun havainto ja odotus eivät kohtaa: huumorista ja hämmennyksestä [When perception and expectation do not meet: humor and confusion]. In H. Laiho, & M. Tuominen (Eds.), *Havainto: Suomen Filosofisen Yhdistyksen yhden sanan kollokvion esitelmiä* [*Observation: Presentations of the One-Word Colloquium of the Finnish Philosophical Society*] (pp. 246–255). University of Turku. Reports from the Department of Philosophy, 40. http://urn.fi/URN:ISBN:978-951-29-7136-7.

Huifen, W., & Qiuhong, T. (2012, July). *Study on socio-materiality convergence of IT architecture and social architecture: From critical realism view*. The 2012 International Conference on Computing, Measurement, Control and Sensor Network (pp. 421–424). IEEE.

Karana, E. (2010). *Meanings of materials*. LAP LAMBERT Academic Publishing.

Knuutila, S. (2018). Huumorin tartunta. In S. Knuuttila, P. Hakamies, & E. Lampela (Eds.), *Huumorinskaalat. Esitys, tyyli, tarkoitus* (pp. 19–35). Finnish Literature Society.

Laitinen, R. (2004). Johdanto tilan kokemuksen kulttuurihistoriaan. In R. Laitinen (Ed.), *Tilan kokemuksen kulttuurihistoriaa* (pp. 1–15). University of Turku.

Lefebvre, H., & Nicholson-Smith, D. (1974/1991). *The production of space*. Blackwell Publishing.

Leonardi, P. M. (2012). Materiality, sociomateriality, and socio-technical systems: What do these terms mean? How are they different? Do we need them? In P. M. Leonardi, A. B. Nardi, & J. Kallinikos J. (Eds.), *Materiality and organizing: Social interaction in a technological world* (pp. 25–48). Oxford University Press.

Luiro, S. (2013). *Lapland, above ordinary. Lapland tourism strategy 2015–2018*. Culture Regional Council of Lapland.

Malpas, J. E. (1999). *Place and experience: A philosophical topography*. Cambridge University Press.

Marchetti, A., Miraglia, L., & Di Dio, C. (2020). Toward a socio-material approach to cognitive empathy in autistic spectrum disorder. *Frontiers in Psychology*, 10 (2965). https://doi.org/10.3389/fpsyg.2019.02965.

Mattelmäki, T., Vaajakoski, K., & Koskinen, I. (2014). What happened to empathic design? *Design Issues*, 30 (1), 67–77.

Mattila, P. (2018). *Luxury 2.0*. https://www.aaltoee.com/aalto-leaders-insight/2018/luxury-2.0.

McDonagh, D., & Thomas, J. (2010). Rethinking design thinking: Empathy supporting innovation. *Australasian Medical Journal*, 3 (8), 458–464.

Morgan, D. (1996). The enchantment of art: Abstraction and empathy from German romanticism to expressionism. *Journal of the History of Ideas*, 57 (2), 317–341.

Nelskylä, L. (2018). *Luksusta*. https://yle.fi/uutiset/3-10425676/.

Niinimäki, K., & Koskinen, A. (2015). I love this dress, it makes me feel beautiful! Empathic knowledge in sustainable design. *The Design Journal: An International Journal for All Aspects of Design*, 14 (2), 165–186. https://doi.org/10.2752/175630611X12984592779962.

Orzulak, M. M. (2006). Reviving empathy and imagination: Arts integration enlivens teaching and learning. *The English Journal*, 96 (1), 79–83. https://www.jstor.org/stable/30046669.

Pajari, K. (2017). *Kiina himoitsee teknologiaa, joka tunnistaisi jokaisen ihmisen kolmessa sekunnissa valvontakamerasta – Hanke on valtava tietoturvariski, sanoo professori*. https://www.hs.fi/ulkomaat/art-2000005420311.html

Pajari, K. (2019). *Kiinan pimeä reuna*. https://dynamic.hs.fi/2019/uiguurimuslimit/.

Paliskuntain yhdistys. (2019). *Miksi poron koparat naksuvat*. https://paliskunnat.fi/poro/poro/usein-kysyttya/miksi-poron-koparat-naksuvat/.

Peloquin, S. M. (1996). Art: An occupation with promise for developing empathy. *American Journal of Occupational Therapy*, 50 (8), 655–661.

Sonneveld, M. H., & Schifferstein, H. N. (2008). The tactual experience of objects. In *Product experience* (pp. 41–67). Elsevier.

Tikkanen, J. (2016). *Nisäkkäiden ääni*. Poro. https://suomenluonto.fi/uutiset/nisakkaiden-aania-5-osa-poro/.

Tilastokeskus. (2019). *Lappi houkutti joulukuussa ulkomaalaisia matkailijoita*. http://www.stat.fi/uutinen/lappi-houkutti-joulukuussa-ulkomaisia-matkailijoita.

Tilley, C., Tilley, C., & Tilley, C. (2006). *Handbook of material culture*. SAGE Publishing.

Veelaert, L., Du Bois, E., Moons, I., & Karana, E. (2020). Experiential characterization of materials in product design: A literature review. *Materials & Design*, 190, 108543. https://www.sciencedirect.com/science/article/pii/S0264127520300769#bb0025.

Verducci, S. (2000). A conceptual history of empathy and a question it raises for moral education. *Educational Theory*, 50 (1), 63.

Walker, S., Evans, M., Cassidy, T., Jung, J., & Twigger Holroyd, A. (2018). *Design roots: Culturally significant designs, products and practices*. Bloomsbury.

Section D

The role of technology in creating empathy

Step 4: Scaling up empathic action

16 Human or nonhuman agent?

Experiences of empathy in a digital customer tourism journey

Päivi Hanni-Vaara

Introduction

Digitalisation of services offers several possibilities to enhance the tourism experience as technology is increasingly mediating experiences. It is essential to note that digital transformation has had several effects on the tourism business itself. For example, digital transformation has drastically altered the roles of the business, from a transaction-based, supplier-oriented business to a customer, network and collaborative-oriented social value creation business along the past decades (Pesonen, 2020, p. 89). Likewise, digital transformation has reinforced business in developing new service concepts that can respond to the needs of value.

As an anthropocentric, interpersonal global business field, tourism continuously aims to develop the digital accessibility of services. The tourism industry has suffered from several pandemics, most recently from COVID-19, which has affected the consumption of tourism-related services. The expectations of customers are that digital services become personalised and able to be accessed pretravel, onsite and post-travel (Neuhofer et al., 2012, p. 36; Reichstein & Härting, 2018, p. 1484).

The digitalisation of tourism services is formed in complex and interdisciplinary ecosystems that represent diverse networks of immaterial and material practices (Kohtamäki et al., 2019, p. 380). To explain this complexity from the customer's perspective, Amadeus (2020, p. 8) indicated that the average customer journey when purchasing hotel or related accommodation may take 36 days and involve 45 touchpoints. Therefore, it is unsurprising that accessibility, convenience, usability, and safety are defined as the most desired functionalities by tourism customers when defining the expectations of a frictionless digital customer journey (Kofoed, 2021).

Along with the development of the service concept, digital transformation has been extended to services in which the customer may interact with a human agent or a technology-provided nonhuman agent. The technology-provided nonhuman agent can become, in a sense, real through artificial intelligence (AI) technology, in which human-simulating service elements function with the aid of machines, devices and programmes (Ailisto, 2019; Jylkäs et al.,

DOI: 10.4324/9781003227557-20

2018, p. 1437). The nonhuman agent is an actor in the activities and operations, resembling a human and mediating the services provided at the various touchpoints of the digital customer's journey (Jylkäs et al., 2018, p. 1438). In addition, AI can conduct frequent and volume-based digital operations by recognising and reacting to the needs of the customer (Ailisto, 2019; Perez-Vega et al., 2021, pp. 902–903).

AI technologies—for example, augmented reality (AR) and virtual reality (VR)—mediate and provide experiences in which the customer is immersed in the service, which is done by using multiple senses instead of reading texts and watching pictures and videos only (Yung et al., 2020). One practical example of using immersive technologies in the tourism business is Carnival Corporation's provision of a VR service as a pre-experience of a cruise, here with the aid of VR glasses (Fortune, 2016). This technology-provided service may be reflected in cognitive empathy, in which the customer obtains value by immersing themselves in the facilities and services delivered during the cruise. An immersive pre-experience demonstrates that the service provider can view things from the customer's perspective (Yalcin & DiPaola, 2018, 22; Chen, 2018, p. 50). This means that with the aid of immersive technology, customers can more easily understand the service concept by gaining insights into the cruise ship and its service. As a result, the VR service aims to support customers' decision-making in purchasing the cruise service.

With digital services increasingly becoming mediating experiences, there is a constant need to balance them with empathetic customer insights to perceive a holistic understanding of each customer's needs (Miettinen et al., 2014, pp. 29, 34). Empathy is valuable for evaluating, apprehending and recognising the genuine value of the customer's individual expectations of the tourism service (Genesys, 2020). Additionally, empathy can help in studying the digital customer journey, its touchpoints and service moments, focusing on the inspiration of the customer's experiences and expectations of, desires for and emotions about the service (Mattelmäki et al., 2014, p. 67). With their touchpoints and service moments, customer journeys are excellent determinants in defining individual customer engagement and the value of the service (Becker, 2020, p. 21; Perez-Vega et al., 2021, p. 902).

In the current study, a digital touchpoint represents the material and immaterial elements that intersect with the experiences of empathy (the emotions and senses)—the moment of the service (time)—and digital space—which defines the service's channels (Risdon & Quattlebaum, 2018). The touchpoint for material elements can be channels, devices and solutions, while the immaterial elements can be the experiences based on cultural and social behaviour (Miettinen, 2011, p. 55). The temporal dimension defining timing at the touchpoint is called a service moment.

The literature (Powell & Roberts, 2017, pp. 137–138) has addressed the idea that empathy is an apparent part of digital interaction in tourism, representing communication in the various service interfaces provided by multiple actors (Miettinen et al., 2014, p. 34; Jylkäs et al., 2018, p. 1437). However, there is insufficient knowledge of empathetic responses in the digital interaction between the customer and service provider (Powell & Roberts, 2017, pp. 137–138). Because digital tourism services customers are segmented based on their motivation to travel, the present study's target group is a leisure traveller whose motivation is to take a holiday outside their usual environment to experience something new or expected (Statistics Finland, 2021).

The present research studies empathy as a psychological phenomenon, analysing a leisure traveller's experiences of empathy in their digital customer journey. The perspectives of empathy are on cognitive and affective empathy. Here, cognitive empathy signifies customers' experiences of the service provider's ability in a context where affective empathy elaborates the findings of shared emotions. The individual who is experiencing this journey in the present study is a leisure traveller who is taking their digital customer journey through the touchpoints, explaining whether the service moment is experienced with a human agent or a technology-provided nonhuman agent. The practical examples explain what the leisure traveller finds the most valuable, convenient and important regarding the digital customer journey.

Reflecting empathy in digital interaction

Empathy is a critical part of ethics and morality because it requires one to experience otherness when acknowledging the perspectives and well-being of others in situations that are not necessarily beneficial to oneself (Ruonakoski, 2019, p. 315; Aaltola & Keto, 2018, pp. 19–20). Empathy is not an emotion, but rather, it is a person's reaction to another actor's emotions (Powell & Roberts, 2017, p. 138). A useful perspective for the discussion of empathy is that one should not confuse empathy with sympathy. In sympathy, we show compassion for the other by directing our distinct feeling for them (Aaltola & Keto, 2018, p. 25). As a result, sympathy is a feeling like joy or pity, but it is not an emotional experience.

Empathy is especially present in situations where a person can use multiple senses and can experience and empathise with the service, instead of simply relying on pure imagination (Shin, 2018, p. 64). The most recognised form of empathy is cognitive empathy, which refers to a perspective-taking ability when one is "sharing others' internal states and explicitly considering those states" (Chen, 2018, p. 50; Zaki & Ochsner, 2012, p. 675). In cognitive empathy, the actor observes and evaluates another actor's reactions by trying to assimilate the other's internal state, for example, what the other is thinking, feeling and experiencing (Kamas & Preston, 2020, p. 2; Zaki & Ochsner, 2012, p. 675). Furthermore, cognitive empathy includes insights into the other's personal, social and cultural norms; values; and beliefs (Belman & Flanagan, 2010, p. 6). In practice, service provider needs the competence of customer insights, in which the provider can walk the digital customer journey in the leisure traveller's shoes to empathise with and perceive their experience.

The present study's other empathy component is affective empathy, which is also called emotional empathy (Aaltola & Keto, 2018, pp. 63–64; Chen, 2018, p. 50; Friesem, 2016, p. 27). Friesem (2016, p. 28) argued that affective empathy is needed when one is willing to interact socially and form relationships. Additionally, a relationship may achieve an emotional level only when there is authenticity, subjectivity, respect, confidence and unreserved atmosphere between the parties (Ioannidou & Konstantikaki, 2008, p. 119; Mattelmäki & Battarbee, 2002, p. 269).

Indeed, affective empathy is reminiscent of a process in which one has an insight that enables the experience of another's emotional state and the equal sharing of emotions (Friesem, 2016, p. 27). However, Yalcin and DiPaola (2018, p. 21) noted that the interconnection with shared emotions may lead to unconscious mimicking of the other. This means the effect of sharing experiences may become so emotional that those involved start to live the role of the other (Friesem, 2016, p. 27). More specifically, the contrasting moment may lead to parallel empathy, which refers to imitating the other when in reactive empathy the contrasting moment leads to irritation (Belman & Flanagan, 2010, p. 6; McQuiggan et al., 2008, p. 167).

Although empathy is generally interpreted as a positive phenomenon, it is important to recognise the potential of 'negative empathy' or 'dark side empathy' (Bove, 2019, p. 32). 'Dark side empathy' describes a context in which a person morally misuses their capability of cognitive empathy to pursue goals in their self-interest (Aaltola & Keto, 2018, p. 52). Another example of 'dark side empathy' is a lack of empathy, which may be the result of having a heavy workload where there is an excessive amount of empathy; this is a situation that can lead to exhaustion (Bove, 2019, p. 38).

Including humane, diversified, social and cognitive contexts, there have been attempts to replace human-provided empathy with AI technology (Bove, 2019, p. 38). Yalcin and DiPaola (2018, p. 20) indicated that cognitive science and AI communities have continuously attempted to prototype and digitalise empathy with artificial and interactive nonhuman agents. Thus far, AI has been able to do statistical learning in categorising information by perceiving and learning from it whereas its' present capabilities in abstracting and reasoning statistical information are minor (Ailisto, 2019, p. 8).

The case study: MyStory—Along the Northern Lights Route

The case for the current study was conducted in relation to the Interreg Nord–funded project called MyStory—Along the Northern Lights Route (NLR). The NLR is more than 600 kilometres long and is a joint Nordic tourist itinerary and scenic route between the Bothnian Bay and Norwegian Sea, covering Finland, Sweden and Norway (Meriruoho et al., 2007). The MyStory project collaborates with organisations from public to private and third-party sectors in Finland, Norway and Sweden. The project's administrator is the Lapland University of Applied Sciences (Lapland UAS) in Finland (MyStory, 2021). The partner network consists of Lapland UAS, the Finland Futures Research Centre at the University of Turku, and Business Pello in Finland with Halti Business Garden in Norway.

One of the project's key objectives is to strengthen the competences of tourism companies in digital storytelling and marketing. Nearly 30 micro-tourism companies from Finland, Norway and Sweden participate in the project's business support programme (SP). The activities of the SP cover webinars, workshops and coaching (MyStory, 2021).

One of the SP programme webinars—Empathising with the customer: creating value with human and tech on a customer journey—was organised on 13 April 2021 (MyStory, 2021). The aim of the webinar was to inspire and support learning in service design and immersive technologies. The webinar delivered information about customer insights while offering practical tools for service design. It also provided useful information about immersive technologies and their role in deepening the customer experience (MyStory, 2021).

After the webinar, the project's participants and subscribers received a semi-structured Google Forms online survey. The survey included a variety of four multiple-choice and open-ended questions asking for accounts of empathy-related experiences of digital customer service touchpoints and service moments. The survey's informants were asked to assimilate the role of a leisure traveller and reflect on their own experiences in purchasing tourism-related services online.

The multiple-choice questions asked the informants the following:

- The most valuable digital service concepts in general
- The most convenient digital channel choices in urgent service needs
- The most attractive digital visual elements
- If the simulated empathy was experienced as authentic or not

The open-ended questions asked the informants to explain their experiences of the following:

- The most important elements of automation from a technological perspective
- Empathy in customer service
- Empathy in digital customer service
- The attractiveness of visual elements

Findings

The data samples, a total of 10 (n=10) responses, were collected in the online survey, which represented the study's empirical evidence. The study's method was to analyse the collected data using a qualitative inductive content analysis. The analysis was carried out in the interplay with theory and data, including the researcher's interpretation, to observe not only the visible, but also the latent content of the informants' leisure travel (Graneheim et al., 2017, p. 32). The role of the researcher as an ethnographer was to make suggestions in the interplay with theory to interpret both the visible and latent content (Graneheim et al., 2017, p. 32).

The data samples were coded and dismantled into pertinent thematic units to explain the correlation with the experience of cognitive and affective empathy in a leisure traveller's digital customer journey (Ignatow & Mihalcea, 2018, pp. 10, 146; Vuori, 2021). The role of the service provider was also analysed to determine whether this provider was a human or nonhuman agent.

The findings of the open-ended questions explained the digital experiences of empathy. The data were placed in a four-square matrix (Figure 16.1). The horizontal line of the four-square matrix illustrates empathy, in which cognitive (perspective taking) empathy was positioned on the left, leading to affective (sharing emotions) empathy on the right. The human and nonhuman agents who primarily provided or mediated the digital customer service were positioned vertically, with the human agent at the top and nonhuman agent at the bottom.

Another illustration of the findings describes the most important, valuable and convenient digital touchpoints (Table 16.1). In addition, the findings were reflected for empathy components, here describing the experience for cognitive or affective empathy. Moreover, the analysis explained whether the agent at the touchpoints was human or nonhuman. The description of the most important elements explained the characteristics and holistic experiences for digitally automated services. The most valuable digital service concepts of the customer journey are positioned in order. The choices for the most convenient digital channels represented the order of digital touchpoints in sensitive and urgent service needs.

Valued and empathetic human agents

One of the challenges in digital customer service concerns situations when the customer is feeling anxious, stressed or somehow vulnerable (Bove, 2019, p. 31). The current study's findings are consistent with those of Bove (2019, p. 31), underlining the importance of empathy with a human agent, especially when the leisure traveller is emotionally charged and seeking a human to take their perspective and even share emotions with them. The multiple-choice alternatives of *human-to-human contact* and *being contactable on the phone* are voted as being fairly valuable touchpoints, in which the most convenient channel of the service moment is a *phone*. The findings indicate that the service moment could be experienced as 'an atmosphere' affected by subjective experiences occurring at the touchpoint of the service moment with a human (Gherardi, 2018, p. 749).

The analyses of the data samples show that the experiences of the leisure traveller informants mainly emphasise cognitive empathy when interacting with human agents. Having a perspective-taking ability is valued when the service is personalised; here, the human agent could understand that "life can take unexpected turns", so the human agent can "adjust behaviour according to the customer". The elements behind the actions experienced are to "listen, react and assist" in resolving problems and to "give information in a friendly manner". However, there are also experiences of affective empathy with shared emotions, where the informants describe their experiences of "living in the moment with the customer" and "treating others as you would expect to be treated". The findings are related to experiences of sharing—and even immersing oneself—at an emotional level with the leisure traveller (Friesem, 2016, p. 27).

The data samples show there is also a risk of 'dark side empathy'. When the leisure traveller meets a human agent, the boundary in maintaining and managing equality, for example, when solving a problem, requires social intelligence and the insights of both participants. The risk of 'dark side empathy' (Bove, 2019, p. 32) can especially appear when the leisure traveller morally misuses their rights in asking the human agent to "resolve the problem, even if it means that the company rules are broken". The case shows that the expectations of a leisure traveller are based on their individual or even emotional needs, in which they ignore the business ethics, morality and sense that the human agent needs to follow (Belman & Flanagan, 2010, pp. 6, 10; Bove, 2019, p. 38; Aaltola & Keto, 2018, p. 52).

Surprisingly, the multiple-choice data show that the least valued service concept of all digital services is the leisure traveller's need for *a longstanding relationship*. Here, digital transformation, like the changes in consuming leisure travel–related digital services, seems to affect service relationships between the customer and the service provider (Pesonen, 2020, p. 89). Namely, traditionally *a longstanding relationship* is experienced as a bilateral relationship between two persons in which the connection is frequent and stable. For example, *a longstanding relationship* may consist of affective empathy with human dimensions like sharing emotions. More specifically, the basis of a longstanding relationship is experienced as including trust, loyalty and shared values covering, for example, the changing roles of personal lives.

However, digital transformation relationships may be changing, emphasising multilateral social networks and cocreation, which create social value (Kohtamäki et al., 2019, p. 380; Pesonen, 2020, p. 89). However, support for the value of *a longstanding relationship* is indirect: the discussion can be extended to relationships as a social phenomenon that is generally valued when moving towards the social-emotive era (Lappalainen, 2018). The argument is that the importance of forming relationships remains valid, but the forms between the participants change to become more amoebic, fragmented and multilateral.

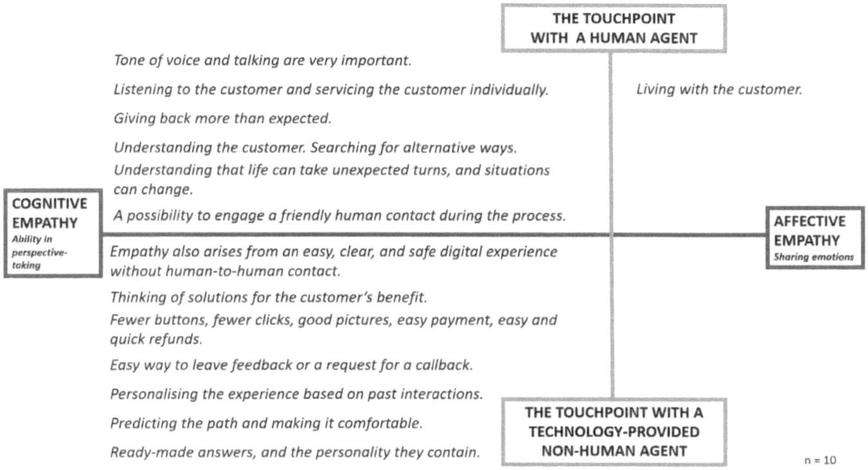

Figure 16.1 Digital experiences of empathy with a human or nonhuman. A four-square matrix, where the horizontal line presents the experiences of cognitive and affective empathy. The vertical line illustrates whether the digital service provider is a human or nonhuman agent.

Technology-provided nonhuman agents

Technology-provided nonhuman agent services have a significant role in digital transformation where traditional services like data and activities are reformed and new services are developed (Pesonen, 2020, p. 70). The very first digital touchpoint is increasingly shared with a technology-provided nonhuman agent. For example, one of the multiple-choice questions asked about the value of the *alternative channels for service (WhatsApp and Facebook)*. This alternative was voted as the third most valuable touchpoint, at which point the nonhuman agent mediates information to connect the leisure traveller with the human agent, if required. For example, a nonhuman social robot—a chatbot—may empathise and create value for a leisure traveller by following the questions and instructing them to proceed further (Belman & Flanagan, 2010, p. 6).

The current study's informants illustrate several digital experiences where the postexperience is reflected in automation, which supports a new experience in repeating the post search as a starting point (Heimbach et al., 2015, p. 129). The examples of the data illustrate the turn from postexperience to new experience with "predicting the customer journey based on the past" and "finding with just a few clicks your trips and stays if you need the information for some reason after years". These experiences are reflected in cognitive empathy, in which the role of automation is to support the experience based on the user's former behaviour.

Moreover, the data samples specify the importance of simplicity in concrete and separate digital actions when the leisure traveller is using various interfaces. The examples cover both devices like mobile phones and the use of solutions that can enhance the digital experience. The experiences of "fewer buttons and clicks", "clear and transparent" visibility, "information that is supported with texts and good pictures" and "safe credit card payment" are some basic, concrete cognitive empathy elements. The data samples are correlated by Amadeus's research (2020, p. 12), which underlines standard language and correct content that can facilitate a customer's experience and that is reflected in empathy.

Likewise, when requesting the informants for the most valuable digital service touchpoint, the findings of *a single point of contact* explain the importance of a model, which emphasises a one-stop-shop principle where customer service covers multiple modes in a single place for personalised service expectations (Eckhardt et al., 2017, p. 28). Another example that is reflected in *a single point of contact* is an omnichannel model, which is used in travel agency business to collect all digital touchpoints in a single place (Amadeus, 2020, pp. 5–6; Genesys, 2020, pp. 6–7). This finding reflects the service provider's ability in perspective taking (cognitive empathy), in which a *single point of contact* represents the leisure traveller's frictionless point of departure. Principally, it emphasises the collection of digital service touchpoints and service moments that define the alternatives for interaction with the tourism service provider.

When asking the informants about the attractiveness of the visual elements throughout their customer journey, the multiple-choice findings indicate the significance and importance of visualisation with photos, videos, movies and graphics. Photos are experienced as the most attractive because of their appeal and the amount of information they contain. The informants experience that the content in photos is realised, understood and more easily lived with, thus being reflected in cognitive empathy. In some cases, visualisation is experienced as humanised, especially when the illustrations are drawn by hand and, hence, seem more authentic. Elements that appeal to emotions, for example, the live images, storified engagement and visual elements, are valued in videos and movies.

Maiz-Arévalo (2015, pp. 140–141) indicated that digital communication is a sequence of actions in which the customer uses signs to send and receive messages to create sense. Typically, the first digital touchpoint is a programmed, solution-based device using, for example, AI to communicate with the customer. A voice user interface (VUI) and a chatbot are examples of a nonhuman agent mediating information and supporting the customer's experience. Jylkäs et al. (2018, p. 1437) suggested that the role of AI is to assist both the customer and the human agent. Therefore, the nonhuman agent's role cannot be diminished because it mediates information and affects the total experience.

Finally, immersive technologies like AR and VR are experienced as some of the least attractive elements of visualisation. Immersive technologies are found to be supportive as an experience, but they are also found "to take a lot of effort" from the customer. However, the findings show that the role of AR and VR is somewhat favoured, as reflected in having the role of an authentic and empathetic simulator of an experience as well. Nevertheless, the findings explain that the variety of immersive technologies is also experienced as negative. Although they are multiple, felt to be engaging and somewhat real, the experience "lacks the final piece, the proximity of a human being".

Table 16.1 The most important, valued and convenient digital touchpoints in order. The table explains the digital experiences of empathy from the perspective of a leisure traveller occurring with a human or nonhuman agent.

The perspective	*The digital experiences*	*The empathy components leading the experience*	*The agent providing the service*
The **most important** element in (automated) digital customer service	• Easiness, usability, simplicity. • Safety, trustworthiness. • Clarity, transparency and visibility of information. • Profiling, predicting of customer path.	Cognitive empathy in which the experiences emphasise the perspective-taking ability of personalised services in the digital touchpoints and service moments of the customer journey.	Nonhuman agent: the data samples indicate technical and technological elements that support the functions when using the interfaces. The content is mainly reflected in digital automation practices.

The perspective	*The digital experiences*	*The empathy components leading the experience*	*The agent providing the service*
	• Direct purchasing transactions with multiple credit cards. • Tested digital customer journey (no bugs).		
The **most valuable** service concepts	1. A single point of contact.	1. Cognitive empathy.	1. Nonhuman agent.
	2. Human-to-human contact.	2. Affective empathy.	2. Human agent.
	3. Alternative channels for service (WhatsApp, Facebook).	3. Cognitive empathy.	3. Human or nonhuman agent.
	4. Being contactable on the phone.	4. Affective empathy.	4. Human agent.
	5. Communication in a friendly manner.	5. Affective empathy.	5. Human or nonhuman agent.
	6. Checking that all is well during the trip.	6. Cognitive empathy.	6. Nonhuman agent.
	7. Longstanding relationships.	7. Affective empathy.	7. Human agent.
The **most convenient** digital touchpoints in sensitive and urgent service needs	1. Phone call.	1. Affective empathy.	1. Human agent.
	2. Sending a message using an app (WhatsApp or similar).	2. Cognitive empathy.	2. Human agent.
	3. Chatting on the internet with service provider.	3. Cognitive and affective empathy.	3. Human or nonhuman agent.
	4. Email.	4. Cognitive empathy.	4. Human or nonhuman agent.
	5. Sending an SMS message (text message by phone).	5. Cognitive empathy.	5. Human or nonhuman agent.
	6. Walk-in (if possible).	6. Cognitive or affective empathy.	6. Human agent.
	7. Completing a form on the service provider's webpage on the internet.	7. Cognitive empathy.	7. Nonhuman agent.

Conclusion and discussion

The present study's findings reveal that digital experiences with a human agent emphasise affective empathy, especially in situations when the leisure traveller is stressed, emotionally charged, feeling vulnerable and needs to share emotions. In general, human agents are experienced as showing cognitive empathy when they take the perspective of a leisure traveller, for example, in listening and understanding "that life can take unexpected turns". However, the findings show that there may be a risk of 'dark side empathy' if the leisure traveller misuses their moral rights by asking the human agent to resolve something, even if the company rules are broken.

The findings in technology-driven nonhuman agent mediating services emphasise cognitive empathy, in which the service provider takes the perspective of a leisure traveller by using technology like automation when mediating services. The customer journey's most valuable touchpoint is *a single point of contact*, allowing the leisure traveller to choose the most suitable channel for each touchpoint of the service moment. Moreover, technology-enhanced services repeating the leisure traveller's former behaviour are reflected in cognitive empathy because they make the journey smoother by showing the history of previous searches (Shen et al., 2020, p. 3). Here, technical elements like the simplicity and safety of the interface with fewer clicks and buttons are valued. When testing the functionalities of the platforms and solutions, these pitfalls may be empathised with and prevented.

The experiences of digitally visual elements stress the use of photos, videos, movies and graphics. The experience is lived authentically with the service provider, especially in visual content that is humanised, for example, when illustrated by hand-drawn content. Perhaps surprisingly, immersive technologies are found to be less attractive. However, they are reflected in cognitive empathy, in which the service provider engages with the leisure traveller in immersing themselves in the experience. Although the aim of AI is to support a leisure traveller's decision-making by analysing, simulating and learning from the customer's behaviour (Shen et al., 2020, p. 3), immersive technologies are experienced as requiring a lot of effort. The experience is somewhat engaging and real, but it lacks the final piece: "the proximity of a human being".

The findings show that the level of empathy is mainly cognitive empathy (perspective taking), covering reflections of technical functionalities like repeating the history of a person's previous searches (Ailisto, 2019, p. 8; Launchbury, 2017). With AI technology mediating services and simulating humans, this study's findings show that the experiences of AI focus on describing, narrating and categorising information. Hence, AI's attempts to simulate cognitive empathy are justified. Although the leisure traveller experiences the service of a nonhuman agent as somewhat empathetic, this does not necessarily mean that the nonhuman agent knows how to abstract and reason about the empathetic contents (Ailisto, 2019, p. 8). Indeed, the current study's argument is that humans are the ones who create the signs, content and reasoning of empathy that AI technology seeks to prototype and learn from.

Future research could explore the effect of emotional stress affecting a leisure traveller's choice of a digital touchpoint and service moment. Moreover, the studies could explore the effect on digital customer experience by comparing the experience of using familiar and unfamiliar technology. Finally, future studies could explore a combination of humane and technological experiences in digital mobility ecosystems that can connect tourists with locals in rural destinations.

Summary 1: Lessons learned that can contribute to the organisational or business context

Digital transformation has diminished the value of *a longstanding relationship*, which is reflected in the roles and changes in consuming leisure travel—related digital experiences. The value of relationships remains, but the forms emphasise multilateral social networks and interest groups, for example, the recommendation systems. The finding is reflected in digital service experiences that explicitly emphasise cognitive empathy—here as a perspective-taking ability—with automated services that are mediated by a nonhuman agent. However, there is a need for affective empathy when a leisure traveller feels emotionally vulnerable. The most convenient touchpoint is a phone, in this case, which can enable affective empathy and shared emotions with a human.

Automation is important because it supports personalised digital service, where simplicity, predicting a customer's path based on previous actions and safe usability of the interface are valued. However, the value in the digital experience comes from the touchpoints that are easily found at *a single point of contact*, emphasising a one-stop-shop with multiple service modes in a single place. Although AI is a mediating service, immersive technologies are experienced as partially authentic but requiring effort from the leisure travellers. Instead of immersive technologies, the visual experiences of leisure travellers emphasise photos, videos, movies and graphics, which are easily accessible, familiar from regular use, and assimilated in empathetic service.

Summary 2: Contribution to organisational or business knowledge or practices

A single point of contact is experienced as the most valued touchpoint in the digital customer journey of a leisure traveller. This shows cognitive empathy, where the service provider can deliver a one-stop-shop or an omnichannel model experience to collect all digital touchpoints at the same place. *A single point of contact* enables a leisure traveller to choose the touchpoint for each service moment based on their needs. Supported by automation elements, the experiences emphasise ease, clarity and safe usability of the regularly used interfaces.

Instead of relying on AI, like immersive technologies the leisure traveller values photos, videos, movies and graphics as visual elements. The value of photos, videos, movies and graphics is reflected in humanised ways to provide information, which is mediated in ordinary, easily accessible digital touchpoints and, thus, can be experienced to include cognitive empathy where the service provider has the ability in taking the perspective of a leisure traveller.

Acknowledgements

This grant-funded research work was supported by the Finnish Cultural Foundation. In addition, this research was supported by the MyStory—Along the Northern Lights Route Project, which is cofinanced by the Interreg Nord Fund EU programme.

References

Ailisto, H. (2019). *Tekoälyaika – vaikutukset työhön*. Paper presented at Lapland University of Applied Sciences Alumni Event, 31 October.

Aaltola, E. & Keto, S. (2018). *Empatia – Myötäelämisen tiede*. Into Kustannus Oy.

Amadeus (2020). *Insights for the new travel – Omnichannel*. https://amadeus.com/en/insights/research-report/insights-for-the-new-world-of-travel-omnichannel.

Becker, L. (2020). *Toward a customer-centric perspective of customer experience* [Doctoral dissertation, University of Turku]. https://www.utupub.fi/bitstream/handle/10024/149688/AnnalesE60Becker.pdf?sequence=1&isAllowed=y.

Belman, J., & Flanagan, M. (2010). Designing games to foster empathy. *Journal of Cognitive Technology*, 14 (2). https://tiltfactor.org/wp-content/uploads2/cog-tech-si-g4g-article-1-belman-and-flanagan-designing-games-to-foster-empathy.pdf.

Bove, L. (2019). Empathy for service. *Journal of Services Marketing*, 33 (1). doi:10.1108/JSM-10-2018-0289.

Chen, C. (2018). Developing EFL students' digital empathy through video production. *System*, 77, 50–57.

Eckhardt, J., Aapaoja, A., Nykänen, L., Sochor, J., Karlsson, M. & König, D. (2017). Deliverable 2: European MaaS Roadmap 2025. MAASiFiE project funded by CEDR.

Fortune. (2016). Carnival sets sail with virtual reality vacations. In J. Gaudiosi (Ed.), *Fortune Section Tech*, 19 February. https://fortune.com/2016/02/19/carnival-sets-sail-with-virtual-reality-vacations/.

Friesem, Y. (2016). Empathy for the digital age: Using video production to enhance social, emotional, and cognitive skills. In S. Y. Tettegah & D. L. Espelage (Eds.), *Emotions, technology, and behaviors* (pp. 21–45) Academic Press. https://doi.org/10.1016/B978-0-12-801873-6.00002-9.

Genesys. (2020). *Empathy in customer service: A consumer survey and practical guide*. https://www.genesys.com/en-gb/resources/empathy-in-customer-service-consumer-survey-and-guide.

Gherardi, S. (2018). Theorizing affective ethnography for organization studies. *Organization*, 26 (6), 741–760. doi:10.1177/1350508418805285.

Graneheim, U. H., Lindgren, B-M., & Lundman, B. (2017). Methodological challenges in qualitative content analysis: A discussion paper. *Nurse Education Today*, 56, 29–34. https://doi.org/10.1016/j.nedt.2017.06.002.

Heimbach, I., Kostyra, D. S., & Hinz, O. (2015). Marketing automation. *Business & Information Systems Engineering*, 57, 129–133. https://doi.org/10.1007/s12599-015-0370-8.

Ignatow, G., & Mihalcea, R. (2018). *An introduction to text mining: Research design, data collection, and analysis*. SAGE Publications.

Ioannidou, F., & Konstantikaki, V. (2008). Empathy and emotional intelligence: What is it really about? *International Journal of Caring Sciences*, 1 (3), 118–123.

Jylkäs, T., Äijälä, M. H., Vuorikari, T. M., & Rajab, V. (2018). *AI Assistants as Non-human Actors in Service Design*. Proceedings of the ADMC18 DMI: Academic Design Management Conference, 1436–1444. https://www.dmi.org/page/ADMC2018Proceedings.

Kamas, L., & Preston, A. (2020). Empathy, gender, and prosocial behavior. *Journal of Behavioral and Experimental Economics*, 92, 101654. https://doi.org/10.1016/j.socec.2020.101654.

Kofoed, A. (2021). *From human touch to human tech: The challenge of frictionless travel beyond COVID-19*. Paper presented at Enter 2021 Conference, 20 January.

Kohtamäki, M., Paridac, V., Oghazie, P., Gebauerf, H., & Baines, T. (2019). Digital servitization business models in ecosystems: A theory of the firm. *Journal of Business Research*, 104, 380–392.

Lappalainen, P. (2018). *Dialoginen ja tunneälykäs johtaminen*. A physical lecture of Dialogical and Emotional Intelligent Leadership at University of Lapland, 11 October.

Launchbury, J. (2017). *A Darpa perspective on artificial intelligence*. https://www.darpa.mil/about-us/darpa-perspective-on-ai.

Maiz-Arévalo, C. (2015). Typographic alteration in formal computer-mediated communication. *Procedia – Social and Behavioral Sciences*, 212, 140–145.

Mattelmäki, T., & Battarbee, K. (2002). Empathy probes. In T. Binder, J. Gregory, & I. Wagner (Eds.), *PDC 02 proceedings of the participatory design conference* (pp. 23–25). CPSR.

Mattelmäki, T., Vaajakallio, K., & Koskinen, I. (2014). What happened to empathic design? *Design Issues*, 30 (1), 67–77. https://doi.org/10.1162/DESI_a_00249.

Meriruoho, A., Rantala, O., & Veijola, S. (2007). *On the Northern Lights Route from Tornio to Kilpisjarvi: Perspectives in tourism studies for developing a scenic road of tourism* (Vol. 3201055). Finnish Road Administration. https://trid.trb.org/view/851020.

McQuiggan, S., Sabourin, J., Phillips, R., & Lester, J. (2008). *Modeling parallel and reactive empathy in virtual agents: An inductive approach*, 7th International Joint Conference on Autonomous Agents and Multiagent Systems (AAMAS 2008), Estoril, Portugal, 12–16 May, Vol. 1, 167–174. doi:10.1145/1402383.1402411.

Miettinen, S. (2011). *Palvelumuotoilu – uusia menetelmiä käyttäjätiedon hankintaan ja hyödyntämiseen*. Tammerprint.

Miettinen, S., Rytilahti, P., Vuontisjärvi, H-R., Kuure, E., & Rontti, S. (2014). Experience design in digital services. *Research in Economics and Business: Central and Eastern Europe*, 6 (1). http://rebcee.eu/index.php/REB/article/view/53.

MyStory. (2021). *Northern Lights Route. Events*. https://northernlightsroute.info/events/.

Neuhofer, B., Buhalis, D., & Ladkin, A. (2012). Conceptualizing technology enhanced destination experiences. *Journal of Destination Marketing and Management*, 1, 36–46.

Perez-Vega, R., Kaartemo, V., Lages, C. R., Borghei Razavi, N., & Männistö, J. (2021). Reshaping the contexts of online customer engagement behavior via artificial intelligence: A conceptual framework. *Journal of Business Research*, 129, 902–910. https://doi.org/10.1016/j.jbusres.2020.11.002.

Pesonen, J. (2020). Asiakassuhde-elämyksiä matkailijoille. In H. Konu, J. Pesonen, & H. Reijonen (Eds.), *Matkailuliiketoimintaa teoriasta käytäntöön* (pp. 69–98). Kustannusosakeyhtiö Vastapaino.

Powell, P., & Roberts, J. (2017). Situational determinants of cognitive, affective, and compassionate empathy in naturalistic digital interactions. *Computer in Human Behavior*, 68, 137–148.

Reichstein, C., & Härting, R-C. (2018). Potentials of changing customer needs in a digital world: A conceptual model and recommendations for action in tourism. *Procedia Computer Science*, 126, 1484–1494.

Risdon, C., & Quattlebaum, P. (2018). *Orchestrating experiences: Collaborative design for complexity*. Rosenfeld.

Ruonakoski, E. (2019). Empatia moraalisen toimijuuden perustana. *Ajatus*, 76 (1), 315–330. https://journal.fi/ajatus/article/view/88195.

Shen, S., Sotiriadis, M., & Zhang, Y. (2020). The influence of smart technologies on customer journey in tourist attractions within the smart tourism management framework. *Sustainability*, 12 (10), 4157. https://doi.org/10.3390/su12104157.

Shin, D. (2018). Empathy and embodied experience in virtual environment: To what extent can virtual reality stimulate empathy and embodied experience? *Computers in Human Behavior*, 78, 64–73.

Statistics Finland. (2021). *Concepts. Leisure trip*. https://www.stat.fi/meta/kas/vapajmatka_en.html#tab2.

Vuori, J. (2021). Laadullinen sisällönanalyysi. In J. Vuori (Ed.), *Laadullisen tutkimuksen verkkokäsikirja*. Yhteiskuntatieteellinen tietoarkisto. https://www.fsd.tuni.fi/fi/palvelut/menetelmaopetus/kvali/analyysitavan-valinta-ja-yleiset-analyysitavat/laadullinen-sisallonanalyysi/.

Yalcin, Ö., & DiPaola, S. (2018). A computational model of empathy for interactive agents. *Biologically Inspired Cognitive Architectures*, 26, 20–25. https://doi.org/10.1016/j.bica.2018.07.010.

Yung, R., Khoo-Lattimore, C., & Potter, L. E. (2021). Virtual reality and tourism marketing: Conceptualizing a framework on presence, emotion, and intention. *Current Issues in Tourism*, 24 (11), 1505–1525. doi:10.1080/13683500.2020.1820454.

Zaki, J., & Ochsner, K. (2012). The neuroscience of empathy: progress, pitfalls and promise. *Nat Neurosci*, 15, 675–680. doi:10.1038/nn.3085.

17 Capitalising on empathic actions

Design principles of digitally transforming business processes

Yangyang Zhao and Timothy K. Craig

Introduction

The megatrend of digitalisation has spurred transformation in nearly every business, at least to some extent. The rapid adoption of digital technologies can propagate powerful means for businesses to sustain their capabilities and gain a competitive edge. Remote work from home using internet platforms, which started to occur more prominently because of the COVID-19 pandemic, is one practical example of this. This so-called 'reimagining the business process' through the use of digital technologies is gradually changing how humans work and interact with each other. Successful businesses are those that empathise with human needs, design for them and integrate them into their new technology applications. These activities define the empathic action–based business transformation in digital realms.

Despite tremendous efforts being expended in digital transformation, many businesses found their improvement results remained at distressing levels and that failed programmes significantly exceeded expected successes (Tekic & Koroteev, 2019). One reason is that most managers failed to grasp the true value of empathic actions to business processes—let alone know how to manage them during the course of the digital transformation. Yet it is underexplored what roles digital technologies play in capitalising on empathic actions for businesses and what businesses must do to exploit them to a strategic advantage.

Some pioneering executives have recognised the link between empathy and the business process and have redesigned the process of how business is done. In line with this attempt, the case study that we explore in this chapter comes from an international company performing preclinical research and development activities for large pharmaceutical companies. As part of its digitalisation strategy, the case company also redesigned its business process through radical acts of empathy, resulting in improved operational performance and employee retention. In this rapidly changing marketplace, the case study offers valuable evidence on how to digitally transform venture-wide operations through empathic actions in a strategic and systematic way. In particular, five design principles with associated structural activities for the organisational (re)design with empathy are outlined and illustrated by the case study.

DOI: 10.4324/9781003227557-21

Related work

The missing link

The discussions about the value of empathy and its related actions in an organisation have been varied. The central value of empathy is deeply rooted in discovering and meeting both human needs and the needs regarding human-to-human relationships and human-to-system interactions. 'Empathy' has been widely recognised as an actional instrument providing access to certain kinds of insights into user/customer needs, perceptions and perspectives that benefit creative problem solving (Delpechitre et al., 2019). Much has been said about the necessity of being empathic to enhance novel ideation and creativity in group activities, for example, within new product/service development (Salminen et al., 2021; Dalton & Kahute, 2016; Brown, 2008). Some scholars have further highlighted the relational values of empathy in fostering emotional connections, moral decision making and collaborations within an organisation (Betzler, 2019). Others, however, have pointed out the potential risks of misusing empathy without proper judgement and reducing otherness to sameness (Bloom, 2017; Baron-Cohen, 2012; Lather, 2008).

Because every instance of empathy is related to humans, the value of empathy originates from the actions of detecting and resolving human needs (Dalton & Kahute, 2016). A proper understanding of human behaviours and human relations could set the basis for our actions when it comes to capturing the value of empathy and mitigating the risk of potential misuse within an organisation. How to engage human empathy in actions is perceived as a skill that can be trained and improved (Holt et al., 2017). Many process-oriented design frameworks, such as the IDEO's design thinking process and Google's five-day design sprint, are populated mostly at individual and group levels. Proper engagement remains a mystery to business-level performance, and a lack of practical guidance exists at the organisation-wide level. Yet exploration here is expected as the adoption of these design frameworks increases.

The engagement of empathy has come to prominence in business management (Ohreen, 2021; Tzouramani, 2017; New & Kimbell, 2013; Pavlovich & Krahnke, 2013). As businesses consistently struggle with scaling up, cost overruns and customer satisfaction, they are under new pressure to redesign their business processes so that they can grow sustainably in digital times. Along with the surge in the use of digital technologies, human interactions within the organisation and with customers in the marketplace have been transformed. To detect and respond to ongoing changes, it is crucial to digitally transform the entire business processes for increased accessibility to external customers while realising efficiency in internal operations, because all human interfaces in product/service design and production are critical for business process success. Although empathic actions are considered the pathway to manage human interfaces, there has been a very limited discussion on the subject of redesigning organisation-wide business operations (Young, 2015).

Therefore, there is a missing link in how to capture the value of empathy in digitally transforming a business process. Redesigning the business process with empathy promises improved business performance, but not at the expense of human stakeholders (such as employees/customers). Many scholars have provided relevant design frameworks for creative problem solving, which are mostly philosophical approaches without deliberate organisational practices; hence, many questions remain unanswered (Agarwal & Weill, 2012; Brown, 2008). For example, how will managers know when their organisations have capitalised on the empathic actions in their everyday operations? What concrete changes in venture-wide business process are required? What technology and transformation programmes must be in place? How do you get from here to there?

The empathic action-based business process

We situate our study in the context of organisational practices as a way to implement the digital transformation of business processes. Many papers have been published and become fundamental in uncovering the key issues in such a transformation (Ivančić, et al., 2019; Zhao, 2019; Schwertner, 2017; Matt et al., 2015). Three key issues are to be resolved. First is a thorough understanding of the process that needs to be changed. A business process is known as the collection of organisation-wide activities performed by stakeholders in developing products or services for customers (Vom Brocke & Rosemann, 2014). The optimisation of the business process usually involves transformation in the cultural, structural and operational aspects across all levels and functions in an organisation. Through empathic actions, the process change that will occur happens through understanding human needs and human-related interactions within an organisation and with the environment, and based on these, it seeks solutions in dealing with the socio-technical complexity involved (Alvarez & Porac, 2020). Thus, the empathic action–based business transformation focuses on process improvement through better knowledge and understanding of the social aspect of the business. Second is the issue of creating a valid (re)design of the process that will result in collecting the value of human empathy. This requires a systematic and holistic design approach to guide the empathic actions at the individual level and to be transformed as the organisational values. The organisational values should help unify all the high-level organisational goals and the bottom level of functional executions by individuals. Through a series of purposeful actions, as every step is accomplished, the organisation moves forward one more step to empathy-empowered business process. Third is the issue of how to incorporate digital technology aids, that is, digitalisation in our context. The (re)design of the business process is associated with the social nature of the business operation but also the technology use in realising the solution. Many management theories (Orlikowski, 2010, 1992) have posited that technology use is inextricable and inseparable from our social interactions and artefacts that were created for problem solving. Technology that aids in the development of better tools helps ensure that the gains from empathic actions are in fact distributed, monitored and assessed. For instance, digital technologies can pave the way for enabling information flow and putting useful information at employees' fingertips at all levels in an organisation. Meanwhile, it can encourage employee engagement with results and satisfaction that their work is being used by others in a productive way. Hence, managers should have a firm foundation to implement a digital transformation towards an empathic action–based business process once these three key issues are addressed.

Research methodology

We employed a case study as the main research methodology to exemplify how the issues are tackled. As Yin (2018) pointed out, a case study is 'an empirical enquiry that investigates a contemporary phenomenon in depth and within its real-life context'. In real-life case scenarios, the link between inductive reasoning and systematic experiments in management practices has been proven to help decode the formula for business success (i.e., design principles generation in our case) (Dimov, 2020).

Introducing the case study

The case company comes from a Contract Research and Development Organisation (CRO) in the life sciences industry, which has been under heavy pressure to deliver timely medications treating a variety of diseases, including COVID-19, cancer and heart disease, among others. Part of the drug discovery process involves a specialised field called structural biology, where atomic resolution using the three-dimensional structures of targeted proteins related to the disease are determined with the initial 'hit' compounds, which can be identified in a number of ways, including but not limited to virtual screening, biophysical/biochemical screening and cell-based assays. The case company mainly performs preclinical research and development projects in structural biology, in collaboration with many multinational companies at the same time. CROs are usually small or medium-sized companies, striving for very competitive performance in time, cost and quality.

Data collection and analysis

The unique data stem from a case study conducted in the US. The participatory methods compose our data collection and analysis, which are seen as integral to the success of the research efforts and to the local adoption of the findings (Brown & Wyckoff-Baird, 1992). We coconstructed the data collection and analysis through partnerships with the local people (the top management in the case company) who had insider knowledge throughout the initial design and execution of the organisational redesign and digital assistant generation. Specifically, the data sources incorporate local knowledge in our case through interviews, cocreation workshops and performance monitors (see Table 17.1). The analysis of the data sources was geared towards the research objective of studying the design principles in digitally transforming the business process with empathy. We first reviewed all the collected data for quality evidence, and based on this, we could seek answers to all the questions posted, including the three key issues. The analysis then took place through working with the collected data along with the theoretical resources to induce the design principles. Finally, we were able to construct the storyline in the form of systematic and sequential activities and to present sufficient details as the case findings.

Findings

We aim for a shared set of design principles derived from our case study, which can be used as value-capturing metrics to track and review all structural activities of organisation-wide digital transformations. An organisation-wide business process redesign usually requires the implementation of five key activities: *initiation and team setup, stakeholder identification and need finding, situational analysis for root causes, experimental design for new business process* and *technological realisation and assessment.* Each activity in our case study was accompanied by a distinctive design principle. Many companies are familiar with the activities to produce new business processes because they are part of the conventional systems approach in solving social-technical problems (INCOSE, 2015). However, little is known about how to practise them in capturing empathic values through those activities. By generating the design principles that support those activities and integrating them into practices of sustaining—and even improving—business performance, the organisation can capitalise on the value from more empathic actions.

Activity 1: Initiation and campaign team setup

After the departure of a previous CEO and the arrival of a new leadership team, the case company had the vision of gaining competitiveness at least in

Table 17.1 Data sources, participants and expected outcomes.

Data sources	*Participants*	*Expected outcomes*
One-to-one face interviews	Board members, (outgoing) CEO, senior managers	Eliciting the list of stakeholders
Semi-structured one-to-one interviews	All company employees, including (outgoing) CEO	Understanding 'as-is' situation and stakeholder needs
Cocreation workshops	Board members, senior managers and other functional groups, respectively	Analysing root causes and conceptualising 'to-be' situation and requirements
Evaluation studies through business performance monitors	Senior managers, functional group leaders	Verifying and validating the new business process for the implementation

part through digitalisation. The leadership team, consisting of the chief scientific officer, chief marketing officer and chief operations officer (i.e., the C-level positions), launched the digital initiative for business process design. The scope of the business process design project was to digitise several business processes, including the establishment of an integrated inventory management, work assignment and completion process and a work-hour reporting system. It was expected that this digitalisation process would result in the generation of customised software created through building on a commercial electronic laboratory notebook platform. With a strong human-centred mindset, an aligned commitment to redesign and digitalisation with a focus on empathy by the top management team, the team was able to set the stage for the later success.

This first design principle is in line with the practicality that all business transformation initiatives require the commitment by top management. Very practically, to redesign large parts of an organisation, people with the authority to authorise such an activity must be convinced of the plan and willing to actively participate as stakeholders with their own human, human-to-human and human-to-system empathic relationships. All the cultural and management support-related factors are important for the successful integration and adoption of the digital technology. Therefore, we propose the following.

Design principle 1. Obtaining commitment from top management

Activity 2. Stakeholder identification and need finding

Identifying stakeholders is the key staple in the problem domain. A stakeholder can be defined as individuals and organisations that have influence and can be affected by the intended digital system's use and performance (INCOSE, 2015). In this case company, the scope of the intended digital initiative was within the organisation's operational process. Thus, we were mainly concerned with the stakeholders identified as the company's employees.

Within the 'as-is' organisational structure, the outgoing CEO was also acting as the project leader, who had the overall responsibility in consulting with the customers and executing all the projects, for example, the proposed timelines, costs and so forth. Other individual stakeholders then performed different job functions, depending on the instructions given by the CEO. The strengths identified through this stakeholder analysis are as follows: 1) the structure was flexible enough to allocate or move individual stakeholders to different projects; 2) the information flow was easily integrated by the CEO; and 3) the decision making was very centralised with little ambiguity. These strengths remain as such only under the assumptions that the CEO has continuous and unlimited capacity and a sufficient pool of other employees able to independently operate in multiple R&D pipeline positions. However, this was not the case. Most employees were well trained and highly educated professionals in a specific field, and so-called full-stack employees were scarce resources in the talent market. Thus, the 'as-is' system exhibited the following weaknesses: 1) business capacity was constrained by one individual's time and capacity as

CEO; 2) top-down directives undermined motivation and the capacity of other individual stakeholders besides the CEO, including both full-stack and non-full-stack employees; and 3) there was a massive risk of project failure if the CEO was absent or even on scheduled vacations. In fact, the CEO resigned rather unexpectedly and put the organisation's survival at risk, but the new top management leadership team, who called for this digital initiative, emphasised the opportunity for an organisation-wide business process redesign.

In the 'to-be' organisational situation, the leadership team (the three C positions) was formed. It is worth mentioning that all the leadership team members had previously served on senior management or advisory board roles in the company and had been trusted and perceived as capable leaders. Their new appointments as the leadership team were an attempt to mitigate the risks of centralised authority and project management responsibilities. A matrix-based organisational structure was envisioned for embracing the motivation and capacity among all the employees by structuring them into functional groups while giving flexibility in applying resources from the functional groups to projects. Table 17.2 lists the five key groups and their functional descriptions.

The need findings for the identified stakeholders are related to the empathic actions for a deep understanding of stakeholder needs and help in assessing their interest regarding both the technical (i.e., conventional functional needs) and social aspects (i.e., emotional needs in our case) in the intended work system (Bryson, 2004). Conducting interviews is a common technique, which was the case for our need finding activities (Goguen & Linde, 1993). We assembled all the relevant personnel from functional groups (a total of 25 personnel) in the company and performed informational one-on-one interviews regarding their needs and how the as-is work system made them feel and how they would like to feel in the to-be state. By analysing the gap between the as-is (old) and the to-be (newly desired) states based on the interview data, we were able to articulate the characteristics of the stakeholders, catalogue the stakeholder

Table 17.2 Functional group and description.

Functional group	*Description*
Project management	Overall designer of project and customer contact.
Cloning and expression	Construction of synthetic genes, cultivation of cells producing (expressing) the recombinant protein.
Protein chemistry	Purification and quality control of recombinant protein from cell pellets or supernatants provided by cloning and expression.
Structural biology	Crystallisation and cryoelectron microscopy performed using proteins supplied by protein chemistry.
Biophysics	Identifying and characterising protein–protein or protein–ligand interactions using the proteins supplied by protein chemistry.

groups and elicit their needs (Franklin, 2006). The identified stakeholder groups and their functional and emotional needs for the company's business process are shown in Figure 17.1.

The identified needs in the social aspects include both positive emotional needs (i.e., things the stakeholders wanted to feel) and negative emotional needs (i.e., things they did not want to feel). Throughout the empathic design process, the leadership team sought to increase the activities or behaviours that encouraged positive emotional responses and minimised activities or behaviours that produced negative emotional responses. It was noted that a critical emotional need was the desire to be valued for scientific expertise and to feel in control of the experiments being performed. The fact that this emotional need is common across all stakeholders presented an obvious challenge in the implementation because it was impossible for all stakeholders to be in control of the entire experiment. However, it was possible for the process to be broken up so that many stakeholders had their own areas of absolute control. Additionally, part of the intended redesign of the business process needed to address the structurally induced conflict rooted in the stakeholder needs. One example of this structural conflict is that project leaders needed to request detailed experiments be done by members of functional groups; however, function group leaders were domain experts who may disagree with the experimental designs of the project leaders. Because the project leaders had the authority to request experiments be done, this structure itself triggered the negative

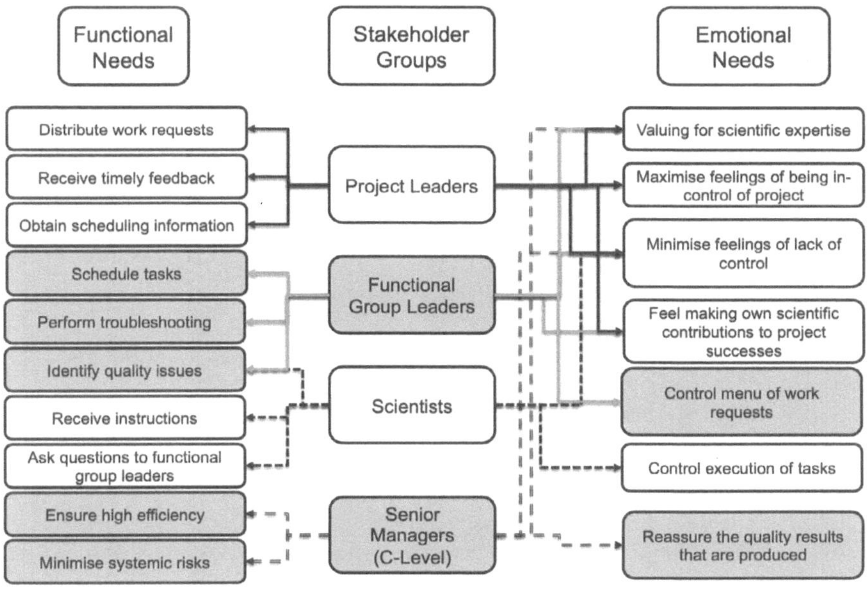

Figure 17.1 Stakeholders and needs.

emotional response of lacking control and minimised the desired positive emotional response of having their scientific expertise valued.

Based on the above, we propose the following.

Design principle 2. Emphasising strengths and working to minimise weaknesses in the social aspects of the organisation

Activity 3.Root causes analysis in human interfaces

Like many project-based organisations, stakeholders in the case study were specialised in different functional parts of the business process, with few members having full-stack expertise. The different subprocesses, standards and best practices of the functional groups and stakeholders would generate challenges in managing the interfaces for the overall business performance. The main issue in redesigning the business process for a project-based organisation is rooted in interface management through the contextual project workflow. Figure 17.2 exemplifies the workflow map of a typical project, along with the timing. The workflow involves a complicated business process consisting of five information-intensive steps. To complete the steps within the expected durations, the case company needed to overcome interface obstacles that appeared at the boundaries between people, concepts, equipment and technical support systems (Nooteboom, 2004). For example, a single purified protein target would be subjected to >4000 chemical mixtures individually, and robotic imagers would capture images of these small volumes over time, with images being manually classified by humans. Often, the rate-limiting step of the process and one of the most critical challenges in the projects would be the expression and production of a pure protein, which was the result of a collaboration between the cloning and expression and protein chemistry groups, which was driven by a number of key stakeholders in this case company.

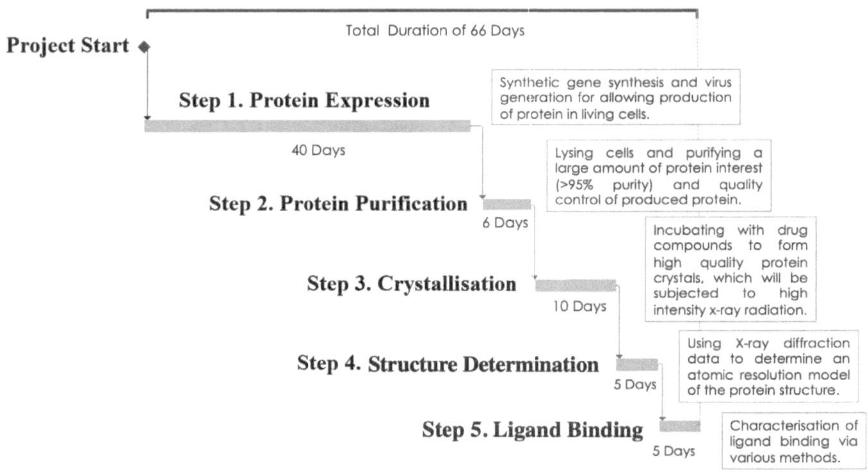

Figure 17.2 Workflow map of a typical project.

With a common goal, the existing interface management method crosscut the organisation's business process (re)design to facilitate alignments among stakeholders in daily operations, such as roles and responsibilities, place and timing for information exchange, highlighting the critical interface challenges earlier in projects (Bible & Bivins, 2019). The (re)design efforts often resulted in a new interface system to help streamline the workflow, communication and satisfaction of the identified stakeholders (system users). According to Conway's law (1968), the main constraint for organisations to produce any design system is the tendency to cope with the existing communication structures. The communication structure resides in human interfaces as the process of acquiring all relevant information, interpreting this information, and effectively disseminating the information to persons who might need it (Zulch, 2014). An effective business processes requires the effective exchange of information from one to another in an effective manner (PMP, 2007). The structure of the relational interfaces between the stakeholders is also the focal point of the relational values of empathy in many informative-intensive companies.

Therefore, from a holistic view, empathic action is required to investigate the causes of the interface challenges among stakeholders. A root cause analysis can help determine the underlying causes behind stakeholder needs in terms of human interfaces (Franklin, 2006). The five whys method is a simple yet powerful method to perform a root cause analysis (Serrat, 2017). When performing a root cause analysis, we started by questioning why the stakeholder needs exist and the linkages to relational interfaces. If the identified cause is not the root cause, we can then work on why the identified cause exists recursively until the root cause has been identified. The process of determining the root causes for a certain challenge may require fewer or more than five why repetitions.

As Rajkumar (2010) pointed out, the most typical interface-related obstacles are found within three main areas: language, political and cultural. The fundamental relationship in the 'as-is' organisational state is not only a source of strength, in that the project leader can communicate easily in a common language with customers on both a scientific and project management basis, but also a source of conflict within the company because many experienced scientists felt they did not get to contribute significantly to the successful design and completion of projects. The root causes were largely attributed to the highly hierarchical and command-control organisational scheme. The project leader (the former CEO) used to be the person who gave instructions to the resources provided in the functional groups and acted as an overall expert across different subjects operated by the functional groups. This leading role gave the project leader a substantial degree of authority over all other employees, who were, in many cases, also experts with many years of experience. Moreover, the relational interfaces for communication among the stakeholders were chaotic and without formal structures, causing a poor culture for collaboration and low employee satisfaction.

Restructuring the organisational scheme as the 'to-be' state presented opportunities and potential benefits. However, this would also create a number of new structural relationships, which may naturally produce similar conflicts with the former. We identified that the fundamental conflict was rooted in the emotional needs of stakeholders, the communication channel among groups and organisational support to the project. Thus, the solution should be able to retain and motivate individual employees, facilitate communications and provide better organisation-wide support for operational efficiency and capacity for those who perform the work by using the newly designed system. Therefore, we propose the following.

Design principle 3. Having a holistic view of a human interface analysis at all business levels

Activity 4. Experimental design for new business process

With a good understanding of the root causes, several design concepts for the new business process system were initially ideated. Only after a few iterations of experimental designs was the final solution that satisfied all critical stakeholder needs accepted by the leadership team in the company. In our case, the redesign of the interfaces between the stakeholders, especially project leaders and functional group leaders, was the key for any effective project operation. Because different stakeholders had different needs at different steps of the project, it was not possible to have each stakeholder be in full control. However, it was possible to have a single stakeholder be in control of one or smaller subsections of the project. As a result, the solution included a new request system where elements of the system were separated into groups and each group was under the control of a single type of stakeholder (see Figure 17.3). Each type of stakeholder was designed with a clear role and responsibility in handling each

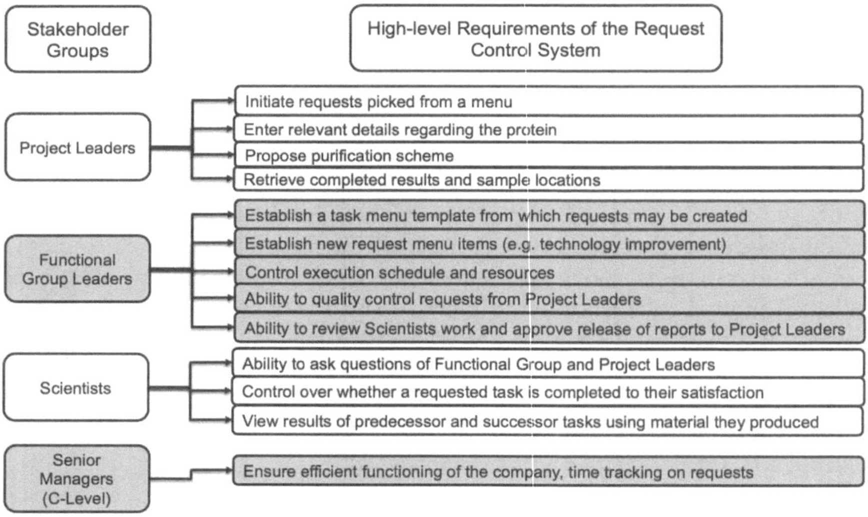

Figure 17.3 High-level requirements for the request control system.

interface area (in terms of the project execution) on both sides of the interface. This type of design reflects one of the most important methods to facilitate efficient project communication by establishing communication lines and information flow (Fisk, 2010; Bible & Bivins, 2019). For each stakeholder, the requirements defined who to contact and request what information from. The information flows across the designed communication lines should complete the high-level interface areas and the overall integration of the workflow steps throughout project execution.

This solution attempted to relieve the past pain of experienced scientists and streamline their relationship with the project leader, but also to set up an online communication platform and increase operational transparency. The solution was set to be realised through a digital platform that would allow all members of the project to track and contribute to the project workflow using narrative formatting. A graphical representation of the communication interfaces with milestones for one request in the digital system is provided in Figure 17.4. Here, there might be many requests, which are hyperlinked to each other, to be put in by the project leaders to complete a single project.

Stakeholders can see how fulfilling the requests for individual steps contributes to overall project progress. This narrative formatting allowed users to see that their contributions helped the success of the project. This format also increased the level of transparency of the project, allowing senior managers to easily overview projects to inform resourcing and capital investment. This increased transparency was expanded to include project and resource planning so that schedules could be planned in view of all stakeholders, who could then ensure proper prioritisation and efficient use of limited resources, such as an incubator space for protein expression. If any request was unclear or required in-process troubleshooting, direct communication among the stakeholders was enabled through online comments. The use of digital channels radically changed the ways stakeholders could

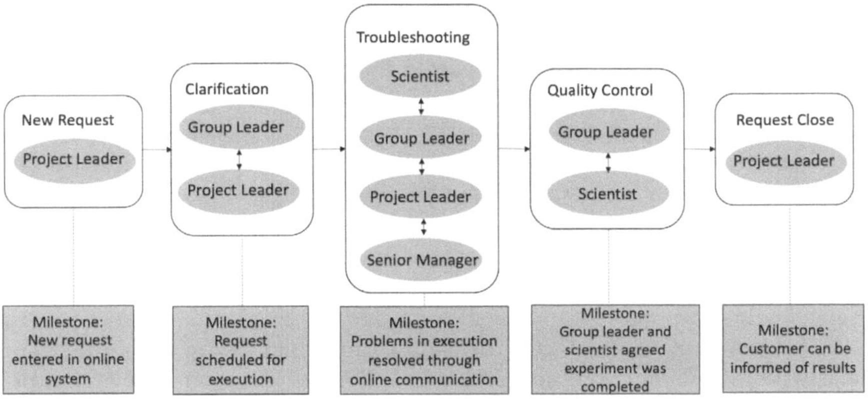

Figure 17.4 Example of a communication interface for one request.

communicate, but it also broke the conventional barriers of the older organisational hierarchy. Therefore, we propose the following.

Design principles 4. Ideating for positive organisation-wide changes in resolving root causes

Activity 5. Technological realisation and assessment

Most digital transformation programmes primarily focus on technical advancement. They yield benefits, especially when project collaboration and coordination are challenging when face-to-face communication is not feasible (Lindvall & Rus, 2000). However, the success of business transformation depends critically on the redesign of human-related interfaces rather than on technology. The adoption of technology in realising a newly designed system is a double-edged sword because not all the 'to-be' business processes can be easily digitalised or automated, and a failure of implementation can result in lost work time, frustration and missed project deadlines. How to harness the appropriate technologies for realising the conceptual solution is key.

Communicating and transmitting information can be aided by technology, such as digital access to, storing and exchanging project data, along with facilitating the communication. In our case, the design for the request control system (see Figure 17.4) was realised through the Labguru commercial software package with significant additional customisation. The digitalised solution was a web-based platform with easy accessibility from commonly available web-browsing software in mobile devices, allowing stakeholders to input and output the status and results of the work in its customised forms, for example, the hours tracking in each request web document while at the laboratory bench. Each request form had comment fields used to collaborate between functional group leaders, project leaders and scientists to exchange opinions and questions and facilitate discussions promoting the valuing of scientific expertise—a key identified emotional need—by all parties while conveniently not requiring all parties to be in the same place at the same time. However, the system users sharing common interfaces had their respective specifications related to personal interfaces because of their distinctive needs. This level of detail was not easily automated and managed organisation wide, but the organisation should build an empathic mindset among all stakeholders to mitigate such interface issues in execution.

After implementation, we found that all the interpersonal communications (both online and offline) were important because they helped avoid overloading one key project personnel with information. As Shuman and Twombly (2010) pointed out, people only collaborate when the benefit they receive from collaboration is greater than the effort. The implementation of the newly designed business process is related to a change management (Bible & Bivins, 2019) for the state of mind of stakeholders, and it can be trained. All stakeholders should obtain a common understanding of the technical and non-technical interfaces they share in the 'to-be' business process. Multiple training sessions and instruction books for the newly designed system and its usage helped new system adoption. Project leaders and functional group leaders also conducted regular meetings to continuously align schedules and the resourcing of projects with the project and group members to identify critical interface issues and to solve potential conflicts that could emerge.

The process of technological realisation is normally subject to testing. Successful transformation of the business process yielded benefits. R&D contractors, like the case company, are usually small- or medium-sized companies, and, thus, struggle to balance project competence and cost-driven competitiveness. Measurable improvements in our case study mainly included efficiency, effectiveness and stakeholder satisfaction. After the implementation of the digitalised business process and all the above empathic actions for one year, the case company's revenue increased about 35%, largely because of doubling the business capacity from 20 to 45 projects; the project overrun was decreased by 30%; employee satisfaction was improved, as judged by reduced turnover and employee survey, which was attributed to the shared ownership of the projects by group leaders, scientists and project leaders, as well as good communication across different business levels. Therefore, we propose the following last principle.

Design principle 5. Implementing an empathic mindset all the time at all business levels

Summary 1: Lessons learned that can contribute to the organisational or business context

Although organisations might realise the value of empathy and digitalisation, many are unsure of how to apply them in an organisation-wide transformation. Through a case study, we have demonstrated the importance of acting empathically across the entire process of digitally transforming a business process rather than the conventional technology focus. It was found that not all human interfaces are to be digitalised but can be managed through empathic actions. We outlined five systematic activities and their associated design principles that resulted in the radical design of the business process and the digital business platform, here with significantly improved performance.

Summary 2: Contribution to organisational or business knowledge or practices

Drawing on theory and novel data, this chapter investigates how a small- to medium-sized company capitalised on the value of empathic action while digitally transforming a business process. It tackles the missing link between empathic actions and business process (re)design. The actionable design principles for business processes (re)design with empathy are outlined and illustrated through a real-life case study in the healthcare industry. It also sheds light on the usage of digital technologies to promote empathic-oriented business transformation and better understanding of the interactions between non-digitalised and digitalised parts of the business process.

References

Alvarez, S. A., & Porac, J. (2020). Imagination, indeterminacy, and managerial choice at the limit of knowledge. *Academy of Management Review*, 45 (4), 735–744.

Agarwal, R., & Weill, P. (2012). The benefits of combining data with empathy. *MIT Sloan Management Review*, 54 (1), 35–41.

Baron-Cohen, S. (2012). *The science of evil: On empathy and the origins of cruelty*. Basic Books.

Betzler, M. (2019). The relational value of empathy. *International Journal of Philosophical Studies*, 27 (2), 136–161.

Bible, M., & Bivins, S. (2019). *Project interface management: Reducing risk on major projects*. J. Ross Publishing.

Bloom, P. (2017). *Against empathy: The case for rational compassion*. Random House.

Brown, M., & Wyckoff-Baird, B. (1992). *Designing integrated conservation and development projects*. The Biodiversity Support Program.

Brown, T. (2008). Design thinking. *Harvard Business Review*, 86 (6), 84–94.

Bryson, J. (2004). What to do when stakeholders matter – Stakeholder identification and analysis techniques. *Public Management Review*, 6 (1), 21–53.

Conway, M. (1968). How do committees invent? *Datamation*, 14 (4), 28–31.

Dalton, J., & Kahute, T. (2016). Why empathy and customer closeness is crucial for design thinking. *Design Management Review*, 27 (2), 20–27.

Delpechitre, D., Rutherford, B. N., & Comer, L. B. (2019). The importance of customer's perception of salesperson's empathy in selling. *Journal of Business & Industrial Marketing*, 34 (2), 317–337.

Dimov, D. (2020). Opportunities, language, and time. *Academy of Management Perspectives*, 34 (3), 333–351.

Fisk, E. (2010). *Construction project administration* (9th ed.). Prentice Hall.

Franklin, M. (2006). *Performance gap analysis: Tips, tools, and intelligence for trainers* (vol. 603). American Society for Training and Development Press.

Goguen, J., & Linde, C. (1993). Techniques for requirements elicitation. In *Proceedings of the IEEE International Symposium on Requirements Engineering* (pp. 152–164). IEEE.

Holt, S., Marques, J., Hu, J., & Wood, A. (2017). Cultivating empathy: New perspectives on educating business leaders. *The Journal of Values-Based Leadership*, 10 (1), 3–25.

INCOSE. (2015). *INCOSE systems engineering handbook: A guide for system life cycle processes and activities* (4th ed.). John Wiley & Sons.

Ivančić, L., Vukšić, V. B., & Spremić, M. (2019). Mastering the digital transformation process: business practices and lessons learned. *Technology Innovation Management Review*, 9 (2), 36–50.

Lather, P. (2008). Against empathy voice and authenticity. In A. Y. Jackson & L. A. Mazzei (Eds.), *Voice in Qualitative Inquiry* (pp. 17–27). Routledge.

Lindvall, M., & Rus, I. (2000). Process diversity in software development. *IEEE Software*, 17 (4), 14–18.

Matt, C., Hess, T., & Benlian, A. (2015). Digital transformation strategies. *Business & Information Systems Engineering*, 57 (5), 339–343.

New, S., & Kimbell, L. (2013). *Chimps, designers, consultants and empathy: A theory of mind for service design*. In Proceedings of the Cambridge Academic Design Management Conference (pp. 1–14). Cambridge.

Nooteboom, U. (2004). Interface management improves on-time, on-budget delivery of megaprojects. *Journal of Petroleum Technology*, 56 (8), 32–34.

Ohreen, D. (2021). The managerial use of empathy: Missteps into the mind of others. *Philosophy of Management*, 1–27.

Orlikowski, W. J. (1992). The duality of technology: Rethinking the concept of technology in organizations. *Organization Science*, 3 (3), 398–427.

Orlikowski, W. J. (2010). The sociomateriality of organizational life: Considering technology in management research. *Cambridge Journal of Economics*, 34 (1), 125–141.

Pavlovich, K., & Krahnke, K. (2013). *Organizing through empathy*. Routledge.

PMP, R. L. K. (2007). *Effective communications for project management*. Auerbach Publications.

Rajkumar, S. (2010, July). *Art of communication in project management*. In PMI® Research Conference: Defining the Future of Project Management, Washington, DC. Project Management Institute.

Salminen, M., Hamari, J., & Ravaja, N. (2021). Empathizing with the end user: Effect of empathy and emotional intelligence on ideation. *Creativity Research Journal*, 33 (2), 191–201.

Schwertner, K. (2017). Digital transformation of business. *Trakia Journal of Sciences*, 15 (1), 388–393.

Serrat, O. (2017). *Knowledge solutions: Tools, methods, and approaches to drive organizational performance*. Springer Nature.

Shuman, J., & Twombly, J. (2010). Collaborative networks are the organization: An innovation in organization design and management. *Vikapla*, 35 (1), 1–13.

Tekic, Z., & Koroteev, D. (2019). From disruptively digital to proudly analog: A holistic typology of digital transformation strategies. *Business Horizons*, 62 (6), 683–693.

Tzouramani, E. (2017). Leadership and empathy. In J. Marques & S. Dhiman (Eds.), *Leadership today* (pp. 197–216). Springer.

Vom Brocke, J., & Rosemann, M. (2014). *Handbook on business process management 2: Strategic alignment, governance, people and culture*. Springer.

Yin, R. K. (2018). *Case study research design and methods*. SAGE Publications.

Young, I. (2015). *Practical empathy: For collaboration and creativity in your work*. Rosenfeld Media.

Zhao, Y. Y. (2019). Transforming systems engineering design for accelerated industrial innovation. In *Managing complexity and creating innovation through design* (pp. 116–130). Routledge.

Zulch, B. G. (2014). Communication: The foundation of project management. *Procedia Technology*, 16, 1000–1009.

18 Empathy and delivery cyclists

Eduardo Rumenig Souza, Luiz E. P. B. T. Dantas, Rosana Vasques, André Casanova Silveira and Maria Cecília Loschiavo dos Santos

Introduction

The democratisation of disruptive informational and communicational technologies (ICTs), such as the internet, smartphones, social media, consumption and navigation apps, have transformed the modes of interactions between human and nonhuman beings, as well as the social environment itself (Helmond, 2015; Horst & Miller, 2020; van Doorn & Badger, 2020). Currently, we can order services and goods or navigate across space in real time with a simple smartphone's touch. Such technologies raise our capacity to connect with other people and our accessibility to opportunities, things and goods (Cass et al., 2005). Moreover, ICTs have widened our extensibility, enabling us to be in multiple spaces simultaneously or grasp multiple temporalities from the same place, hence disregarding physical distance (Miller, 1999).

In the labour context, ICTs have engendered new market arrangements headed by digital platforms (DPs), that is, technological companies able to decentralise data production by customers, entrepreneurs and workers, merge and process these data—through application programme interfaces and software development kits—and trade them on the global stock market, mainly for advertising companies (Srnicek, 2017; van Doorn & Badger, 2020). This form of accumulation has underlined huge differences from previous means. One difference is how this current way has deployed unpaid work performed by consumers to build big data banks, currently known as digital oil (Siegele, 2020).

Another one is that DPs have enabled the recruitment of workers based on the demand of consumption, remunerating them only for work effectively performed—also named on-demand or piecework— in turn allowing a piecemeal, flexible and intermittent labour arrangement (Antunes, 2018; Dubal, 2020; Huws, 2014). A real-time surveillance system also converts them (the workers) into (self-)managers who dispense human supervision, saving on the corporation's costs regarding management procedures (Cherry, 2016; Rogers, 2015).

The gamification of work, offering rewards or sanctions depending on the performance of the individuals, is another aspect of the DP arrangement.

DOI: 10.4324/9781003227557-22

Gamification increases the competitiveness among DP workers and encourages them to extend their workload beyond the point at which the labourers produce equivalent production costs (absolute surplus value). Similarly, DPs encourage them to work more efficiently to raise their scores on DPs (relative surplus value) (Antunes, 2018; van Doorn & Badger, 2020).

Therefore, the facilities offered by DPs are underpinned by raising the working time, reducing salaries, worsening the working conditions, depersonalising social relations and blurring the boundaries between working/nonworking time, as well as who are workers/nonworkers (Alves et al., 2020; Antunes, 2018). As claimed by several authors (Antunes, 2018; Dubal, 2020; Huws, 2014; Srnicek, 2017; van Doorn, 2017; van Doorn & Badger, 2020), DPs change the labour market and the economic arrangement, negatively affecting ethnic minorities and socioeconomically vulnerable groups.

However, in the Global South, such social and economic disarrangements are not new. Historically, Global South countries (like Brazil) have had to address successive crises involving economic and labour market deregulation—aside from ethnic-racial exploitation, structural under- and unemployment (Instituto Brasileiro de Geografia e Estatística, 2021b)—and fiscal austerity policies, especially regarding the lower working classes (de Oliveira, 2015). DPs only have accentuated this process, boosting neoliberal, individualistic and competitive behaviours among workers, entailing new ways of sociability (*geselligkeit*). Curiously, despite these social changes, few studies have shed light on the social outcomes engendered by DPs in the Latin American context.

This chapter assesses the ways of sociability among DP cyclists enrolled in logistic platforms, such as UberEats, Rappi or Ifood, during their labour routine in one of the biggest Latin American conurbations: São Paulo (Brazil). This municipality has been characterised by informal economic activity (without legal rights or labour guarantees), higher rates of unemployment (14%) and substantial socioeconomic inequalities (Instituto Brasileiro de Geografia e Estatística, n.d.). We surmised that DPs fostered competitive, individualistic and antisocial behaviours, affecting the human ability to feel and think from the perspective of others, that is, to think about or reflect on others' actions and emotional states despite not having the same experiences (Battarbee et al., 2015; Molnar-Szakacs, 2011; Sevillano et al., 2007).

The ability to recognise the otherness and understand another person's perspective has been designated as empathy and identified as a precondition for prosocial behaviour and moral judgements (Battarbee et al., 2015; Molnar-Szakacs, 2011; Sevillano et al., 2007), even though authors like Prinz (2011) have claimed that empathy might compromise the human capacity to judge, given preferential treatment to ingroup rather than outgroup members because of prejudices. Empathy underpins social evaluations based on moral thoughts and actions because it 'elicits feelings of concern for the other' and 'prompts behaviour aimed at helping', modulating fairness perceptions and inhibiting 'behaviours that are harmful to others' (Molnar-Szakacs, 2011, p. 81). This is especially true when it comes to emotional empathy, which involves intersharing experiences, emotions and feelings in an unconscious, precognitive and more general state-matching reaction (Molnar-Szakacs, 2011).

We draw on the ethnographic perspective—particularly to the phenomenological technique called 'ride-along' (Kusenbach, 2003)—to assess if the sociability among DP workers and between DP workers and other urban actors is led by moral values, mutual aid behaviour, solidarity and recognition of alterity or, conversely, if it is led by prevailed individualism, competitiveness and apathy concerning others.

To explore these hypotheses, we segmented the chapter into six sections, including the introduction (first). The second section situates São Paulo and the platform works in the literature. The third discusses the ethnographic method, the fieldwork challenges and the delivery cyclists' characteristics. The fourth stresses the labour routine of the cyclists enrolled in the field research. The fifth section is dedicated to sketching the ingroup and outgroup empathy behaviour, while the sixth section summarises some key findings.

São Paulo context and its digital platform workers

The São Paulo metropolitan region (SPMR) comprises 39 municipalities and more than 22 million inhabitants (Instituto Brasileiro de Geografia e Estatística, 2021a). The municipality has 13 million inhabitants distributed in 1,521 km^2. Since 1960, São Paulo was the most important economic conurbation of the country, representing 30% of the country's GDP, with the tertiary sector corresponding to 70% of the jobs, most of them informal. It has a substantive rate of unemployed (12%), underemployed (24%) and discouraged workers (5%). The average income of its inhabitants is €316.77, a bit more than the minimum wage (€179.00) (Instituto Brasileiro de Geografia e Estatística, 2021b).

Since the twentieth century, governmental decision-makers have allowed for a private motorised transport system, which has brought forward negative externalities such as air pollution (Andrade et al., 2017), congestion (de Sá et al., 2017), socio-territorial exclusion and mobility inequalities (Giannotti et al., 2021; Marques, 2016). To overlap decades of urban plunder (Kowarick, 1977, 1980) promoted by this 'asphaltic magic circle', which privileged motorway construction, stimulating the purchase of automobiles, requiring additional motorways that stimulate more automobile purchases (Lefebvre & Nicholson-Smith, 1991, p. 374), decision-makers have designed public policies to transform the city into a more sustainable place. Among these best practices, the municipal Master Plan of 2014 encompassed a bold cycling network plan, building more than 600 km of cycle lanes and cycle paths, as well as several bicycle parks and bike-sharing services over the course of less than one decade (Bonduki, 2011; de Sá et al., 2019).

Such non-motorised infrastructure contributes to questioning the hegemony of motor vehicles, as well as to attracting global logistic DPs that offer bicycle delivery services, resulting in an expansion of the number of platform 'green jobs': a common term to designate delivery cyclists who work for DPs (Scotini et al., 2017). Currently, São Paulo has a plethora of delivery services (e.g., UberEats, Ifood and Rappi, among others) that are usually performed by cyclists hired in an informal labour regimen. The majority are young males (75% were under 27 years old), black or mixed race (71%), and with a low educational level (incomplete high school), remaining available to work more than ten hours daily for little more than the minimum wage (€170.00) (Aliança Bike, 2019).

These underpaid platforms' green jobs conceal juridical and legal deregulation, structural unemployment, racial and gender exploitation and socio-economic vulnerabilities: the last estimates count 300,000 DP cyclists and motorcyclists in São Paulo alone (Antunes, 2018, 2019). As a result, these technological revolutions fostered first by GAFAM (Google, Amazon, Facebook, Apple and Microsoft) and second by lean platforms (UberEats, Rappi and Ifood) exacerbated an ongoing process of decentralisation, informatisation and globalisation of productive chains, disrupting the labour market in Global South countries that are unable to follow the technological transformations boosted by Global North corporations (Antunes, 2019; Marques, 2016; de Oliveira, 2015; Smyrnaios, 2016; Srnicek, 2017).

Aside from this precariousness, these DP workers must face scarcity and inaccessibility to urban facilities in a city that prioritised motorised instead of active transportation. The lack of facilities such as bathrooms, shelters to take a rest or cyclo-friendly infrastructure increases the traffic risks and compels DP cyclists to remain on the streets without access to facilities, which compromises their quality of life. The COVID-19 outbreak worsened this scenario, closing down those private facilities that informally supported DP cyclists, such as shops, grocery stores and services (Abílio et al., 2020).

To summarise, there was an increase in health risks without either public/private support or financial compensation to DP cyclists, bringing to light the historical injustices concerning the lower classes. Although the service is considered essential, the workers are disposable. Therefore, in Global South countries, the platform green jobs have also been identified as '*precariat*' (Huws, 2014; Standing, 2016), '*info-proletarian*' or a 'disorganised, unstable, ideologically diffuse, and a quite vulnerable group' performing intermittent work under a juridical regime of exception (Antunes, 2019, p. 58).

Ethnographic methods and field research

I (first author) performed six months of ethnography with five delivery cyclists in São Paulo (Brazil) during the first wave of the COVID-19 pandemic, from March to August 2020. The participants who enrolled in the research showed interest in the notices published on social media (Instagram, Facebook and WhatsApp). Hence, the researcher explained the criteria of inclusion (to be healthy and to work for more than six months for DPs) and obtained written informed consent, which was previously approved by the ethics committee of the University of São Paulo's under the inscription 35886620.2.0000.5391.

During the research period, the participants were supported with physical and psychological care, such as bike fit services, workout routines and psychoanalysis sessions, to reduce the occupational health labour risks. The ethnography was performed during peak order times (11 a.m. to 3 p.m.), always on weekdays and once a week. We choose a phenomenological ethnographic approach named 'go or ride-along', which enabled us to observe the delivery cyclists while they worked.

In general, a ride-along consists of stalking a person while the stalker observes: (i) the environment perception; (ii) space practices; (iii) biographies; (iv) social architecture or urban materialities; and (v) social relationships with non/human beings (such as urban actors or technological tools [smartphones or bicycles]) (Kusenbach, 2003). Thus, through the embodied interaction of the cyclists (on movement) with other bodies, objects and urban space, I grasped the cyclists' social relations and empathic interactions during their labour journeys.

All five subjects (Rodolfo, Adolfo, Quixote, Juan and Dante, which are fictitious names adopted to preserve their identity) are male (40 ± 10 years) and working for DPs or a big retail national company (NC). They cycle around 70 km per day, although with distinct working journeys. DP cyclists (DPc) work 10 to 12 hours a day, whereas national company cyclists (NCc) work half of this time (6 hours). Invariably they inhabit the outskirts of the city, with a Human Development Index (0.76 ± 0.02) lower than their labour territories (0.84 ± 0.07), which encompass the inner city and south region of São Paulo, which is characterised by a higher HDI (Gonçalves & Maeda, 2015). Dante identifies himself as white, while the other four identify as black.

The streets were adopted as the unit of analysis. Since the beginning of the twentieth century, social anthropologists have considered the street as a metaphor of the city, constituted by a socio-spatial relationship that unveils the urban and social practices (Frehse, 2011; Park, 1915; Simmel, 2012). It is the scenario where the cyclists, in interaction with other human/nonhuman artefacts, perform their social roles, mostly through their body practices. The researcher is a spectator of this social reality composed from relationships conceived and (re)constructed by social practices consolidated over time (Lefebvre, 2004).

We privileged the 'passage situations' during the fieldwork, highlighting the relationships between the individual and space (Agier, 2019, pp. 93–96). The passage situations are social practices circumscribed by individualisation and the absence of personal relations with the social environment because of their ephemerality. There is no crystallisation of personal relationships with urban space or urban agents. Hence, we also resorted to photography to register these ephemeral social practices. The images complement the ride-along performed by the cyclists moving through the city. After each field incursion, a fieldwork notebook—filled with both images and text—was analysed from an anthropological gaze as what seems to be familiar to one may seem strange to another.

Labour routine

The first aspect disclosed by the ethnographic fieldwork was that the delivery cyclists are not a homogenous group. We identified that NCc (Adolfo and Rodolfo) demonstrate better work conditions than DPc (Juan, Quixote and Dante). NCc, for instance, have access to a company's shed close to the commercial inner city, where they might have lunch, take a rest, go to the toilet, access safe water, gather with other cyclists or load their bicycles every morning. They previously know their route, the number of deliveries by day and remuneration—commonly higher than that of the DPc—reducing unforeseen economic issues. They can also access their bosses upon demand, for example, disagreements about their incomes, routes, number of deliveries by day, suitable products for bicycle transport, timetabling of labour or shipment schedule. Their routines are shorter, more predictable and transparent (fieldwork notes).

NCc bicycles are customised with back and front rumps to carry additional goods. These upgrades increase the physical effort but also their earnings. In addition, plastic strips, woven bags and plastic bags are creatively used to raise their transport capacity. In other words, their bicycle's materiality expresses the NCc's agency over their vehicles, ascribing a particular way to customise their bicycles and new uses for disposable materials (Figure 18.1).

In contrast, DPc do not even know if they will have orders during their workday once they are submitted to an on-demand labour regimen. They receive a lesser remuneration for each delivery: 50% less than the NCc, even though DPc work twice as long. They have no communication channels with their superiors to complain about the work conditions or imponderables because algorithms have overtaken the role of bosses. Their bicycles also evidence lower quality than that of the NCc, requiring ongoing and more frequent repairs. Unlike NCc, DPc do not have any official place to gather during their work breaks. Such a lack of predictability, difficulties in accessing operational managers, lower wages and worsened labour conditions make their routines more difficult.

Unlike the NCc, DPc are compelled to stay available to work full-time without any compensation. Free time is the only resource that someone can afford gratuitously, yet it is replaced by the time available to work. DPc remain connected to the DPs through their smartphones around the clock, blurring the boundaries between work/nonwork time. Even physiological demands must be fitted with the rhythm of the orders forwarded by the DPs. For instance, lunchtime is done amid orders, commonly standing up on the sidewalks. If the DPs send an order, the DPc discontinue their meals to attend to the consumers' necessities.

Another aspect that impairs both groups is the scarcity of urban facilities, even when working in high-quality urban areas. Dante (DPc), for instance, tried to access a bathroom in a parking lot. However, the guard did not allow him to use it, compelling Dante to urinate on the street while protecting his privacy behind a tree trunk. He claimed, 'The guard did not allow me to go to the toilet because they guessed I want to see a car and steal something'. It was

Figure 18.1 Adolfo's customised mountain bike (top) and Juan's e-bike (bottom). The customisation allows Adolfo (NCc) to accommodate several items on his bicycle, while the e-bike reduces the physical effort performed by Juan (DPc), evidencing some agency over their work tools. Photograph by Eduardo Rumenig.

one of the reasons for cyclists rarely drinking water during the labour routine, evidencing a martyrdom that the body must ride out. Although physically close, cyclists remain socially distant from urban facilities.

This scenario became more dramatic after the COVID-19 outbreak. Some restaurants and grocery stores that supported cyclists were closed by governmental decree. Those that remained open casually charged €0.33 for the bin, heating lunch boxes or going to the toilet. Earning less than €16.28 a day, these cents may represent a considerable expenditure for the cyclists (fieldwork notes).

The pandemic also contributed to downsizing the remuneration of the DPc because of an overflow of unemployed from the sectors closed by government decree (Instituto Brasileiro de Geografia e Estatística, n.d.), setting forth a work schedule (one workday and two days off) that reduced the number of people available to work simultaneously (fieldwork notebook).

Our fieldwork disclosed the exploitation and expropriation that cyclists suffer, especially from DPs, disregarding elementary human necessities, such as eating or drinking water. The 'sustainable' jobs that enable cyclists to work 'whenever [they] want—anytime, during the weekend, or throughout the week' while they enjoy and 'discover new sides to the city' in fact are disguising precarious labour conditions. For these reasons, authors such as Antunes (2018, 2019) have named DP jobs as 'modern servitude'.

Ingroup and outgroup empathy

Nevertheless, the same ICTs that contribute to degrading the cyclists' work conditions might be handled empathically to outdo (or mitigate) some adversities. As defined previously, empathy means the 'art of stepping imaginatively into the shoes of another person, understanding their feelings and perspectives, and using that to guide your actions' (Krznaric, 2014, p. 68). Empathy embraces emotional and cognitive components (Sevillano et al., 2007), changing the ability to receive and process information and one's moral judgement about others (Battarbee et al., 2015; Molnar-Szakacs, 2011).

Molnar-Szakacs (2011) argued that emotional empathy is an autonomic and precognitive state-matching reaction, embodied unconsciously and being more effective among the ingroup rather than outgroups (Gutsell & Inzlicht, 2010). For instance, Caucasians show more emotional empathy attunement (feel what another feels) for Caucasians (ingroup) than Africans or Hispanics (outgroup) (Gutsell & Inzlicht, 2010). Hence, emotional empathy is higher among equals.

However, cognitive empathy can be evidenced among outgroup members if individuals develop cognitive flexibility, which allows them to consciously assume the perspectives of others, leading to moral judgements and actions concerning others. Empathy can be considered an ability that counteracts individualistic and blasé behaviour, which means the incapacity to respond appropriately to the stimulus of urban life. The blasé spirit is commonly observed in urban societies, arousing estrangement and impersonal relations among individuals (Simmel, 2012).

We surmise that the DPs would enhance blasé and individualistic behaviour through the gamification of work and algorithmic management. Conversely, embodied social relations, mostly among cyclists (ingroup), would evoke emotional and cognitive empathy, engendering the ways of sociability underpinned on solidarity and mutual aid.

Meanwhile, the agency of the cyclists over the ICTs contradicts our initial hypothesis, showing that even the DPc might assume empathic ingroup and outgroup social interactions during their labour routines. For instance, one of

Juan's friends (DPc) complained about his exhaustive labour routine on social media. Then, Juan decided to offer his rented e-bike to mitigate the strenuous effort of his fellow. Later, the new e-bike owner sent a message to Juan claiming that he was facing difficulty replacing the discharged battery. So Juan met and taught him how to switch the item, hence, in the process, refusing orders and losing money.

Delivery cyclists also handled the ICTs to share information about urban facilities and opportunities, such as (1) the cheapest groceries or bicycle repair shops; (2) services that hired cyclists without the mediation of DPs (which helps them raise their wages); (3) shops to store or heat their lunch boxes for free; (4) accessible bathrooms; (5) safest public places to take a rest; (6) shorter routes; or (7) urban areas that should be avoided because of a lack of security. These embodied acknowledgements about the city seem to mitigate everyday adversities, especially for the DPc, who do not have the same facilities as the NCc.

Expert cyclists also invoke such embodied acknowledgements to surpass geography hurdles, such as uphills, high-speed tracks or high-traffic volume routes, sharing these bodily acknowledgements with less-skilled cyclists, usually through social media. Some of them can realise even the air quality or wind intensity, pick out the most favourable routes and share these tips with other cyclists. Such appropriation of the urban space overlaps its conceived notion, replacing it with a lived and perceived one that is underpinned by bodily apprehension of the urban space.

Overall, conceived space is apprehended as Euclidean and rational, that is, an abstraction or mental construction disassociated from the physical and social realities of lived experience, one that is guided by efficiency and rationality. The bodily appropriation of conceived space might produce a different kind of space, created by a lived experience that embodies complex symbolism linked to the clandestine or underground side of social life. The perceived space, which is set up by a close association between daily routines and urban reality, is also present in its process of the embodiment of the city. Thereby, 'The form of social space is encounter, assembly, simultaneity [... of] everything that is produced either by nature or society' (Lefebvre, 2004, p. 101). Conceived, lived and perceived space produce the most concrete expression of the social space, which is understood as the sovereignty of human beings over the space, leading to tactics that allow cyclists to bear labour hardships.

The bodily appropriation of the city transforms it into a field of possibilities, which is in opposition to the homogeneous and contemplative conceived one (Lefebvre & Nicholson-Smith, 1991). Understood 'as a material and energetic fabric, both mobile and unstable; it is moved by driving forces, with its remission to the objects and marked by interference of internal and external intensities, constituting a field of forces and proto-meanings' in the interaction with other elements and other corporealities (Coelho Jr., 2010, p. 59), the body gives rise to unforeseen ways of sociability and acknowledgement of the city, which is quite distinct from those outlined by the DPs, guided by rationality and capital accumulation. This body cartography—or 'bodygraphy'—denotes an urban experience inscribed under varying degrees of stability in the body of who experiences it, simultaneously reconfiguring the urban space, the body and the sociability between the urban actors (Britto & Jacques, 2010).

One unforeseen way of sociability and appropriation of the city engendered by the bodily empathic interactions was a political mobilisation held on 1 July 2020, on Paulista Avenue, one of the most important financial and commercial territories of São Paulo. This protest gathered thousands of DP workers, journalists and supporters to denounce the exploitation perpetrated by DPs, overflowing public opinion with empathic feelings concerning the DP labourers.

The 'BrequedosApps', as it was named, was a political movement organised through social media to claim better labour conditions. Using their smartphones, bicycles and thermal backpacks, the cyclists (and other DP workers) partially suspended the activities of DPs in São Paulo and other Latin American metropolises abroad, such as the city of Guatemala (Guatemala), Buenos Aires (Argentina) and Bogotá (Colombia), evidencing the agency of the cyclists and their extensibility—the possibility to be in multiples places simultaneously engendered by ICTs (Delgado Neves & de Carvalho, 2020). These political demonstrations have neither a hierarchical structure with formal institutions as protagonists nor long-term sociability among workers. Moreover, it is not an exclusivity of Global South countries. Similar demonstrations took place in the Global North, as in Portugal ('Precari@s inflexíveis'), the UK ('No money, no Food') or France ('Deliveroo protests').

The BrequedosApps highlighted how ICTs might be handled to support collective workers' demands. Emotional and cognitive ingroup empathy added to solidarity and mutual aid networking provisionally subverted the cyclists' routines, ascribing new uses to the streets and disclosing the multiple uses/meanings that ICTs, body, work tools and streets might assume. BrequedosApps raised even the outgroup awareness about the adversities experienced by DP workers. Figure 18.2 illustrates some passage situations witnessed during the BrequedosApps.

As expected, empathy is more evident in ingroup rather than outgroup agents. Nonetheless, outgroup empathic relations were also observed during the cyclists' routine. For instance, a steakhouse's owner provided meals for the DPc who have eaten nothing. Juan (DPc) said,

> Last week I picked up delivery here at the end of my journey, around 10 p.m. Then, an employee asked me if I was hungry, offering a generous steak sandwich. These guys are amazing. They offer water, let you use the toilet, and sometimes offer snacks with the leftover meats. They are *steadfast*.

In another 'passage situation', a police officer approached us while Juan (DPc) and I were doing therapeutic exercises in a public square (Praça Roosevelt) to reduce his chronic back and hip aches. We thought that the cop would bother us, but instead, the cop shared some stretching tips with us to mitigate Juan's soreness: 'Sciatic? Is it sciatic? I have the same problem, and I perform the same

Figure 18.2 A DPc enjoys the free space among the protesters to make tricks and stunts with his bicycle during the BrequedosApps in Paulista Avenue (left side), denoting new uses of the bicycle, body and urban space. On the right side, cyclists drive on a blocked highway. One of them put his hand on the central cyclist, evidencing ingroup empathy through a body practice. Photograph by Eduardo Rumenig.

exercises every day'. Both situations evidence that outgroup empathic interactions may occur, though they are mostly restricted to physical interactions.

DP decision-makers should take these embodied acknowledgements about the city and the empathic sociability into account to design ICTs that are able to improve the labour conditions of DP cyclists. Moreover, DPs' CEOs should 'ride someone else's bicycle' to understand the perspectives and necessities of cyclists. This cognitive flexibility, which is built by empathic feelings, should guide the forward decision-making process of these companies, taking into account the human dignity that cyclists deserve.

Conclusion

Foucault stated that 'every exercise of power presupposes forms of resistance. [The] problem is to know where the resistance will arise' (cf. Foucault, 1994). The ethnography of the NCc and DPc grasped some of these clefts where cyclists exert some agency against the exploitation of the DPs through empathic sociability and ICT appropriation. The 'blasé' spirit that guides urban life—and the platform economy—is countered by empathic ingroup interactions, reverberating in ways of sociability quite distinct from those fostered by DPs over the past few decades. Embodiment interactions between outgroup agents also seem to mitigate the harsh routine of cyclists, engendering unforeseen ways to occupy and produce the social space.

The BrequedosApps revealed that ICTs, body, labour tools and urban spaces might assume distinct roles, contributing to setting up social arrangements distinct from the hegemonic, engendering—at least provisionally—a micro-urban revolution. The empathic feelings and the solidarity embodied in BrequedosApps turned these nonhuman agents into instruments to improve the labour and living conditions of delivery cyclists to the detriment of exploiting them.

Such social arrangements underpinned by empathic ways of sociability unveil others' political, moral and social possibilities of existence.

It is pivotal to realise that DPs rely on their workers to solve the precarious labour conditions that DPs are responsible for. Therefore, DPs' decision-makers should embed this unfair scenario into the ICTs' design to atone for the negative externalities fostered by them in the Global South. The CEOs of such platforms should offer cyclists better contracts, higher salaries, safer working conditions, appropriate equipment and the possibility to manage their nonwork time, here to the detriment of algorithms. This would contribute to the workers' auto-organisation and agency over their routine. The DP cyclists, in turn, must wield even more agency over the ICTs to empower these empathic networks and their struggle for decent labour conditions.

Summary 1:Lessons learned that can contribute to the organisational or business context

The implications of digital platforms (DPs) on the sociability of their labourers, as well as the workers' agency over these DP technologies, have been little explored in the Brazilian context. Performing ethnography with delivery cyclists, we discovered that these companies and their algorithms have harshened their labourers' routines. Nonetheless, ingroup and outgroup empathy might contribute to overtake this plight. DPs' decision-makers should take the empathic social interactions among the DP cyclists into account to attain cognitive flexibility and foster decent labour conditions for the workers of the Global South.

Summary 2: Contribution to organisational or business knowledge or practices

Digital platforms (DPs) and algorithmic management of the workforce have changed the labour market worldwide. Although these technologies have facilitated access to goods and services, they have also led to the decline of salaries, blurring the borders between work/nonwork time and loosening the labour contract's rules. Nonetheless, mutual aid networks built informally by DP cyclists and other urban actors have contributed to mitigating such negative externalities, especially in the countries of the Global South. DPs should embed this empathic sociability set up by delivery cyclists and urban actors to design new technologies that engender decent labour conditions.

References

Abílio, L. C., de Almeida, P. F., Amorim, H., Cardoso, A. C. M., da Fonseca, V. P., Kalil, R. B., & Machado, S. (2020). Condições de trabalho de entregadores via plataforma digital durante a COVID-19 [Working conditions of couriers via digital platforms during Covid-19]. *Revista Jurídica Trabalho e Desenvolvimento Humano*, 3. https://doi.org/10.33239/rjtdh.v.74.

Agier, M. (2019). *Antropologia da cidade: lugares, situações, movimentos* [*Anthropology of the city: places, situations, movements*]. Editora Terceiro Nome.

Aliança Bike. (2019). Pesquisa de perfil dos entregadores ciclistas de aplicativo [Survey of the cyclists' profile of platform delivers]. *Aliança Bike*. https://aliancabike.org.br/pesquisa-de-perfil-dos-entregadores-ciclistas-de-aplicativo/.

Alves, A. C., Bagno, L. I. M., & Gonçalves, N. (2020). Entregas mediadas por aplicativos e o mito do empreendedor de si mesmo na pandemia do coronavírus [Delivery mediated by mobile apps and the myth of self entrepreneurship in the coronavirus pandemic]. *Revista de Direito da UNB*, 4 (02), 85–116. https://periodicos.unb.br/index.php/revistadedireitounb/article/view/32329.

Andrade, M. F., Kumar, P., de Freitas, E. D., Ynoue, R. Y., Martins, J., Martins, L. D., Nogueira, T., Perez-Martinez, P., de Miranda, R. M., Albuquerque, T., Gonçalves, F. L. T., Oyama, B., & Zhang, Y. (2017). Air quality in the megacity of São Paulo: Evolution over the last 30 years and future perspectives. *Atmospheric Environment*, 159 (3). https://doi.org/10.1016/j.atmosenv.2017.03.051.

Antunes, R. (2018). *O privilégio da servidão: o novo proletariado de serviço na era digital* [*The privilege of serfdom: the new service proletariat in the digital age*]. Boitempo Editorial.

Antunes, R. (2019). *Riqueza e miséria do trabalho no Brasil (volume IV): trabalho digital, autogestão e expropriação da vida* [Wealth and misery of work in Brazil (volume IV): digital work, self-management and expropriation of life]. Boitempo Editorial.

Battarbee, K., Suri, J. F., & Howard, S. G. (2015). Empathy on the Edge. *Rotman Management*, 60–65.

Bonduki, N. (2011). The urban development model of São Paulo needs to be reversed. *Estudos Avançados*, 25, 23–36.

Britto, F. D., & Jacques, P. B. (2010). *Corpocidade: debates, ações e articulações* [*Bodycity: debates, actions and articulations*]. EDUFBA.

Cass, N., Shove, E., & Urry, J. (2005). Social exclusion, mobility and access. *Sociological Review*, 53 (3), 539–555. https://doi.org/10.1111/j.1467-954X.2005.00565.x.

Cherry, M. (2016). Beyond misclassification: The digital transformation of work. *Comparative Labor Law and Policy Journal*, 37 (3), 544–577.

CoelhoJr, N. E. (2010). From intercorporeality to co-corporeality. Elements for the clinical practice of psychoanalysis. *Brazilian Journal of Psychoanalysis*, 44 (1), 51–60.

Delgado Neves, G., & de Carvalho, B. V. (2020). Breque dos aplicativos: direito de resistência na era digital [Breque of the apps: right of resistance in the digital age]. *Le Monde Diplomatique*, 27. https://diplomatique.org.br/breque-dos-apps-direito-de-resistencia-na-era-digital/.

de Oliveira, F. (2015). *Crítica à razão dualista/O ornitorrinco* [*Criticism of dualist reason/The platypus*]. Boitempo Editorial.

de Sá, T. H., Edwards, P., Pereira, R. H. M., & Monteiro, C. A. (2019). Right to the city and human mobility transition: The case of São Paulo. *Cities*, 87, 60–67. https://doi.org/10.1016/j.cities.2018.12.024.

de Sá, T. H., Tainio, M., Goodman, A., Edwards, P., Haines, A., Gouveia, N., Monteiro, C., & Woodcock, J. (2017). Health impact modelling of different travel patterns on physical activity, air pollution and road injuries for São Paulo, Brazil. *Environment International*, 108, 22–31. https://doi.org/10.1016/j.envint.2017.07.009.

Dubal, V. B. (2020). The time politics of home-based digital piecework. *Center for Ethics Journal: Perspectives on Ethics, Symposium Issue 'The Future of Work in the Age of Automation and AI*, 50.

Foucault, M. (1994). *Dits et écrits, 4 volumes*. Éditions Gallimard.

Frehse, F. (2011). *Ô da rua! O transeunte e o advento da modernidade em São Paulo [Ô from the street! The passerby and the advent of modernity in São Paulo]*. EDUSP, Editora da Universidade de São Paulo.

Giannotti, M., Barros, J., Tomasiello, D. B., Smith, D., Pizzol, B., Santos, B. M., Zhong, C., Shen, Y., Marques, E., & Batty, M. (2021). Inequalities in transit accessibility: Contributions from a comparative study between Global South and North metropolitan regions. *Cities*, 109, 103016. https://doi.org/10.1016/j.cities.2020.103016.

Gonçalves, A. D. F., & Maeda, M. T. (2017). IDH e a dinâmica intraurbana na cidade de São Paulo. In B. O. Marguti, M. A . Costa, & C. B. Favarão (Eds.), *Territórios em números: insumos para políticas públicas a partir da análise do IDHM e do IVS de UDHs e regiões metropolitanas brasileiras* (pp. 171–191). Instituto de Pesquisa Econômica Aplicada.

Gutsell, J. N., & Inzlicht, M. (2010). Empathy constrained: Prejudice predicts reduced mental simulation of actions during observation of outgroups. *Journal of Experimental Social Psychology*, 46 (5), 841–845.

Helmond, A. (2015). The platformization of the web: Making web data platform ready. *Social Media and Society*, 1 (2), 2056305115603080. https://doi.org/10.1177/2056305115603080.

Horst, H. A., & Miller, D. (2020). *The cell phone: An anthropology of communication*. Routledge. https://doi.org/10.4324/9781003086949.

Huws, U. (2014). *Labor in the global digital economy: The cybertariat comes of age*. NYU Press.

Instituto Brasileiro de Geografia e Estatística. (n.d.). *PNAD contínua - pesquisa nacional por amostra de domicílios contínua [Continuous PNAD – Continuous national household sample survey]*. https://www.ibge.gov.br/estatisticas/sociais/trabalho/17270-pnad-continua.html?=&t=o-que-e.

Instituto Brasileiro de Geografia e Estatística. (2021a). *Censo demográfico [Demographic census]*. https://cidades.ibge.gov.br/brasil/sp/sao-paulo/pesquisa/13/5908.

Instituto Brasileiro de Geografia e Estatística. (2021b). *Desemprego [Unemployment]*. https://www.ibge.gov.br/explica/desemprego.php.

Kowarick, L. (1977). *The logic of disorder: Capitalist expansion in the metropolitan area of Greater Sao Paulo* (Vol. 102). Institute of Development Studies.

Kowarick, L. (1980). *A espoliação urbana [The urban plunder]* (Vol. 44). Editora Paz e Terra.

Krznaric, R. (2014). *Empathy: Why it matters, and how to get it* (Vol. 4). TarcherPerigee. https://books.google.com/books?id=I1h9AwAAQBAJ&pgis=1.

Kusenbach, M. (2003). Street phenomenology: The go-along as ethnographic research tool. *Ethnography*, 4 (3), 455–485. https://doi.org/10.1177/146613810343007.

Lefebvre, H. (2004). *A Revolução Urbana [La Révolution Urbaine]. (Trad. Sérgio Martins)*. UFMG, Belo Horizonte.

Lefebvre, H., & Nicholson-Smith, D. (1991). *The production of space* (Vol. 142). Oxford Blackwell.

Marques, E. C. L. (Ed.). (2016). *São Paulo in the twenty-first century: Spaces, heterogeneities, inequalities*. Routledge. https://doi.org/10.4324/9781315622422.

Miller, H. J. (1999). Measuring space-time accessibility benefits within transportation networks: Basic theory and computational procedures. *Geographical Analysis*, 31 (1), 1–26. https://doi.org/10.1111/j.1538-4632.1999.tb00408.x.

Molnar-Szakacs, I. (2011). From actions to empathy and morality – A neural perspective. *Journal of Economic Behavior and Organization*, 77 (1), 76–85. https://doi.org/10.1016/j.jebo.2010.02.019.

Park, R. E. (1915). The city: Suggestions for the investigation of human behaviour in the city environment. *American Journal of Sociology*, 20 (5), 577–612. https://doi.org/10.1086/212433.

Prinz, J. (2011). Against empathy. *The Southern Journal of Philosophy*, 49, 214–233.

Rogers, B. (2015). The social costs of Uber. *SSRN Electronic Journal*, 82, 85. https://doi.org/10.2139/ssrn.2608017.

Scotini, R., Skinner, I., Racioppi, F., Fusé, V., De Oliveira Bertucci, J., & Tsutsumi, R. (2017). Supporting active mobility and green jobs through the promotion of cycling. *International Journal of Environmental Research and Public Health*, 14 (12), 1603. https://doi.org/10.3390/ijerph14121603.

Sevillano, V., Aragonés, J. I., & Schultz, W. P. (2007). Perspective taking, environmental concern, and the moderating role of dispositional empathy. *Environment and Behavior*, 39 (5), 685–705. https://doi.org/10.1177/0013916506292334.

Siegele, L. (2020). A deluge of data is giving rise to a new economy. *The Economist*, 5, 2–7.

Simmel, G. (2012). The metropolis and mental life. In J. Lin & C. Mele (Eds.). (2012). *The urban sociology reader* (2nd ed., pp. 37–45). Routledge. https://doi.org/10.4324/9780203103333.

Smyrnaios, N. (2016). L'effet GAFAM: Stratégies et logiques de l'oligopole de l'internet. *Communication Languages*, 2, 61–83.

Srnicek, N. (2017). *Platform capitalism*. John Wiley & Sons.

Standing, G. (2016). The precariat, class and progressive politics: A response. *Global Labour Journal*, 7 (2), 189–200. https://doi.org/10.15173/glj.v7i2.2940.

van Doorn, N. (2017). Platform labor: On the gendered and racialised exploitation of low-income service work in the 'on-demand' economy. *Information Communication and Society*, 20 (6), 898–914. https://doi.org/10.1080/1369118X.2017.1294194.

van Doorn, N., & Badger, A. (2020). Platform capitalism's hidden abode: Producing data assets in the gig economy. *Antipode*, 52 (5), 1475–1495. https://doi.org/10.1111/anti.12641.

19 AI innovations, empathy and the law

A user-centric perspective on copyright and privacy

Robert van den Hoven van Genderen, Rosa Maria Ballardini and Marcelo Corrales Compagnucci

Introduction: Empathy a missing piece of law's puzzle?

Legal communication and precontractual communication depend on a mutual understanding and acceptance by the participants. Here, an understanding is based on the underlying ethical norms and empathy based on a sense of cognitive empathetically basic elements. These elements must be integrated in the development and use of artificial intelligence (AI) in legal processes, specifically in the context of intellectual property rights (IPRs) and privacy. Notwithstanding the lack of research in this specific field, for the future of business relations, becoming more conscious of the importance of cognitive empathy in legal relations should be recognised to create a smooth and mutually trusting framework on all legal levels. This is particularly prominent in cases concerning the processing of personal data and protection of creative products through the use or further development of AI.

This chapter focuses on the role of empathy in the context of the regulation of AI[1] innovations, with a particular focus on intellectual property (IP) law (especially copyright) and privacy laws. Empathy is often missing in the development and application of law because of the idea that the law must be neutral and objective. However, the law is an instrument that creates communications and relations between (natural) persons and legal persons (companies, states and institutions), so when studying the law, greater consideration should be given to empathy. The introduction of AI could help in this area.

Empathy is notoriously not easy to define, even though the term 'empathy' is used to describe a wide range of experiences. For the purpose of this chapter, we rely on the general definition that understands empathy as the ability to sense other people's emotions, coupled with the ability to imagine what someone else might be thinking or feeling. Moreover, both the concepts of 'affective' and 'cognitive' empathy are important for our analysis. Affective empathy refers to the sensations and feelings we receive in response to others' emotions; this might include mirroring what the other person is feeling or just feeling stressed when we detect fear or anxiety in others. In contrast, 'cognitive

DOI: 10.4324/9781003227557-23

empathy' (sometimes called 'perspective-taking') refers to the ability to identify and understand other people's emotions.[2] This concurs with the definition given in the introductory chapter in this book, according to which 'empathy is the capacity to understand the elements that underpin the realities and situations that are experienced by people'.[3] This is also in line with the perspective of the draft AI Regulation of the European Commission, which is based on a human-centric approach (Commission Proposal 2021 O.J. (C. 206 final)). This means that the capacity to understand what someone else means, the possibility to agree on this, and the acceptance of the result can be considered important aspects of cognitive empathy in legal relations. As a result, these communication processes need to be transparent to the contracting parties and based on fairness.

Interactions in law between human beings (in legal terms referred to as 'natural persons') as well as between enterprises such as organisations and governments (in legal terms called 'legal persons') govern the realities and situations within society. Generally speaking, it could be argued that in law, empathy should be a leading concept for creating a better understanding between parties. Traditionally, the law sets the rules for human behaviour, here based on certain key ethical and empathetic principles such as fairness and transparency. This emotional understanding of the other parties' objective and anticipation of that party's reaction and expectation is needed to create a successful legal framework. At the same time, however, even if empathy is a more or less hidden element in rulings by judges—and, thus, influences the interpretation and creation of the law—the challenge lies in finding a proper balance between embedding empathy and maintaining objectivity in the law and decision-making. For this reason, it has long been questioned whether—and to what extent—empathy should actually form part of the legal norms and legal systems. We believe it is important to integrate empathy in decision-making and normative systems. Indeed, if empathy is compared with ethics, insecurity is associated with ethics because of contextual differences—social, functional, era related, geographical, cultural and political—on a global scale. Therefore, the uncertainty of ethical norms based create a feeling of insecurity within human relations. On the other hand, empathy possesses a universal character in terms of not being influenced by the factors that make ethics difficult to apply in law and in using AI because of the volatile character.

While looking at the specific case of AI technology, combining AI with empathy for better engagement is clearly one of the main targets in the development of several AI applications. Indeed, one could question whether it is even possible to embed empathy in the development of AI technology but not in the regulatory framework that drives AI innovations and developments. However, several of the legal fields that are the most relevant for AI regulation, such as copyright and privacy laws, do not appear to explicitly endorse or holistically hold empathetic visions. This leads to the question of whether this level of (non)empathy in the key areas of laws for AI is sufficient to drive empathetically steered AI systems and the entities of near-future appliances performing tasks with legal effects.

This chapter addresses this challenge by analysing selected situations that are particularly relevant in the context of businesses and organisations. We first briefly present the possible role of empathy in the context of AI developments to position the current discussions related to embedding empathy in AI technology. We then move on to discuss the role of empathy (both as a general concept and more specifically as cognitive and affective empathy) in AI regulation through law, here with a focus on some areas of European Union (EU) law. In this exercise, we start by presenting a general overview of the role of empathy as a general concept in law for AI, subsequently discussing two selected areas related to the regulation of AI innovations: first, we look at the case of AI-generated works and European copyright law before then exploring the case of AI and privacy laws in the EU. Our analysis shows that embedding empathy—especially the principles of fairness and transparency—in the regulation of AI innovations is not only possible, but also a necessity to achieve empathetic AI applications in the future, allowing us to enhance humans' understanding and acceptance of AI technology and AI-supported decision-making. Thus, we propose how empathy could be better embedded in the regulation of both AI-generated works through copyright and the regulation of situations that are relevant to privacy laws. We conclude that empathetic elements could create a better understanding and acceptance based on the principles of transparency and fairness in the same legal framework; this can also govern the implementation of AI in industrial and social processes.

AI technology and empathy—Some starting points

When looking at the specific case of AI developments, the first remark relates to the fact that empathy is seen as a human virtue. This might imply that a virtual artificial system would not be capable of empathetic behaviour because of its rational nature. Yet for AI to be accepted in society, it should be developed in an emphatic, human-centric manner. This is especially found to be the case once we look at current AI developments. Currently, we are in the early stages of developing AI applications, and most systems are based on so-called 'weak' AI and machine learning.[4] There is a tendency in AI evolution towards deep learning and self-learning, whereby other aspects of human behaviour (such as empathy) can be integrated in the learning process of AI systems. A clear example is the emotional behaviour of robots such as Sophia,[5] where 'she' reacts with emotions in a humorous way (Uploader, 2018). Of course, robot Sophia's behaviour is largely created by mimicking other human (or animals in the case of robotic pets) parties and anticipating their reactions. The more automated AI becomes, the greater the need to establish a way to keep it as human-centric as possible as a way to enhance trust in and acceptance of AI.

Although empathy is largely based on physiological signals, this is only one of its elements; as previously mentioned, there is a difference between affective and cognitive empathy. Affective empathy is estimated to be between 52% and 57% heritable, whereas cognitive empathy is less determined by genetics, with only about 27% being heritable and the rest presumably being influenced by environmental and learning experiences (Allen, 2016). Therefore, it cannot be denied that opportunities might arise to train artificial systems, at least in cognitive empathy. This is in line with experiences with the robot Sophia. Cognitive empathy is based on the recognition of a reaction and anticipating the possible expectations of the other person on an emotional and other more rational levels of expectation. This is a learning exercise and could be acquired similarly to how human actors, with training through experience, can recognise and anticipate circumstances and situations. Because humans learn by experience, AI systems could learn by training, for example, by machine learning or by self-learning capabilities. Of course, as with human actors, success is based on the acceptability and capacity to make oneself conscious of these signals and act in conformity with those signals and the behaviour of the other party. All those rules and norms of behaviour, even with empathetic elements, must be learned by AI for it to be able to operate in accordance with our key societal principles, such as mutual understanding and fairness.

Regulating AI—Is there a role for empathy in current laws?

Empathy, law and AI—Some general remarks

Because empathy is considered a human quality, forming the basis of creating moral behaviour, one would expect that empathy would be an essential element of the legal system because the law creates norms to regulate societal behaviour. However, law and law-making very rarely rely on empathy as a concept, but rather, they mainstream other sets of similar principles, such as those related to ethics. For example, the English philosopher John Locke, whose theories have built the foundations of several of today's laws, affirmed the importance of using the powers that we have as human beings to act in such a way that we obtain things that are good and useful. Specifically, ethics (note, not empathy) is 'seeking out those rules, and measures of human actions, which lead to happiness, and the means to practice them' (Locke, 1690b).

However, even if ethics and ethical requirements are not specifically comparable to empathy, one could say that ethical guidelines could create the basis for the rules for understanding the theatre of relations between actors, thus being the foundation of empathy.

An interesting and recognisable development is that—concerning the implementation of AI in societal processes—the first reaction of national and international interest groups and authorities, besides warning of the risks, is creating so-called ethical guidelines that are also recognisable in the field of human relations as empathetic behaviour (High-level Expert Group on Artificial Intelligence, 2019). For example, some ethical principles, such as fairness and transparency, could be considered basic learning data for developing empathetic behaviour. They create a starting point for human understanding of the rules in interhuman relations, ultimately leading to trust and behavioural acceptance. These same rules are also intended to be applied in developing and employing AI systems. Indeed, these principles are currently included in the draft Regulation on a European Approach for Artificial Intelligence (Commission Proposal 2021 O.J. (C. 206 final)), which recognises that AI development and use should be guided by certain essential (human) value-oriented principles. The rules for AI that are available in the EU market or otherwise affecting EU citizens should put people at the centre (i.e., they should be human-centric) so that people can trust that AI technology is being used in a way that is safe and compliant with the law, including respect for fundamental rights. Ultimately, this will lead to better acceptance of AI in society. All this could also be considered a large-scale empathetic approach that considers citizens' feelings and emotions, creating better understanding and acceptance between all actors.

In the draft Regulation on AI, empathy could be considered a prerequisite for respect for fundamental rights. With a set of requirements for trustworthy AI and proportionate obligations on all value-chain participants, the proposal will enhance and promote the rights protected by the Charter of Fundamental Rights of the European Union (2000/C 364/01), such as the right to human dignity (Article 1), respect for private life and protection of personal data (Articles 7 and 8) and nondiscrimination (Article 21) because the draft affirms the importance of creating transparent processing (Article 10).[6] Defining the neutralisation of these risks would be considered an 'empathetic' requirement, increasing transparency and fairness for initiating AI interactions with natural persons, other (natural) entities, other legal persons or autonomous artificial entities. Empathetic risk issues exist regarding bias and discrimination arising from the use of AI. Poorly designed algorithms or poor-quality data can adversely affect one or more population subgroups. Even when sufficient care is taken to programme algorithms without errors, data collection may still reveal past patterns of discriminatory activity. Where AI is developed to serve as an enhancement for medical devices, for instance, discriminatory patterns of the underlying algorithm can have significant implications. Indeed, AI accuracy can only be as good as the data used to train it. In training AI with input data, the principles of fairness and transparency should always be taken into account to foster understanding and generate acceptance.

Taking into account the fundamental values for its functioning will generate acceptance by people of AI-generated decisions. Next, we proceed with applying these general principles to two fields of law relevant for AI regulation: IP rights with a focus on copyright law (3.2) and privacy law (3.3).

Regulating AI-generated works via copyright—Is there a place for empathy?

Generally speaking, the IP rights system aims at rewarding those who develop innovations and creations with an exclusive, temporary and limited right, while also balancing societal interests. For instance, IP rights entail the right to exclude or deny use by others of the subject matter in question. IPRs comprise a diversity of rights, including copyright, patents, trademarks and design rights. For simplicity, in this chapter, we will only focus on copyright-related issues, which, in simplified terms, are attached to original works of intellectual effort created by (human) authors (see Kur, 2019).

Issues related to the inter-relation between IP law, AI developments and empathy have been vigorously discussed since the advent of AI-generated works and innovations. From among the several challenges that AI and automation bring to the current IPR framework, we focus on some of the most controversial topics related to copyright and AI: issues related to the authorship and originality of AI-generated works (see Aplin & Pasqualetto, 2019; Ballardini et al., 2019; Ginsburg, 2018).

First, in terms of authorship, key questions have revolved around whether—and to what extent—it is legal and/or justified to extend copyright entitlements (and ownership) to creations generated by nonhumans.

Under EU copyright law, the concept of 'author' has always been the starting point and centre of this discussion. If we look at justification theories for copyright protection, for instance, copyright entitlement is often justified based on deontological theories, such as natural law and natural rights theories (Locke, 1690a), as well as theories focusing on IP as an inherent ingredient of personality.[7] According to these theories, the intellectual labour of the author, mixed with other resources, justifies the author's right over the fruit of their labours. Moreover, these theories also justify IP rights as an inherent ingredient of the self or of personality. In addition to theories, European copyright law—including the international copyright treaties to which the EU is a party,[8] EU legislation (see Council Directive 93/83/EEC, 1993 O.J. (L 248); Council Directive 96/9/EC, 1996 O.J. (L 77/20); Council Directive 2006/115/EC, 2006 O.J. (L 376); Council Directive 2009/24/EC, 2009 O.J. (L 111)), cases from the Court of Justice of the European Union (CJEU) and the national laws and cases of the EU member states tend to interpret the concept of 'author' as a natural person (understood as a human being, as mentioned earlier). The concept of authorship should be interpreted and understood in line with the concept of 'originality', which is a *conditio sine qua non* for copyright protection in the EU. Here, an important issue that AI-generated works raise is the fundamental question of whether a nonhuman author can ever be able to produce an 'original' work of art as understood under current EU copyright doctrines. Also, the numerous decisions of the CJEU interpreting originality seem to stick to the romantic concept of the author as a natural person. This can be deduced inter alia from the emphasis placed on the interpretation of originality as reflecting the authors' 'own intellectual creation', 'personality' and 'personal touch' (e.g., Case C-5/08, Infopaq International A/S v. Danske Dagblades Forening, 2009; Joined Cases C-403/08 and C-429/08, Football Association Premier League Ltd et al. v. QC Leisure et al., 2011; Case C-145/10, Eva-Maria Painer v. Standard Verlags GmbH et al., 2013; Case C-604/10, Football Dataco Ltd et al. v. Yahoo! et al., 2012).

What does all this reveal in terms of empathy and copyright law, especially in relation to AI? First, the primary focus on the 'author' makes the copyright system quite apathetic—at least in terms of issues of protection. For copyright purposes, it is only relevant what authors think and how they feel or perceive their work, without considering how other parties think, feel or perceive of that same work. Second, because the copyright framework for protection is apathetic, the activities of an AI entity that fall under the domain of copyright (as in cases where AI creates a work of art) have also followed this pattern. As a result, the mainstream line of interpretation currently argues that because AI-generated works are created by entities that are not human beings, they cannot be protected under copyright law (both because a nonhuman cannot be an author and because a nonhuman cannot fulfil the criteria needed for protection, such as the criterion of originality). In other words, this implies that works that are automatically generated by AI should fall into the public domain and be available to anyone. However, in a world where AI is increasingly being used in the arts and literature and where human and AI contributions to creative works are increasingly mixed together, is an approach that categorically excludes AI as a contributor to a work from the copyright domain sustainable? In particular, does this way of (apathetically) regulating AI follow the principles developed by the draft Regulation on a European Approach for Artificial Intelligence (Commission Proposal 2021 O.J. (C. 206 final)); thus, is it able to mainstream principles such as fairness and transparency to foster understanding among parties and promote the acceptance of AI overall?

As presented below, the lack of empathy in our copyright laws for AI has already led to complications in relation to the regulation of AI and its creations, hampering the realisation of these fundamental principles.

Regulating privacy in AI—The need for a user-centric empathetic approach

Although there is no universally accepted definition of privacy, broadly speaking, privacy is 'the right to be let alone, or freedom from interference or intrusion. Information privacy is the right to have some control over how personal information is collected and used' (International Association of Privacy Professionals, n.d., para. 1). The right to privacy is recognised as a human right in the Universal Declaration of Human Rights (UDHR) (Article 12), the European Convention of Human Rights (ECHR) (Article 8) and the Charter of Fundamental Rights of the European Union (2000/C 364/01) (Article 7) and is alluded to as a constitutional right in most countries around the world.

Because of the exponential growth of technology, privacy has become one of the most dynamic and disrupted sectors of law. AI and data-driven companies are adopting platform-based business models (Corrales Compagnucci, Fenwick et al., 2019), offering new products and services that process large amounts of data in unprecedented ways. The healthcare, fintech and banking sectors are prime examples of these changes (Corrales Compagnucci, Kono et al., 2019).

These AI technologies, however, also create new uncertainties and risks. In turn, those uncertainties and risks have a complex character that requires going beyond a single discipline because they comprise technological, ethical, legal and organisational aspects. We believe that this new risk profile requires multiple perspectives—and the role of empathy with a user-centric approach can fill the gap. In particular, embedding cognitive empathy concepts such as fairness and transparency in the user interfaces of AI computer software products and services will create trustworthiness and acceptance. This will enhance the mutual understanding among the stakeholders involved.

One interesting point in common with data protection laws, such as the GDPR (Council Regulation 2016/679, 2016 O.J. (L 119) 1) and the California Consumer Privacy Act of 2018 (Cal. Civ. Code § 1798.100, 2018), is the focus on empowering individuals by granting them more rights and control over their personal data as having informational sovereignty. However, despite these new regulatory efforts and several institutional changes to improve data protection regimes, policy makers have not truly been discussing issues of respect to consumers (Corrales Compagnucci, 2020). The discussion concerning empathy is inherently rooted in the concept of respect regarding the origin and source of personal data: the individual. We provide a concrete example of this below.

Embedding empathy for human-centric AI regulation

Empathetic, fair and transparent copyright promotes understanding and AI acceptance

As presented above, empathy as a general concept seems to be an unknown characteristic of copyright protection rules, especially for the purpose of interpreting concepts of authorship and originality. One of the main consequences already perceived in the context of copyright regulation of AI-generated works relates to the fact that the current rules are unable to prevent (mal)practices such as the misappropriation of fully AI-generated works by human authors. As previously explained, the current apathetic copyright approach leaves no room for automated AI-generated works to be copyrightable because there is no legitimate (human) author and because the originality requirement for protection is not met. At the same time, however, it is not an easy task to separate or understand how to draw the line between what is fully AI generated as opposed to what is instead a work created by a human author using AI as a tool. Normally, in situations of this kind where human authors are involved, copyright law offers the so-called 'sufficiency test', according to which to be an author, someone needs to have contributed to a work with sufficient originality. Where authors are humans, the criterion of sufficiency is based on how authors perceive their contribution to a work. Indeed, it can be argued that this doctrine links the parties through empathy. However, in a situation where the creators are a human author and AI—or even an AI alone—how can such a level of understanding be enshrined? Cases where these types of issues are disputed have already begun to appear. For instance, in a case from Japan, an AI-generated book almost won a prize, even though the book was found to have been fully AI generated (Olewitz, 2016). We can easily see similar situations in many other areas of the industry, notably in the field of media, where these days, a large percentage of news is already AI generated. This trend in the nontransparency of sources has already diminished many people's trust in news.[9] Indeed, the more AI technology advances and the more complex AI becomes, the more situations of this kind are expected to increase. At the same time, these cases do not promote trust in the use of AI in literature and the arts. On the contrary, AI has become a place for suspicion, and its use is starting to be seen more as a questionable method for illegitimate appropriation by human authors who are taking works that they did not create. Ultimately, this cannot promote—but will rather hinder—the social acceptance of AI. Instead, it would be desirable to integrate the fundamental rights of the Charter of Fundamental Rights of the European Union (CFR), which recognises human centrism, into the core copyright system, for example, via better including respect for the principles of fairness and transparency in the copyright rules for protection, especially in the context of AI-generated works. This could better foster an understanding among humans as to the role of AI in activities caught by copyright law; consequently, it could promote the acceptance of AI. The fairness and transparency of decision-making in the legal context or by means of AI should pave the way to integrating empathetic elements in the process compared with Locke's feelings and therefore empathy-oriented (1721) idea of transparency of the senses, which runs in contrast to the Cartesian idea of mechanical functioning of the mind (Rozemond, 2006).[10]

Privacy and empathy by design in AI systems

Small- and medium-sized enterprises (SMEs) are searching for new alternative sources of data that would help them understand their customers better and become more competitive in the market. Because of market asymmetry, they cannot obtain accurate and updated data. As a result, start-ups are creating new ideas and business models, including user-centric/user-held approaches (Heinerth et al., 2011). This kind of bottom-up movement could be seen as a sign of empathy emanating from the market. It helps individuals exert more control over their data but also obtain value from it.

One of the defining features of this technological disruption is the emergence of new products and services such as smart wearable (eHealth) devices and 'apps' that leverage algorithm-based AI systems. These new developments create challenges for regulators and other policy makers, particularly in the context of privacy (in the context of healthcare, see Corrales Compagnucci et al., 2020). These challenges, however, can also bring new opportunities for AI regulation. How can we design a legal system that empowers individuals with their personal data and helps them obtain value from it? Empathy—in particular, cognitive empathy—plays a crucial role here: it allows us to put ourselves 'in the individual's shoes'. Private citizens strongly believe that they own their personal data. Personal data should be owned as a human right and compensated for when used by third parties for commercial purposes (Will.I.AM, 2021). This is in line with Locke's depiction of individuals as proprietors of their own person (Olsthoorn, 2019). Crucially, personal data should be treated as an extension of the individual's own personality rights, granting protection to their personal development (Van der Sloot, 2015). This new approach is gaining momentum not only among individuals, but also among companies searching for new ways of interacting with their customers. This, in turn, will open new opportunities for individuals.

The starting point of the user-centric/user-held data approach is the individual. Thus, individuals hold the ultimate power to make decisions over their personal data, particularly how they want to share it with third parties. In practice, however, the individual must have the appropriate tools to collect and exercise control over that data. By way of illustration, cloud-based applications are increasingly using AI and machine learning tools to collect, analyse and share large amounts of data.

A prime example of this user-held data model has been developed by the Silicon Valley company Prifina (www.prifina.com), which helps individuals connect personal data sources and bring in data from different sources such as wearables, sensors and online services into one single place (the so-called 'personal data cloud'). A personal data cloud enables not only the storage of the most up-to-date personal data from multiple sources, but also opens opportunities for individuals to obtain everyday value. This value is generated on the individual's side: individuals can gain better insights, recommendations and nudges utilising apps that 'activate' user-held data.

The developer community plays a vital role in the user-held data model. With Prifina's proprietary and open-source resources, software developers can build serverless apps that run on top of user-held data in each individual's personal data cloud. These new types of data applications are very easy to build because they do not require back-end solutions. Developers can build these apps overnight. It is like giving them a palette with a paint and brush to draw.

From the economies of scale perspective, the user-held data model opens new opportunities with data that originate from individuals. These new technological approaches to data, such as edge computing, federated learning and blockchain, help turn the tables in the personal data market and capture value from personal data on the user side. The user-held data model also has the potential to help brands and businesses—other than the five data titans (Google, Facebook, Amazon, Apple and Microsoft)—directly interact with individual customers. It also taps into the creative output of individual developers, who can build new applications and personal data use cases for the next decade.

Conclusions

The (draft) Regulation on a European Approach for Artificial Intelligence (Commission Proposal 2021 O.J. (C. 206 final))—deals with the risk assessment of the use of different AI applications based on the effects on the natural person and society as a whole. In this regulation, as well as existing rules for legal practice, ethical and empathetic guidelines are increasingly gaining importance in human-centred legal relationships. This certainly is the case if we look at the use of new disruptive technologies such as AI in processing personal data and the protection of people's fundamental rights. This type of privacy/empathy-driven innovation follows the user-centric/user-held data movement, concentrating on the transparency of AI-generated processing (Senarath et al., 2017), which is based on the principle that granting individuals more control over their own personal data will empower and liberate them (Jurcys et al., 2020). Moreover, it is also crystalline for the creation of works that mutual understanding based on empathetic principles such as fairness and transparency will create a basis for the acceptance of the functioning of new and often disruptive ways of working with and communicating through AI. In the creation of works with AI, ethical and empathetic building blocks should be required and regulated as integrated essential elements of the IP system.

Bringing empathetic requirements into the regulation of new disruptive technology such as AI (especially stressing the elements of fairness and transparency) and within business and other societal activities will enable a better understanding and acceptance of the technology itself, fostering our global cooperation in AI developments and uses. Nevertheless, empathy in law will not be the only way to generate an understanding and acceptance of AI. As Bloom (2018) states in his book *Against Empathy, the Case for Rational Compassion*, he has doubts as to his own proposed book title, thus referring to a different title in the text: 'Empathy plus reason, make a great combination because as with cholesterol there is a good type and a bad type' (p. 12). Certainly, fairness, transparency and understanding to create acceptance and empathy in all legal and societal processes—by both humans and AI—will be an indispensable combination.

Summary 1: Lessons learned that can contribute to the organisational or business context

Legal communications and precontractual communications depend on understanding and mutual acceptance by participating parties. Understanding is based on the underlying ethical norms and empathy, in the sense of cognitive empathically basic elements. These elements must be integrated in the development and use of AI in legal processes, certainly in the context of intellectual property rights and privacy.

Summary 2: Contribution to organisational or business knowledge or practices

Notwithstanding the scarce emphasis on this approach at the moment, for the future of business relations, the consciousness of the importance of cognitive empathy in legal relations must be recognised to create a smooth and trusting framework on all legal levels. This is particularly prominent in cases that concern the processing of personal data and protection of creative products by the use or further development of AI.

Notes

1 The term AI was first introduced by J. McCarthy and M. L. Minsky at the Dartmouth Conference in 1955.
2 See Chapter 1 of this book, where Sarantou and Miettinen refer, inter alia, to Ashworth and Lucas (2000), Rumble et al. (2010), and Saarikivi (2018).
3 See Chapter 1.
4 Weak—or narrow—AI is designed for specific and limited tasks such as in the production industry, as well as speech recognition and translators; even face-recognition technology and artificial personal assistants such as Apple's Siri and Amazon's Alexa are forms of weak AI. In addition, decision-supporting systems based on the use of algorithms can be considered weak (although the effects can be strong; see Stanford, n.d.).
5 Sophia, a robot developed by Hanson Robotics (n.d.), is currently the most developed household robot and was even granted a citizen's rights by Saudi Arabia.
6 The degree of transparency should take into account the intended purpose of high-risk AI systems and the need to ensure compliance with applicable legal obligations of the user and provider, as appropriate.
7 For example, Immanuel Kant's and G. W. F. Hegel's 'self-fulfilling or self-flourishing arguments' (Acton, 1967, p. 442).
8 See, e.g., 'Berne Convention for the Protection of Literary and Artistic Works' as amended on 28 September 1979, WIPO Copyright Treaty (WCT) and Agreement on Trade-Related Aspects of Intellectual Property Rights (TRIPs) of 1 January 1995.
9 Because people can hardly see the difference between AI-generated real news and fake news (Site AI Generate Fake News, n.d.).
10 Descartes developed a conception of the physical world as purely mechanical in nature, thus making it possible for his view that all physical phenomena can be explained mechanistically.

References

Acton, H. B. (1967). Hegel, Georg Wilhelm Friedrich. In *The encyclopedia of philosophy* (p. 442). Macmillan.

Allen, S. (2016, 6 December). Is your empathy determined by your genes? A new study of twins explores where empathy comes from: nature or nurture? *Greater Good Magazine.* https://greatergood.berkeley.edu/article/item/is_your_empathy_determined_by_your_genes.

Aplin, T., & Pasqualetto, G. (2019). Artificial intelligence and copyright protection. In R. M. Ballardini, O. Pitkänen, & P. Kuoppamäki (Eds.), *Regulating industrial internet through IPR, data protection and competition law* (pp. 81–97). Kluwer Law.

Ballardini, R. M., He, K., & Roos, T. (2019). Digital distribution of AI generated content: Authorship and inventorship in the age of artificial intelligence. In T. Pihlajarinne, J. Vesala, & O. Honkila (Eds.), *Online distribution of content in the EU* (pp. 117–135). Edward Elgar.

Bloom, P. (2018). *Against empathy, the case for rational compassion.* Vintage.
California ConsumerPrivacy Act of 2018, *Cal.* Civ. Code § 1798.100 (2018).
Case C-145/10, Eva-Maria Painer v. Standard Verlags GmbH et al., 2013, *E.C.R.* #, ECLI:EU:C:2013:138.
Case C-5/08, Infopaq International A/S v. Danske Dagblades Forening, 2009*E.C.R.* #, ECLI:EU:C:2009:465.
Case C-604/10, Football Dataco Ltd et al. v. Yahoo! et al., 2012, *E.C.R.* #, ECLI:EU:C:2012:115.
Charter of Fundamental Rights of the European Union (2000/C 364/01). https://eur-lex.europa.eu/legal-content/EN/TXT/?uri=CELEX:12012P/TXT.
Commission Proposal2021*O.J.* (C. 206 final).
Corrales Compagnucci, M. (2020). *Big data, databases and 'ownership' rights in the cloud.* Springer.
Corrales Compagnucci, M., Fenwick, M., Haapio H., Minssen, T., & Vermeulen E. P. M. (2020). Technology-driven disruption of healthcare & 'UI layer' privacy-by-design. *SSRN.* https://papers.ssrn.com/sol3/papers.cfm?abstract_id=3611702.
Corrales Compagnucci, M., Fenwick, M., Haapio, H., & Vermeulen, E. P. M. (2019). Tomorrow's lawyer today? Platform-driven legaltech, smart contracts & the new world of legal design. *Journal of Internet Law*, 22 (10), 3–12.
Corrales Compagnucci, M., Kono, T., & Teramoto, S. (2019). Legal aspects of decentralized and platform-driven economies. In M. C. Compagnucci, N. Forgó, T. Kono, S. Teramoto, & E. P. M. Vermeulen (Eds.), *Legal tech and the new sharing economy* (pp. 1–14). Springer.
Council Directive 93/83/EEC, 1993*O.J.* (L 248).
Council Directive 96/9/EC, 1996*O.J.* (L 77/20).
Council Directive2006/115/EC, 2006 O.J. (L 376).
Council Directive2009/24/EC, 2009 O.J. (L 111).
Council Regulation2016/679, 2016 O.J. (L 119) 1.
European Convention of Human Rights. 1950 https://www.echr.coe.int/documents/convention_eng.pdf.
Ginsburg, J. (2018). People not machines: Authorship and what it means in the Berne Convention. *International Review of Intellectual Property and Competition Law*, 49 (2), 131–135.
Hanson Robotics. (n.d.). *Sophia 2020.* https://www.hansonrobotics.com/sophia-2020/.
Heinerth, C., Keinz, P., & Lettl, C. (2011). Exploring the nature and implementation process of user-centric business models. *Long Range Planning*, 44 (5/6), 344–374.
High-Level Expert Group on Artificial Intelligence. (2019, 8 April). Ethics guidelines for trustworthy AI. *European Commission.* www.aepd.es/sites/default/files/2019-12/ai-ethics-guidelines.pdf.
International Association of Privacy Professionals. (n.d.). *What is privacy?*https://iapp.org/about/what-is-privacy/.
Joined Cases C-403/08 and C-429/08, Football AssociationPremier League Ltd et al. v. QC Leisure et al., 2011, *E.C.R.* #, ECLI:EU:C:2011:631.
Jurcys, P., Donewald, C., Globocnik, J., & Lampinen M., (2020). My data, my terms: A proposal for personal data use licenses. *Harvard Journal of Law & Technology Digest.* https://jolt.law.harvard.edu/digest/my-data-my-terms.
Kur, A. (2019). *European intellectual property law: Text, cases and materials* (2nd ed.). Edward Elgar.

Locke, J. (1690a). *An essay concerning human understanding*. https://www.gutenberg.org/files/10615/10615-h/10615-h.htm#link2HCH0006.

Locke, J. (1690b). *The second treatise of civil government*. https://rintintin.colorado.edu/~vancecd/phil215/Locke.pdf.

Locke, J. (1721). *An essay concerning human understanding* (vol. 2, 8th ed.).

McCarthy, J., & Minsky, M. L. (1955). *Dartmouth conference*. http://www-formal.stanford.edu/jmc/history/dartmouth/dartmouth.html.

Olewitz, C. (2016). Japanese AI writes novel passes first round national literary prize. *Digital Trends*. www.digitaltrends.com/cool-tech/japanese-ai-writes-novel-passes-first-round-nationanl-literary-prize/.

Olsthoorn, J. (2019). Self-ownership and despotism: Locke on property in the person, divine dominium of human life, and rights forfeiture. *Social Philosophy and Policy*, 36 (2), 242–263.

Rozemond, M. (2006). The nature of the mind in the Cartesian circle. In S. Gaukroger (Ed.), *Blackwell guide to Descartes' Meditations*. Wiley-Blackwell.

Senarath, A., Arachchilange, N., & Slay, J. (2017). *Designing privacy for you: A practical approach for user centric privacy*. https://arxiv.org/pdf/1703.09847v2.pdf.

Site AI generate fake news articles. (n.d.). *Futurism*. https://futurism.com/site-ai-generate-fake-news-articles.

Stanford. (n.d.). Artificial intelligence. *Stanford encyclopedia of philosophy*. https://plato.stanford.edu/entries/artificial-intelligence/.

Van der Sloot, B. (2015). Privacy as personality right: Why the ECtHR's focus on ulterior interests might prove indispensable in the age of 'big data'. *Utrecht Journal of International and European Law*, 31 (80), 25–50.

Will.I.AM. (2019, 21 January). We need to own our data as a human right - And be compensated for it. *The Economist*. www.economist.com/open-future/2019/01/21/we-need-to-own-our-data-as-a-human-right-and-be-compensated-for-it.

Universal Declaration of Human Rights. *United Nations*, 1948. https://www.un.org/en/about-us/universal-declaration-of-human-rights.

Uploader. (2018). Will Smith wants to do it with Sofia the Robot [video]. *YouTube*. www.youtube.com/watch?v=4q5ITqQuiT0.

Index

Note: Information in figures and tables is indicated by page numbers in *italics* and **bold**.